MAFIA

Also by Ryan Gingeras

Sorrowful Shores: Violence, Ethnicity, and the
End of the Ottoman Empire 1912–1923

Heroin, Organized Crime, and the Making of Modern Turkey

Mustafa Kemal Atatürk: Heir to an Empire

Fall of the Sultanate: The Great War and the
End of the Ottoman Empire 1908–1922

Eternal Dawn: Turkey in the Age of Atatürk

The Last Days of the Ottoman Empire

MAFIA
A Global History

RYAN GINGERAS

**SIMON &
SCHUSTER**

London · New York · Amsterdam/Antwerp · Sydney/Melbourne · Toronto · New Delhi

First published in Great Britain by Simon & Schuster UK Ltd, 2026

Copyright © Ryan Gingeras, 2026

The right of Ryan Gingeras to be identified as the author of this work has been asserted in accordance with the Copyright, Designs and Patents Act, 1988.

1 3 5 7 9 10 8 6 4 2

Simon & Schuster UK Ltd, 1st Floor
222 Gray's Inn Road, London WC1X 8HB

For more than 100 years, Simon & Schuster has championed authors and the stories they create. By respecting the copyright of an author's intellectual property, you enable Simon & Schuster and the author to continue publishing exceptional books for years to come. We thank you for supporting the author's copyright by purchasing an authorised edition of this book.

No amount of this book may be reproduced or stored in any format, nor may it be uploaded to any website, database, language-learning model, or other repository, retrieval, or artificial intelligence system without express permission. All rights reserved. Enquiries may be directed to Simon & Schuster, 222 Gray's Inn Road, London WC1X 8HB or RightsMailbox@simonandschuster.co.uk

www.simonandschuster.co.uk
www.simonandschuster.com.au
www.simonandschuster.co.in

Simon & Schuster Australia, Sydney
Simon & Schuster India, New Delhi

The authorised representative in the EEA is Simon & Schuster Netherlands BV, Herculesplein 96, 3584 AA Utrecht, Netherlands. info@simonandschuster.nl

The author and publishers have made all reasonable efforts to contact copyright-holders for permission, and apologise for any omissions or errors in the form of credits given. Corrections may be made to future printings.

Simon & Schuster strongly believes in freedom of expression and stands against censorship in all its forms. For more information, visit BooksBelong.com.

A CIP catalogue record for this book is available from the British Library

Hardback ISBN: 978-1-3985-3165-9
Trade Paperback ISBN: 978-1-3985-3166-6
eBook ISBN: 978-1-3985-3167-3

Typeset in Sabon by M Rules
Printed and Bound in the UK using 100% Renewable Electricity at CPI Group (UK) Ltd

As ever, for Mariana

Contents

Foreword: The View from Zulette Avenue   1

Introduction: 'The true princes who govern us'   5

Part I: Genesis

1. The Long Scourge: Banditry and the Pre-History of Mafias   15
2. Love and Relaxation for Sale: Vice and the Roots of Organised Crime   44

Part II: Consolidation

3. Origins: Mafias of the Early Twentieth Century   75
4. From Booze to Dope: The Advent of Global Mafias   117

Part III: Transformation

5. Godfathers: The High Tide of Old Mafias   153
6. Between Decline and Revolution: Mafias at Century's End   220

Conclusion

The Great Dilution: Making Sense of the
Twenty-First Century   310

Notes   345
Bibliography   381
Acknowledgements   411
Index   413

FOREWORD

The View from Zulette Avenue

Around 1912, my great-grandparents bought their house on Zulette Avenue in the Bronx. Pop was in the ice-delivery business and ran it partially out of the backyard. When he and my great-grandmother Maisie bought the place, most considered Pelham Bay the country. The extension of the subway in 1920 helped turn the neighbourhood into its present-day collection of single-family homes and low-rise apartment buildings. Central European motifs found on some of the buildings testify to the smattering of Germans and Hungarians who once lived there, but most of Pelham Bay's earliest residents were Italian or Irish. Two funeral homes, Giordano and McNulty, served their respective clients. I attended several wakes at McNulty over the years. Recently, they went out of business, underscoring the slow extinction of Pelham Bay's Irish.

The last of our family to pass through McNulty's on the way to St Raymond's Cemetery was my grandfather, Charles Fitzpatrick, or Charley, as I always knew him. Charley was not a Bronx native. He spent his first years in Canary Island, a Harlem neighbourhood long forgotten by most New Yorkers, and came to Pelham Bay just ahead of the Depression. Charley lived an extraordinary life, despite spending most of it as either an elementary school teacher or principal. He joined the Marines after Pearl Harbor and managed to survive the worst of Guadalcanal, Bougainville and Guam. Though he loathed Communism, he resisted the urge to re-enlist ahead of the Korean War. In the mid-1950s, FBI agents enlisted Charley as an informant. With their blessing, he became a member of the American Communist Party. No one, save my grandmother, knew of his double life until the US Congress called him to give testimony in 1971. He never shied from talking about the people he came to know while in the Party. To the end, he believed American communists did take orders from Moscow and did threaten America from within. Nevertheless, his memories of their sincere kindness and intelligence were heavily tinged with hints of regret.

To walk the streets of Pelham Bay with Charley was to receive a tour of his life and times. Crossing a corner here or passing a house there often came with a story or an aside. At Keane Square he would mention his childhood friend, the park's namesake, Larry 'Killer' Keane, who died at Guadalcanal. Not too far from the Square is the site of the Ye Olde on Crosby Avenue. Charley would speak of tending bar there after he came back from the war. Serving drinks at Ye Olde, as he told it, was a ringside seat to the neighbourhood's underworld. Although he never handled the action himself, the bar was full of gamblers and bookies, some who dealt in jukeboxes and vending machines, and those euphemistically 'involved' in construction and certain other trades.

This sort of clientele brought in the likes of Willie Moretti. Back then, Charley only knew Moretti as a big-drinking wise guy from New Jersey, who would hang around the Ye Olde for hours. One evening, when Moretti was the worse for wear, a man who identified himself as 'the Beak' telephoned and asked for Willie. My grandfather tried to hand Moretti the receiver but was waved away. When Charley told the Beak that Moretti was unavailable, the Beak imparted a message: deliver the five large or Willie's going for a dip in the Hudson in cement shoes. Many decades later, I told my grandfather that Moretti was likely the inspiration for Luca Brasi in *The Godfather* (which I learned from watching *The Sopranos*). I never learned who 'the Beak' was, but I suspect it was Paul Castellano.*

Charley's Willie Moretti story was only one of many mob-related tales that peppered my childhood. It required little prompting for him to muse at length about friends, acquaintances and family members connected, in some way, to the Mafia. Walking to place our bets at the local off-course betting parlour often came with comments about the neighbourhood restaurants or businesses that he suspected were mob hangouts. Between 1990 and the early 2000s, there was a social club on Crosby Avenue with a bright blue awning with the name 'Vito's' emblazoned on it. In the window was a common poster featuring several Hollywood gangsters all seated at a card table together. Not subtle, Charley and I agreed.

In my early teens, Charley recommended a book that served as the first mob history I read: T. J. English's *The Westies*, an account of the Irish mafia in Hell's Kitchen. I was delighted to learn that our family possessed tangential connections to characters detailed in its pages, though I'll admit I have, from time to time, inflated or perhaps embellished this family connection just a bit in the retelling. During the 1980s and '90s, news coverage of the Mafia gave us a lot to talk about: the murder of Paul Castellano, John Gotti's various trials and the slow demise of Vincent 'the Chin' Gigante.

---

* Castellano's biographers, Joseph O'Brien and Andris Kurins, described the gangster as possessing 'a strong Picasso nose' that sat in the middle of a 'massive head [that] hung slightly forward on his heavy neck, creating a buzzard-like effect'. See Joseph O'Brien and Andris Kurins, *Boss of Bosses: The Fall of the Godfather: The FBI and Paul Castellano* (New York: Simon & Schuster, 1991), p. 25.

Our shared interest in the Mafia formed only one aspect of a deeper bond. An impassioned storyteller, Charley loved history. It was his influence, more than anything, that made me consider becoming a historian. But never in my years at university or graduate school did the thought of studying the Mafia occur to me. A different set of circumstances led me to learn Turkish and to specialise in Middle Eastern history. Then, as I was doing my doctoral research in Istanbul in the early 2000s, the mafia wormed its way back into my life and studies. Among the first promises of the newly elected prime minister, Recep Erdoğan, was the imposition of a 'clean hands' reform agenda, one that echoed Italy's fight against corruption and organised crime in the 1990s. Voters and pundits applauded Erdoğan's determination as evidence that the country was reforming after a decade of economic hardship and instability. Many of my Turkish friends spoke often of the 1990s as an era when the mafia held sway over both politics and the underworld. Augmenting this early introduction to Turkey's mafia was the release of the country's first made-for-TV mob drama, *Valley of the Wolves*. The show is not great. Yet its existence captured my imagination, especially as it aired in parallel with my beloved *Sopranos*. I could not help but find so much of the Bronx and America in Istanbul and Turkey. The similarities and differences, to my mind, begged investigation.

Wanting to know more, I ventured to the National Archives in College Park, Maryland; there I found a trove of American diplomatic and police reports. From this archival base I composed much of my second book, *Heroin, Organised Crime and the Making of Modern Turkey*. In time, I came to see a much bigger story about how mafias and their crimes shaped other countries across the world. Those revelations became the basis of this book. In my heart, however, it is an homage to my family and the place we called home for over a century.

INTRODUCTION

'The true princes who govern us'

Stories about the making of *The Godfather* are now the stuff of popular lore. Before its release in 1972, gangster pictures, at least according to legendary movie producer Robert Evans, were passé. Attempts during the 1960s to recapture the genre's earlier mystique offered few positive indicators. 'Except for a B-picture or two,' Evans wrote in his memoir, 'every film about Sicilians and organised crime had one thing in common – red ink.'[1] Mario Puzo's novel, which sold nine million copies after its 1969 release, ultimately persuaded Evans and others at Paramount Pictures to believe that *The Godfather* might be different.

In selecting a young Francis Ford Coppola to direct, the studio aimed to give the film both a contemporary edge and a sense of authenticity. Coppola, for his part, wanted his movie to be something more than just a crime drama. 'Coppola will make the picture on one condition,' Evans was told: 'that it's not a film about organised crime but a family chronicle. A metaphor about capitalism.' With the studio's future at stake, Bob Evans wasn't amused. 'Fuck him and the horse he rode in on. Is he nuts?'[2] The fights got worse once Coppola was formally announced as the film's director. There were bitter arguments over casting, including the choice of the film's leading man, Marlon Brando. Tensions between Coppola and the studio escalated as creative differences emerged over music and editing. In Hollywood, rumours held that the film was doomed after it failed to open as scheduled during Christmas 1971.

Of course, history unfolded differently. *The Godfather* dominated the American box office and earned ten nominations at the 1972 Academy Awards ceremony. Still more impressive is the immediate effect the movie had upon audiences worldwide. For at least one French reviewer, the film's premise, more than its artistry, was what made *The Godfather* so evocative. Even though the word 'mafia' is never mentioned, the movie fulfilled the audience's expectations of its 'occult power'. 'Consciously or not,' he supposed, 'people are inclined to believe that the true princes who govern us are hidden masters, all-powerful [but] anonymous.' The belief that the audience was finally allowed entrance into a world long forbidden to them was what made *The Godfather* a hit.[3]

When Coppola took on *The Godfather*, he insisted the film had to be a period piece for it to be received as genuine. Yet for many cinemagoers in 1972, there was nothing historical about the gangsters portrayed on screen. For many Americans, the Mafia was a contemporary reality. With his election as president in 1968, Richard Nixon promised voters 'a war on organized crime', one that would target 'narcotics peddlers' responsible for corrupting 'the lives of the children of this country'.[4] Nixon was not the first American president to prioritise the fight against drugs. Every president dating back to Harry Truman had labelled the struggle against narcotics abuse and trafficking a national crisis.[5] The growing visibility of the country's heroin epidemic, as well as rising urban crime rates, appeared to warrant something akin to a declaration of war. For many Americans, gangsters had been fixtures of neighbourhood and city life for generations. Television news in the 1950s and '60s had introduced many more Americans

Introduction

to real-life godfathers such as Vito Genovese or Carlos Marcello. Senate hearings and national scandals did much to sustain one of the film's key premises: mob families lorded over a vast criminal underworld and exercised undue influence over American politics and the economy.

For the millions who went to see *The Godfather* outside the United States, the film was no less timely and relevant. A viewer in Tokyo or Rome could draw parallels between Coppola's Corleone family and crime groups native to Japan and Italy. At the time of the film's release, France was in its own crusade against the racketeers and drug traffickers associated with Marseille's infamous crime bosses. In Turkey, the film resonated so strongly with moviegoers that locals adapted the Turkish translation for 'godfather' (*baba*) as the new collective name for gangsters living in Ankara and Istanbul.[6] Over time, 'godfather' became shorthand for crime lords and sinister political bosses in countries worldwide. Yet it is also possible that the characters and culture represented in *The Godfather* were entirely alien to audiences outside the United States. In 1972, there was nothing comparable to the American Mafia in places such as Colombia, Nigeria or India. Though it was unlikely that many Chinese or Soviet citizens could even have seen the film after its initial global release, there were few godfathers in China or the Soviet Union that audiences could use as local points of reference.

In the decades that have followed, *The Godfather* has become even more relatable to audiences worldwide. Now, more than ever, there is nothing that appears exceptionally American about the background or motivations of the Corleone family. A powerful Russian *vor* or Mexican *patrón* could replace Michael Corleone in a more contemporary adaptation. A present-day Chinese triad or Jamaican posse could wield the influence of the Corleone criminal empire. The film's implicit commentary on the nature of political power and business could be applied to real-life affairs in Eastern

Europe or South America. Why has *The Godfather* become so adaptable? The film was prescient about forces reshaping the world in the late twentieth century, and even though it is a work of fiction, contemporary viewers continue to see it as a depiction of core truths about life today and in the past.

Coppola's conceptual vision for *The Godfather* was not cut from whole cloth. Elements of the film's critique of American politics, society and capitalism can be found in earlier classics, such as *Scarface* (1932) and *The Public Enemy* (1931). One may argue that its timely arrival to theatres, as well as its artistic brilliance, earned the film its place within modern consciousness. As a template for other treatments of organised crime, *The Godfather* and its sequels introduced tropes that are now critical to the perception of mafias across the globe. The conceit of many mafia films and television shows is the principle that the viewer is seeing either the past as it really was or the present as it genuinely is. A story set in the underworld reveals the true history of a city, country or nation – a history that is often suppressed or unacknowledged. To borrow the words of James Ellroy, the motivation behind many fictional accounts of organised crime is to demythologise the past. To dive meaningfully into the history of the mafia, any mafia, is to build a more authentic history of politics and society, one that spans what Ellroy calls 'the gutter to the stars'.[7]

These sentiments are at the core of this book. What follows is not so much a strict history of mafias and mobsters; the intent is instead to explore the rise, consolidation and denouement of mafias on the global stage. As in *The Godfather*, the book draws upon the history of mafias and organised crime to tell a much larger, more complicated story. To understand where modern-day gangsters come from, and why they have assumed such global significance, is to delve into several critical, and generally familiar, historical tropes. The narrative ahead returns time and again to

Introduction

a basic question: how have mafias reflected or helped define the making of the modern world?

The historical evolution of modern-day mafias tells us a lot about the countries in which we find them. To piece together the history of the Camorra or the tongs or to lay out the biography of Escobar or Capone, requires an appreciation of the places and eras that produced them. In principle, mafias teach us a lot about the ever-growing power of states. Governments, after all, are the fundamental agents that define what is a crime and who is a criminal. Those who enforce the law, more than gangsters themselves, are typically the ones who identify and explain the significance of a gang or thug who comes into view. Above all, the history of mafias tells us a great deal about the physical limits of state power. Every state today, and all the great empires of the past, have been tormented by organised crime (or something analogous to it). Even with all the benefits of modern technology and law enforcement know-how, no present-day state has found a way to immunise itself from the dangers of mafias. More often than not, history suggests that mafias play notable roles in the making of governments, economies and epochs. Michael Corleone's rebuke of Senator Geary holds true. Mafiosi, politicians and industry executives are often expressions of the same hypocrisy.

The more one looks critically at the history of gangsters and their trades, the more one must also contend with the extent to which they are the product of popular and elite imagination and paranoia. Mobsters, to varying degrees, are boogiemen. They embody many of the worst fears of a society. We almost always imagine them as rough men from the lower ranks of society. They often appear to us as outsiders, most likely immigrants, minorities or both. Their trades, such as prostitution and drug trafficking, are often conceived to be dangerous in moral and physical terms. Popular culture has exploited the social anxieties that undergird how most people perceive mafias. Without fictional characters such as Scarface, Michael Corleone and Tony Soprano, gangsters would possess far less political significance than they do in the world today.

The United States, of course, plays an important role within the broader global history of organised crime. American movies and television shows, as well as actual American gangsters, have contributed mightily to how many around the world think about and see mafias closer to home. The influence of the United States is not limited to the legacies of Capone and his Hollywood equivalents. An American first coined the phrase 'organised crime'. American reformers, diplomats and academics have long been at the forefront in raising awareness of organised crime on the global stage. American law enforcement agents have led the way in introducing many of the strategies that have defined local and transnational campaigns against mafias. Understanding criminal syndicates in this regard demands greater appreciation of the rise of the United States as a world hegemon.

A global history of mafias cannot be about politics solely. Mafias often constitute an economic construct, and membership, particularly in the contemporary world, is a form of employment. The most lucrative criminal trades tend to concern the buying or selling of commodities and services. To understand something about the making of specific mafias or mobsters is to explore the economic development of their preferred trades. With the passage of time, it is necessary to look at the power dynamics that have governed the global marketplace. Whether one talks of the trade in terms of narcotics, weapons or people, one must confront the centrality of European and American commercial interests around the globe. Westerners have long been the most active traders and consumers of certain illicit goods. The laws and prohibitions around these goods and services have largely been the product of Western diplomacy and power politics.

*

Introduction

The word 'mafia' is often used permissively. In English, it passes as shorthand for groups involved with organised crime. Mafia, however, is a term imbued with gravitas. Mafias do not come and go; they persevere or grow despite the passage of time or changes in leadership; they possess a culture, history or pedigree that adds to their status; their mythos overshadows the exploits or dangers of the common criminal. Policy experts and scholars tend to favour a host of other terms to describe the existence or nature of enduring gangs and criminal conspiracies (be it 'organised crime groups', 'transnational organised crime groups' and so forth). Academic debates over nomenclature often tend to avoid a critical question: how did the word 'mafia' enter the lexicon? Why is it that states and societies came to perceive the presence of local mafias in their own midst?

A coherent series of events may help provide an answer to these questions. The word 'mafia' has an Italian root. Yet it required outsiders, particularly Americans, to give it its modern meaning and endow it with global significance. Sensational revelations in the United States during the 1960s appeared to confirm the existence of invisible empires that ruled underworlds at home and beyond. Filmmakers and journalists devoured these admissions and made them the basis of movies and exposés consumed by tens of millions. Thereafter, mafias were not just a source of frontpage news and popular entertainment; they became integral to how people see their past, present and future.

PART I

GENESIS

Mafias are not ancient. The name and concept originates no earlier than the early 1800s. Nevertheless, to begin this history then would be wrong. Present-day mobsters and mafias may best be described as late descendants of bandits and brigands. Banditry is an ancient form of organised crime, where the criminal action seldom outlasts the life of the proponent. To be considered a bandit or brigand, one only need to commit acts of robbery (the most likely target being a traveller or someone from out of town). Though seemingly less sophisticated, bandits share similarities with their more modern counterparts. Both mafias and brigands terrorised the weak and powerful in great states and petty kingdoms. Yet they have done more than inspire fear. Both, at times, have been seen as avatars for peoples, regions and nations. Their legacies often invoke a certain amount of romance or nostalgia. They are both, in many ways, the quintessential anti-hero.

Groups such as La Cosa Nostra or the yakuza did not spring from the earth. Like bandits before them, mafiosi are born into worlds shaped by the states that govern them. The laws that brigands and mobsters defy are the product of the regimes, norms and economies that envelope them. How successful or endemic bandit gangs and mafias are tells us a lot about the weaknesses or limits of their native states and governments.

There is a critical point of rupture in this story. There came a time in world history when bandits, as a global phenomenon, began to die away around much of the globe. Why this is the case is the combination of several factors, the most important being the advent of industrialisation. As industrialised forms of work and consumption took hold, states grew stronger. As cities became the focal point of rapidly diversifying economies, landscapes became more urbanised. Many of the world's governments vanquished banditry on the back of these changes. This was one factor that gave states the confidence to pass stricter laws, which they believed to be more closely aligned with modern social mores. Following their victory over banditry, states imposed more rigorous penalties and regulations upon those who gambled, sold sex or dealt in intoxicants. Those who defied these laws most often did so as members of groups and gangs. As the twentieth century dawned, it appeared even more the case that organised crime was the province of a specific class of criminal. In due course, in various parts of the globe, such criminals typically came to be seen as members of the mafia.

1

The Long Scourge: Banditry and the Pre-History of Mafias

Lord Byron had yet to find poetic fame when he arrived in the mountains of northern Greece. A search for inspiration and adventure had moved him, in 1809, to take his 'grand tour' of Europe's east. The fruit born from this trip to the Ottoman Empire's Balkan provinces was his epic poem, 'Childe Harold's Pilgrimage', the first of his many contributions to the Romantic movement. Among the central characters of this work is Ali Pasha of Ioannina, an Ottoman governor who reigned over much of the southern Balkans. In the poem, Byron presents Ali as a metaphor for what he experienced during his journey through Greece's highlands. Ali, as he described him, was 'a man of war and woes'. Though he never reveals what made Ioannina's governor so rugged or worn, Byron upholds Ali as the epitome of the Balkans, a place with all the allure and cruelties of the ancient Orient.

Byron's travelling companion, Lord Broughton (aka John Hobhouse), was less artful in relating his memory of their visit. According to his account of the trip, Ali was simply 'indistinguishable from the shabby-looking Albanian guards that surrounded him'.[1] Though he prided himself as a man with a noble pedigree, there was something that appeared common and crude about the pasha. Ali, as Lord Broughton understood it, began his career as a 'freebooter' at the head of a large gang. Banditry was a profession that ran in the family, one plied by his father and grandfather before him. His reputation for sadism was part of local lore. After clashing with an opposing village, Ali invited a local elder to his home for a parley. The meeting purportedly ended with the man's corpse roasting on a spit. Through wily navigation of local politics, coupled with his willingness to marshal troops for the sultan in Istanbul, Ali Pasha had become a ranking lord of the Ottoman Empire by the time Byron arrived at his court. At the height of his power, Ali Pasha ruled his fiefdom as a state within a state, with his influence stretching through much of the western Balkans. Amid the Napoleonic Wars of the early 1800s, both France and Britain courted him as an ally.[2]

Unsophisticated and rapacious though he may have appeared, Ali fancied himself a state-builder and patron of commerce and learning. It was possible that the 'Lion of Ioannina' could have founded a kingdom of his own in what is today Albania and Greece. His overthrow and execution in 1822 ended this dream. Other Ottoman aspirants succeeded where Ali failed. At the time of Ali's reign over Ioannina, another Albanian from northern Greece, Mohammed Ali, installed himself as governor of Egypt after a series of extraordinary, bloody events. Like Ali Pasha, Mohammed's good fortune was indebted to the loyalty and service of hundreds of cutthroats and former bandits who followed him to Egypt. Unlike the former 'Lion of Ioannina', Mohammed Ali managed to secure Egypt's governorship as a hereditary title. Both he and his heirs came to be seen as the seminal rulers and reformers of the modern state of Egypt. The last of his line, King Faruk, abandoned the throne in 1952 after a military coup that gave way to the dictatorship of Gamal Abdel Nasser.

Ali Pasha's story is not atypical from the perspective of history. His path represents a common arc for those who excelled at murder, theft and extortion. Yet his life provides several useful points of reference in confronting the subject of banditry in world history. Ali's tour de force illustrates the way many young states are formed. He first gathered local authority as a brigand. For European observers such as Lord Broughton, Ali's good fortune was symptomatic of the corruption and decay of the late Ottoman Empire. But one could be more charitable towards Ali and his ambitions as a state builder. Promises of plunder aided in the construction and growth of Charlemagne's empire in the latter part of eighth-century Western and Central Europe,[3] and the avarice of Hernán Cortés and his men was a seminal force in laying the foundation of the colony of New Spain in the early sixteenth century, yet neither Charles the Great not Cortés are typically called bandits.[4]

Reverence for the founders of Mexico or the Holy Roman Empire is not a testament to the adage of 'might makes right'. The uncomfortable origins of many states speak to what sociologist Charles Tilly has euphemistically characterised as the 'organised crimes' of state-making and war-making. Young states are often born resembling a 'protection racket'. Demands for taxes, tribute or spoils are among the essential features of a proclaimed state. Fear, more often than not, compels those conquered to accede to these demands. Driving this fear are often explicit and implicit threats of violence. Mobilisation for war is an equal part of this foundational relationship between the government and the governed. It is the threat of harm (be it from outside enemies or from the government itself) that often compels people to fight on behalf of their lord and state. How then, Tilly asks, do the subjects or citizens come to see this kind of relationship as valid?

What endows a Cortés, or even an Ali Pasha, with the legitimacy to rule and extract wealth from their people? What sets Cortés or Ali apart from base thieves and brigands? Successful rulers and states, Tilly explains, tend to purvey 'violence on a larger scale, more effectively, more efficiently, with wider assent from their subject populations'.[5] Extended periods of time tend to solidify the durability, and the legitimacy, of this relationship between ruler and ruled.

It is hard to say when banditry, as a crime and as a trade, was born. What is clear is that classical states and societies grappled with what separated theft or extortion from otherwise 'legitimate' appropriation of wealth by the politically powerful. Poetry and other writings from ancient Greece regularly engage with the prickly issues of power and force in the relationship between landed elites and those who laboured beneath them. A principled aristocrat, some argued, should not resort to violence in growing wealthy. Nor was it right for landowners to abuse tenants who rendered a share of their crops as payment. Nevertheless, powerful individuals did often rob to get rich and exploit the weak for their own material gain. Such unrestrained exercises of force frequently led to disorder and rebellion in Greek society.[6] Violence in the pursuit of wealth and power was not just a moral issue; the wanton use of violence by rapacious elites jeopardised a state's survival.

These ancient Greek sources were not specifically speaking of *kleptes* or bandits. A *klept* was a character of low repute. Nevertheless, both the Greeks and Romans understood that the specific crime of brigandage undermined the state's political legitimacy. *Latrones*, or Roman bandits, represented a unique class of criminal, one distinct from those who generally stole from others. Under Roman law, what made them unique was 'their use of weapons (*vis armata*), their forming of bands (*factiones, homines armati coactive*), and their aim of plunder (*spoliare*) with malice aforethought (*dolus malus*)'.[7] Why the Romans made such a key distinction between banditry and other forms of theft may relate to the political implications of the crime. The conceit of government lies in the principle that only sovereign rulers may apply the threat of violence in extracting wealth from their peoples. By banding together and seizing property under the threat of harm, a clutch of bandits represented something akin to an army, a force that challenged the state's monopolisation of violence. Bandits upset the natural order of politics and their presence may highlight the corruption or incompetence of governing regimes. Many Romans drew this lesson from the legend of Bulla Felix, a brigand chieftain active in central Italy during in the early 200s. Like the Robin Hood myth of a different era, Felix purportedly possessed noble intentions in leading his 600-strong band of thieves. His looting at the expense of the rich, as well as his flagrant disregard for the state, endeared him to critics of the reigning emperor and the Roman system. When asked why Bulla had chosen to become a bandit, his reply to his praetorian accuser was simple. 'Why,' Bulla countered, 'are you a prefect?'[8]

Bulla Felix's retort underscored an anxiety many great lords of history would have understood. Prefects, vassals and satraps often behaved like bandits. Yet rulers of various types relied upon such men to govern in their name. Marshalling soldiers and materiel for war, as well as the maintenance of something like order, was often not possible without them. A retainer's authority, however, often became a licence to exploit the weak.

But Felix's point could be construed in an even more nuanced way. It was not simply that provincial governors or estate holders often stole from local communities at a whim. The nature of political systems appeared compromised or prone to violence and expropriation. Throughout the world, rulers found themselves defending their regimes from charges that they, as a collective, were nothing more than bandits. In medieval Japan, peasants, magnates and religious leaders lobbied the shogun to fight against 'evil bands', or *akutō*, responsible for acts of carnage and theft. But according to one recent study, petitioners often used the term akutō as a vague pseudonym for various kinds of conflicts between elites and communities over agricultural rights, taxes or power.[9] 'Evil bands', in a way of speaking, could refer to genuine brigands as well as characters associated with the political system itself.

History is rife with cases where brigands lorded over large swaths of land and people at a government's expense. Depending upon the time and place in history, states had to deal with enormous bandit gangs. At the turn of the eighteenth century, a rogue named Louis Dominique Cartouche claimed leadership over an immense body of thieves that pillaged farms and interdicted traffic outside of Paris. Over the course of a seven-year period, French courts tried Cartouche alongside 742 accomplices for various crimes.[10] For French kings, gangs of this size were a rarity. In other parts of the world, it was not uncommon for significant portions of the countryside to fall under the rule of violent bands that numbered in the hundreds or thousands. Eliminating such brazen demonstrations of lawlessness, particularly before the modern era, often proved costly or perhaps fruitless. The likelihood of failure led states to ignore or put off their suppression. In many cases, regimes sought compromises to mitigate the threat they posed to public order. The kingdom of Hessen in early modern Germany was the site of one particularly curious arrangement. There, local authorities sanctioned the creation of 'crook villages' comprised of resettled criminals, transients and other undesirables. Though the residents of the villages vowed to abide by the law, they grew notorious for larceny under the complicity of provincial officials. Their concentration in one location, it seems, at least limited the scope of their crimes.[11]

To try and not succeed could empower an outlaw leader,

leading local populations to look leerily at the state's legitimate rulers. One alternative to punitive action was to co-opt bandits and incorporate them into the works of the regime. Sultan Abdülhamid I of the Ottoman Empire pursued this tactic in awarding Ali Pasha his local governorship. While constituting an admission of state weakness, the recruitment of a rogue such as the Lion of Ioannina afforded potentially mutual benefits. Ali's acceptance of an official rank came with the promise of submission and fidelity to the state. With that title in hand, Ali could continue to wield local authority without fear of official reprisal. A hard character such as Ali could conceivably govern as competently, if not better than, other imperial appointees. Colonial and post-independence Latin America is rife with instances where states and elites wilfully inducted bandits into the ranks of the powerful. The archetypal *caudillo*, or provincial strongman, was often associated with one-time bandits as well army officers and aristocrats. Far less successful bandits, for example in Mexico, could theoretically look forward to obtaining employment in the police or as frontier guards if they gave up a life of crime. Their reliability as state officials, of course, was another matter.[12]

Granting bandits concessions, let alone incorporating them into the workings of government, is a testament to the basic limits of statecraft. Until relatively recently, states were comparatively simple organisms. Bureaucracy, in the modern sense of the term, was absent or rudimentary even among the most powerful empires of history. Rule tended to be personalised, as opposed to being institutional or corporate, and those who held power, regardless of their station, typically possessed no specialised education that prepared them to govern. The levers of government, for most of history, were also basic and blunt. Reigning over a district beset by bandits may have entailed nothing more than indiscriminate punitive actions such as mass burnings and public executions. In the absence of modern technology, long distances slowed the spread of news and prevented governments from responding swiftly or decisively. Before the dawn of global capitalism, money and credit were regularly in tight supply. Few states possessed the financial or human resources essential for maintaining regular, efficient institutions; schools, hospitals and prisons were scarce. Even the building or expansion of roads took money that was not always readily available. The weak nature of states contributed to the proliferation of bandits for most of recorded civilised history.

The historical struggle between bandits and early states offers us a series of signposts with which one can better comprehend the origins and significance of modern mafias. Contemporary criminal syndicates, like bandits in the past, represent something more than threats to public order and safety. In their actions and by their nature, they constitute a challenge to the legitimacy of states and regimes. Among the telltale signs of a modern-day 'failed state' is the presumption that cartels or gangs hold authority.

Banditry's long historical arc also reveals the fine line that may separate those who hold power legitimately from those who appear to be out-and-out rogues. History is replete with tyrants and lords who behaved like brigands. Among the things historians have come to appreciate in more recent years is the degree to which *de jure* bandits contributed to the making of states in history. Banditry, in many cases, served as a means of upward mobility for those with political aspirations. Rulers also saw utility in recruiting brigands into their service. At a time when the bar for state service was low, there was no reason why a brigand such as Ali Pasha couldn't be as effective in governing as anyone else. Indeed, having the likes of an Ali Pasha on the government's side was better than gambling that he could somehow be defeated or crushed.

The Long Scourge

BETWEEN WEALTH AND THE WEAK: THE ECONOMY AND CULTURE OF BANDITRY

Tepelenë, the town of Ali Pasha's birth, resides in the midst of hard country. Located in what is today southern Albania, the landscape is riven with high mountains and deep ravines, making it ill-suited for intensive farming. During Ali's youth, there were few passable roads. Chronic outbreaks of disease, such as malaria, were common. Its physical proximity to Gjirokastër, the provincial capital, did little to compensate for the lack of economic opportunity in the region. Tepelenë's hard-scrabble fortune was typical of many places inhabited by Albanians in the late eighteenth century. The wars of this period added even greater pressure on similar mountain communities. In addition to the burden of military service, the state's requisitioning of food and higher taxes compounded the poverty and instability. Many Albanians from the western Balkans left their homes looking for work and a better life. Year after year, thousands migrated south and east where they found seasonal employment. Contemporary place names in Turkey, such as Arnavutköy, as well as surnames in Syria and Egypt, such as al-Arna'ut (the Albanian), reflect this historic diaspora.

Albanian migrants were not a welcome sight for residents in many Ottoman towns. The presence of large numbers of destitute, homeless men compelled local authorities to ban Albanians from settling in several cities (including Istanbul). In the countryside, large numbers of Albanians resorted to banditry to compensate for the lack of opportunity, and travel through much of the Balkans was precarious through the eighteenth and nineteenth centuries due to the activities of brigands. The repute earned by Albanians during this period tarred their reputation among large numbers of Ottoman citizens. The effect these trends had upon popular consciousness is evident from scenes found in the shadow puppet plays of Karagöz. A common stock character in the Karagöz adventure stories is 'the Albanian', a man who is typically rough, prone to anger and violent.[13]

The plight of Ali Pasha's native land is typical of the places associated with banditry's evolution in world history. Brigandage is fundamentally a rural profession, particularly in places afflicted with chronic levels of poverty. Many of these same areas also tended to be geographically remote or seasonably inaccessible. For states the world over, areas known for their dense forests, high mountains or rugged terrain were often infested with bandits. It was possible, however, for territories known for prosperity and peace to fall victim to brigandage. War, famine, mass migration and economic collapse drove otherwise prosperous individuals and communities to resort to violence and theft. Whether in times of conflict or peace, a central factor in the propagation of banditry was of the lack of sustained government presence. In Ali Pasha's native Albania, few residents outside major towns would have seen any physical trace of the Ottoman imperial administration. Law and order, as defined by Istanbul, was an intermittent feature of daily life in southern Albania well into the twentieth century. Similar travails plagued various portions of imperial China despite its historical wealth, might and sophistication. During a relatively affluent period in the sixteenth century, Beijing struggled mightily to halt bandit attacks within proximity of the capital. Among the factors responsible for this trend was the impoverishment of local soldiers, who supplemented their income with brigandage, as well as the region's marshy terrain, which gave shelter to criminals fleeing the law.[14]

Many of the dynamics that gave rise to banditry on land – poverty and desperation, as well as war and economic uncertainty – also led to the proliferation of pirates on the high seas. Geography, however, figured into piracy's evolution in more discrete ways. Pirates relied upon bays and waterways that were far from centres of power for protection. Physical choke points, such as narrow seas and straits, proved attractive locales for corsairs and raiders. The combination of these factors led to entrenched patterns of piracy. For example, Japan's proximity to lucrative sea-lanes, as well as endemic droughts and economic hardship, contributed to the proliferation of *wokou* pirates during the sixteenth century.[15] Other pirates displayed far greater mobility and range than bandits. Captain William Kidd's career as a privateer and cutthroat in the seventeenth century took him from the Caribbean and the North Atlantic to the shores off Surat in southern India.[16] For even the most powerful states in early modern history, combatting such arrant activity across the open ocean posed a challenge. The financial and physical difficulties that came with stopping piracy inspired many states to seek their co-operation. As with banditry, employing pirates brought benefits beyond reducing the threat they posed to commerce, property and public safety. Recruiting privateers such as Kidd also allowed states to avoid the fiscal burden that came with building and maintaining a navy.

Residing somewhere on the margins of the social and economic history of banditry are nomads. Migratory peoples, as a whole, bear no resemblance to bandits or pirates. To move from place to place is not so much a conscious choice of profession as it is a societal state of being. Yet one of the core attributes of many nomadic societies is raiding. Plundering other settled and nomadic communities fulfilled multiple needs for migratory groups. Augmenting the size of animal flocks, or even the population of the nomadic community itself, often came from kidnapping. Raids also inflated the status of individuals and groups within certain migratory communities. Townspeople and farmers naturally possessed little empathy with raiding nomads. This inherent antagonism extended towards both nomads who resided within the borders of both established empires and those who marauded on the frontier. As late as the twentieth century, several major states, such as China, Iran, Russia, British India and the United States, worked to bring predatory nomadic groups under their control. Like the case of banditry and piracy, reining in migratory bands of Bedouin, Comanche and Nogay tested the efficacy and capacity of governments. In addition to their fluid patterns of movement, nomadic groups tended to reside in areas far from centres of power and in locations that facilitated their evasion (such as deserts and steppe). The historical record often conflated nomads with brigandage and barbarism. The 'bandit Apache', as one Arizona historian put it in 1916, possessed no land or property to fight for save for the 'rugged hills' and 'his share of deer and rabbits'. What drove the Apache to take up arms was 'the loss of supremacy – the right of the red man to do as he chose, at the expense of his weaker or richer red brothers'.[17]

Such observations reflect how many in the past equated banditry with the character or culture of certain peoples or communities. From the perspective of governments and citizens alike, indifferent economic or social factors were not always enough to explain why someone became a highwayman or brigand. Banditry's prevalence among a group was enough to associate an entire people with criminal proclivities. Historical observers construed Albanians, Chechens, Mongols, Corsicans, Circassians and Yaqui as cast from a similarly defective mould. The development of biases does not seem to stem purely from perceptions about the essential nature of a group's culture. Instead, as with the case of the Albanians in the Ottoman Empire, the connections drawn between crime and regional or ethnic identity may have been a product of government thinking. To identify and stop the spread of banditry, state administrators resorted to makeshift, coarse policies. Targeting groups associated with crime was often seen as the only effective course of action. Associating Albanians and others with banditry often left a lasting stigma.

The Long Scourge

These historic links between specific groups and banditry invoke an exceedingly sensitive question for scholars today: can it be possible that banditry, or 'criminal' behaviour more generally, was or is a facet of a group's culture? Scholars tend to differ on this issue. Some sociologists and anthropologists have broached these links in proposing the existence of certain 'honour culture' societies. Such cultures permeate certain places in the world, such as in the lands encompassing the Mediterranean. In these locales, residents tend to construe acts of violence and theft as masculine behaviour. The notion of honour reflects a person's successful 'control over resources by means of physical force'.[18] Why such cultures exist in some places as opposed to others is a matter of dispute. Scholars tend to link honour cultures to the historic absence of stable, legitimate states capable of exercising the unquestioned use of force. In these environments, banditry takes on more noble or legitimate contours. Locals may admire someone who robs, intimidates and kills because they make themselves 'respectable'.[19]

There are risks in believing local cultural traits help determine banditry's prevalence within certain areas. One cautionary lesson can be found in south Asia. In the early nineteenth century, British imperial officers and adventurers published lurid accounts of their encounters with what they perceived to be a vast, indigenous criminal conspiracy. Indians themselves termed the phenomenon as *thuggee*. Thuggee, from which the term 'thug' is derived, constituted a loose association of gangs who strangled and robbed hapless travellers. What appeared to bind many of the 'stranglers' together was their collective devotion to their patron goddess, Kali. Though thuggee gangs appeared to have comprised both Muslims and Hindus, the cult had passed from generation to generation. The lurid nature of their killings and rituals underscored what appeared to many to be the primitive nature of Indian culture. Hindus, *The Times* declared in 1838, were 'the only people amongst whom a sect has been found who seriously believed that they were pleasing and propitiating Heaven by murdering their fellow-citizens, and appropriating the plunder to their own use'.[20] The seriousness of the problem compelled British Indian officials to engage in a campaign to combat thuggee throughout the subcontinent. More contemporary scholars have cast doubt on the existence of a criminal cult devoted to Kali. Rather than a genuine cultural phenomenon, critics have argued that thuggee was more likely the product of British prejudice, false reporting and a general misunderstanding of south Asian society. Other scholars are not so sure. A survey of archival records from periods predating the arrival of the British suggest that thugs may indeed have existed for some time. Either way, colonial officials saw thuggee as confirmation of Britain's modus vivendi in India. For administrators in London and Delhi, to rule the subcontinent was to civilise it. Thuggee was one of many practices, such as infanticide and *suttee* (widow burning), that had to end for India to be ruled and reformed.[21]

Whatever the case, cultural bias and politics continued to influence India's relationship with banditry well after thuggee was declared extinct in the mid-nineteenth century. Officials in Delhi today still speak of the existence of people belonging to 'Other Backward Classes' or OBCs. As groups found towards the bottom of India's caste system, OBCs tended to be associated with what the British colonial government once referred to as 'criminal tribes'. Under British imperial rule, 'criminal tribes' faced draconian restrictions on their movements and activities. Elements of this colonial administration remained in force in India despite the country's independence in 1947.

Historians have tended to look at the issue of banditry's relationship with culture in a different way. What has intrigued historians the most about brigandage is what it reveals about the development of class and social consciousness. In 1959, Eric Hobsbawm published his influential work *Primitive Rebels: Studies in Archaic Forms of Social Movements in the 19th and 20th Centuries*. As a Marxist scholar who had first dedicated himself to the study of labour activism and social reform, Hobsbawm took up the subject of banditry as a potential window into the politics of the European underclasses. Brigandage, he proposed, at times represented a mode of rebellion against those who exploited the peasantry and urban poor. These 'social bandits', as he called them, were primitive expressions of discontent and mobilisation aimed at exacting vengeance on landowners, tax collectors and others who gained wealth and power over them. The earliest iterations of the Mafia of Sicily, he assumed, emerged from these same impulses. Even though its first leaders were drawn from the elite, the Mafia usurped many of the elite's prerogatives in ways that favoured peasants and workers. It was, in Hobsbawm's estimation, 'a parallel system' of governance 'that grew out of the needs of all rural classes'. This system, it seemed, was preferable to what the government in Rome had to offer in the nineteenth century. 'For the weak – the peasants and the miners – it provided at least some guarantee that obligations between them would be kept, some guarantee that the usual degree of oppression would not be habitually exceeded; it was the terror which mitigated traditional tyrannies.'[22]

Subsequent iterations of *Primitive Rebels* excluded discussion of the Mafia as an example of Hobsbawm's thesis. This revision aside, the book remains a cornerstone. For decades now, scholars have built upon the supposition that social bandits offer insights into the struggles and aspirations of the weak and the poor in history. Hobsbawm's work energised debate within the study of the Balkans over the historical relevance of the legendary *hajduk*s, or mountain bandits, of early modern Bosnia, Greece, Serbia and Bulgaria. Social banditry as a supposed global phenomenon gave comfort to those who argued that hajduks represented the will of peasants to be free from Ottoman rule. Such a contention is not without its detractors. There are broad disagreements over whether peasant bandits possessed political motives besides a disdain for landlords or provincial governors. It is doubtful that hajduks consciously fought for nationalist causes.[23] Nevertheless, the myth of the nationalist hajduk has inspired more recent waves of activism and militancy. The infamous Serb paramilitary leader and crime boss, Arkan, claimed that he was carrying on the hajduk tradition during his murderous campaigns waged during the Yugoslav Civil War.[24] Suspicions that the social bandit is more myth than legend has spawned broader revisions with respect to the social relevance of banditry. Rather than an archaic form of peasant resistance, more recent scholarship has tended to emphasise the roles of elites in either supporting or perpetrating acts of brigandage.

A prime example of this paradox can be found in the myths and realities surrounding the figure of Jesse James. As the leader of the dreaded James-Younger Gang, which terrorised the American Midwest for much of the 1870s, James assumed folk hero status. Newspapers from the time popularised the gang's brazen murders and bank heists as acts of revenge against those who sought to swindle the common man. Jesse's brother, Frank, declared that if America ever fought a second Civil War, it would be one between 'capital and labor' or 'greed and manhood'.[25] A closer look at his life does not reveal Jesse James to be much of social bandit. As the son of prominent slaveholding family from central Missouri, James was a virulent white supremacist and supporter of Southern succession. During the Civil War he served as a Confederate guerrilla under the command of infamous leaders William Quantrill and 'Bloody Bill' Anderson. James viewed his post-war reign of terror as a continuation of the Civil War itself. Due to the support of sympathetic journalists, politicians and commentators in Missouri, the James-Younger gang assumed its contemporary mythos. Though the press convinced many to see him as a folk hero, James fancied himself as a man principally dedicated to resurrecting the old political order, the Confederacy and the Southern 'way of life'.[26]

That Jesse James's exploits remain the stuff of legend is testament to the romantic power of literature, film and song. Bandit tales are adventure stories, but they are also often metaphoric in their construction. This served as the basis for Hobsbawm's insights into banditry's historical resonance. Whether they tell of the deeds of Jesse James, Mexico's Malverde, Brazil's Lampião or China's Bai Lang, art that glorifies bandits tells us something of the people who compose it or embrace it. Ballads and folk yarns about highwaymen, hajduks and other 'noble robbers' point to popular and genuine yearnings for power and justice. The appeal of the bandit stems from his (or her) ability to smite those who rule at the expense of the weak.

Robin Hood epitomises this sort of outlaw, despite the fact that no one with that name ever lived. The first known reference to Robin Hood is in ballads dated to 1377.[27] One of the earliest stories, *A Gest of Robyn Hood*, emphasises that he was a robber and thief prone to violence (on more than one occasion, Robin beheads or mutilates his victims). Though his thievery served to punish the wicked, it is far less clear whether he stole or killed for the benefit of the poor. His generosity among the downtrodden was likely meant to imply his commitment to 'Christian charity rather than any conceived social policy'.[28] Nothing in these early ballads suggests that his life and exploits were meant to be seen as an indictment of a corrupt or illegitimate state.

The earliest tales of Robin Hood were also generally ambivalent to matters of class and status. Robin, in these first adventures, is a free-born yeoman and therefore someone comfortable around people of higher status. His persona did not assume more subversive implications until centuries after his conception. In sixteenth-century Britain, popular May Day celebrations included performances of plays and other rituals that celebrated Robin Hood as a champion of the common people. The pageantry and stories associated with these local festivals, one nobleman complained to the king, not only led to 'lewdness and ribaldry', but also taught disobedience to the crown and for the law.[29] Yet by the reign of the Tudors, elite audiences also took greater interest in Robin Hood. Writers and playwrights increasingly reimagined him as a lord who embodied the virtues of chivalry and loyalty. Like King Arthur, Robin Hood came to be seen as an unmistakable representation of historic England and the English nation. Walter Scott's *Ivanhoe* reintroduced him to British readers in the nineteenth century. Scott's Robin Hood became Robin of Locksley, a nobleman and kind-hearted rebel who had fought in the Crusades alongside Richard the Lionheart. These and other embellishments upon the Robin Hood myth transformed him into a humble patriot who defied the tyranny of Prince John and the oppressive Normans in the name of England's Anglo-Saxons.

Robin's lasting artistic influence, as well as his applicability across different cultures, is indicative of the evocative nature of the outlaw. It may not matter that Robin Hood did not always rob the rich and give to the poor; in the long run, the character proved supple enough for audiences to embrace him in contrary ways. Be it in the *Gest of Robyn Hood* or Kevin Costner's *Prince of Thieves*, a Robin Hood may be powerful or oppressed, dashing or crass, terrifying or lovable, loyal or rebellious, vengeful or gracious, generous or indifferent. Though defiant of authority, Robin Hood almost always appears to represent the common folk. This kind of bandit, like the gangster or mafiosi of popular media today, is the everyman.

The Long Scourge

'BURIED UNDER ACRES OF MORTAR AND BRICK': BANDITRY'S LONG ROAD TO EXTINCTION

On the morning of Ned Kelly's hanging, 11 November 1880, a crowd of 5,000 formed outside Melbourne's Old Gaol. Among the mix of curious onlookers were relatives and well-wishers. Kelly's notoriety was what drew such a large crowd. Over the previous years, his exploits as a bank robber and murderer had become a regular feature of Australia's daily newspapers. His final showdown with the authorities, during which he wore an elaborate suit of armour, sealed his place in the colony's popular consciousness. Kelly, from the perspective of the press at least, was no hero. He had killed three policemen while his gang terrorised the interior of rural Victoria. His transformation into a popular icon, however, was already in the making. 'We hear people talking of the poor Kellys,' one journalist noted, 'recounting in glowing terms their now famous raid upon Euroa; extolling their cleverness on evading capture, and holding them up as men to be admired rather than reprobated.'[30] Despite fears of a riot that morning, the men and women who assembled before the jail melted away as news of his death seeped through the crowd.

A good amount of nostalgia is responsible for Ned Kelly's metamorphosis into Australia's Robin Hood. He and his brother were born of immigrants from Ireland. Like tens of thousands of others, his father Red came as a convict deported by the British crown. The romance that colours how many Australians perceive him, however, is only partially rooted in his defiance of the police and the British imperial government. His connection to the countryside and to a more bucolic time in the country's past plays some role as well. In the century that preceded Kelly's dramatic rise to prominence, the Outback had been a refuge for escaped prisoners and outlaws fleeing the penal settlements along the coasts. Bushrangers epitomised those who embraced and thrived in Australia's rough wilderness. By the time of Kelly's hanging, his native Victoria, including its inland districts, had changed. A gold rush in the 1850s brought an onslaught of settlers and investors to the colony. By 1880, 'Marvelous Melbourne' had grown into a city with a half a million residents.[31] Together with other booming centres like Sydney, the colonies of Australia had assumed more affluent and cosmopolitan attributes. The economy continued to diversify and expand, bringing in more immigrants from both Europe and Asia. City life, with all of its economic, social and cultural trappings, increasingly defined day-to-day tastes and routines. Politics, too, was becoming more democratic and urbane. By the time Victoria joined the continent's other five colonies in creating a united federation, women had attained the right to vote in several parts of the country. As the twentieth century beckoned, Australia was no longer a distant repository for Great Britain's convicts and outcasts. It was evolving into a sophisticated state and an increasingly self-confident and self-aware nation.

Ned Kelly's demise speaks to a quandary: why does brigandage begin to disappear throughout much of the world by the twentieth century? To date, no scholar has proven precisely when, how or why banditry went into decline or vanished. Nevertheless, to talk of banditry as an ongoing phenomenon in the twenty-first century is moot. The major newspapers of the Western world do not lament brigandage as a social or political strain. It is even harder to find modern prominent officials or parties campaigning to end brigandage. A bandit now seems like a profession reserved for a wilder, more backward place and time. Why?

Banditry's end is symptomatic of states that developed robust systems of administration and commerce. Steady shifts in the world economy have led to the modern states we know today. The beginning of the colonisation of the Americas in the late 1400s, coupled with increased patterns of trade across the Indian and Atlantic Oceans, prompted dramatic changes in the daily lives and habits of people all over the world. People soon ate better due in large measure to crops imported from the Americas. The increased availability of New World commodities augmented improvements in agricultural practices by the sixteenth century. Meanwhile, silver mined in the Americas inundated trade networks and marketplaces throughout the globe, leading to increased amounts of liquidity and spending. Intensifying patterns of commerce and production enhanced the numbers and the fortunes of urban merchants, bankers and professionals. All of this led to more efficient and lucrative economies. While states in Western Europe benefitted the most from this revolution in commerce and finance, state treasuries everywhere soon reaped increasing windfalls from the rise of trade after the 1500s. Through the imposition of new port duties and other commercial taxes, governments around the world looked upon trade as a more reliable and lucrative source of revenue. With the aid of new-found fiscal reservoirs, states could do more than build larger palaces and finance more protracted wars. The onset of this commercial revolution permitted rulers and attendants greater latitude to assert their power over those they governed and to create more rigorous forms of administration.

As agricultural yields and mortality rates improved, rural populations expanded. While trade may have enriched merchants and professionals living in town, unemployment and landlessness increased in the countryside. Desperation compelled untold millions to migrate to market towns and ports between the fifteenth and twentieth centuries. Most of the work that greeted them was for unskilled positions as labourers, porters, mill workers and weavers. The arrival of these newcomers to town became the initial workforce for the first industrialised trades. The eighteenth century saw this shift towards mechanised mass production within towns in Northern Europe. A hundred years later, industrialised patterns of labour became the global norm. The wealth this generated profoundly changed the nature of work and production. As tax receipts pushed upwards, governments financed reforms that made states more centralised and professionally run. New formal ministries, staffed by ever larger numbers of bureaucrats, undertook increasingly more ambitious projects in the public interest. Enhancing the physical growth of the public and private sectors were rapid breakthroughs in technology and scientific know-how. Old problems that afflicted agrarian society, such as sanitation, urban fires, epidemics and chronic hunger became increasingly more manageable. The complexion of society also began to change. By the middle of the nineteenth century, the number of urban dwellers began to overtake the number of residents in the countryside in several areas around the world. An 1851 census of Great Britain estimated that the country's urban population comprised 50.2 per cent of the whole. Sixty years later, that number would jump to 78.1 per cent.[32]

The dual forces of industrialisation and urbanisation created increasingly difficult environments for bandits to survive. As employment opportunities drew ever larger numbers of people to cities, there were simply fewer residents travelling country roads or living on the land for bandits to victimise. Although some rural crime lingers on within many modern societies, urban crime rates, particularly in matters of theft and armed robbery, grew more serious over time. The development of industrialised, commercially driven economies created new incentives for would-be highwaymen and stickup artists. To paraphrase the famed bank robber Willie Sutton, crime came to prevail in urban centres because that's where the money was.

The growth of the state placed brigands in even graver jeopardy. By the opening of the nineteenth century, a structural revolution had begun to gather momentum in various parts of the world. Government funding for projects such as road and bridge construction increased. Investment in new technology, particularly after the advent of the telegraph and steam engines, led to the rapid expansion of communication and transport networks. Greater financial resources also allowed for the increased management of natural resources such as water, minerals and wood. Forests and mountains, once the refuge of isolated and rebellious communities, came under more direct supervision of governments.

Complementing these advancements was the establishment or enlargement of state institutions. Before the nineteenth century ended, public education became a standard practice. Even in once-remote places one could find post offices, courts, hospitals, jails and barracks. All of these changes left bandits fewer and fewer places to hide.

For many areas once troubled by brigands, the coup de grâce came in the form of more regular, professional policing. Few states previously maintained constabulary forces exclusive of the military. Crime detection, let alone prosecution and punishment, often relied heavily upon the initiative of local communities and private citizens. England's overworked and untrained village constables were a mainstay of public law enforcement in the countryside through to the nineteenth century. Searching for suspects and raising public awareness of criminal acts depended on the raising of a 'hue-and-cry', as opposed to a set of standardised legal procedures.[33] Ivan the Terrible (1530–1584) had the foresight to establish a 'Banditry Office' in the middle of the sixteenth century in his position as Grand Prince of Moscow and all Russia. This too was no professional police force but rather a personal army that served his will alone.[34] It was only later, beginning in the eighteenth century, that permanent, regular rural constabulary forces came into being. France led the way with its reorganisation of the medieval *maréchaussée* system. Rather than a hodgepodge of various court-appointed or ad hoc officers, the *maréchaussées* constituted a force that was centralised, organised, professionally trained and regularly paid. Paris redubbed the force the Gendarmerie Nationale in 1791 in the wake of the Revolution. Napoleon prized its ability to surveille the whole of the countryside, often providing 'the most precise information' of the nation's mood and doings.[35] Other European nations followed in the early nineteenth century. With the spread of European empires, imported models, be it Britain's constables, Italy's carabinieri or French gendarmes, helped inspire the development of rural police forces worldwide.[36]

Until these changes, travel out of many major cities carried with it the distinct possibility of being held up and robbed along the highway. London, for example, had more than its share of bandits blighting the roads out of town. After the 1795 execution of the last notorious highwayman to plague London, that danger subsided, thanks to the establishment of nighttime patrols and regular tolls, the increased use of traceable banknotes as opposed to gold and, perhaps most of all, London's own growing city limits. As would be the case for bandits outside of other towns in the world, outlying ravines, forests and swamps previously favoured by highwaymen were increasingly 'buried under acres of mortar and brick'.[37]

Nevertheless, a number of factors did stymie the elimination of banditry through the nineteenth and twentieth centuries. Downturns in the economy, as well as recurrent problems of unemployment, low crop yields and landlessness, periodically sparked sudden surges in brigandage. During the early 1800s, economic upheaval, brought on by industrialisation, helped sustain the proliferation of rural gangs in southern England.[38] As in the past, war and mass mobilisation ignited even larger outbreaks of banditry. The end of the First World War led to a wave of rural crime in multiple portions of the world. Before the close of fighting in 1918, close to half a million men deserted the ranks of the Ottoman imperial army, precipitating widespread acts of brigandage.[39] The collapse of the Qing monarchy in 1912, coupled with the outbreak of civil war and Japan's invasion, led to decades of lawlessness in the Chinese countryside. Our understanding of banditry in more contemporary times becomes more convoluted in cases where pedantic crime overlapped with acts of popular resistance. British troops stationed along Kenya's colonial border frequently complained of 'raiders' invading from neighbouring Ethiopia. In the context of the late nineteenth century, imperial officials and locals on the ground interpreted these incidents as attacks upon the legitimacy of British colonial rule.[40] In the decades that followed the October Revolution of 1917, Bolshevik bureaucrats lamented what they often referred to as banditry in Chechnya. Chechens, as one official put it in 1952, 'refuse to work, organize mass disturbances, get involved in fights with local inhabitants, and continue their bandit-like activities', such as plundering collective farms. Officials, however, did not perceive such acts as an indictment against Soviet rule. It was indicative instead of their belief that Chechens 'have a specific genotype and are fanaticized by pan-Islamism'.[41]

These late struggles with banditry are not irrelevant to our understanding of organised crime and mafias today. The historical forces that led to the gradual end of brigandage tend be associated with states that first developed more centralised governments and more industrialised economies. Most of these states are located within the confines of Western Europe and the western hemisphere. Conversely, countries with lasting economic or political impediments continued to struggle with banditry into the twentieth century. These difficulties, brought on by war or political upheaval, tended to lead to delays in industrialisation and generally weaker systems of administration. Banditry's varied history in the nineteenth and twentieth centuries, in other words, reflects a widening disparity between the so-called West and the proverbial 'rest'. This gap, which mirrored a more generalised divergence in the nature of commerce and state-building, remains an integral part of how we often perceive incidents of banditry in the twenty-first century. News coverage, as well as academic studies of more contemporary bandits, tend to depict the phenomenon as illustrative of issues such as poverty, corruption and inequality in the developing world.

Banditry also reflects profound disparities within societies and states, regardless of whether they are in the developed or developing world. Areas that remained notorious for banditry during the nineteenth and twentieth centuries were often among the most remote, underdeveloped or impoverished territories of a state. In many cases, the peoples who lived there retained or earned reputations for unruly behaviour. The perception that certain types of peoples or localities fostered cultures of banditry pervaded both the colonial world as well as established nation-states. France put its last great bandit to death in 1935. Newspapers in the country treated the arrest and execution of André Spada, Corsica's 'Tiger of Cinarca', as an event of national significance. Spada's early years of destitution reflected the island's long-standing association with poverty. He murdered twelve men in his life of crime although locals on the island appeared to hold him in high esteem. Yet Spada claimed to have never robbed to get rich but to avenge those who had wronged him, particularly those in power. For the press, his crass temperament and virility epitomised the rustic qualities of his native Corsica. 'No doubt we came to see Spada and to hear him respond to his ... romantic crimes,' one journalist wrote. It was, for many who attended the trial, equally 'the funeral of a romantic'.[42] An era long in the making seemed to have ended.

And yet one may still find faint traces of banditry's historical endurance. Just after the turn of the twenty-first century, officials in India proudly announced they had killed two of the country's last great bandits: Rambabu Gadariya and Koose Munisamy Veerappan. Both men came from humble stock before amassing small fortunes as kidnappers. Both were known to be exceedingly violent. After an early life as a goat herder, Rambabu had accrued scores of criminal charges and had murdered at least thirty-five people.[43] Veerappan, meanwhile, had claimed the lives of over 150 people and over 2,000 elephants in his thirty-year career as a kidnapper and poacher.[44] Nevertheless both men were upheld as local Robin Hoods with deep ties to the communities that harboured them. It was with support of locals in his native Tamil Nadu that Veerappan grew wealthy from the illicit trade of sandalwood and ivory. His willingness to donate money for dowries and building temples was essential to his evasion of the authorities. Before police killed him in 2004, Bollywood producers had released two films devoted to his exploits and mystique.

The BBC, the *New York Times* and other international news agencies took an intense interest in the demise of these two bandits. Why their deaths drew such publicity was, in many respects, a reflection of the context. Both men were killed amid America's War on Terror and the hunt for Osama Bin Laden.[45] Their deaths also seemed to reveal something far more meaningful about the country where they were born. India's prospects as an emerging nation appeared bright and luminous in the early 2000s. As one of the foundational BRIC (Brazil, Russia, India, China), India was seen by economists to have great potential for economic growth and prosperity. Its status as the world's largest democracy further buoyed hopes that India would mature into a global power. The very existence of Veerappan and Rambabu, however, contrasted sharply with these expectations. Veerappan's jungle fiefdom was near to Bangalore, India's prospective Silicon Valley. 'As the South Indian states strove to be seen as forward-thinking hotbeds of technology and development,' one *New York Times* commentator noted, 'it seemed ridiculous that they couldn't catch a bandit in their own backyard.'[46] The critical lessons local commentators drew from the killing of the two bandits concerned issues of economic sustainability and good governance. The life both men lived appeared to point to the larger challenge of India's endemic poverty, particularly among marginal social groups.

Banditry's waning relevance, of course, did not relieve governments from worrying about crime. As states asserted greater control over the countryside, administrators struggled to maintain control over their growing cities and ports. The terror that brigands once inspired on the periphery of towns soon transferred to neighbourhoods and whole cities in various parts of the world. The pervasiveness of urban crime drove political debates over matters of reform and public safety. Greater care and energy were spent gathering statistics on the spread and nature of urban crime. Newspapers, followed by radio, film and television, fanned popular anxieties with lurid tales of malice and depravity. Even in the most industrialised and affluent of societies, to stroll around town after dark, or to tread into certain quarters at any time, appeared to carry risks of theft or bodily harm.

The Jack the Ripper murders of 1888 were an early example of the sort of fears urban crime stirred at the end of the nineteenth century. The Ripper's reign of terror over London's old East End did not last long. 'Ripperologists' tend to agree that he was responsible for the deaths of five women between August and November that year. His brief scourge, however, summoned a wave of fright and outrage in Britain. Leading the way in interpretating the murders were London's newspapers. 'Penny dreadful' tabloids, as well as the more established *Times*, cast the killings as the natural outgrowth of urban poverty and blight. It seemed natural that Jack haunted the likes of Dorset Street in Spitalfields. It was a place, as one reformer avowed, where hunger 'walks prowling in its alleyways' and where 'the criminals of to-morrow' were born.[47] Consternation at Scotland Yard's failure to nab the murderer did little to prevent public speculation as to the Ripper's identity.

News editors and retired policemen offered a number of competing theories: Jack was alternately a loathed immigrant from Eastern Europe, a mad doctor driven by blood lust, a deranged West End playboy with a taste for low-class women or perhaps a leftist radical seeking attention. Whatever the case, Jack the Ripper essentialised, for many in the city, the loathing, ills and bigotries spawned by late nineteenth-century London.[48]

What also drew the public's attention to Jack the Ripper were his victims. All the women he murdered were prostitutes. At the time of their deaths, a campaign aimed at ending the sex trade was gathering strength in Britain and beyond. By the 1880s, other trades and practices of ill-repute, such as gambling and narcotics consumption, acquired new significance as officials, as well as activists and newspaper editors, sought to make towns healthier, safer places. Growing apprehensions about prostitution and other 'vices' were not restricted to the physical or moral threats associated with them. Eliminating vice was increasingly seen as critical to the maintenance of a well-ordered economy and society.

Many of the characteristics that defined state efforts to do away with banditry echoed in this new struggle to combat different forms of vice. There was, however, an essential difference that made the prohibitionist campaign to end prostitution and other vices different from the historic fight against brigands. Governments before the nineteenth century had long wavered in their efforts at regulating gambling, prostitution and the consumption of alcohol and narcotics. Nor was vice consistently viewed or construed as a crime worthy of the state's attention. Moreover, unlike bandits, card sharks, pimps and lotus eaters did not necessarily leave bloodied corpses behind. Gambling, sex and intoxicants were enjoyed by large numbers of people. This allure made these trades cornerstone industries of the emerging mafias of the modern era.

2

Love and Relaxation for Sale: Vice and the Roots of Organised Crime

San Francisco's transformation into a great metropolis was slow and laboured. The town, originally dubbed Yerba Buena, remained small and isolated during its first years as a Spanish and then Mexican outpost. When the United States conquered California in 1846, there were fewer than a thousand residents. Though it sat at the heart at an immense harbour, significant obstacles constrained San Francisco's long-term growth. The terrain enveloping the Golden Gate was marshy and windswept. The rough hills that sprawled south offered little flatland for development. Despite the immense wealth that poured into San Francisco after the discovery of gold in California in 1848, the city's leaders fretted over the lack of fresh water well into the twentieth century. Decades passed before engineers, backed by an immense fortune in private and public capital, completed the aqueducts and dams necessary to store and transport water into the growing metropolis. It took a similarly gargantuan effort to rebuild San Francisco after the disastrous earthquake of 1906. As the city recovered, its skyline soared higher, with buildings of steel replacing older structures of wood and brick. Less than ten years after the quake, San Francisco welcomed the world to its shores with the opening of the Panama–Pacific International Exposition. Like other grand fairs held in London and Paris at the end of the nineteenth century, the San Francisco exhibition was meant to celebrate the wonders of the day as well as the wealth and sophistication of the United States. One speaker touted America's intrepid nature as the force that founded 'this beautiful city of dreams'. 'The greatest adventure is before us,' he boomed, 'the gigantic adventures of an advancing democracy – strong, virile and kindly – and in that advance we shall be true to the indestructible spirit of the American pioneer.'[1]

San Francisco did not always invoke such sentiments. Aspects of the city's culture and history sullied San Francisco's status as an American jewel on the Pacific. Since its heyday as a mining hub, the town had developed a reputation for corruption, crime and loose morals. Single men seeking to strike it rich in the nearby Sierras gave life to hundreds of gambling establishments in the city. Local card halls and betting parlours attracted punters as well as legions of thieves and ruffians. Casual violence was commonplace at the many saloons and dancehalls of the city's core. By the 1870s, several neighbourhoods fell under the influence of gangs comprising young miscreants and petty crooks. San Francisco's prostitutes attracted the greatest attention. With tens of thousands of would-be fortune seekers arriving in the San Francisco Bay year after year, the city's sex industry drew large numbers of girls and women, lured or kidnapped from far and wide. Xenophobia and other anxieties, such as widespread alcoholism and opium use, coloured local impressions of those involved in 'trade'. The local press heightened these fears with lurid exposés drawn from the streets of notorious districts such as the Tenderloin and the Barbary Coast. Each of these neighbourhoods were tantamount to a 'school of vice', as one paper put it – places where children learned at the feet of 'ragpickers, scavengers, prostitutes and their "men"'.[2]

San Francisco's leaders worked to curb the city's worst excesses in the decades before the quake of 1906. The city's first police officers were generally underpaid and often unreliable. At various points in the nineteenth century, vigilante committees served as the real keepers of the peace. What passed for justice, however, was often no better than the vilest of crimes, including murder and rape. Ordinances meant to discourage lewd or repugnant behaviour often went unenforced. The justice system used many of the laws, such as local and state-imposed penalties on opium smoking, to target Chinese and other Asian immigrants. Yet by the start of the new century, a more earnest effort at good government gathered momentum. Reformist politicians, backed by social activists, gained power at the expense of well-heeled 'machine bosses'. Newspapers played a critical role in bringing down corrupt luminaries such as lawyer and kingmaker Abe Ruef, who helped manage a 100-room brothel.[3] In the wake of the Panama–Pacific Exposition of 1915, San Francisco's oldest red-light district, the Barbary Coast, came under fierce pressure as police and other city officials sought the closure of establishments known for prostitution and kink. One public enquiry in 1921 declared the Barbary Coast 'theoretically dead', with only 'a few straggling resorts remaining open for the meager profit afforded to visiting sailors and tourist slumming parties'.[4]

The development of San Francisco's 'underworld' bears many similarities to other histories found across the globe by this point in time. Far older cities came to similar points of reckoning in dealing with issues of crime, vice and reform. As industrialising urban centres grew and became precarious places to live, governments took greater interest in the security and welfare of their citizens. Yet unlike banditry, what came to define certain types of wrongdoing was not simply the threat of violence or unruly behaviour. Rather it was the belief that certain vices were too corrosive, degenerative or loathsome to be allowed to flourish unchecked. Three particular services – gambling, sex and the sale of intoxicants – were central to these fears.

Efforts to end the sex trade, curtail gambling and forbid the sale of intoxicants reflected a spirit of reform and revitalisation found throughout the Western world. The power and influence of Western empires helped introduce these campaigns to large portions of Asia and Africa too. Putting prohibitions into place often failed to curb the public's demand for these illicit industries; however, many mafias originated simultaneously with the creation of these newly 'organised crimes'.

'DIRTY TRADES' AND THE LAWS THAT MADE ORGANISED CRIME

Cairo, as a city, did not exist during the time of the pharaohs. Yet by its founding in the tenth century, prostitution had been a feature of Egyptian life for millennia. Lore dating back to the time of Herodotus held that one of the pyramids of Giza was built to honour a famed Greek courtesan. More direct evidence suggests that prostitution was integral to the rhythms of life, commerce and religion in Ancient Egypt. Relief images and written sources from the pharaonic, Hellenic and Roman periods detail the proclivities and decorum surrounding the trade.[5] Neither the spread of Christianity, nor the Muslim conquest in the seventh century, ended the importance of the profession in Egypt, despite its condemnation in both the Bible and Quran. Like many urban workers, prostitutes donned telltale articles of clothing and went about their business in select neighbourhoods, and successive dynasties and regimes saw the practice was to some degree regulated. In the seventeenth century, a troop of forty constables watched over local brothels. Regular taxation on the city's prostitutes paid for this force, as well as other services provided by the local administration.⁶

There were times, however, when officials sought to curb or ban the trade. In 1798, Napoleon Bonaparte landed in Egypt to use it as a base to threaten the British colony of India. After making quick work of the local Ottoman garrison, he and his soldiers settled into Cairo with the belief that French government could reform the city. Among the measures the French imposed were new regulations directed at the city's sex industry (such as improved street lighting outside brothels and greater transparency when it came to the costs of a prostitute's services). Years into the French occupation, however, Napoleon soured on Cairo's sex workers. Outbreaks of venereal diseases claimed the lives of nearly 2,500 soldiers. As punishment, French officials drowned 400 prostitutes in the Nile and shuttered Cairo's brothels.⁷ Mass killings and greater oversight failed to end the trade. Many prostitutes carried on with their business in towns just outside Cairo as Napoleon's men floundered in their effort to hold Egypt. With Napoleon's defeat, Cairo's brothels reopened and continued to thrive despite intermittent acts of government suppression.

The gambling industry possesses a somewhat similar hold over the history of Bath in Western England. From Bath's days as a Roman settlement, gaming and wagering were common practices among its residents. Archaeological finds in the nineteenth century, including the discovery of dice made from bone, affirm that the city's famous baths were often the setting for games of chance.⁸ The development of England's gambling culture likely shaped the tastes of Bath's residents through the Middle Ages. Knights and pilgrims returning from the Crusades, for example, helped introduce Near Eastern versions of card playing as a game of chance. With the ascendency of Elizabeth I in the late sixteenth century, the British government approved the creation

Love and Relaxation for Sale

of a national lottery, an innovation meant to raise money for the maintenance of the country's navy. It was also under Elizabeth that Bath earned a reputation as a resort town for the nobility and the well-to-do. Gambling became an important attraction in the town in the early 1700s.

One particular figure proved instrumental in Bath's transformation into a city of leisure and vice. Richard 'Beau' Nash was a well-born gentleman and gadfly of no great distinction before his arrival in Bath. Yet as a self-declared professional gambler, he assumed the title 'master of ceremonies' and introduced the town to much of the decorum associated with London's gaming houses. He cleaned up the streets and forbade gamblers to wear swords (a gentleman's right, but one that resulted in the death of Nash's predecessor). He added to Bath's charm by organising elaborate balls and hiring musicians from London. His efforts paid dividends. Large 'companies' of noblemen and middle-class patrons flocked to Bath in the hopes of taking in the glamour and excitement of establishments such as the Pump Room and the Assembly Room.[9] Although the town featured a variety of gaming attractions, including horse racing, raffles and early iterations of roulette, card playing brought in the greatest number of gamblers. With lords and ladies forgoing their fortunes over games of chance, the British parliament intervened for fear of the moral and economic consequences of Bath's gambling culture. When a number of popular card games were made illegal in the 1730s and '40s, Nash and others invented new games. Bath eventually lost its appeal despite Beau Nash's best efforts. As British laws governing gambling grew stricter in the nineteenth century, wagerers in Bath went underground. For Britain's higher rollers, the end of the Napoleonic Wars allowed the well-heeled to explore new playgrounds, such as Saxon-les-Bains in the Alps and Monte Carlo on the French Riviera.[10]

These stories, drawn from places as different from each other as Cairo and Bath, attest to the disjointed histories of prostitution and gambling. For much of history, nothing akin to modern-day mafias claimed these trades as a part of their raison d'être. Why? Simply put, they were not necessarily considered crimes. Those who partook in either certainly drew the condemnation of religions, states and societies. But before the modern era, though a variety of different governments attempted to ban, discourage or regulate gambling and prostitution, they were inconsistent in their treatment. As late as the seventeenth century, German officials shaved women bald if they were found guilty of prostitution. Emperors in Beijing imposed harsh penalties upon Chinese gamblers, including fines, caning and imprisonment, but it failed to deter them. And yet, those same regimes sought to benefit from the proceeds generated by prostitution and gaming. Issues of morality or religious proscription tended to have little to do with why states began to take a harder, more consistent approach. The transformation of prostitution and gambling into 'organised crimes' stems from misgivings that were both universal and timeless. From classical times, areas euphemistically designated for 'trade' and 'sport' were places known for theft or violence. Betting parlours and brothels were associated with drink and other intoxicants, which often contributed to the raucousness or dubiousness of the clientele. Governments rarely expected gamblers and prostitutes to police themselves or ward off troublesome elements. The state was often obliged to step in.

Concern for the public's safety only partially accounts for why governments increasingly sought to rein in vice. As with banditry, more consistent and effective policing ensured fewer places and fewer citizens escaped the gaze of the modern state. Improved government revenue streams, as well as better state services and offices, incentivised administrators to do more for the citizens they served. The desire and the will to impose greater discipline and regimentation on people grew in tandem with state oversight.

Love and Relaxation for Sale

Conducting more rigorous censuses did more than improve a government's ability to tax or conscript: detailed census data offered greater insight into the location, composition and character of a state's citizenry. It was often on the basis of these statistics that administrators divined new regulations meant to nurture and protect the populace, as well as improve a government's effectiveness. As services improved – be they courts, police stations or schools – citizens increasingly acquired habits and licences that would make them more responsible and dutiful.

Stricter legal regimes imposed upon gambling and prostitution echoed global concerns stemming from accelerated urban development and industrialisation. For much of history, a slow and organic process shaped the development of modern towns. Few cities, such as China's imperial capital of Xian, emerged from a pre-planned vision. More often than not, unique geographic quirks and haphazard design formed the basis of a prosperous town. Efforts at redevelopment or renovation also tended to be incidental as opposed to preordained. What frequently passed as urban renewal was often the result of fire or earthquake, not a preset agenda.

The increasing pace of urbanisation, particularly by the eighteenth century, changed the organisation and construction of cities. A boom town such as San Francisco represents an extreme historical case. In the year before the start of the gold rush, the town's population hovered around a thousand. Four years later, in 1852, over 36,000 people lived in San Francisco. By 1900, the city claimed 342,000 residents.[11] As the town's original adobe architecture gave way to a rising metropolis made from wood, brick and steel, overcrowding became a chronic challenge. Neighbourhoods known for housing the down and out, such as the Tenderloin south of Market Street, became synonymous with ills such as malnutrition, unemployment, abuse, crime and hopelessness. The city's ten-cent boarding houses, one journalist mused in 1890, 'were grand dispellers of illusions and most of the weary sleepers who stretch out their limbs on [their] hard mattresses have little left to live for'.[12] While its relative newness and compact landscape contributed to San Francisco's struggle with poverty, other, more established cities witnessed similar trends. Mexico's capital experienced no less a boom in urban growth. With its population nearly doubling between 1895 and 1921, Mexico City swelled with residents living in impoverished, rundown neighbourhoods. Newspapers documented families having no place to cook but in the hallways of buildings or outside. Stray dogs roamed the street while transients raided homes and menaced residents. Those who endured these conditions often paid high rents.[13]

State investment in public infrastructure addressed some of the troubles caused by rapid urbanisation. Mass projects dedicated to improving public lighting, sanitation, heating, transport and drinking water were among the hallmarks of the nineteenth century. But for many civic leaders, the problems brought about by urban growth and declining standards of living were not solely material in nature. It appeared to many that what plagued the downtrodden were intellectual, moral or perhaps spiritual afflictions. Those who lived in squalor, some claimed, often did not know how to clean or care for themselves. Those who could not work simply needed greater discipline and spiritual maturity. 'Proper living' became the solution to disease, child abuse and destitution. For those who saw modern problems in these terms, government was the essential instrument of reform. Intense public campaigns compelled officials to implement school curricula that included lessons on hygiene and civic morality. In Britain, debtors and petty criminals could be confined to workhouses to learn the supposed discipline that came with hard labour. In the United States and other countries, activists and local governments opened homes for 'fallen women' who sought a more respectable life away from prostitution and poverty. The imagined benefits went beyond remedying the physical blight associated with urban poverty. A modern citizen, particularly one living in town, needed to cultivate the sort of restraint and dedication required for work in factories, warehouses and offices. The state, guided by right-minded leaders, was seen as the most effective means of instilling these ethics.

The ascendency of nationalism helped mould this shift around the philosophy of government. As the nineteenth century progressed, officials, ideologues and activists increasingly saw the work of the state as vital to the preservation of the nation. Nationalists came to understand that what bound a people together was not an attachment to a specific language, history, religion or territory. Nations also possessed values, values that enabled them to survive and thrive. Citizens of the nation, any nation, were meant to work hard, be frugal, obey the law, strive to be healthy and be attentive to the needs of the state. Reformers and conservatives tended to agree that men and women were obliged to abide by specific codes of behaviour. A nation, many believed, would not endure unless its men became good fathers, responsible husbands and steadfast workers and soldiers. A nation and its children depended upon the dedication of dutiful mothers and wives. Certain vices threatened the nation from within.

This desire to steel or revitalise society brought about a general reassessment of how states regulated gambling and prostitution. Beginning in the early 1800s, Western states and empires set a critical precedent for how vice was to be regulated or eradicated. Under a restored Bourbon monarchy, France declared all forms of gambling illegal in 1836. As other continental European states followed suit, calls to outlaw wagering grew louder in Britain and the United States. Gambling on horse racing, lotteries and other events grew in popularity through the nineteenth century as faster forms of transport and communication enabled punters and bookies to participate from far away. As wages improved through the century, larger numbers of urban workers splurged on boxing matches, parlour games and raffles. Anti-gambling advocates understood these new trends in apocalyptic terms. Games of chance, in the words one British critic, created 'feverish excitement in the place of work and industry', unsettled 'the labour market and the working classes' and encouraged 'crime and general recklessness'.[14] Lawmakers in London and in various American states agreed. After 1853, the British parliament took steps to curb the public's ability to gamble. Complaints over match fixing, as well as the moral dangers of gambling, led to blanket bans on horse racing and other games throughout America by the end of the nineteenth century.

Beyond the North Atlantic, British and French colonies rigorously sought to police gambling. In Hong Kong, British administrators cracked down on horse betting after introducing thoroughbred racing in the mid-nineteenth century, though the colonial government reluctantly eased restrictions after attendance at the Happy Valley racetrack plunged. Such exemptions or rollbacks tended to be rare. The most likely groups to enjoy gaming during this era were wealthy people with access to private clubs. While much of Europe grew more intolerant of wagering, the newly independent state of Monaco transformed itself into a gambling mecca. Although its principal casino, Monte Carlo, drew a crowd of 60,000 visitors during its opening year in 1868, the island developed a reputation for catering to the continent's elites.[15]

Prostitution acquired even greater significance among modern reformers. In 1791, France required all prostitutes to register with the state and undergo regular medical inspections performed by government authorities. The 'French system' mirrored broader state efforts to manage aspects of the economy and promote healthier social standards. 'Like begging, like gambling,' one French reformer declared, '[prostitution] is an industry, a resource against hunger or against dishonour, because one does not know to what ends an individual will go when they have no resources.'[16] As governments elsewhere sought to place similar controls over the sex trade, grassroots activists pushed for more stringent regimes that would outlaw prostitution. Advocates, such as English reformer Josephine Butler, reviled prostitution as an institution that enslaved mothers and daughters. In appealing to the public's humanity and patriotism, Butler and other strident feminists construed prostitution as a purveyor of disease, immorality and crime. Aiding them were their allies in the press, such as the famed editor W. T. Stead. Amid the hysteria generated by the Jack the Ripper killings, Stead's paper seized upon the murders as an instructive example of the mania, violence and depravity the sex trade inspired. Britain's decision to outlaw prostitution in 1885, as well as noted cases like the Ripper killings, spurred other countries in Europe and beyond to suppress prostitution altogether. As with the imposition of anti-gambling laws, European empires influenced governments in Africa and Asia to regulate sex work. Even independent states such as Japan and China drew upon European models in imposing government oversight of brothels as well as outlawing tabooed practices like child prostitution.

Legislation is one thing, enforcement another. Like the establishment of rural gendarmes, the organisation of modern urban police forces gave states increased confidence in their ability to oversee gambling and prostitution. As in the countryside, professional constabulary services were slow to take shape in cities, with law enforcement left to an array of ad hoc watchmen and 'committees' assembled by local authorities. Urban policing in many eighteenth-century European capitals was not restricted to keeping the peace. Constables in Louis XIV's Paris also kept tabs on the city's intellectual classes and urban poor to stymie dissent and revolt.[17] It was not until the mid-1800s that more recognisably 'modern' police forces emerged. Cities everywhere tended to draw inspiration from London's Metropolitan Police. As the first centralised uniformed service staffed by salaried, trained professionals, Britain's 'Bobbies' exemplified a commitment to dispassionate law enforcement. London raised standards further with the advent of its specialised investigative units, housed at Scotland Yard, which aided in both solving and pre-empting crimes.[18] By the end of the nineteenth century, major cities throughout the world adopted more invasive practices meant to make law enforcement more precise and effectual: this ranged from techniques such as fingerprinting and complex filing systems, to the adoption of more exacting guidelines and philosophies deemed critical to maintaining the professionalism of their craft.[19] Embracing psychology, for example, allowed local policemen to understand the personal motives and pathologies that drove criminals, making them easier to catch or interdict.

It is now clear that flaws and misconceptions tainted the invention of modern policing. Initially there was hope that new police forces would be more reliable than the amateurs they replaced. Uniformed constables, however, often proved to be as corrupt and incompetent as their predecessors. Bribery scandals, and accusations of brutality and ineptitude, were commonplace in both the Old and New World during the 1800s. Even the impeccable Scotland Yard endured a period of public outrage when four seasoned detectives were arrested for taking payments from known swindlers in 1876.[20] A less obvious failing can be sourced to the biases of lawmen and experts. Convention dictated that criminal behaviour was an innate trait of large groups of people. Anglophones spoke ominously of the threat posed by the 'dangerous classes' among the impoverished. Racism augmented the belief that the indigent formed an undifferentiated mass of real and potential criminals. The Buenos Aires police ranked among the first bureaus in the world to adopt fingerprinting, a move dedicated to tracking, as one officer put it, 'unruly, mobile and highly foreign' migrants from Southern and Eastern Europe.[21] Biological and social sciences became important for many who sought to understand and monitor groups with supposed propensities towards crime. Anthropologist Cesare Lombroso (1835–1909), as author of *The White Man and the Coloured Man*, proved especially influential in leading officials and reformers to believe that criminality was hereditary. Lombroso argued that southern Italians were criminally inclined since their 'inferior civilisation' was the product of their improper race-mixing with Africans across the sea.[22]

As gambling and prostitution drew increased public scrutiny, many frailties of modern policing were exposed. San Francisco's early history attests to the uneven and capricious results that came with enforcing anti-vice laws. As a frontier town, it saw licentious behaviour reign in the years following the American conquest. Its early justice system often differed little from mob law. Among the earliest groups to patrol the town's streets was a band of Mexican-American War veterans called the Society of Regulators. The Hounds, as they were better known, were notorious for wanton acts of rape, theft and murder. Among their most frequent victims were Chilean migrants, particularly women pressed into the sex trade. Local law enforcement gradually became more legalistic and less violent as the San Francisco Police Department grew. The policing of morals, however, remained discriminatory. An 1890 law forbidding persons from maintaining or visiting 'any house of ill-fame' led the police to corral the vice trade to a select number of neighbourhoods.[23] Meanwhile, lawmakers targeted Chinatown as a haven for sex slavery and wanton behaviour. Mass arrests of Chinese men became commonplace after the California legislature expressly banned games of chance (including fan tan, a favourite among new Chinese immigrants).[24] Public scrutiny of the police department increased as evidence of official misconduct mounted. Successive official enquiries at the turn of the century accused officers of taking bribes from madams and gambling-house proprietors both inside and outside San Francisco's red-light districts.

One state investigation made clear that 'visits of white men and white boys' to 'Chinese brothels and gambling resorts' were so open that there was 'no reasonable excuse' for the police not to know.[25] Signs of improvement were visible by the end of the First World War, driven by the intervention of the state government in Sacramento and the demands of local voters. In 1921, the San Francisco chief of police issued a ban on licensed tours and 'slumming parties' through the Barbary Coast and other areas known for loose morals.[26] Though vice remained in San Francisco, more regular government oversight made it seem far less rampant.

Regardless of their success, local enforcement efforts led many activists to see their cause as one without borders. Expanding the campaign was more than just a matter of conscience. For policing to be effective, the suppression of vice had to be co-ordinated beyond the confines of any one town or country. Officials and campaigners understood prostitution to be a global problem because many of the women counted or apprehended as sex workers were migrants of some kind. Administrators in colonial Bombay noted that, in addition to women from different parts of India, there were women who had travelled from as far away as Romania, Poland and Japan to work in the city's brothels.[27] For anti-vice advocates, economics alone did not account for why women worked in far-off bordellos. The true culprits were the 'procurers' who forced impoverished girls and mothers into the trade. The moral outrage inspired by these observations gave birth to a global crusade against what came to be known as 'white slavery'. The British parliament was among the first to take action with the passage of an 1885 law making the 'procurement' and transport of women across international borders a crime.[28] As other governments followed Britain's example, European and American news agencies printed lurid exposés of white slavery's local effects. Across the world, anxieties about race and race-mixing tended to colour how officials and the public understood the significance of white slaving. It was not that women were forced to endure such vile treatment at the hands of men, but rather it was the abject horror that it was often West Indians, African Americans or Polish Jews who 'stole' white girls from their families and subjected them to inhumane treatment. 'The white-slave traffic,' as one American congressman put it, 'while not so extensive, is much more horrible than any black-slave traffic ever was in the history of the world.'[29]

The feverishness surrounding white slavery reflected the phobias and prejudices of the nineteenth century. Some of the attention it drew, however, appears to forecast the rise of mafias in the twentieth century. The extraordinary career of Joseph Silver is especially illuminating in this regard. Born Joseph Lis in Galicia, in Russian-administered Poland, he pursued a decades-long criminal career spanning four continents at the turn of the century. From London to New York to Johannesburg to Buenos Aires, Silver travelled among networks of men and women who slummed across the world seeking to set up shop or evade arrest. He particularly relied upon the aid and services of fellow Jews, who, like Silver, left home in the hopes of escaping the poverty and anti-Semitic violence of Eastern Europe. Silver enjoyed his best years in South Africa as the 'king of pimps'. Johannesburg in the late nineteenth century was 'a man's town' on account of the large numbers of European and African mineworkers residing there.[30] With men outnumbering women in some parts of the city by as much as ten to one, Silver had a reservoir of steady customers for his bars and hotels. However, in addition to the threat of prosecution, Silver had to compete with rival pimps and hustlers. In addition to German, French and Polish 'white slavers', Johannesburg's underworld hosted a set of Americans calling themselves the 'Bowery Boys' in honour of the storied gang from Manhattan's Lower East Side. None of these groups could be called mafias; the networks established by Silver and others proved transient and brittle. Silver himself was often destitute and on the run. He died, ironically enough, in his native Poland, where Austrian authorities likely executed him for operating a smuggling outfit during the First World War.

Unlike prostitution, illicit gambling operations were typically the province of local entrepreneurs. Yet as with 'white slavery', there is little evidence that durable criminal syndicates reigned over illegal gaming by the turn of the twentieth century. There were early signs that criminals did manage to fashion fleeting networks that operated across large swaths of territory. Hodge-podge campaigns aimed at outlawing lotteries in portions of the United States led to the proliferation of organised schemes. During the late nineteenth century, operators based in Louisiana sold lottery tickets all over the country despite state and city prohibitions. By the 1880s, up to five million Americans had bought into the Louisiana state lottery, so much so that over half the mail posted from New Orleans contained tickets purchased out of state.[31] A more dramatic revolution in illegal gambling occurred with the development of the famed 'race wire' at the turn of the century. With the advent of the telegraph, bars and pool halls across America transformed into betting parlours featuring live horse racing results. When public pressure forced Western Union, the popular telegraph company, to end its association with gambling in 1904, smaller, private operators stepped in. Among them was Jacob 'Mont' Tennes, a prominent bookmaker from the north side of Chicago. His Illinois-based wire service, dubbed the General News Bureau, amassed a fortune from illicit wagering by the early 1910s, with an estimated $25,000 made in monthly profits.[32] Tennes's management over the bureau concluded with a whimper. His decision to sell off his stake in the company in 1927 gave way to an even more complex gambling racket, one engineered by the notorious Chicago Outfit founded by Al Capone.

What the likes of Tennes and Silver had in common was the

extent to which both ably co-opted politicians and the police. Both men prospered most when they received the protection of government officials. By the turn of the twentieth century, this cosiness between vice lords and elements of the state drew increasing ire from activists. Local corruption scandals across the Western world spoke to an undeniable fact: a larger system of wrongdoing sustained and abetted prostitution and gambling. The phrase 'organised crime' first entered the English language in this context. Its usage began in the United States. For reformers and opponents of 'machine' politics in many American cities, 'organised crime' in part denoted the entrenched corruption of the day. The obvious permissiveness with which gambling dens and brothels continued to do business appeared symptomatic of the vote-rigging and self-dealing evident in urban centres across the country. In New York, those who worked to eradicate vice felt certain that the Democratic Party, which had ruled over the city for much of the nineteenth and early twentieth centuries, deserved the blame. Saloons that illegally dispensed beer on Sunday, the *New York Times* observed, were 'more or less connected with every variety of professional and organised crime' and doubtless 'most intimately connected with professional and organised politics'.[33] Increased use of the phrase 'organised crime' also reflected the ways in which reformers perceived the fundamental nature of the vice trade. In 1909, Theodore A. Bingham, a former police commissioner, published an article in New York's *McClure's Magazine* entitled 'The Organized Criminals of New York'. In the piece, Bingham acknowledged that the police and city officials often protected purveyors of gambling and prostitution. Yet what made the trades organised was not solely the result of government complicity. Those who dealt in vice, particularly on Manhattan's Lower East Side, did not form a 'loose mass' of operators. They were, in his opinion, 'thoroughly organized, financially, politically and legally, for offence and defense'.[34]

Bingham's conclusions correspond to a critical moment in the formation of modern-day mafias. Since the beginning of modern Western efforts to control or eradicate vice, many presumed that the force of law could prevent the masses from indulging in prostitution and gambling. By the early twentieth century, it appeared in many places, first perhaps in the United States, that this assumption was wrong. The state itself was a part of the problem. But why petty officials and local policemen allowed vice to go unchecked spoke to something more than just political corruption. As 'organised crimes', prostitution and illicit gambling drew upon the support and complicity of a range of conspirators, including representatives of the state. The development of the white slave trade showed that the laws of supply and demand were making prostitution an increasingly globalised trade. What appeared to drive vice was not simply venality, but the profits it could generate. Vice had become an industry.

When the phrase 'organised crime' entered English parlance, few among the wider Western public knew of 'the Mafia'. By the time of Police Chief Bingham's condemnation of Manhattan's 'organised criminals' in 1909, American newspapers were just beginning to speak of the scourge of 'black hand' mafiosi in cities like New York. 'Organised crime' during this brief window had yet to be connected to anything like the gangs or syndicates now associated with mafias.

At the moment of its conception, 'organised crime' tended to be exclusively linked with gambling and prostitution, yet efforts to stamp out the use of intoxicants had begun to take shape in the same decades. Campaigners believed narcotics and alcohol were an equal threat to the health and integrity of societies and nations: fomenting crime and bringing out the worst qualities of marginal, uncivilised or undesirable people. There was a correspondingly fervent belief that governments could police the personal habits of drinkers and drug users. This belief led to the signing of the first international accord dedicated to regulating the sale and transmission of opium everywhere. Few, of course, foresaw the damage these prohibitions would inflict in the years come.

'THE ABYSS OF DIVINE ENJOYMENT': NARCOTICS AND THE GLOBALISATION OF CRIME

As addiction took hold of Thomas De Quincey, his dreams became darker and more frightful. In one instance his nightmares transported him to the jungles of Asia. There animals surrounded him, chirping and screeching at his appearance. He felt himself entombed 'with mummies and pyramids, in narrow chambers at the heart of eternal pyramids'. For what seemed like an eternity, his only company was a crocodile who scorched his skin with 'cancerous kisses'.[35] The arrival of these nightmares caused De Quincey to grasp the costs that came with consuming laudanum. He first took the drug to treat the discomfort he felt as a result of a toothache. As time went on, he increased his consumption to maintain the euphoria and enlightenment he felt during his waking hours. The onset of bad dreams gave way to a profound sense of pain and shame. It was this sense of helplessness that led De Quincey to compose his memoir, *Confessions of an English Opium-Eater.* Though now recognised as a landmark book on the perils of drug use, *Confessions* incited rage among readers after it was first published in 1821. The bulk of De Quincey's account, critics noticed, could be interpreted as a celebration of opium's many pleasures. Most of his recollections, after all, could be read as a eulogy to his early indulgences. He evinced little guilt in recounting the sublime thrills that drew him into addiction.

Thomas De Quincey was not the first artist to discover the joys and sorrows of what he called 'the abyss of divine enjoyment'.[36] But, in the years following publication, *Confessions* came to be cast as a premonition of a larger societal conflict between social order and inebriating substances. It is now recognised as a milestone for the movements that compelled states to demonise and punish anyone found dealing in 'dangerous' intoxicants.

Why *Confessions* would have such a profound effect speaks to the culmination of several overlapping forces that came to shape modern times. De Quincey's memoir reflects many of the sentiments that helped bring about prohibitions on gambling and prostitution. Like the evils of vice, opium and other intoxicants debased the individual and was unbecoming of a man of intellect. De Quincey admitted that there was nothing 'more revolting to English feelings' than a man who exposed 'his moral ulcers and scars'; yet he deduced that if educated men like himself could be ensnared by narcotics, British society was in danger and needed to be warned.[37]

How intoxicants such as opium drew the ire of the public differs from the history of vice in several significant ways. Certainly, there were times and places where the use and abuse of certain substances were stringently policed. Church authorities in colonial Mexico meted out harsh penalties against those found to have ingested hallucinogens.[38] Early modern jurists in Iran and the Ottoman Empire condemned the drinking of coffee as an act that led to heresy and debauchery. And by the Middle Ages, municipalities throughout Europe instituted bans on the sale and consumption of alcohol on Sundays. Alas, edicts issued by political and religious leaders often went unheeded. Gluttony or rebelliousness were not the sole causes of the public's willingness to resist different forms of regulation: some intoxicants were embraced for their healing properties; some possessed religious significance. And by the pre-industrial era, many governments looked upon alcohol and other drugs as important sources of tax revenue. As transoceanic trade grew during the seventeenth century, northern European capitals levied duties and surcharges upon imported spirits. For Great Britain, the nation's rivalry with France overshadowed the revenue collected from duties on imported French brandy and wine. At the turn of the eighteenth century, lawmakers in London encouraged citizens to take up gin as a more 'patriotic drink'. To stimulate consumption, parliament even allowed the public to distil the spirit themselves, as long as they paid a low summary tax of tuppence for every gallon produced.[39]

Britain's imperial ambition, as well as the allure of private gain, lay at the heart of opium's emergence as a global commodity. From pre-classical times, people traded and ingested opium for relaxation and convalescence alike. But in the late 1700s, Dutch and British merchants seized upon the drug as a commodity that they could sell; in defiance of an outright ban issued by Beijing against the selling and smoking of opium, they targeted the restrictive Chinese marketplace. Neither the British government nor East India Company traders necessarily sought to use opium as a political weapon against the Chinese government. Tantalising profit margins provided more than enough reason for merchants and commercial agents to invest in opium. Nevertheless, as high officials from Beijing began cracking down on foreign importers of the drug in the 1830s, London dispatched the Royal Navy in response. Britain's victory over China in the First Opium War in 1842, as well as a series of agreements between Beijing and other European states thereafter, opened China to a tidal wave of opium. The promise of high profits in the Far East led speculators from across the world to invest heavily in the sale and transport of the drug. Meanwhile, production spiked in poppy-producing regions such as Bengal, Vietnam, Anatolia, Iran and the Balkans, as producers sought to meet and feed demand. After lifting their prohibitions against opium, China's Qing government initially sought to tax the trade both to raise revenue and stymie consumption. The ultimate impact opium had upon China's population was profound. By 1869, up to 60 per cent of Beijing's general population partook in the use of opium.[40] Of the millions of migrants to leave China during the nineteenth century, a great many would take their habit with them.

China's opium epidemic occurred in the shadow of an even more dramatic trend. Western doctors and apothecaries had prescribed opioids for centuries. Laudanum, the drug that first hooked Thomas De Quincey, was originally concocted in the 1500s and used widely thereafter. In the early 1800s, two inventions heightened their impact and appeal: morphine and the syringe. Paving the way was the German manufacturer Merck, which pioneered the mass production and marketing of morphine, securing wide distribution and a revolution in pain relief. By the middle of the century it became a staple remedy for treating headaches, dysentery, menstrual pain and surgical wounds. Union soldiers fighting in the American Civil War were issued over ten million opium pills, as well as two million doses of powdered morphine, during the course of the conflict in the 1860s.[41] In the second half of the century, the pantheon of pain medication expanded to include heroin and cocaine. Both drugs, first isolated and synthesised in Germany, represented significant improvements in the treatment of a variety of ailments. Sigmund Freud famously experimented upon himself to understand cocaine's wonderous effects. Its potential as an anaesthetic, Freud posited, was only one of the drug's many applications. Depression, anaemia and indigestion as well as impotence could be treated with doses of cocaine. Freud found no indication that it produced a 'compulsive desire to use the stimulant further; on the contrary one feels a certain unmotivated aversion to the substance'.[42]

The growing availability of narcotics did not immediately lead to regulation; however, attempts to prohibit opium use would eventually run parallel to campaigns aimed at reducing rampant alcohol consumption. Civic leaders, particularly in Europe, had long drawn a connection between public disorder and drinking spirits, but the rapid increase in the urban population saw officials move to curtail the availability of alcohol among the metropolitan poor. Adding to the problem was the rise of mass-produced liquors such as brandy, gin, whisky and rum. Soon after promoting gin as a patriotic drink, British authorities feared a 'gin craze' among Britain's lower classes. After levying a series of draconian laws, parliamentarians hoped to deny 'people of lower and inferior rank' the means to render themselves 'unfit for useful labour and business', let alone commit crimes.[43] Critics denounced the laws as an attack upon personal liberty, leading officials to deem the prohibition unenforceable. Reversal of the legislation in the 1750s stymied the temperance cause but did not bring it to an end. Over the course of the nineteenth century, an alliance of religious activists, feminists and social progressives pressured national and local administrations throughout the West to check uninhibited alcohol consumption. As with the campaigns to rid society of prostitution and gambling, the temperance cause appealed to the anxieties and aspirations of the day: alcohol, like vice, ruined families, debilitated workers, incited criminals and debased the nation and its manhood.

As the temperance movement gained strength, Western reformers took increased note of the harm caused by narcotics. European clinicians were among the first to advocate prohibition. In the 1890s, Max Nordau, a Hungarian physician, published a treatise on the degenerative effects of certain modern habits. For Nordau, individuals who were incapable of restraining their indulgence faced mortal doom. The use of intoxicants, be it alcohol, opium or hashish, potentially led whole nations to 'descend to the lowest degrees of degeneracy, to idiocy, to dwarfishness'.[44] Racism fed the ease with which anti-drug activists associated narcotics with brutishness. The people of China, one French doctor noted, owed 'their current decadence and their decrepitude' to the ravages of opium. The one advantage of the drug, as he saw it, was that it would likely stifle 'the prodigious faculty of reproduction of these races' and therefore 'save Europe from the invasion of the yellow barbarians'.[45] Loathing directed towards China and Chinese immigrants was not the only source of anti-drug sentiment. Before the First World War, newspapers published a wave of reports detailing a crime wave carried out by African American cocaine users. Among those who subscribed to the scourge of the 'Negro cocaine fiend' was the surgeon general of the United States, who warned that the drug made offenders virtually invulnerable to bullets.[46] Others drew connections between cocaine and the rising plague of white slavery. One doctor testified to his belief that the drug was the essential agent used to 'corrupt young girls'. Once the victim succumbed to the habit, it was, he warned, 'but a short time before such girls fall to the ranks of prostitution'.[47]

It was Asia, and not the West, where modern drug prohibitions were born. Fear of a China-style explosion in opium use led Japan to pursue a rigorous anti-narcotics regime beginning in 1870.[48] In 1906, China's ruling Qing dynasty declared a nationwide campaign to end opium use. Imperial officials banned poppy cultivation across the country and compelled users to register with the state. The initial successes of this campaign, however, came to a halt after the overthrow of the Qing in 1912. Imperial China's collapse occurred as a far more robust and influential drive to eradicate opium came into effect in the Philippines. After seizing the Spanish colony in 1898, American administrators took hold of a land where opium production was legal and the drug widely enjoyed. It was also a lucrative source of revenue, netting American authorities hundreds of thousands of dollars a year after the conquest.[49] Reformers and religious conservatives were aghast. Popular anger in the United States compelled the new colonial governor to form a commission to investigate the matter. Leading the commission was an Episcopal bishop, Charles Brent, whose recommendations compelled Washington to change course. Brent's suggested controls led to a ban on imported opium, the closure of smoking dens and the registration of known users. Opium consumption in the Philippines declined after passage of the 1906 measures but remained visible as a result of illicitly imported stocks from China. Brent resumed his lobbying efforts, demanding now that the United States take a greater role in leading an international campaign. Heeding his call was Theodore Roosevelt, who endorsed, as president, the bishop's suggestion that an international convention be held in the hopes of tackling the problem of opium use globally. The convening of the summit in Shanghai in 1909 marked the beginnings of a universal regime dedicated to regulating the consumption and sale of narcotics.

Brent's proposal was not without precedent. The levying of customs duties, as well as attempts to outlaw trade in contraband goods, dates to classical times. Yet it was only in the modern era that governments sought to regulate the sale or shipment of certain products on a global scale. The British decree of 1807 outlawing the international slave trade constituted the first of such endeavours. London's near monopoly over the shipping lanes between Africa and the Americas, coupled with its naval might, helped curtail the scope of the trade dramatically. By the 1840s, the Royal Navy deployed up to a quarter of its fleet in interdiction operations against slavers.[50] Amid negotiations to end the Napoleonic Wars, signatories attending the peace conference in Vienna finally agreed to join Britain and condemn the Atlantic slave trade. Subsequent diplomatic engagements, as well as armed coercion, aided London in seeing through its wishes. Piracy met a similar end during this era. As with the transnational slave trade, changing social norms in Europe led to a growing consensus among the continent's imperial powers in the aftermath of the Napoleonic wars. In 1856, all of Europe's foremost states agreed to outlaw privateering as a means of waging war. The Royal Navy enforced this accord more than any other body. For the delegates who met in Shanghai in

1909, the proposition of an international convention ridding the world of opium's evils was not without merit. By then, slavery and piracy were generally considered practices of the past.

The agreement forged in Shanghai provided the basis for a succession of local and international laws mandating strict controls on the production, shipment and sale of narcotics. A second and still larger congress in the Hague in 1912 recognised two other drugs, heroin and cocaine, as substances worthy of global regulation. Among the amendments to the Treaty of Versailles, drafted and adopted at the close of the First World War, signatories also consented to uphold the Hague agreement. Narcotics control fell under the authority of the League of Nations, which sought to co-ordinate between member states on matters of suppression and prosecution. Meanwhile, governments in various parts of the world passed national laws meting out stiff penalties to individuals found distributing or even using banned substances. In the United States, in addition to passing strict regulations on opiates and cocaine, Congress and majority state legislatures endorsed the Volstead Act of 1919, which led to the complete prohibition of alcoholic beverages.

The question of who or what would serve as the enforcement mechanisms of many of these regulations often went unanswered. Those states that signed the 1912 Hague convention may have presumed that the British navy, as well as those of other amenable governments, would stand as a deterrent against smuggling on the high seas. Both of these suppositions proved flawed. No country in the world at this time possessed specialised police agencies assigned to supervise or implement prohibitionist laws. Moreover, citizens of many countries, including in the West, doubted the overall professionalism of law enforcement officials. What many did not foresee was the impact the Great War would have upon the policing of the world's oceans. In 1922, each of the world's major maritime powers agreed to reduce the size of their standing navies. Further cuts to the budget, as well as lingering anti-war sentiment, compelled London to shrink the Royal Navy further. With that, the world lost the principal instrument that had helped suppress piracy and slaving over the previous century.

At the dawn of this new era, there was nothing akin to the contemporary mafias that now dominate the global trade in drugs and other commodities, but there were signs of their imminent emergence. In the United States and Britain, press agencies covered the consumption of opium among Chinese migrants and their accounts of what passed for the seedier side of local Chinatowns were often lurid to the point of fantasy. Yet among the trends both journalists and police officials noted was the influence of clandestine societies over local opium markets. These fraternities, or tongs, resorted to violence when competition gave way to conflict. No one drew ready comparisons between them and the mafiosi of the world's Italian diaspora. Those connections would come later.

PART II

Consolidation

Though we know nothing about the precise moments of conception of the oldest mafias, it is clear their earliest members cultivated similar cultures and rituals. The ranks of these societies were closed and exclusive. Members tended to abide by strict codes. They carried on hidden feuds and generally haunted the poorer quarters of their environs. These groups appeared in different parts of the world under very different conditions. No history of the Camorra of Naples or Sicily's Mafia is complete without understanding the revolutionary forces that created a united Italy. The story of the triads reflects the breakdown of imperial rule in China. The yakuza began in an earlier period in the country's history but matured alongside Japan's reinvention as a nation state. Ironically, all four of these groups teetered on the verge of collapse at the close of the Second World War.

As the twentieth century began, each of these criminal fraternities found their way to the United States. These expatriates were already inspiring fear and curiosity when Washington decided to criminalise alcohol and narcotics consumption. Prohibition laid the foundation for a loose collection of crime families and syndicates that grew in tandem with one another across the country. Most, but not all, drew inspiration from the criminal fraternities of Italy. It is in this light that the personality and legacy of Al Capone assumed global significance. His crimes, as well as the films that celebrated him, seemed to confirm that the American gangster was a modern force unlike any other.

No one spoke of an 'American mafia' at this stage in history. Yet the elements that led many to see the United States as the heart of the mafia world were already taking shape. A host of international actors aided in the flow of drugs and alcohol across US borders. By 1950, more ambitious American gangsters were themselves looking for opportunities to invest and get rich abroad. How we came to understand this is largely the work of one of the most important, yet least recognised, figures in American history: Harry Anslinger. The founder of Washington's first counter-narcotics service, Anslinger was one of the earliest to investigate and identify the transnational traffickers known for trading in heroin and other drugs before the Second World War. It was Anslinger who contended that a singular conspiracy dominated the narcotics trade inside the United States and it was the result of his work that the notion of the mafia gained currency across the world.

3

Origins: Mafias of the Early Twentieth Century

William Trollope was a man of letters with no special passion for stories of crime or violence. He was an accomplished novelist and travel writer with an affection for Italy. When he first wrote about the existence of the Mafia in 1877, Italy had only recently celebrated its sixteenth year as a nation. Though well acquainted with the country, Trollope never encountered any mafiosi himself. His discovery came primarily from press clippings and books. At that time, no group or conspiracy in the English-speaking world claimed any connection to the Mafia. For Trollope, to understand Sicily's mafiosi was to comprehend Italy's basic dysfunction.

Italy, he cautioned readers in his native Britain, was a country confronted by massive challenges. There were disparities in wealth and sophistication between northern cities such as Milan and Florence and southern ones such as Naples and Palermo. Across the country, people differed profoundly in terms of their temperament and lifestyle. As a consequence, authorities in Rome struggled to govern and unite Italians as a nation. 'The fact is,' he lamented, 'that in Italy one travels from civilisation to barbarism, as one goes from the north southwards.'[1] With this in mind, Trollope considered Sicily's Mafia to be a conspiracy that permeated the elite and the poor of the island. Brigand gangs who robbed travellers on the roads were bound to the Mafia. Large landowners and government officials abetted the murders, thefts and acts of extortion mafiosi committed. Evidence of the Mafia's influence was visible even in Rome. When the government attempted to adopt extraordinary powers to combat banditry on the island, Sicily's parliamentary representatives denounced the plan as unwanted meddling. This was proof, as Trollope saw it, that the island's political leaders wished to 'live in their social sty such as they have made it and cry aloud against any attempt to cleanse it!'[2]

Just what the Mafia was proved harder to define. Trollope quoted one authority as saying it was 'a medieval sentiment' stemming from Sicily's history. The island, after all, had never known good government. Locals simply preferred lawlessness and were willing to go to great lengths to protect their way of life. A specific code of silence, known as *omerta*, trumped the rule of law. Trollope interpreted the word as being derived from *homo* in Latin and therefore relating to manliness. Omerta allowed one licence to exact vengeance. It privileged the strong, notably those who took the law into their own hands. No citizen, even the most noble, was above omerta. It was for this reason that juries regularly acquitted bandits and killings went unpunished. Whether there was anything singular about the Mafia, Trollope could not say. The Mafia's leaders, the true 'organizers of crime', blended seamlessly into high society. They wore frock coats and gloves and found willing patrons and compatriots among each of Italy's main political parties.

A British officer posted far across Asia wrote of a similar world decades earlier. Frederick Forbes, a lieutenant in the Royal Navy and a veteran of the First Opium War, travelled through China during the 1840s. In his memoirs, he referred to 'a mysterious freemasonry' known throughout the country. Like Trollope, Forbes drew more from books than observation. Things he had read made him aware that a feared 'triad society' was present in and beyond China's borders, and composed of 'the most depraved dregs of the people, the idlers, gamblers, opium smokers, and such like vermin'.[3] Ruling over the triads were elders who inducted members through a series of secret rites, with the initiated then making their living by theft and robbery. Less clandestine, and more comprehensible, was the triads' engagement in acts of political revolt. During Forbes's time in Asia, anti-government societies were multiplying in response to rising hatred of the ruling dynasty, the Qing.

The writings of William Trollope and Frederick Forbes contain few original insights but are of interest because they exemplify their times. By the early twentieth century, stories dealing with the development of modern mafias were becoming commonplace in Western newspapers and books. Most who wrote about these conspiracies learned of them through second-hand reporting. A precious few, such as Trollope and Forbes, had been to the countries about which they wrote. As points of reference, they are indicative of the sort of reports that introduced the readers to the world's oldest mafias: the Camorra, the tongs or triads, the yakuza and, most of all, the Mafia of Sicily.

The early histories of the triads, yakuza and Italy's mafias are not exclusively bound to the lands of their birth. By the outbreak of the First World War, a great many cities, particularly in the United States, became stomping grounds for syndicates and conspiracies inspired by these original mafias. The criminals who imported these subcultures retained many of the traits associated with the compatriots they left behind. This transference from the Old World to the New marked a critical turn in the making of modern mafias. As the shadow of the Great War faded, the yakuza, triads and Italian mafias were no longer purely provincial conspiracies. As they integrated into their American surroundings, they assumed new dimensions and features. After the christening of a new era of peace in Versailles, mafias forged in the diaspora became the purveyors of an increasingly globalised culture of organised crime.

FREEMASONS OF CRIME:
EUROPE AND THE ADVENT OF THE ITALIAN MAFIAS

By the time the Netherlands attained its independence from Spain in 1648, Amsterdam had grown into a city of approximately 200,000 people. Trade via both the Atlantic and the North Sea brought with it money, goods and newcomers. Amsterdam's largesse also fed the growth of neighbouring towns such as Leiden, Delft and the Hague, all of which flourished through the seventeenth and eighteenth century. This golden era came with a cost. By the end of the seventeenth century, Amsterdam was the setting of an expansive underworld. The city's pickpockets, burglars and robbers were a fluid community of men and women who arrived and departed with the trading ships. Nevertheless, court records describe a coherent criminal subculture. Though there were no discernible kingpins, it was commonplace for cheats and thieves to operate within large networks. Most of those brought before the court possessed distinct nicknames or monikers: Henrik Hallow Eye, the Heathen, Claes the Vicar and Jack of Clubs. A discrete slang dotted their speech, some of which remains untranslatable in either Dutch or English. A code of behaviour was observed by the criminals of Amsterdam, including special parameters governing duels and knife fights.[4]

Early modern Europe boasted other towns and cities with their own criminal subcultures. London under the Stuart monarchy possessed a sizable underworld of crooks and purse-snatchers. Many peasants from the countryside became urban pickpockets, burglars or smugglers. Though most criminals operated alone, networks of fences, brokers, shopkeepers and denizens gave sanctuary to hustlers of all types. Savvier thieves co-operated with the authorities in order to avoid arrest. There was the fabulously named Moll Cutpurse, who started as a lowly pickpocket and became London's premiere dealer in stolen goods. Between the 1620s and '30s, Moll operated a warehouse catering to thieves seeking to stash looted jewellery and other valuables. She was also an invaluable informant and agent for those seeking the return of filched property. Many of Moll's conspirators learned their trade from family, particularly as children who first acted as lookouts or lures. The city's jails also gave life to schemes and the culture of London's underworld.[5] There, as well as in other parts of Europe, prison was a place where criminals perfected their craft and developed their own manner of speech, dress and behaviour. Throughout central Europe, for example, transients and lawbreakers used a slang known as Rotwelsch. This 'cant of thieves', whose origins date back to the thirteenth century, comprised an amalgam of expressions rooted in Latin, German, Yiddish and Romani. In practice, Rotwelsch was more than coded talk among wrongdoers. It was a marker and source of identity for marginalised people in various parts of Europe.[6]

The prevalence of sophisticated gangs and criminal subcultures before 1800 is critical to the context in which Europe's first mafias were born, but to understand the Camorra and Sicily's Mafia solely as an expression of Europe's vast underworld would be a mistake. After all, in London or Amsterdam, the early modern era did not beget criminal societies or syndicates that endured past the nineteenth century. By the mid-1800s, the criminal cultures of pre-industrial Europe had begun to vanish. Like the bandits of

Europe's countryside, criminal underworlds that once thrived in some European cities became weaker as local governments grew in size, authority and complexity. The introduction of factory work, as well as the arrival of still more migrants, transformed historic neighbourhoods once known for lawbreaking. Trappings of Europe's criminal subculture, including Rotwelsch, fell victim to state efforts aimed at stamping out deviance in the name of national purification and unity. All of these trends make the emergence and endurance of groups like the Mafia all the more intriguing. To understand the forces that produced and helped sustain Italy's mafias, one must look elsewhere.

Nineteenth-century observers often agreed that the Mafia and the Camorra constituted secret fraternities of crime. As outsiders learned more of Italy's mafiosi, the more likely they came to see these groups as partially inspired by the Freemasons. This perception reflected both reality and popular imagination. By the mid-nineteenth century, Freemasonry had existed, in one form or another, for more than a century. Though its reputed origins date back to the habits of stonemason guilds in Scotland in the late sixteenth century, fraternal lodges first proliferated throughout Europe in the 1700s. Freemasonry's devout affiliation with Enlightenment principles drove its popularity among middle-class men. As industrialisation gathered pace, and the British Empire expanded, lodges took root in cities elsewhere in the world. The nature of their meetings, particularly their rituals and ranks, quickly attracted the attention of outsiders. Masonry's code of secrecy inspired wild suggestions as to 'the craft's' true intentions and character. In 1884, Pope Leo XIII declared that Freemasons concealed themselves in building churches or accepting peoples of different faiths. Their true 'master and god' was Satan, to whom they built altars and proclaimed as 'the avenging force of reason'.[7]

It was masonry's reputation for anti-conservatism that made it the subject of political repression and suspicion. In 1784, Bavarian

Origins

authorities outlawed secret societies when they uncovered a cadre of so-called Illuminati planning to usurp the governments of various German states. The outbreak of the French Revolution followed the collapse of the Illuminati conspiracy, an event many opponents decried as a co-ordinated Freemason revolt. States throughout Europe cracked down on the brotherhood after the execution of Louis XVI. Though French Jacobins succeeded without the help of any lodges, the belief lingered that the Freemasons constituted a shadow society with links to political circles throughout Europe.[8]

It is not clear if Napoleon was a Freemason. Politics, however, compelled him to forge alliances with the masons. With his invasion of southern Italy in 1806, France's emperor installed his brother-in-law and cavalry commander, Joachim Murat, as ruler of the Kingdom of Naples. Upon taking his throne, Murat hoped to anchor his rule by establishing close ties with the masonic lodges of southern Italy. The young monarch's decision was well-founded; elements of the Neapolitan elite, particularly adherents to 'the craft', had cheered the French Revolution and had loathed the kingdom's previous Spanish rulers. Murat's relationship with the masonic lodges eventually turned foul as local opposition to the Napoleonic regime intensified. Fractures developed among Freemasons in Naples, leading to the creation of a fiercely rebellious and nationalistic splinter lodge calling itself the Coal Burners or Carbonari. Between the overthrow of the French and the restoration of Spanish rule, the Coal Burners were instrumental in inciting public opinion against foreign overlordship. Events came to a head in 1830 when royalist forces crushed a Carbonari-led revolt, forcing many of its leaders to flee Naples.[9] Still more Coal Burners ended up in the town's medieval prison. It was there that many revolutionaries came to know and influence another secret society: the Camorra.

As is the case with most mafias, no written record of the

Camorra's moment of invention exists. Like the term 'mafia' itself, even the origin of the name is a matter of dispute. One policeman testified in 1915 that the fraternity took its name from a Spanish adventurer, Raimondo Gamur, who founded the group in the seventeenth century (an event many scholars doubt ever happened). Camorra might derive from the Spanish word *camorra*, meaning a quarrel or fight, or *chamarra*, meaning jacket, in reference to the tight waistcoat worn by those who gave their allegiance to a gang.[10] What we know of the Camorra's origins largely comes from fellow prisoners, most notably dissidents inspired by the Coal Burners. These first sources testify to the existence of an 'honoured society' birthed around the middle of nineteenth century. As a gang, they imposed a rigid system of order and tribute over inmates in the city's central jail. No one, as one witness recalled, was 'allowed to eat, drink, smoke or gamble without a *camorrista*'s permission'. Those who defied these impositions 'ran the risk of being clubbed to death' or worse.[11] Any convenience or allowance came with a tax, or *pizzo*, to be paid. The Camorra possessed unique rituals and customs. New members swore an oath over crossed daggers and were compelled to duel a more senior camorrista with a knife. Most duels did not end in death but with slashes to the arms and body. Many of the initiated eventually sported elaborate tattoos on various parts of their body. All were bound to a secret code of conduct, such as not prostituting one's wife or sister. Though perverse, one early researcher likened the Camorra's inner culture to a 'pseudo-Masonic phantasmagoria'.[12]

Why the Camorra chose to adopt rituals mimicking those of the Freemasons is not clear. They were, however, not alone. The Charcoal Burners, as well as more mainline lodges, likely influenced the rituals associated with Sicily's Mafia. By the 1870s, Italian investigators uncovered sources detailing the initiation rites and codes associated with the Mafia's *cosche* or clans. Outsiders learned that young mafiosi sealed their loyalty after pricking their finger and smearing their blood on an effigy of a saint. Older members then set fire to the image, an homage to the literal and figurative hell awaiting anyone who betrayed their brethren.[13] Now there is nothing secret about the Mafia's initiation rites. The public confessions of well-known informants, such as Joe Valachi, as well as film depictions, such as from *The Sopranos*, have made the Mafia's customs into the stuff of popular lore. Revelations such as these carried a different weight in the mid-nineteenth century. For outsiders, as well as perhaps for mafiosi and *camorristi* themselves, mimicking the rituals of the Freemasons underscored the solemnity of their 'honoured societies'. Freemasonry invoked notions of a power or an authority that was not evident to the naked eye. Adopting the culture of masonic secrecy was not simply a tool to maintain discipline and order within their ranks. It became instrumental to the mystique cultivated by the Camorra.

As with the Camorra, we possess no evidence of when or why Sicily's Mafia crafted their own rituals. The question of its genesis is an even greater mystery. 'Mafia', or terms to that effect, were part of Italian parlance well before the nineteenth century. Florentines, for example, have used the word as a synonym for poverty and misery. Yet in Sicily, *mafia* may have come from a different root. Some scholars speculate it derives from Arabic and was used in reference to someone who is bold or brags.[14] A *mafioso*, in this respect, could mean virtually anyone who was tough or domineering. Indeed, many officials and investigators in the 1800s came to conclude that the Mafia, more than anything, was a state of mind as opposed to a coherent organisation. There may be, ironic as it may sound, some truth to this. In the absence of certifiable sources, it could be the case that the Mafia was, at one point, a way of being. Yet by the establishment of a united Italy, it is clear that a cross-section of Sicilians formed a coherent subculture of crime and conspiracy in the western portion of the island.

Sicily, like Naples, entered the nineteenth century as a land long governed by foreign lords from Spain and Austria. The politics of administering the island and its people was a far more complicated arrangement. By 1800, much of the Sicily's nobility left behind their feudal estates and resided in larger towns and cities. For absentee landowners living in the western city of Palermo, managing their lands, orchards and mines was a task assigned to renters or hired overseers, a group largely referred to as *gabellotti*. A *gabellotto*, conceivably, could have come from any walk of life. What was paramount for local lords was the maintenance of good order among their tenant farmers and contracted miners. Upholding the peace required individuals capable of imposing their will upon others. Gabellotti did not always perform this task alone. Some formed militias made up of local thugs to serve alongside them as overseers.[15] By the mid-century, this system of land tenure and authority came to compromise the fabric of local government. One magistrate swore that 'there is not a single official who does not prostrate himself before the local men of influence and power and who does not intend to profit from his office'. From his vantage point, there were fraternities or 'sorts of sects' whose bosses reigned over this culture of corruption.[16] Though no one can say for sure, this arrangement between landlord, overseer, militiaman and peasant helped engender the Mafia. The earliest mafiosi were not necessarily criminals per se. Instead, they composed an informal class of enforcers, extortionists and arbiters. Although the job of a gabellotto was a cornerstone of this order, the Mafia's earliest generations may have been made up of anyone who wielded power through their personal authority and threat of violence. What mattered most was that Sicily's elites depended upon this system for their benefit and the benefit of the kingdom.

Further waves of upheaval would bring both the Camorra and the Mafia into the centre of politics. Amid the Napoleonic wars, British troops occupied Sicily. In the spirit of progress, occupation authorities abolished the feudal rights under which the island's nobility owned and administered their land. The restoration of Spanish rule after Napoleon's defeat compounded the breakdown of this system. Provincial communities grew more unsettled as land changed hands, a process that further empowered the surrogates of the old nobility. The imposition of monarchical rule drove Sicilian converts to the Carbonari cause and successive revolts led to the mass imprisonment of would-be revolutionaries. As in Naples, it was in the dungeons of Palermo's central prison that the Charcoal Burners came to know the Mafia. The synergy between mafiosi and imprisoned rebels led some Italian commentators to suggest the Mafia was 'a form of Freemasonry or Carbonaria' since both 'hated all despotic governments'.[17]

All those who reviled Spanish rule were redeemed in 1860. In the spring a raucous army led by famed revolutionary Giuseppe Garibaldi marched into Palermo. By September, Naples also fell to Garibaldi, paving the way for the unification of what became the Kingdom of Italy. Among those who rejoiced in the capture of Palermo and Naples were members of the Camorra and the Mafia. In advance of Garibaldi's victories, frantic government officials in Naples attained the services of camorristi as informants and policemen in a vain attempt to forestall the tide of revolution. With the fall of the monarchy, many in the Camorra effortlessly switched their allegiances. Having abandoned their habits when they became policemen under the Spanish, many 'went back to being camorristi but did not stop being policemen' under a united Italian government.[18]

The retention of Camorra members became indicative of the problems the Italian state faced in Naples after unification in 1860. Within a year of Italy's birth, a rebellion rocked Naples when camorristi resisted being disciplined for their wanton criminal behaviour. Mass round-ups did little to stem their influence. Over the following decades, the Camorra became further entrenched within Neapolitan society. In addition to extracting a pizzo from neighbourhood shops, camorristi exploited wealthy business leaders and rival criminals. Italy's testy electoral environment created opportunities for the Camorra to ingratiate themselves with politicians. Above all, their dominance over the Neapolitan underworld made them partners and allies of corrupt and desperate officials. One newspaper complained in 1879 that gambling houses 'subsidised' local constables to the tune of ten lira a day. 'One could say the Camorra was always around, all that changes is the uniform of the lazy bourgeois [elite] and that of the idle police official.'[19]

Politicians from Rome, as well as foreign visitors, tended to attribute the power of the Camorra to the character of the city's inhabitants. Why the Camorra thrived, however, tended to be the result of widespread poverty. Despite earlier periods of prosperity, listless periods of economic growth, as well as outbreaks of cholera, took a terrible toll on workers and families in the late nineteenth century. Destitute residents of Naples' urban grottos provided the Camorra with many willing recruits. For visitors like William Trollope, one could empathise with the city's poor since it was their oppression that supplied camorristi with 'its first and bottomless foundation'. It did not change the fact that Naples, as he heard it said, was a Mediterranean 'paradise inhabited by devils'.[20]

Economic hardship was no less common in Sicily. But poverty was not the only factor to influence the rise of the Mafia on the island. In 1866, anti-government sentiment again surged, leading to acts of rebellion in the streets of Palermo. Many Sicilians, including former soldiers in Garibaldi's army, came to reject unification as yet another expression of foreign rule. More random and endemic forms of violence shook western portions of the island. Bandits plagued the countryside, leading to a raft of kidnappings, animal thefts and blackmail. Ongoing disputes over land led to daring assassinations and massacres of whole families. Violence loomed over the most basic forms of trade. Rising European demand for lemons and oranges in the mid-nineteenth century saw citrus cultivation become a staple of the Sicilian economy. Yet by the 1870s, few in the citrus industry could operate free of extortion or the threat of harm. Competition over the right to extort and extract eventually produced states of war in villages and towns throughout Sicily's western highlands. In Uditore, a district lying just beyond Palermo, fighting between rival clans in 1874 left thirty-four people dead, a number totalling more than 4 per cent of the population.[21] Outsiders interpreted all of these signs of upheaval as the telltale traits of the Mafia.

By then, authorities in Palermo and Rome understood that Uditore's clans, or cosche, were but one component of Sicily's Mafia. Other conspiratorial forces appeared to dominate the island but pinpointing them was a matter of heated debate. Among those who tried to grasp the essence of the problem was Leopoldo Franchetti, an intellectual and one-time parliamentarian from Tuscany. Franchetti arrived in Sicily in 1876 to conduct what he called a private enquiry into the troubles plaguing the island. He found no shortage of evidence of some kind of malevolent force that exploited innocent victims and undermined the state's authority. Clarifying exactly what was at the heart of these troubles was more difficult to explain. 'Mafia is an extremely difficult thing to define,' one policeman told him. 'You would need to live in Sambuca to get an idea.'[22] As a liberal thinker, Franchetti interpreted the Mafia as a kind of rogue entrepreneurialism or, as he called it, 'an industry of violence'. A mafia boss, or *capo*, used murder and the threat of harm to regulate 'the division of labour and function' and impose the sort of discipline that business demanded to 'achieve an ample and constant flow of profits'.[23] Franchetti's high-minded explanations, however, had little effect upon Italian perceptions of the Mafia. Local politicians, as well as members of Italy's literati, often cast it as something more benign and less structural. Mafiosi, Palermo's mayor told one public enquiry, could be 'anyone who has self-respect and has a certain exaggerated pride, and the inclination to not be overwhelmed but to overwhelm others, the will to appear courageous, to be ready to fight, and so on'.[24]

Some, however, were convinced that the Mafia was more than a culture of bravado and thuggishness. Police in Palermo had evidence of the Mafia's elaborate initiation rituals as early as 1876. This led one senior prosecutor to conclude that there were 'groups or associations of criminals of various sizes here and there in Sicily', though they were not necessarily 'confederated or bound to one another by links of mutual complicity'.[25] Historians tend to agree that what was called 'the Mafia' by 1900 constituted a spectrum of behaviour and conspiracy. Cosche in Uditore and other parts of Sicily formed a constellation of small and often competitive bands who taxed and monopolised businesses such as the citrus industry. Bandits who looted the countryside often did so under the patronage of powerful landowners and petty officials who received a portion of their spoils. Petty criminals in Palermo and other towns similarly paid tribute to men of authority, be they policemen or political leaders. All of these instances at times were expressions of the Mafia's power. They did not, however, emanate from a singular organisation or source of authority.

Before the turn of the century, trials and scandals associated with the Mafia and Camorra became subjects of interest for journalists and commentators throughout Italy. More remarkable is the speed with which the Mafia became a theme within the arts. In 1863, a play entitled *The Mafiosi of Vicaria Prison* opened to rave reviews in a Palermo theatre. *Vicaria* was a redemption story featuring of a group of *capo*s who ruled over a band of abusive inmates. At no point in the play is the word 'mafia' ever mentioned, but the play's dialogue, composed in the Sicilian dialect of Italian, is peppered with unmistaken allusions to mafia culture: the paying of a pizzo, talk of 'humility' and 'respect' and the sacred rituals of initiation.[26] The publication of detailed studies, such as Leopoldo Franchetti's two-volume tome, added to the public's fascination. A common theme found in all of this work was the backwardness of Italy's southern provinces. For authors and readers in more affluent parts of Italy's north, mafiosi and camorristi were avatars representing the south's primitive, and genuinely foreign, culture. Lurid accounts of crime in Naples and Sicily struck a chord among nationalists and reformers of the time. When northerners such as Garibaldi engineered the unification of Italy in 1860, they did so with the belief that all Italians were descendants of the same history and civilisation. The pervasive influence of the Mafia and Camorra compelled many Italians to reassess this premise. Popular writers, such as criminologist Alfredo Niceforo, argued that Italy was functionally divided between a white Aryan north and a more 'mongrelised' south. Similar to Cesare Lombroso's theory of 'Criminal Man', published in 1876, the Mafia, as he understood it, was the genetic and cultural remnant of Arab African rule over Sicily during the ninth and eleventh centuries. It was, in his words, a continuation of 'the feudal spirit, the Arab spirit of independence, [and] the medieval spirit of chivalry'.[27]

Readers and visitors from outside of Italy often embraced these interpretations wholeheartedly. Sicily, as well as much of the mainland, was on the fringe of Europe. Like the continent's extreme east, it was a place where the remnants of old institutions such as serfdom and banditry still appeared to be visible just below the surface. There was no wonder, as one German scholar understood it, 'that in a country like southern Italy, where so many medieval customs and abuses still prevail', that groups like the Camorra and the Mafia survived and thrived.[28] Sordid depictions of Sicily and its Mafia resonated with Europeans in other ways. By the end of the nineteenth century, newspapers brimmed with stories of dangerous secret societies. The decades that preceded the First World War were an age of violent extremism. Radical politics, as opposed to crime, lay at the heart of most these news accounts.

To attain national independence, or to resist the encroaching hand of government, a wide host of groups adopted clandestine measures. Many drew direct or indirect inspiration from the mystique of the Freemasons. In the US, the Ku Klux Klan's adoption of distinct robes, rituals and ranks reflected the masonic roots of many of its founders and members. The Internal Macedonian Revolutionary Organisation, which sought to free portions of the southern Balkans from Ottoman rule, similarly aped the rites and secrecy of the mason lodges found in cities such as Thessaloniki, Sofia and Istanbul. For the passive observer, the terror inflicted by these revolutionaries appeared comparable to the sort of violence and subversion perpetrated by the Mafia. It was this sense of equivalence that led to the wider use and corruption of the term 'mafia'. In 1903, for example, journalists at the *Manchester Guardian* quoted a Russian news account of an assassination in the Caucasian town of Alexandropol. The British journalists referred to the killers as members of the 'Armenian mafia'. It was more likely the culprits were nationalists belonging to the Armenian Revolutionary Federation.[29] The Serbian press similarly referred to Albanian rebels in southern Yugoslavia as 'mafia bands'.[30] British newspapers also spoke of an 'Irish mafia' after the murder of the lord mayor of Cork in 1920. The crime, which authorities later attributed to rogue police constables, spoke to the restlessness and disorder that plagued Ireland during its war of independence. The core difference, as one correspondent put it, was that Ireland 'has no such excuse as Sicily had when the Mafia was formed to check the atrocities of [Spanish] military rule'.[31]

Oddly enough, as the notion of the mafia gained currency outside Italy, there were signs that Mafia and Camorra influence

Origins

was beginning to wane. As socialism's popularity surged, significant numbers of Italians saw both secret societies as oppressors of the nation's workers. Electoral success emboldened socialists in Naples to demand greater accountability from public officials corrupted by the Camorra. In 1901, a sprawling public enquiry concluded with the publication of a two-thousand-page report indicting the Neapolitan political establishment. There was in the city, the report declared, both a 'low' and 'high' Camorra that brokered nearly everything. Camorristi catered to everyone, be they 'the rich industrialist who wants a clear road into politics or administration to the small shopowner who wants to ask for a reduction in his taxes; from the businessman trying to win a contract to a worker looking for a job in a factory ... they all find somebody stepping into their path, and nearly all make use of them.'[32] Mass dissatisfaction culminated with the close of the so-called Cuocolo trial in 1912. The trial centred on the death of a Camorra boss, Gennaro Cuocolo, and his wife, a reputed prostitute, who were found stabbed, bludgeoned and mutilated years earlier. The bloody details of the killings intensified media scrutiny of the Camorra's grip over the police and the city. A sixteen-month trial and media circus ensued, leading to dozens of indictments. The drama of the Cuocolo affair reached its climax when the court rendered guilty verdicts for all charged. Upon conviction, one man grabbed a piece of glass and slit his own throat.

Few in Naples emerged from the Cuocolo trial unscathed. Witnesses levied a bevy of accusations at public officials, politicians and policemen. But the Camorra suffered most, as hundreds were jailed in the wake of the Cuocolo killings and continued social and political change whittled away at what was left.[33] 'High' Camorra bosses disappeared from city's political scene as Italy mobilised for war in 1914. The carnage of the Great War, followed by nationwide political upheaval, introduced an even more decisive force bent upon eradicating both the Camorra and Mafia as a whole: fascism.

Sicily witnessed similar trends. Peasants and townspeople increasingly decried the exploitation practised by large landowners and corrupt politicians as socialism gained popularity. In 1893, violent protests in Palermo compelled the government to dispatch tens of thousands of troops to the island to maintain order. Though fundamentally threatened by the prospect of revolution, a few mafiosi capitalised upon the socialist cause for their own gains. For more prominent mafiosi, Benito Mussolini's power grab in 1922 provided greater solace. Fascism's uncompromising stance towards socialism was welcomed as a reprieve from both government and popular pressure. When elections were held in 1924, mafia intimidation aided a pro-fascist coalition in achieving a resounding victory against Sicily's socialist candidates. To mark his success, Mussolini visited the island that spring. While touring a municipality south of Palermo, he arrived accompanied by Don Francesco Cuccia, the local mayor and a reigning capo. The visit, by all accounts, ran smoothly until Cuccia loudly rebuked Mussolini for travelling under guard. 'There is no need for so many cops,' he told him. 'Besides me, your Excellency has nothing to fear because I give the orders around here.' Two months later, Cuccia was behind bars.[34]

Mussolini's petulant act of retribution was less personal than it was political. Ahead of his trip to Sicily, the fascist press lobbied him to destroy the Mafia rather than let it coexist as a potential rival. To bring the island to heel, Mussolini appointed a loyal Blackshirt and seasoned veteran of the police, Cesare Mori, as prefect to the district of Palermo. Mori took to the post with vigour. Through the course of a three-year campaign, authorities placed 11,000 people in prison. Mussolini publicly swooned over Mori's results. He had, he declared, conducted surgery and taken a scalpel to the Mafia. By 1927 the number of murders on the island was less than half of what it was three years earlier. Incidents of cattle rustling dropped to even lower levels. There would be no let-up in the campaign until Sicilians could 'no longer even remember the mafia'.[35] Yet in 1938, police inspectors in Sicily reported that 'all that happened is that there were a few pauses, creating the impression that everything was calm' so that it would appear that the 'mafia had been totally eradicated'.[36] Regardless, Mori's assault on the island left a lasting scar upon the generations that survived the crackdown. In 1986, one Mafia informant told prosecutors that memories from the 1920s remained fresh among older mafiosi. Mori sent many to languish in prison. His uncle, once a boss, was 'reduced to stealing to earn a crust'. Under fascism, no one could deny that the 'music changed'.[37]

At the time Mussolini sent the Mafia reeling, organised crimes such as gambling, prostitution and narcotics trafficking were little known on the island of Sicily. Extortion, more than anything, was what gave life to the Mafia. By contrast, the Camorra of Naples were purveyors of vice. Several women even distinguished themselves as both prostitutes and members of the 'honour society'. It was commonplace for male and female members to bear tell-tale scars on their face as testament to their hard lives. Camorristi also promoted gambling and loan sharking. A fixed chain of conspirators, as one officer testified, was central to the society's success. Camorra preyed upon young men whom they drove 'into the arms of light women', who then 'took them to gambling hells [sic] where they were ruined'. Once stripped of their money, 'the usurer completed the work'.[38] These and other schemes that sustained Italy's mafias were thrown into chaos as war began again in 1939. When the fighting concluded, political changes forced both to adapt to a dramatically transformed world of crime. Aiding them in this transition were mafias and industries based abroad.

FROM SHAOLIN TO THE ISLANDS OF JAPAN: THE RISE OF THE TRIADS AND YAKUZA

Lore has it that the triads were conceived out of the violence of the seventeenth century. Their origins are often traced to events following the fall of China's Ming dynasty, which ran from the mid-fourteenth to the mid-seventeenth centuries. A new line of emperors came to the throne after an invasion by peoples referred to as the Manchus or Jurchen. The Jurchen founders of the new Qing dynasty assumed power as a distinct caste, one that was separate and superior to those who served below them. Early Qing emperors used war and conquest to establish their hegemony. According to legend, their more notable supporters included monks from the Shaolin Monastery in central China. Despite helping the government to fight off an invasion from Mongolia, the Qing emperor grew suspicious of the monks and ordered their temple to be burnt to the ground. Only five monks survived the attack. Together the escapees formed a secret fraternity known as the Heaven and Earth Society and swore to exact revenge. One of the branches of this group subsequently assumed a different name, the Three United Society, from which the term 'triad' was born. Members of the Heaven and Earth sect later rebuilt the Shaolin Temple, transforming it into an early centre for the training and development of martial arts. The society's motto, 'Oppose the Qing, Restore the Ming', remained a part of its creed well into the 1800s.[39] The 1979 film *The 36th Chamber of Shaolin* celebrates the glories of the Heaven and Earth triad as a story of one monk's decisive victory over his Qing oppressors. A shared affection for this kung fu classic later helped inspire the look and energy of the hip-hop group, the Wu Tang Clan.

Though the Wu Tang Clan became the subject of an FBI investigation into possible ties to organised crime in the 1990s, the original Heaven and Earth society bore no resemblance to Sicily's

Mafia.[40] Italy's prisons nurtured the Camorra and Mafia, with the differences between them rooted in their local history. Neither imprisonment, nor association with crime, nor anything distinctively regional or provincial defined the triads. Though largely comprising men and women of low social standing, members of both the Camorra and Mafia became deeply embedded within the elites of their home regions before the Second World War. This was far less the case for the triads. Where their collective histories meet is in their relevance and longevity as secret societies. To understand these differences and similarities, one must appreciate China's travails in the modern era.

Secret societies have been fixtures of Chinese political and spiritual life for centuries. It is hard to distinguish the earliest development of secret societies from general folk practices found throughout China. The one trait most share is their collective devotion to mysticism and ritual. Subversive politics was the potent factor aiding the growth of the most well-known societies. Opposition to the Qing dynasty catalysed the spread of several conspiratorial groups with august names: the Elder Brother Society, Society of the Righteous Harmonious Fists, the White Lotus Society and the Heaven and Earth Society. Most societies also provided help to men of the same social class, point of origin or trade. It is for this reason that men who were poor, marginalised, far from home or without families tended to flock to these groups. Why some societies became enmeshed in crime tended to reflect the economic desperation of those who joined them.

The many crises that enveloped Qing China after 1800 were critical to the growth and appeal of the Heaven and Earth Society. Following the empire's defeat in the First Opium War, the dynasty's legitimacy eroded rapidly. The Qing battled successive waves of insurrection, many of them brought on by a variety of secret societies, until their final overthrow in 1912. The empire's woes, as well as increased exposure to the West, imbued many of these anti-government movements with nationalist overtones. Sun Yat Sen, the founder of the modern Chinese Republic, shrewdly joined one secret society in order to further his own fortunes and that of the nationalist cause. As anarchy swept over the countryside, increased foreign trade lured millions of migrants to the coastal cities, where they sought employment, aid and security. Many of these newcomers became opium addicts amid the growth of the opium trade during the nineteenth century. Triad societies offered a sanctuary and a source of opportunity for millions of Chinese citizens. Being in a triad, as one popular verse went, was significantly 'better than renting an ox to farm bad soil'.[41]

The frenetic pace of urbanisation expanded and diversified the ranks of secret societies. One spin-off from the Heaven and Earth order, calling itself the Elder Brother Society, boasted an extensive following across the towns that lined the Yangtze River. Like all triads, the Elder Brothers had a complex membership hierarchy and engaged in elaborate oath ceremonies. The ritual decapitation of a white chicken sealed a member's initiation, with the presiding officer declaring that all traitors 'would become like this cock' if they ever broke their vows. As with Italy's mafias, the Elder Brothers were bound to a specific code of conduct, including prohibitions on acts of thievery and murder that didn't benefit the society as a whole. Violence and deception in the service of their fellowship, however, was intrinsic to their cause. The Elder Brothers, like other triads, bitterly opposed the Qing as well as the growing presence of Westerners operating in China. In the 1890s they organised a series of riots targeting government offices and European missionaries. To sustain the activities of the order, the Elder Brothers committed acts of armed robbery and ran gambling houses that catered specifically to the destitute.[42]

The triads left an even bigger impression in Hong Kong. As one of the spoils of Britain's victory over the Qing in the 1840s, the colony's importance grew as London's influence in east Asia deepened. Popular unrest in central and southern China also made Hong Kong a haven for refugees and migrants looking for work. Market competition and job placement soon became the province of competing triad interests. Their involvement in organising and profiting from Hong Kong's labour market drew the ire of local British administrators who viewed the principle of 'free labour' as sacrosanct. Piracy on Kowloon Bay, as well as armed robbery and extortion, became synonymous with the triad presence in the early twentieth century.

The fall of the Qing in 1912 did little to diminish the influence and popularity of secret societies. As Sun Yat Sen's republican government succumbed to infighting and disorder, the rule of law collapsed through much of China. Warlords and bandits sped China's fall into chaos and dominated much of the country's landscape through the 1920s and '30s.[43] Secret societies offered peasants and townspeople protection from outlaws and marauding armies. An order calling itself the Red Spears, for example, waged a bloody campaign against brigandage on the Shandong Peninsula before its 50,000-man army became the purveyor of terror in the countryside.[44] An even more complex situation unfolded in Shanghai on the central coast. Triads and other secret societies ranked among the brokers, fixers and ruffians prowling the town's docks, warehouses and urban quarters. Yet by the 1920s, a new group, one that was only loosely related to the triads, came to dominate Shanghai and its budding underworld. Unlike most triads, this fraternity readily integrated into the power structure of the town. More striking is the extent to which it came to be associated with vice and the sale of narcotics. This order, the Green Gang, is now fairly remembered as China's first modern mafia.

The men who joined the Green Gang in the early twentieth century shared much in common with members of older societies such as the Elder Brothers or Heaven and Earth. Its earliest inductees were men who worked on the ships or along the docks of the Grand Canal connecting the Yangtze and Yellow Rivers. There was nothing inherently political or rebellious about them; the chief benefits of 'the family', as its members called the group, were status, protection and kinship. As in the triads, a rigid system of rites and rank defined Green Gang membership. Power within the ranks was also defused among the many lodges (or tongs) that made up the Green Gang's base. Competing tongs, as well as competing triads, enriched themselves by way of armed robbery and kidnapping, the two most common crimes in Shanghai, but the order's main criminal activity was salt smuggling along the Grand Canal. As it matured, the Green Gang entered the opium trade.[45]

Shanghai's unrelenting growth helped power the Green Gang's sudden emergence. The city's population tripled in the years between 1910 and 1930. Administratively, it was a queer place. Shanghai roughly constituted three cities: an internationally governed enclave, the French Concession and the remaining Chinese core and quarters. When it came to matters of municipal cooperation, such as fighting crime and public safety, Shanghai's constituent parts acted more like rival states. What gave the city a greater sense of integrity was commerce as well as entertainment. Electricity and concrete transformed the harbour front of the French Concession. Multi-storey office blocks, streetcars and neon lights turned old thoroughfares into promenades. Nightclubs and motion picture houses, some thirty-six in 1930, were crucibles of the city's nightlife. Sin, more than any other form of entertainment, was what truly defined inter-war Shanghai. Despite being illegal, gambling brought in profits in excess of a million US dollars a week by the 1930s. Sex was no less profitable. As early as 1915, one out of every sixteen women living in the French and international concessions was a prostitute. In addition to the tens of thousands of Chinese women, war, poverty and adventure brought girls from all over the world to Shanghai's brothels.[46]

Origins

Shanghai in 1930 was a hub for the trade and consumption of both foreign and domestic derivatives of opium. Illicit sales skyrocketed thanks to a government ban, and monopolising this trade, as well as other forms of vice, eventually became a part of the modus vivendi of the Green Gang. The order's rise to power made its main architect, Du Yuesheng, one of the most powerful men in Shanghai and, arguably, China.

The path that led Du to join the Green Gang resembled that of most members. The son of a petty clerk and shopkeeper, he was born in 1888 and raised in poverty across the river from Shanghai. He was orphaned at an early age and received no more than four months of an elementary education. At fourteen he moved to the city and immersed himself in its underbelly. After years of eking out a living as a petty extortionist, opium dealer and armed robber, Du Yuesheng was taken in by a local madam and employed as a minder and bouncer in her small brothel. The patronage of his 'foster mother' hardened Du's reputation as a gangster and helped him gain purchase in the Green Gang.[47] 'Big-eared' Du moved up quickly in the order despite his low birth and rural origins. By the late 1920s, he mediated the incorporation of dozens of Green Gang affiliates within the French Concession neighbourhoods of the city. All manner of vice, as well as opium trading, became a Green Gang monopoly within the city's most glamorous and prosperous borough. Du did not rule over this fiefdom alone. A critical member of the Green Gang's collective leadership was a seasoned policeman, Huang Jinrong. As a trusted constable who had served the French administration as far back as the 1890s, Huang ascended to the rank of chief superintendent both despite and because of his Green Gang affiliation. Huang's superiors valued his place in the Shanghai underworld. He was a man who could be counted on to maintain peace and minimise the worst excesses of the concession's shadow economy. As in other colonies, local officials were more than willing to 'let the "natives" go to degradation and demoralisation' since their fate 'was of no concern to the French nation'.⁴⁸ The arrangement between the Green Gang and French officials netted both sides extravagant profits. According to authorities in the neighbouring International Concession, Du and his compatriots lavished the French with a monthly payoff of $180,000 (over $3 million today). Appointees from France claimed to be in charge of the police, but as one British diplomat said, 'the real power was in the hands of Mr Du Yuesheng and his friends'.⁴⁹

Du's influence allowed him and his brothers to further enrich themselves as China descended into chaos. Through the 1920s, rival warlords tussled for control of Shanghai's arsenal and opium exports. Rising anti-Japanese sentiment, as well as the surging popularity of the Communist Party, added more complications. Then there was growing influence of China's new central government under Nationalist leader Chiang Kai-shek. In 1927, Chiang seized the city of Nanjing and declared it the capital of the Chinese Republic. His hold over the country was presumptuous as vast swaths of territory remained under the control of warlords or foreign occupiers. Chiang's administration was desperate for money and allies and Du proved eager to provide both. In 1927, Du assisted in the round-up and massacre of Communists living in Shanghai. His willingness to weed out Chiang's rivals helped facilitate a more lucrative relationship. Despite Nanjing's avowed commitment to eradicate the production and sale of illicit opium, officials loyal to Chiang's Nationalist Party worked with the Green Gang to consolidate and monopolise the trade. While serving as a formal member of Shanghai's official opium suppression committee, Du led the Green Gang into a new era of power and wealth. It was under his watch that Shanghai became Asia's primary port of call for opium smugglers operating throughout the world. His ill gains from the opium trade, as well as profits from gambling, prostitution and other rackets, elevated Du to the top of Shanghai society. He took on the veneer of a philanthropist, opening schools, temples, hospitals and relief agencies that cared for the poor. Du also hired scholars and writers to promote his image among the public (with one going so far as to fraudulently trace his ancestry back to an emperor from China's classical past).

While the influential publication *Who's Who in China* cited Du as a prominent 'liberal contributor to philanthropy and education', other Western observers possessed no illusion as to who he really was.[50] When Nanjing awarded him and other leading Green Gang brothers with honours for their relief work, one foreign correspondent was unamused. China's recognition of Du was as if 'President Roosevelt had brought Al Capone out of [the] clink and presented him with the Congressional Medal for his distinguished public service'.[51]

For all of Du's standing and wealth, he was incapable of escaping the consequence of the Second World War. Japan's invasion of China in 1937 brought his city under full military occupation. Du, as well others in the Green Gang, lit out for Hong Kong and the safety of British rule. For a time, he did what he could to maintain his empire. With Japan's attack on Pearl Harbor and the opening of a wider conflict in the Pacific, trafficking in opium dropped to a trickle, devastating the Green Gang's political and economic fortunes. Du survived the conflict with his ties to Chiang Kai-shek intact. He returned to Shanghai a shadow of his former self and left his hometown for good after Mao Tse-tung's victory in China's civil war in 1949. He died two years later in poor health and politically friendless. Other Green Gang refugees fared better. Younger members who re-established themselves in Hong Kong quickly rebuilt their organisation. The order's criminal activities became so flagrant and widespread that colonial officials were forced to seek out new officers who spoke the Shanghai Chinese dialect. As late as 1960, British police officials still claimed that the Green Gang remained as 'strong as at any time since its establishment on the local scene'.⁵² But a larger wave of refugees eventually eclipsed Du's successors from Shanghai. Between the war and Mao's victory, thousands of displaced triads sought refuge in Hong Kong. In interwar Shanghai, Du Yuesheng deftly coerced Shanghai's triad lodges to operate under his leadership. In his absence, none of his former followers possessed the skill or ruthlessness necessary to maintain the Green Gang's primacy. The future of post-war Hong Kong belonged to the triads alone.

At the height of the war in the Pacific, entrepreneurs from Japan partially filled the vacuum left by the triads and the Green Gang. Chief among these beneficiaries was a Japanese imperial officer named Yoshio Kodama. At first blush Kodama had much in common with Du. Their shared background as boys born into poverty made them into men who were driven and restless. Kodama, however, called no single place home. Though born in the colony of Korea, he returned to Japan where he became embroiled in right-wing politics. His activism and affiliation with militant organisations landed him in jail several times in the 1930s. Kodama's anti-government aspirations changed upon his release from prison. With the Japanese invasion of China, he enlisted in the army, working as a staff officer and aide to occupying forces in China.

In 1941 he struck out on his own and formed a procuring company dedicated to supplying the Japanese war machine. His company metastasized as the fighting intensified, accruing an equity base of $175 million dollars before Japan's surrender. Though Kodama's co-operation specialised in providing the military with precious metals, many of the deals he pursued on the Chinese mainland were sealed through the sale of heroin. With Japan's surrender in 1945, American officials had him arrested and imprisoned as a war criminal. He was one of many to profit from Japanese expansionism, including a slew of lesser-known men who made a fortune from Chinese opium, morphine and heroin.

Origins

They, alongside Kodama, often fancied themselves as modern-day *ronin* or masterless samurai from Japan's past. All, to some extent, were also connected to the yakuza.

Like the triads, Japan's yakuza possesses a history that dates back many centuries. Its mythology, however, differs in significant ways. The term yakuza originates from the phonetics of the word, ya-ku-za, meaning 8-9-3, the worst hand to hold in a game of cards.[53] Who coined the name, let alone when precisely it entered Japanese parlance, is not clear. The name alone confirms that gamblers were the first to acquire a connection to yakuza culture. As far as back as the seventh century, rulers in Japan aspired to outlaw games of chance. Nevertheless gamblers, or *bakuto*, persevered, often forming self-regulating bands managing local gambling houses. Many of these groups fancied themselves as families, or *ikka*, headed by a boss (or father) and his followers (whom he referred to as his children).[54] Violence was intrinsic to this culture. Those who led and were counted among these bands were often capable fighters. The services they provided to local communities often endeared them to the poor and the marginalised. Elites, as well as the government, tended to be more ambivalent about the bakuto. Efforts to combat gambling, as well as other vices, did lead officials to employ bakuto as informants and overseers of neighbourhoods known for crime. In times of desperation, some willingly hired themselves out as warriors.[55] Nevertheless, bakuto and other early yakuza tended to be drawn from the lower ranks of society. To this day, yakuza membership is strongly associated with Japan's historic caste of outsiders, the *burakumin*. As a hereditary group associated with 'unclean' professions such as butchers or leather workers, burakumin often found opportunity for work and status in the company of bakuto gangs. This strong association with outlaws and the unwanted fostered many of the yakuza's cultural traits. Elaborate tattooing, for example, likely originated as a state practice of marking the skin of known criminals. By the twentieth century, full-body art, or *iruzemi*, became a fixture of yakuza pride and stature. Among the things that make the early Japanese underworld distinct from Italy's mafias was its near universal nature. The yakuza entered the modern era as a generally unorganised caste of individuals and gangs. No particular part of Japan claimed any special relationship with these early iterations of yakuza. Above all, there is no evidence of any ikka claiming great wealth or power at the expense of the established order.

As European empires made inroads into Asia, Japan's reigning dynasty of military leaders, the Tokagawa, grew weaker in the face of rising dissent and unrest among provincial lords. The arrival of an American fleet in 1853 dealt the Tokagawa a fatal blow after the Americans forced them to sign a trade treaty that diminished the country's sovereignty and security. Fearing they too could succumb to the same colonial calamities as China, revolutionaries overthrew the Tokagawa and replaced the ruling monarch with a more pliant, reform-minded successor, Emperor Meiji. In the decades that followed Meiji's ascendency in 1868, a strict regime of modernisation and state centralisation transformed Japanese politics and society. Reformist conformity became an absolute for Japan's new ruling class. The dramatic changes that swept over the country placed the bakuto in a tenuous position. The reissuance of laws prohibiting gambling threatened every ikka in the country. However, the state's heavy-handedness spurred many bakuto to engage more directly in politics. By the early twentieth century, ikka leaders and followers joined political parties, particularly on Japan's right. Together they blended into a larger cohort of ideologues prone to violence. As newly remade 'men of chivalry', vice lords joined self-styled 'political ruffians', or *soshi*, in becoming radical activists, party patrons and adventurers.

In advance of the Second World War, the world of the yakuza became even more intertwined with Japan's rightward shift.

Origins

Tokyo's colonial empire in Asia brought opportunities to serve the state and get rich. Though not a yakuza himself, Yoshio Kodama was one of many right-wing nationalists to profit from the empire's growth. When Kodama arrived in China in 1937, he joined a loose collection of freelancing fixers, exporters and agents who took advantage of the local opium trade. As the rule of law deteriorated in China's interior, Kodama and other self-styled ronin ran heroin and engaged in illegal schemes.[56] Labelling this the work of Japan's yakuza is not possible, but Kodama's experience aligned with the yakuza's eventual trajectory. By the time of Japan's surrender to the United States, the yakuza operated both as an extension of Japan's imperial system and as a separate, self-serving and inherently criminal entity.

We know precious little about the evolution of Japan's underworld up until the point the atomic bomb was dropped on Hiroshima. For at least one reflective yakuza, the early iteration of a bakuto was decidedly pedestrian compared to the gangsters who succeeded him. Ijichi Eiji, as he told his biographer, was not born into the life but became a bakuto as a young and aimless man. He embraced the rituals that accompanied his acceptance into a gang in the 1920s. What membership did not necessarily entail was an opportunity to grow rich. 'Yakuza nowadays are mixed up in all kinds of things – in the construction business, drugs, real estate, loan-sharking, you name it – but it wasn't like that in the old days.'[57] In his youth, a bakuto who could not make a living as a gambler was a failure and, perhaps worse still, a fraud. The police did not take kindly to him or others he knew in Tokyo's underworld. During multiple periods of incarceration, authorities subjected Eiji to torture, while larger events, such as war or natural disaster, provided more drama in his life. Yet in contrast to the post-war era, there was little violence and animosity among the gangs of his time. 'In movies and novels, the yakuza are always reaching for a sword or a gun, but that's just bullshit,' he later explained. For him, crime was a profession. 'There were bosses who didn't see eye to eye, of course, but if they'd started carving each other up just because they didn't get on well, the police would have clamped down on them, and their business would have folded.'[58]

Tokyo's defeat in 1945 left the yakuza devastated in Japan and its colonial territories. The peace following Emperor Hirohito's surrender created an altogether new set of conditions governing the country. American occupational authorities ensured Japan became a democracy in more than name. Its economy, though initially decimated, rebounded and its cities rose again. Like the mafias of Sicily, the yakuza who survived confronted the post-war era as a kind of zero hour. To flourish in this new world meant adapting and maturing.

HIGHBINDERS AND BLACK HANDS: THE EARLY MAFIAS ABROAD

In the winter of 1893, a violent coup overthrew the royal family of Hawaii. The plotters, most of them American, prosecuted their attack with the expectation that Washington would annex the islands. Congress fulfilled these expectations and, within five years, Hawaii became an American territory. Washington's complicity in the coup made the strategic and economic value of the islands clear. Sitting halfway between North America and Asia, Hawaii was one of the world's most lucrative centres of sugar production. Its plantations were magnets for migrants of various types. At the time of annexation, newcomers dwarfed Hawaii's native population. While most immigrants lived in the countryside, the fledgling capital of Honolulu drew people looking for respite or relief from the hellish work of the plantations. Alongside the dance halls and bars in town came the gambling dens and whorehouses, the latter inevitably attracting violence and crime.

Origins

Stories of depravity were common in the daily reporting of Honolulu's early newspapers. Among the most consistent subjects were the activities of the town's Japanese gangs. By the time of the coup in 1893, Japanese migrants represented a quarter of the territory's population.[59] A disproportionate number of these settlers came from the lowest rungs of Japanese society. Journalists came to understand that Japanese gamblers and 'procurers' represented a stratum unto themselves. 'The better class of Japanese do not take much interest in the gambling, over which the American press is making so much,' one journalist wrote in 1904. 'The Japanese gamblers are a class apart.'[60] Much the same was said of pimps, who were likened by one Hawaiian editor to a separate criminal caste 'not unlike the soshi in their native land'. For readers in the US, Japan's soshi had become a vaguely familiar subject. In an era rife with anarchist violence and political terror, soshi assassins had been blamed for a string of attacks on Americans living in Japan at the turn of the century. The Japanese pimps in Hawaii were no less violent. 'Procuring with these Asiatic outcasts is but one phase of their vicious activity,' a different editor wrote. 'They also levy blackmail, commit open robbery, interfere by threats of court witnesses, bribe where threats fail, do mob violence ... and now and then commit murder.'[61]

No editor or journalist referred to these offenders as yakuza. In fact, the word makes no appearance in any American discussion of Japanese crime during this time. Though their hallmarks are unmistakable, tracing the origins of these criminals back to the yakuza in Japan remains difficult. Journalists in Hawaii and elsewhere rarely paid attention to the identities or the backstory of the pimps or gambling gangs they featured. There was also no Japanese law that forbade individuals from recruiting or forcing women abroad to work as prostitutes. One Japanese census from 1890 projected there were at least 1,100 Japanese women in brothels between Vladivostok and Vancouver.[62] Whether anything like the yakuza had a hand in this industry is not known. If the gamblers and pimps of Honolulu were indeed transplanted yakuza, the stories of their journeys abroad went untold.

Despite the limits of what we know, the emergence of a Japanese underworld in Hawaii represents a broader trend during this era. The flow of millions of men and women across the world's oceans brought with it a new blending of cultures. Crime, among other things, became an important lens through which many understood the meeting and mixing of peoples. The enthusiasm with which the popular press pursued stories of migrant criminals produced a rich corpus of accounts detailing what was believed to be the existence of conspiratorial societies and gangs. Many of these stories provide a critical link in the history of modern mafias. In them, evidence emerges of how the triads, the Camorra and the Sicilian Mafia took root in the New World. This is especially the case of the United States, a country which became home to many migrant gangs. Decades before the heyday of Capone and New York's Five Families, Americans had come to terms with some of the basic facets of the mafia. This can be seen not only in the pages of the American press but also in contemporary motion pictures. These narratives, journalistic and creative, set important precedents for why mafias grew in importance later in the twentieth century.

The doings of Japanese gamblers and pimps registered far beyond Hawaii. Stories of yakuza-like groups appeared in newspapers in places such as Fresno, Spokane, Butte, Santa Cruz and elsewhere in the western parts of the United States.[63] Their activities, however widespread, paled in comparison to the spectre cast by the so-called tongs. Before the First World War, newspapers from coast to coast carried stories filled with harrowing details of deadly wars waged by these mysterious societies. America's tongs were one manifestation of a wider phenomenon shaping the Chinese diaspora. They were, to a large extent, an outward expression of the secret fraternities that peppered the towns and villages of Qing China.

Origins

Westerners noted the spread of Chinese secret societies during the first half of the nineteenth century. In Singapore and other Malay ports, reports of triad activity emerged before the Opium Wars. Triads arrived in the United States by way of San Francisco. The first of these triad fraternities, the Kwong Duck Tong, was established in 1850, just two years after the California gold rush began. At the time, San Francisco was home to no more than 800 Chinese migrants (the United States had a total of about 8,000 Chinese residents). The size of this diaspora swelled to over 100,000 by the start of the 1880s. Tongs such as Kwong Duck spawned new satellite lodges. Other tongs, such as the Hip Sing, On Leong, the Suey Sing and Hop Sing, eventually took the place of Kwong Duck as they spread to major cities, small towns and mining camps across the country. In some instances, tongs possessed three to four branches within one neighbourhood alone.[64]

Tongs were not strictly criminal enterprises. For Chinese men looking to settle and find work so far from home, they served as pillars of sanctuary, identity and communal welfare. Leaders of a lodge were advocates for its members in dealing with local authorities and employers. Some rallied their members to aid causes back in China. By 1900, tong activists transformed the United States into a bastion of the anti-Qing movement. Like the triads at home, rituals bound members of a lodge together. Several tongs, such as the Chee Kong, placated the public by affirming they were nothing more than a Chinese version of the Freemasons.[65] The multitude of fraternities also reflected inherent communal fissures. Though the majority of migrants came from provinces in southern China, rival lodges drew in congregations of men with the same surname or place of birth. Ethnic differences, particularly estranged minority groups such as the Hakka, also gave birth to independent lodges. Issues of personality and individual grievances were no less important to their establishment and behaviour. According to lore, the first of the 'tong wars' in America began over the custody of a woman. In a struggle that began in a mining camp east of San Francisco, the Hop Sing battled the Suey Sing for nearly twenty years after a leader's mistress was kidnapped. The fighting between the two tongs spread across northern California until 1901 when a peace agreement was finally reached.[66]

By 1900, competition over tribute and vice became the most frequent source of conflict. As Chinatowns multiplied across the country, rival tongs grew to manage and extort all forms of entrepreneurial activity. Launderers, saloon keepers, grocers and dry goods dealers were frequent marks for tongs seeking exorbitant rents or protection money. Gambling houses were establishments where tongmen socialised and muscled unlucky dealers and gamblers. With many migrants arriving in America with an opium addiction, or soon acquiring one, dispensing the drug and opening smoking dens became central to a tong's profits and influence. The brothel, perhaps more than any other institution, connected tongs to one another and to procureurs far off in China. With sex ratios often ranging between 100 or 200 men to one woman, there was no Chinatown in America that did not have at least one house of prostitution. Demand for sex among Chinese migrants led to steady streams of women kidnapped or lured into the trade. Tongs accrued fortunes from the sale of sex as well as the purchasing and selling of abducted women. One lodge, the Hip Yee, supplied Chinatown brothels with up to 87 per cent of women sold into sex slavery in the United States, a total of 6,000 women in all.[67]

Death was a frequent penalty for those who tested the will of a tong. Personal slights, random killings and competing interests also produced grave consequences. In the decades between the 1860s and 1930s, broadsheets in the United States documented the outbreak of scores of so-called 'tong wars'. By the start of the Second World War, the phenomenon had assumed international dimensions. In 1924, a feud between the Hip Sing and On Leong lodges resonated in Chinatowns as far away as Ottawa and Hermosillo.[68] Rival tongs fought one another in other locations in Mexico, Canada and other Pacific Rim countries. In America, however, tong wars took on near mythic proportions. Journalists peppered accounts with lurid details of beheadings, sabre slashings and gunshot wounds. The fact that street battles included fighters armed with axes, spears, swords and staves added to local impressions that the tongs grew out of a crueller, more primitive time and place. Newspapers took to calling the combatants hatchet men and highbinders, a word historically used for Irish bandits during the early 1800s.[69]

The toll from these battles often failed to live up to the attention lavished upon them. For all the hysteria with which New York newspapers covered the 1904 war between the Hip Sing and On Leong, only one lodge member was killed during the whole year. The extremes to which the press publicised the threat of tong violence appears even more jarring when compared to the overall state of crime in New York City. Policemen in 1904 reportedly arrested 334 Chinese suspects for various infractions. During that same year police imprisoned another 20,000 individuals of Irish descent as well as tens of thousands of offenders of Russian, Italian and German background.[70] The consequences of this media attention proved significant. The apparent freedom with which tongs warred with one another while profiting from vice stirred the public's rage. Heartfelt accounts of women forced into prostitution at the hands of the tongs provided reformers with ammunition to end 'white slavery'. Exposés documenting the squalor and hopelessness of Chinese opium dens aided those who called for an end to the opium trade. Opponents of gambling rarely failed to highlight the moral and physical dangers that came with the proliferation of Chinatown gaming houses. All of these hazards underscored the threat of the great 'yellow peril'. The intensity of anti-Chinese sentiment, in part driven by the dangers posed by the tongs, led to action. From 1882 to the Second World War, Congress forbade Chinese nationals from entering the United States. Violations of the 1882 Chinese Exclusion

Act were frequently attributed to the tongs. 'The purpose of the high binder, of the high binder organization, is vicious and criminal,' one California advocate declared. Crushing the tongs, he added, demanded the closure of all lodges and the deportation of all Chinese nationals found in violation of the law.[71] Sometimes members of the public took the law into their own hands. In an era that featured waves of anti-Chinese violence by white mobs, one police raid on a lodge in New York's Chinatown descended into pandemonium as onlookers demanded that someone 'lynch the Chinks'.[72]

In New Orleans, one self-appointed 'committee of public safety' succeeded in stringing up suspected gangsters of another sort. In the spring of 1891, mobs shot or lynched eleven Italian men across the city. Their crime was a presumed connection to the murder of the Chief of Police, David Hennessey. Before his assassination the previous year, Hennessey began investigating a gang referred to in the press as 'the mafia'. At the head of this group were two brothers, Charles and Tony Matranga. Newspapers reported the Matranga mafia comprised 300 members and that its inductees swore an oath to the brothers upon a skull with two daggers shoved in its eye sockets. While Charles Matranga escaped the lynch mob's fury, others killed in the 1891 attacks were innocent of any connection to the case.[73] There had been occasions when other Italians were suspected of mafia-like crimes in New Orleans, including as far back as the 1860s. The 1891 lynchings, however, were the first of many to occur throughout the American South. Though it constitutes the largest mass lynching in American history, no official enquiry has ever taken place.* By 1910 an Italian consular official recorded a total of thirty-four deaths attributed to

---

* In 2019, the city government of New Orleans issued a public apology for the lynchings, some 128 years after the fact. See Ryan Prior, '128 years later, New Orleans is apologizing for lynching 11 Italians', *CNN* (https://www.cnn.com/2019/04/01/us/new-orleans-mayor-apologizes-italian-americans-trnd/index.html, consulted 3 July 2023).

mob lynchings, making Italians the third largest number of victims of such attacks after African Americans and Chinese.[74]

The New Orleans killings mark an important moment within American mafia lore: it introduced the American public to the existence of an indigenously grown version of the Italian mafia. Yet the New Orleans case did not set off a wave of investigations into mafia conspiracies across the country. This inaction did not mean that Americans were necessarily ignorant of the Sicilian Mafia's contemporary significance. The press had been tantalising readers with garish tales of Mafia and Camorra scandals in Italy since the late nineteenth century. By the First World War, American press stories of murders and other crimes committed by local Italian thugs were commonplace.

The opening of the twentieth century came as a surging tide of migration from Italy washed over the United States. Between 1900 and 1910, a record 2.1 million men and women, mostly from Italy's south, arrived at various American ports.[75] The majority of migrants passed through the gates of Ellis Island. Most lived, for a time at least, within the boroughs of New York City. Endemic poverty and faint hopes of opportunities west of the Hudson drove them further on. At least some among this wave of immigrants arrived already initiated into the Mafia or Camorra. Counted among this generation of newcomers was Giuseppe Morello, the reputed founder of New York's first mafia family. A Sicilian court had convicted Morello in absentia for counterfeiting and other crimes when he arrived in America at the age of twenty-seven. At some point, one of the ruling cosche of his native town of Corleone had inducted him into their clan. Between 1894 and 1903, Morello pulled together a crew of fellow Sicilians, including mafiosi sworn into rival cosche back in Italy. His resurgent career as a counterfeiter and extortionist came to an abrupt halt when police arrested him for murder. The victim was a man found cut in half and stuffed inside a cigar barrel. After 1903, Morello spent several decades going in and out of prison. Some members of his gang escaped to Italy in the hopes of evading arrest or re-establishing ties with mafiosi they left behind. Others remained in the US long enough to enjoy a revival of their fortunes under Prohibition.[76]

New York's first mafia family represented a certain exception rather than a general rule. Newly arriving camorristi and mafiosi tended to work alone or assembled gangs that failed to evolve into durable syndicates. Above all, the crimes most associated with this first generation of gangsters were crude and uncomplicated. Rather than becoming purveyors of vice, most resorted to extortion and kidnapping to make a living. Their collective activities inspired a groundswell of media attention into what was generally called the 'black hand'. We don't know the first criminal to claim the black hand moniker or where the phrase comes from. At the time the first black hand accounts surfaced in the United States in the 1890s, stories of Spanish 'black hand' anarchist activity filled European newspapers. Unfortunately, there is no way of knowing whether American criminals adopted this moniker for themselves or were labelled as such by American journalists.[77] Regardless, by the First World War, black hand crimes plagued cities and towns throughout America. The local newspaper of Pittsburg, in eastern Kansas, warned residents in 1905 of a scourge of black hand attacks in the small town's Little Italy. Like black hands elsewhere in America, the culprits sent notes threatening death or kidnap unless the victims paid them off. No one living in Little Italy dared even to speak the name of their oppressors. Police found many who crossed them dead with a blue sash draped around them. Other corpses had multiple stab wounds. The paper concluded that there was simply no punishment too severe 'for those who discuss the methods of the Mafia's successors'.[78]

Witnesses in Pittsburg and elsewhere in the United States understood that the black hand was not the work of a single monolithic conspiracy. Nevertheless, the frequency of these crimes left a dark stain upon Italian migrants. Nativists seized upon these stories as confirmation that Italians were both loathsome and undesirable as American citizens. Others presented the problem as a wider issue confronting the country. An occasional offence could be forgiven, as one Mississippi editor put it: 'But when foreign groups transport and carry on here their Tongs, mafias, vendettas, class enmities and hostilities, it is a disturbance of such alien ... and bloody character that America is not obliged to endure it and should not.'[79] As in the case of the tongs, these sentiments helped catalyse forces in Congress to eventually pass restrictive anti-migrant legislation in 1924.

Newspapers were not the only vehicle that fostered negative perceptions of Italians – moving pictures did too. In the spring of 1906, Biograph, a New York-based film company, released the one-reel short, *The Black Hand*. The plot of this silent picture is conspicuously simple: a band of kidnappers, assumingly Italians, seize and ransom the daughter of a prosperous grocer. The film is more comedic than frightful. The kidnappers are drunken oafs and a less insipid troop of police detectives apprehend them in their lair. Despite its standing as the first gangster movie, *The Black Hand* is most compelling for the grainy scenes that are photographed on the streets of early twentieth-century New York.[80] A handful of other films followed *The Black Hand*'s lead over the next decade. Before producing his epic account of race and American history, D. W. Griffith released several films that alluded to the black hand and the mafia. Like his 1915 opus *Birth of a Nation*, these early 'revenge' pictures, such as *In Little Italy* and *The Musketeers of Pig Alley*, reflected the director's obsession with violence and ethnicity. As silent classics, they provided early precedents for many of the tropes found in more celebrated Hollywood mafia movies.[81]

These first cinematic gangsters were also premonitions of other turns that took place after the First World War. The adoption of the Volstead Act outlawing the consumption and sale of alcohol touched off a renaissance in American organised crime. By then the mafia entered a far more familiar chapter for students of history. There is no question that Prohibition gave life to a coherent system of syndicates ultimately known as the American Mafia. This critical moment of conception was well documented and inspired new developments in both politics and popular culture. What is perhaps less appreciated is the extent to which American Prohibition reflected a global effort to combat the illicit transshipment and production of narcotics. As in the United States, this massive undertaking produced a revolution in criminal activity.

4

From Booze to Dope: The Advent of Global Mafias

Howard Hawks claimed he met Al Capone on more than one occasion around the release of his landmark 1932 film, *Scarface*. The first time Hawks flew to Chicago, Capone sent heavies to pick him up. The men came late, which miffed Hawks, though they apologised and said they had been at a funeral for someone killed the night before. 'Do I have to ride with you if there was a killing last night?' he asked them. Catching his drift, they allowed Hawks to go in a separate car. He then arrived at a café, where he found Capone with some 'damn pretty girls', who were 'a bit brassy but very pretty'. Hawks found the real-life Scarface welcoming, perhaps even affable. The mob boss loved *Scarface* and, if Hawks is to be believed, watched it five or six times after obtaining a print of the reels. Capone enjoyed how close events in the film mirrored the reality of his rise to power. When he asked Hawks how he could have possibly known about some of the details, the director played coy. 'Look,' he told him, 'you know how somebody can't testify if he's a lawyer? Well, I'm a lawyer.' Hawks professed Capone liked the joke.[1]

Aspects of this story do not necessarily jive with history. By the time *Scarface* arrived in theatres, Capone was serving an eleven-year jail term for tax evasion. Whatever the case, Hawks may be forgiven for taking licence with the truth. The film received no financial backing from the studio system, forcing Hawks to rely on the support of the eccentric aviation and entertainment mogul, Howard Hughes. The censors hated the picture for its violence. In one cut of the movie, lead actor Paul Muni falls dead on the street in a pile of manure. The censors ordered the finale be reshot. In his retelling of this ordeal, Hawks hardly contained his pride. *Scarface* was no box office success, but it engaged meaningfully with mob activity in America. Hawks wanted the audience to embrace and recognise the gross corruption and wantonness of his characters. For this reason, he insisted that Muni appeared to have an incestuous relationship with his sister, alluding to the rumours surrounding the Borgia family during the Renaissance. Towards the end of his life, Howard Hawks remained resolute. 'I wish it had come out in a day when *The Godfather* did, because it's a better picture,' he boasted. To him there was nothing about *The Godfather* that hadn't already been done.[2]

In the same year that Hawks released *Scarface*, another titan of crime told his story for the first time. Elie Eliopoulos sat before an audience of two officials, both in the employment of the Egyptian police. He was not under arrest but still on the run. Months earlier German authorities had apprehended a partner of his by the name of 'Little Augie' Del Gracio with 250 kilos of heroin in possession. Yes, Eliopoulos claimed, he knew Del Gracio, but he was not involved in his dealings in Germany. Elie's denials did not prevent him from waxing poetic about his life and fortunes to the two Egyptian officers. Born in Greece at the turn of the century, he had come from a good family. His interrogators found him 'Mephistophelian [sic] in appearance' and bearing a striking resemblance to German actor Conrad Veidt (who later played the Nazi antagonist Major Strasser in the film *Casablanca*). He was fluent in both French and English but puffed harshly when he spoke. Eliopoulos acknowledged that he was indeed one of the largest traders in heroin in the world and spoke openly of his influence in the Chinese opium market. He refused to acknowledge, however, that he had ever trafficked drugs into the United States.[3] Newspapermen and American agents tended to disagree. During the 1930s newspapers in Asia and the Atlantic world had documented the exploits of Eliopoulos and his accomplices in great detail. As in the case of Capone, an American crusade to bring him to justice was among the chief sources of his international notoriety. Before the end of his career, investigators in the United States calculated that he had accrued a fortune of fifty million dollars by trading heroin. In 1943 he finally stood trial in Brooklyn for his crimes. The effort to bring Eliopoulos before the court was gargantuan, involving investigators in eight countries. Though Eliopoulos was convicted, the judge threw out the jury's ruling after discovering the statute of limitations had been exceeded. At the time of his release, Eliopoulos owned homes in both New York and California. Rumour had it that he was cultivating his own Hollywood friends. Yet to this day no one has ever attempted to bring his life to the big screen.

The American ego may explain why Hollywood made Capone famous while leaving Eliopoulos to languish in anonymity. Despite all the chases and gunfights, *Scarface* (1932) is a soulful meditation on cardinal American sins: avarice, gluttony, violence and lust. Brian De Palma hammers upon all these themes with even greater strength in his 1983 remake. It's unlikely a director could have framed the life of Elie Eliopoulos in a way that spoke to the American experience because the officers described him as demure and remote. Where Eliopoulos shunned attention, Capone sought the eye of the world's media.

The United States survived the First World War intact and free from the upheaval and physical carnage that blighted large portions of Europe, Asia and the Middle East. Its booming economy made its society the heart of a new culture of consumerism and artistry. Yet both despite and because of its prosperity, Capone appeared to be at the forefront of a crime wave that held the country captive. He was the irrefutable face of the violence and corruption of this period. His gaudy, vulgar persona embodied the indulgences and excesses of the Roaring Twenties. Audiences abroad didn't need to see Hawks's *Scarface* to understand – Capone was covered endlessly by the media.

Inter-war newspapers did not speak of Capone or any other American as members of the mafia. The real mafiosi were still perceived to be an obscure criminal class that resided in Mussolini's Italy. This changed in 1950, when a new, more compelling narrative emerged – one that linked Capone and other Prohibition era mobsters to a nationwide criminal syndicate. It was a conspiracy formed and maintained by 'ethnics', men who were either immigrants or the children of immigrants. Capone-like kingpins ruled over these 'combinations', which were bound together by their shared interest in vice and dope. For the Americans who crafted this narrative, the fight against the American Mafia was not one that ended at the Atlantic and Pacific. A global effort was needed to bring them to heel. After 1950, the world came to see mafias on virtually every continent.

BIG SHOTS: NEW YORK AND THE BIRTH OF GANGLAND AMERICA

Paul Kelly was 'aggrieved' when journalists from the *New York Times* visited him in 1912. He had a new social club just north of Times Square and wished to be left in peace. The police felt differently. When the cops raided his establishment and uncovered a roulette wheel, he explained that it belonged to a customer who was storing it there. The police kept an eye on the place, especially when they learned that several 'lucky' customers had been robbed shortly after leaving Kelly's premises. Kelly planned to complain to the mayor. Should his petition fail, he at least had the parking garage he owned to fall back on. The irony of it all is clearly what brought journalists to pay Paul Kelly a visit. A decade earlier, he had led the Five Pointers, one of the most feared and storied gangs in the city. His reputation as a one-time leg-breaker and vote-getter for New York's Democratic Party still lingered. And above all, he had fought Monk Eastman and lived.[4]

Paul Kelly's chosen name was a tribute to the legacies he inherited and the prejudice of his day. Born Paolo Vaccarelli in Naples, Italy, Kelly was a diminutive bantam boxer in his youth. Becoming a Kelly was an homage to Irish pugilists such as John L. Sullivan and Tommy Burns. It was also a custom among Italians and other fighters who wished to conceal their origins. When he took over the Five Points Gang at the turn of the century, he assumed the mantle of one of the fiercest gangs New York had ever known. The Five Pointers represented a consolidation of several of the most notorious gangs of the Lower East Side: the Dead Rabbits, the Pug Uglies and the Whyos. By 1912, the neighbourhood and thugs that gave Paul Kelly's band its reputation had largely ceased to exist. Back in the early 1800s, The Five Points had been the location of the cesspool New Yorkers had used to discard their waste. It became best known as a neighbourhood that housed many of the city's Irish immigrants during the blackest years of the Potato Famine in the 1840s. For much of the remainder of the nineteenth century it was synonymous with crime and dire poverty. Civic reformers laid waste to the Five Points from 1895, tearing down most of its original dwellings. The ethnic persuasion of the Lower East Side also began to change. The mass arrival of Italians, Jews and Chinese immigrants displaced most of the area's Irish residents before the new century began. The Five Pointers reflected this evolution. Its headquarters moved uptown and most of its new members were Italian.[5]

What had not changed from the era of the Dead Rabbits was the multitude of gangs that divvied up New York's underworld. At peak strength, Paul Kelly's Five Pointers ruled over most of the tenement blocks in the Lower East Side. None of Kelly's rackets were especially sophisticated operations. His estimated 1,500 followers mostly engaged in petty crime, such as larceny and extortion. They lorded over, but did not necessarily manage, the humble gambling dens, dive bars and whorehouses they claimed as theirs. As with the old gangs, what distinguished the Five Pointers was their physical prowess. Their street fights were often massive and the wars they waged against their fiercest rivals, the Eastmans, garnered the greatest attention. The Eastmans were unmistakably named after their monstrous-looking leader, the famed Monk Eastman. Born Edward Osterman, he had a crushed nose, jagged teeth and lumpy features that testified to his life of violence. The intensity of the battles Kelly and Eastman waged in 1903 led to the intervention of New York's political establishment. In a deal brokered by city hall, the two men agreed to a bare-knuckle boxing match held in a warehouse close to what is today Yankee Stadium. Their two-hour tumble in the Bronx ended in a draw.[6]

New York's Democratic Party was a pillar of continuity in Kelly's quaint era of crime. Neighbourhoods central to the reign of the Five Pointers and Eastmans formed the bedrock of the turn of the century Democratic machine. Long before Kelly rose to notoriety, a history of mutual interest and co-operation had bound gangs to the party. Generations of aspiring men, particularly those who belonged to the Tammany Hall social club, relied upon the likes of the Five Pointers to intimidate rivals, marshal votes and rig elections. In 1900, Kelly became well acquainted with his state assemblyman, 'Big' Tim Sullivan. As a Lower East Side representative in the state house in Albany, he shamelessly promoted himself as the voice of his downtrodden district. Accusations of profiting from gambling and sex dogged his lengthy career (even though he swore he would rather 'break into a bank and rob the safe' than take a penny from a poor prostitute).[7] For Kelly and Eastman, having the backing of Sullivan meant protection from the police and respectability among their peers.

Systemic alliances between political parties and urban gangs were not uncommon in America by the early twentieth century. Newspaper accounts of battles fought between two bands of thugs over the outcome of a municipal Chicago election in the 1890s likely gave birth to the word 'gangster'.[8] As millions of migrants were establishing new lives in America, both the Republican and Democratic Parties desperately sought potential middlemen and operatives capable of mobilising voters The likes of Paul Kelly provided party bosses with this service and often expected jobs and security in exchange. The muscle and graft that came with patronising gangs were added benefits. The corruption of this period did more than inspire pleas for local political reforms. It became the grist for a series of national campaigns. Amid demand to stem the tide of immigration came calls for a crackdown on vice and intoxicants. By 1910, Congress began to act. An alliance including suffragists, ministers and advocates of urban renewal secured passage of the Mann Act, which imposed federal penalties on anyone found 'trafficking' women across state lines. Four years later Congress considered legislation prohibiting the sale and consumption of alcohol. It was impossible, as one Pennsylvania congressman put it, not to support such a law. Those who rejected Prohibition were 'vultures of vice, the corrupt combinations of politics, the grafters and gangsters', not to mention 'the parasites that clothe themselves in the proceeds of women's shame'.[9] Before Prohibition became law in 1919, Congress also passed the Harrison Act, which made the unlicensed use, import, manufacture or distribution of coca and opium a crime.

Of all the achievements of the so-called Progressive Era, Prohibition was the only legislation to face serious opposition. 'Wet' politicians spoke out vigorously on behalf of several large districts throughout the country. Following the Eighteenth Amendment's ratification, unorganised resistance broke out almost immediately. Homebrewing became rampant. In the place of saloons, which were closing at precipitous rates, 'kitchen-table drinkeries' did their best to take their place.[10] Schemes to import alcohol via Canada, Latin America and Europe proliferated. Outfits such as the Five Pointers were well positioned to capitalise on Prohibition's unpopularity. Yet by 1920, many of the old guard of New York's street gangs were moving on. After Monk Eastman volunteered to fight in the First World War, he returned home with the desire to go straight. A gunman took his life within a year. Paul Kelly got into the bootlegging business for a short spell, but his powers began to fade. In their place came a younger generation of criminals who drew on their experiences under their leadership. The Five Points Gang fostered the careers of two of the most prominent names associated with the American Mafia: Charles 'Lucky' Luciano and Alphonse Capone. Pre-Prohibition New York sired a great many more men who helped construct a nationwide network of mafia families and operations. These ties did not make New York the birthplace of the modern mafia, but it most certainly transformed it into a centre of gravity for mafias in the United States and much of the rest of the world.

New York's first established mafia family, the Morellos, was in a state of a flux as Prohibition came into effect. Terms in prison had forced its founder, Giuseppe, to relinquish control over its former factions. New families in Manhattan and Brooklyn came to prominence. Among them was 'Joe the Boss' Masseria, who may have begun his criminal career as a black hand and kidnapper. After his release from prison, Giuseppe Morello elected to join Masseria's growing family. Joe the Boss was counted among the first mafiosi to enjoy the rising proceeds that came with bootlegging. But he did not control or engineer the networks that brought alcohol to his saloons or speakeasies.

The man credited with innovating and financing the supply of illicit alcohol to New York was no mafioso. The son of a pious Jewish family from contemporary Moldova, Arnold Rothstein secured his reputation as a high-stakes gambler when he convinced the 1919 Chicago White Sox to throw the World Series. His familiarity with the Lower East Side's gambling establishments also brought him to the attention of Tammany Democrats such as Big Tim Sullivan. Legend has it that Rothstein was the first New York big shot to invest in bootlegging, putting up $175,000 of his own money to pay for a shipment of Canadian booze smuggled into the country. The score transformed Rothstein's agents, Big Maxey Greenberg of Detroit and Waxey Gordon of the Lower East Side, into two of the earliest titans of the Prohibition era.[11]

Meyer Lansky was no more than seventeen or eighteen when he met Arnold Rothstein at a Brooklyn bar mitzvah. Rothstein immediately took a liking to the 'hungry' young man. Lansky already had a criminal record and consorted with other young miscreants who grew into lifelong friends. There was Bugsy Siegel, who was younger, tougher and also the son of Jewish immigrants. Charlie Luciano was also close to Lansky, even though he was older, even more bruising and born in Sicily. He boasted of being a one-time Five Pointer and attained his first felony conviction at the age of sixteen. Rothstein took Lansky and his friends under his wing and counselled them to seize the moment when it came to the liquor trade. He introduced them to Al Smith, New York's powerful Tammany Hall governor. When Smith ran for president in 1932, Lansky and Luciano attended the Democratic nominating convention in Chicago as representatives from the Lower East Side. Rothstein, however, did not live to see them become giants of the American underworld. Gambling got the better of him as the 1920s progressed. He bet and lost staggering sums until an unknown gunman murdered him in 1928. Rothstein's pathetic end taught Lansky a valuable lesson when it came to risk: no matter what the game is, every player, 'even Arnie Rothstein, king of them all, loses in the end'. 'That's why,' he later explained, 'I gave up firsthand gambling at an early age. I ran crap games and dice games; I set up gambling joints and casinos. I knew I would always win that way. And I knew I would not end up like Rothstein.'[12]

Prohibition enticed many to diversify their interests and tap into new ones. The desire to supply customers with higher quality alcohol, as well as pressure from the United States Coast Guard and other authorities, led bootlegging operations to pivot between different suppliers in Canada, the Caribbean and Europe. Rising proceeds from liquor allowed entrepreneurs to expand their operations through the opening of new clubs and other businesses. It also led to an incredible amount of movement among aspiring gangsters, many of whom struck out from New York. Johnny Torrio, once a lieutenant in the Five Pointers, moved to Chicago before Prohibition at the invitation of one of the city's most prominent mafiosi, Vincenzo 'Big Jim' Colosimo. As business boomed, Torrio invited other New Yorkers to follow, most notably the young Five Pointer, Al Capone. Other aspiring toughs just passed through the Big Apple. Two Sicilian-born brothers, Stefano and Gaspar Magaddino, left their adopted home of Brooklyn to establish their own crime families in Buffalo and Detroit. Before becoming known as the American Mafia's ambassador-at-large, the Boston-raised Johnny Rosselli started out as a New York bootlegger and hired gunman for Capone's outfit in Chicago.

The steps taken by some bootleggers to co-ordinate their activities in the illicit liquor market were remarkable. In spring 1929, newspapers got wind of a conclave of gangsters in the resort town of Atlantic City. Capone, who was named among the attendees, swore he only came to New Jersey to 'bury the past' amongst his counterparts after years of gang warfare in Chicago. The Atlantic City meeting likely led to more regular gatherings, and though they hardly constituted a board of directors, similar meetings of bootleggers took place as late as 1933.[13] Nor did this 'Commission' of underworld luminaries disappear with Prohibition's end; used as an ad-hoc tool to maintain peace and order, it became one of the defining features of the American Mafia. It gave the impression that a senior cadre of mafiosi orchestrated the most serious crimes in the United States and implied there was something singular about the culture, organisation and interests of the men who met or were represented by this Commission. The American Mafia may have comprised rival families and syndicates spread across the country, but they appeared to be united in their intent to dominate all manner of vice.

In the early stages of Prohibition, harmony proved difficult to maintain. As bootlegging outfits expanded and competition increased, armed clashes and bloodshed ensued with greater regularity. Rising crime rates in the 1920s produced a slew of modern idioms: 'gangland', 'big shots', 'mobsters', 'underworld', 'combinations', and 'criminal syndicates'. Major disturbances in Chicago and New York commanded much of the public's attention but evidence of Prohibition's deadly consequences could be found throughout the United States. In Detroit, the country's fourth largest city in 1930, a split between contending Italian-born mafiosi resulted in a string of killings that grabbed headlines nationwide.[14] By the summer of that year, Detroit and its twenty-one murdered mobsters outpaced Chicago for gang violence.[15]

The profits and notoriety enjoyed by some underworld figures became licence to expand their reach. Emblematic of this pattern of consolidation was the takeover of the Harlem numbers racket. The numbers or policy game was a popular neighbourhood lottery staged on a daily or weekly basis; popular in many cities, it had an especially close following in the Harlem section of Manhattan, an area known for its growing black middle class. Proceeds from numbers were estimated in the millions of dollars by the early 1930s. The fruits of the game drew the attention of successful bootlegger and killer, Dutch Schultz. With the backing of Tammany Hall and associated gangsters, Schultz outmuscled the predominantly West Indian and African American bookmakers and bankers who ran Harlem's numbers game. As many as forty people were murdered in the course of 1930 during his coup. Schultz enjoyed his newfound fiefdom until someone gunned him down in 1935 and associates of Lucky Luciano took over.[16]

Dutch Schultz's murderous ascendency occurred while other dramatic events were remaking New York's underworld. In 1930, assassins gunned down Giuseppe Morello, then the city's premiere mafioso, in Harlem. His death was soon followed by the killing of 'Joe the Boss' Masseria in the beachside community of Coney Island. Police initially downplayed Masseria's death, calling him 'a piker', and, true to form, no one involved in the rackets was willing to talk about it.[17] The truth behind the murder of these two men is now largely lost in the mythos of what witnesses at the time called the Castellammarese War. The full extent of this war will never be known. It may have begun in 1930 with the killing of a mobster in Detroit. It may have left as few as fourteen dead. Some participants later claimed that there were dozens or perhaps even hundreds of casualties.[18] What inspired the war is no less clear. Joe Bonanno, then a newly arrived mafioso, argued that Morello and Masseria met their deaths due to the jealousies of rival transplanted mafiosi from Castellammare, a quaint town on the northwest coast of Sicily. Their murders, as well as the deaths of other old-fashioned 'Mustache Petes', initiated the decline of what Bonanno called the 'men of the old Tradition'. Leading the upstarts in the new generation, Bonanno asserted, was Lucky Luciano, who had served under Masseria. Despite his fidelity to

Joe the Boss's family, Luciano also thrived outside of it. His ties to Jews such as Lansky, whose 'views on life and moneymaking were alien' to more provincial mafiosi, set the 33-year-old Luciano apart from his elders.[19] A new order, Bonanno later testified, came into being under Lucky's stewardship after the Castellammarese War. Five newly consolidated families emerged and took hold of New York's underworld. The heads of these families did not necessarily get along. Beyond their personal interests, Bonanno claimed that the new bosses were divided between those who possessed either a 'Sicilian' attitude or an 'American' one towards their livelihood of being a mafiosi. Yet each would agree that they possessed an equal say in adjudicating areas of conflict and interest among the Five Families.

Whether Bonanno's account is true or not is hard to say. As the founder of one of New York's five canonical families, he refrained from speaking of dealings with Luciano until the 1980s. It was not until the 1960s that the world even learned of the Castellammarese War and its potential consequences. The year 1930 may be best understood as a signpost marking where New York had been and where it was headed; by then, old gangs akin to the Five Pointers were extinct. Though no one referred to Luciano as a mafioso or referenced the existence of a singular mafia in New York, Prohibition sired a new culture of crime in the city. Unlike like the thugs of Monk Eastman's day, this class of criminal operated their gangs and families like corporations, not feudal retinues. Business, more than anything, drove their decisions on affairs of war and peace. What mattered most was money. The thirst for profit – attained through the sale of alcohol, vice or other rackets – pushed them to look beyond their own environs, making them less constrained in their ambitions and thinking. How similar their organisational structures were to Sicily's mafias was yet to be revealed. Yet it was also understood that luminaries such as Luciano and Lansky were linked to other fearful characters outside of New York. Their stature was comparable to, but by no means exceeded, that of Alphonse Capone.

AL'S TOWN: CAPONE'S MOMENT IN THE SUN

At the beginning of the twentieth century, Chicago was notorious for filth. Initially, the blame fell on its physical location and ecology: its surrounds were marshy, making the streets of the old city unbearably muddy. Its earliest citizens lived with the terrible smells that came with the city's poor drainage system. It acquired the nickname 'Slab Town' on account of the shoddy buildings thrown up by its rapidly growing population. Rebuilding in the wake of the great fire of 1871 alleviated some of these problems. Other sources of grime proved more stubborn. As a jumping-off point for migrants heading west of the Mississippi, Chicago had a reputation for transience, loose morals and corruption. As America's progressive movement reached the height of its power between the 1890s and the 1920s, there were at least 500 well-established storefront operations that dealt in sex (with undoubtedly many more never counted).[20] The freedom enjoyed by madams and gaming proprietors charted closely with the city's evolution into a Democratic Party stronghold. Machine politics roared to life in the 1870s under prominent gambler Michael Cassius McDonald. His private fortune and connections to local muscle gave him the leverage to choose which candidates stood for municipal elections. Corruption was the order of the day under his reign. It was Chicago that gave the world the saying, 'Vote early and vote often'.[21]

The city already had more than its share of gangs and big shots before Al Capone came to town. His arrival could not have been better timed: it coincided with the shooting of 'Big' Jim Colosimo, one of Chicago's more feared gangsters. Dubbed 'the most notorious Mafia murder in America' at the time, it remains officially unsolved. There is no question, however, that the men who benefited most from Colosimo's murder were the heirs of his criminal empire.[22] As his former number two, Johnny Torrio inherited Big Jim's brothels, saloons and gambling halls. He assigned the young Snooky, as Capone was known to his friends, to work the door of his club, the Four Deuces. The steady money Alphonse made was better than anything he saw in New York. Business opportunities grew plentiful as he fell into his own diverse crowd of confidants and henchmen. There was Jake Guzik, who came from an extended family of Russian-born pimps and bookmakers, and the bootlegger and fence, Frank Nitti, who had also moved to Chicago after a childhood spent in Sicily and Brooklyn. Their partnership netted Capone an estimated $40 million fortune by the end of the 1920s.

Gangland violence, more than anything, was the bedrock of Capone's fame and fortune. New York's Castellammarese War was a trifling affair in comparison to the bloodshed witnessed in Chicago over booze distribution and other vices. Seven hundred people in Chicago were killed before Prohibition was lifted. In some months the city averaged a murder a day.[23] Well-heeled gangsters took advantage of the black-market sale of military issue 'Tommy guns', often referred to as 'Chicago typewriters'. None of the city's mobs were above the use of dynamite in getting rid of shops, clubs and warehouses belonging to their rivals. It was his battles with Dean O'Banion and Bugs Moran from the north side of the city that brought Capone into a position of leadership. After Johnny Torrio succeeded in rubbing out the mentally unstable O'Banion in 1924, Irish triggermen ambushed Torrio and left him for dead. Torrio survived, but his decision to retire allowed Capone to fully take the reins of his organisation. The war came to a head on Valentine's Day 1929. The machine gun massacre of seven men in a north-side garage included all of Moran's senior lieutenants. Capone, of course, was widely implicated but never charged.

Capone openly bragged of the newspapermen in his pay. Yet there was no need to bribe journalists to write about him. His activities and antics made outstanding copy nationwide. He embraced the attention of cameramen and freely gave interviews. His dress was outrageously gaudy, a fact he recognised and revelled in. Capone's public persona was disarming and even lovable. 'His whole demeanor,' as one journalist found him, 'is that of an overgrown child.' He could easily persuade a know-nothing stranger that he was as 'harmless as a big St Bernard dog'.[24] He had a wit about him as well, a trait that reflected his earthy environment. When he came to Chicago, he had business cards made up while he worked the door at Torrio's Four Deuces. They introduced him as Al Brown, second-hand furniture salesman. When one john asked what sort of furniture he sold, he replied, 'Any old thing a man might want to lay on.'[25] His façade only partially obscured a core truth about Capone: he killed with no hesitation or remorse. Having committed his first murder in his teens, he lured three of his own henchmen to a private party, drugged them and then bludgeoned them with a baseball bat.

The baseball bat murders were one of many anecdotes repeated in the first biography published about Capone in 1930. Its author, *Chicago Tribune* reporter Fred Pasley, also gave credence to less likely stories, such as the claim that Capone fought in France during the war (a tale he used more than once to explain away the scars on his face). Pasley's portrait of Capone as a 'self-made man' resonated with audiences long after Capone's fall. Many echoed Pasley's belief that he had revolutionised 'crime and corruption' by making it more efficient and businesslike in its nature.[26] The notion of Capone as a hyper-malevolent Henry Ford certainly chimed with the times. Mass production and mass consumerism had changed the lives of Americans in the 1920s. Ironically, the first fictionalised account of his life, the novel *Scarface*, offers readers no allegorical lessons. Released the same year as Pasley's biography, author Armitage Trails's story of the gangster Tony Camonte is nothing but pure pulp. Camonte, like Capone, does become powerful and famous, but there's little overt moralising in his dramatic rise and fall.

Hollywood kept all the excitement of both Pasley and Trails's interpretations of Capone's life but added far heavier doses of piety. Before Hawks completed *Scarface*, two other films were released: *Little Caesar* and *The Public Enemy*. *Caesar* and *Enemy* contain only vague references to Capone. The performances of the leading men of each of the Capone movies, Paul Muni, Edward G. Robinson and James Cagney, leave no doubt as to who inspired their parts. Unlike the real-life Capone, the title character of each picture dies violently. The lack of ambiguity was intentionally blunt. Considering the Depression, Hollywood intended audiences to leave the theatres with the same lesson: don't give in to easy money. Crime doesn't pay.

Foreign critics, like many in the United States, had trouble looking past the violence of *Scarface*. A reviewer for *The Times* of London understood that it was Metro-Goldwyn Mayer's stated desire to expose viewers to 'the savagery of the "gangster" world' in order to denigrate it in the public eye. 'That, of course, is nonsense.' *Scarface*, as the reviewer saw it, was 'a brilliant and unscrupulous exploitation of the dramatic possibilities of the gang-war'. It most certainly was 'not a pamphlet on social ethics' for audiences to take home and digest. There were things to like about the picture, however. It was well acted and well shot, although why the main character treated his sister with 'so strange and fierce a possessiveness' came across as a bit of a puzzle.[27]

Hawks's purposeful allusions to incest may have been lost on many viewers but his dramatisation of Capone's life tapped into a groundswell of international fascination. In the age of radio, newsreels and increased syndication, the violence of America's gangland sustained the interest of people all over the world.

Capone became its most recognisable face. Observers abroad, however, drew different lessons from what was happening in Chicago and elsewhere in the United States. 'We don't need to turn our noses up at this America that has to let its prominent criminals roam free,' one German editor counselled its readers. They had their own devils, such as the Sass brothers, who were accused a string of robberies in Berlin the late 1920s. The Sass brothers did not rise to the stature of Capone. But they too rarely faced more than a few weeks in prison even though 'everybody knows about them'.[28] A French commentator agreed. There was no doubt the '"bandits of Chicago" currently hold the limelight in the popular imagination' due to the influence of cinema and the serial novel. But in truth these 'luxurious bandits of America are no more [or] no less bloodthirsty and brutal than the villainous Apaches from other major cities of the world'.[29] Taking their cue from European accounts, a Turkish daily crowned Capone 'the bandit king' of America. Writing from a country where actual bandits still haunted the countryside, one commentator found it shocking that brigandage had taken the lives of over 12,000 Americans. Capone was an 'exemplary threat to American civilization' but he was not alone. After all, Arnold Rothstein was at one time 'as powerful as the American president'.[30]

AFTER PROHIBITION:
THE AMERICAN MAFIA GOES INTERNATIONAL

Eliot Ness loved the spotlight no less than Alphonse Capone. He went out of his way to have film crews at the ready when he staged raids on bootlegging establishments throughout Chicago. Yet the man who inspired the film and television series *Untouchables* was not the man who put Capone behind bars. That honour belonged to Elmer Irey, chief of the enforcement branch of the US Department of Treasury. It was his agents who investigated

From Booze to Dope

Capone's financial records and collected evidence documenting his failure to pay federal income tax. In assembling their case, prosecutors played upon the jury's heartstrings, cautioning them not to see the defendant's crimes as harmless or without consequence. Capone, they insisted, was not Robin Hood. He did not buy $6,500 in meat or $8,000 belt buckles for the benefit of those left unemployed by the Depression. While ordinary citizens earning far less paid what they owed, Capone hid his exorbitant fortune and spent it on himself. His transgressions mattered for what it meant for the greater good. The rule of law had to be enforced to the fullest, regardless of how trivial it may seem. All citizens had to voluntarily report their earnings and remit what they owed. Otherwise, the jury was warned, justice would disappear and organised society would 'revert to the jungle'.[31]

The victory scored by Irey and federal prosecutors spoke to a deeper truth about the nature of the American state during this time. Under Herbert Hoover, the arms of the federal government grew in size and strength. By the end of 1920s, the Department of Treasury, to which both Ness and Elmer belonged, possessed the mandate and the funds needed to crush bootleggers like Capone. In 1930 its Prohibition Bureau employed around 4,000 people and had a $13 million budget. Years earlier, J. Edgar Hoover took hold of what was then called the Bureau of Investigation. As an executive office first tasked with policing white slavery under the Mann Act, Hoover's bureau was smaller and boasted a budget of only $2 million in 1930. His later crusade against bank robbers and public enemies such as Machine Gun Kelly and Babyface Nelson made him a household name in America. His budget consequently rose to a still modest $5 million. Nevertheless, Washington's influence over local law enforcement and administration was expanding.[32]

The American public's exhaustion, more than anything, ended the tyranny of Prohibition. Wild scenes of merriment greeted the rescinding of the Eighteenth Amendment in 1933. For those who amassed fortunes from bootlegging, efforts to pivot away from the booze business had already begun. Some looked to reinvest in legitimate businesses or more stable rackets such as labour extortion. Others slipped into obscurity. Still more went to jail. In New York, a political revolution devastated the underworld. In 1934, voters in the city elected the Republican Fiorello La Guardia as mayor. The son of Sicilian immigrants himself, La Guardia made a name for himself denouncing mobsters and the politicians who protected them. Adding to his leverage as a reformer was the appointment of a Republican special prosecutor, Thomas Dewey, who took on the city's vice industry. With the help of the city's first African American assistant district attorney, Eunice Carter, Dewey convicted Lucky Luciano on charges of running prostitutes. In 1936, a New York judge sentenced him to no less than thirty years in prison. Dewey then went on to aid in the collapse of one the city's more feared syndicates, Murder Inc. Its leader, Louis 'Lepke' Buchalter, was instrumental in sealing Murder Inc.'s place as a dominant force in drug trafficking and labour racketeering in the city of New York. By the end of the decade, successful prosecutions and mysterious killings decimated the ranks of Murder Inc. Thomas Dewey saw to it that Lepke died in the electric chair in 1944.

Luciano's imprisonment and Al Capone's demise at the hands of syphilitic dementia were only stutter steps for the crime syndicates spawned under Prohibition. Rule over the Chicago underworld passed to a consortium of veterans from the Beer Wars, including men like Jake Guzik and Frank Nitti. Nitti's suicide in 1940 paved the way for new blood at the top of what came to be called Chicago's Outfit. Assuming the lion's share of responsibilities was Joe Accardo, one of the supposed gunmen at the St Valentine's Day massacre, and his protégé, Sam Giancana. New York's Five Families also saw changes in leadership and orientation. But they, along with other stalwarts of the Prohibition era, were beginning to think bigger. During the 1920s some syndicates developed large geographic spheres of influence. Under Capone, Chicago ruled over much of the American Midwest. His purchase of a large estate in Florida, as well as Meyer Lansky's purchase of a Miami racetrack, were milestones in the state's budding relationship with organised crime. During one famed gangster conclave, Johnny Torrio raised the idea of a mutual understanding when it came to expansion. The country was big enough for there to be 'open cities' where northern and eastern families could be free to exploit opportunities. And gangsters were already looking to cities west of the Mississippi.

Among the first to arrive at the Pacific was Jack Dragna. In his youth, Jack floated between New York and his native Corleone in Sicily. He cut his teeth as a member of Giuseppe Morello's family but left town to escape the law. Amazingly, he came to Los Angeles in 1915 knowing no one and with no apparent plan for making it big. By the late the 1920s, his control over the city's vice trade compelled newspaper men to dub him the 'Al Capone of the West'. Dragna's young family gradually welcomed others from the east. One noteworthy arrival was Johnny Rosselli. After a stint with Capone in Chicago, Johnny embraced California and the opportunity for reinvention. He shunned the crude brashness associated with Capone's brand of gangster. He worked to drop his accent and adopted a sleeker, more polished appearance. 'John was very observant,' one friend remembered, 'and obviously when he was quite young, he realised that good manners and grooming and the right things to do and the right wines to order and the right food and everything was very important if you were going to be a gentleman.'[33] In the end he put his experience to good use. While maintaining close ties with families back in New York and Chicago, he made inroads into Hollywood as a bookie and strike-breaker.

Soon to follow in Roselli's footsteps was Bugsy Siegel. The New York bootlegger also came hoping for a new start – a longing

Roselli helped fulfil. The two became fast friends. Before the 1930s were through both gangsters catered to the business and carnal needs of Hollywood stars and executives. The two then joined forces in purchasing a share in a racetrack in Tijuana, Mexico. Acquiring this stake girded Siegel's appetites and ambitions. His first foray into Las Vegas came when, alongside Meyer Lansky, he bought a hotel in town. There were casinos on what became the Vegas Strip, but the place 'was in sorry shape', Lansky recalled. 'Living conditions were bad. No one wanted to go to Vegas to gamble. Air connections were bad. And the trip by car was bothersome. It was so hot that the wires in the car would melt.'[34] Siegel saw it differently. By 1945 he usurped an investor's plan to build a luxury resort, the Flamingo. Over the next two years he poured his all into the project. Song and dance man Jimmy Durante headlined the first night of entertainment in December 1946 and a cavalcade of Hollywood talent attended the opening. Industry insiders lauded Las Vegas as a cleaner, more glamorous version of San Francisco's Barbary Coast.[35] Yet Siegel accrued terrible debts and bad blood in realising his dream. Gunmen saw to it that his glory was short-lived.

Meyer Lansky almost certainly knew and approved of his childhood friend's murder. The money he and other East Coast big shots invested in seeding the Flamingo made them silent partners for many years thereafter. By the time of Siegel's murder in 1947, Lansky had already become something of an international gambling magnate. He bankrolled a casino in the racing and spa town of Saratoga in the early 1930s, a place that had previously welcomed Arnold Rothstein. He saw even greater opportunities in Cuba. When Lansky arrived, he found the country reeling from the Depression and a violent change in government. Before the crash of 1929, local promoters had enticed legions of American tourists to come to the island and revel in its offerings of cheap sex, cheaper rum and easy living. By the latter stages of the Depression, things were beginning to change. The tense climate that followed a 1933 coup led tourism companies to advise passengers that cruise ships docked in Havana only 'if conditions permit'.[36] Lansky devised a plan to help revive Havana's casinos and bring the country's tourism industry back to life. With financial contributions from Bugsy Siegel and former Cleveland bootlegger Moe Dalitz, Lansky acquired a stake in the Hotel Nacional and other gambling establishments.[37] There was nothing illegal in the growing interest of mafia figures in Cuba. With the backing of dictator Fulgencio Batista, he and other American gangsters enriched themselves while remaining at arm's length from Thomas Dewey and internal revenue agents. They also set a new standard for international tourism. Their hotels and casinos were classy, well run and affordable. Havana was accessible by air and sea, making it ideal for tourists coming from further away. These were the standards by which Las Vegas was later measured.

The start of the Second World War stunted, but did not undo, Havana's resurgence. With America's entrance into the conflict in 1941, patriotism compelled some mobsters to join the fight. Lansky's partner in Cuba, Moe Dalitz, enlisted in the army and rose to the rank of second lieutenant while overseeing the army's laundry department. With the war's conclusion, Dalitz leaned on his service record and re-established himself as the legitimate financier of the Desert Inn Resort and Casino in Las Vegas. For Lucky Luciano and others in New York, joining the war effort came by happenstance. In February 1942, a steam liner caught fire while docked on the Manhattan harbour front. An investigation of the incident proved inconclusive. Nevertheless, the US Navy feared it was sabotage. To hedge against a future attack, counter-intelligence officers received authorisation to approach members of the New York underworld. Meyer Lansky welcomed the chance to help. Before the war, he organised the beatings of Nazi sympathisers. Now he volunteered to act as a middleman between the government and Luciano. From his prison cell in upstate New York, Lucky agreed to assist the Navy's efforts to police longshoremen activity on the city docks. Lansky brokered similar deals with other New York family heads in establishing surveillance operations of local cafés, hotels and bars. In exchange for his services, some government agents returned the favour by helping Lansky collect debts on his behalf. 'They handed over the money they collected and were always honest in their dealings,' Lansky later bragged. 'I think this must be the only time the US Navy ever directly helped the Mafia.'[38] Luciano reaped a handsome reward for his assistance. In 1946, Thomas Dewey, now governor of New York state, commuted his sentence and set him free. Navy officials who employed him during the war spoke defensively of their collaboration to members of the press. 'Luciano was like all other informers used by our intelligence work,' one claimed. 'He did no more than any good American citizen would have done.' Though the government deported him to Italy as an undesirable alien, Luciano was not done with his former life. By early 1947, newspapers were circulating rumours that he was in Cuba 'negotiating a narcotics deal'.[39] Out west, reporters touted the death of a 'Mexican dope chieftain' as evidence of 'the Mafia's grab for the Mexican dope supply'. The killing appeared to be proof positive that Lucky Luciano, reputed head of 'the Mafia', exercised influence beyond the US. The American underworld was an international force to be reckoned with.[40]

Senior US officials undoubtedly were the source of these revelations. Yet the larger narrative linking Luciano to the drugs trade came almost exclusively from the insights of one man. Before the Second World War, Harry Anslinger's stature as a crime fighter paled in comparison to J. Edgar Hoover. His agency, the Federal Bureau of Narcotics (FBN), was smaller and received far less media attention than Hoover's FBI. But in the latter stage of Prohibition, Anslinger's men were tasked with policing the sale and use of drugs in the United States. Unlike Hoover, Anslinger took his fight abroad to Europe, Asia and Latin America. His case files from this period laid the foundation for much of what we understand of the modern narcotics trade and its origins. It was his sleuthing, alongside his trusted agents, that introduced Elie Eliopoulos and inter-war traffickers to the world. Anslinger's contribution to law enforcement did not stop there. He, more than Al Capone or any other figure in the twentieth century, defined the meaning and the significance of the Mafia in our time.

DRUG BARONS: HARRY ANSLINGER AND THE ORIGINS OF THE MODERN NARCOTICS TRADE

Anslinger's first confrontation with the Mafia, as he told it, occurred in his early twenties. He was fresh from college and had found a job in 1915 supervising construction projects on the Pennsylvania railroad system. Most of his workers were Italians, many of them recent immigrants from Sicily. Early on, a labourer named Giovanni appeared in a ditch by the side of a road. There were twenty-five bullet holes in him. Word was that a black hand, Big Mouth Sam, had done the deed. Anslinger claimed he confronted the culprit and guaranteed that, if Giovanni died, he would see him hang or kill him himself. Giovanni miraculously lived. Even more surprisingly, Big Mouth left him in peace. For Anslinger, the black hand was proof that 'the future has its roots in the past'.[41]

Anslinger included this vignette in his autobiography, *The Murderers*, published soon after his retirement from the Federal Bureau of Narcotics. Although his tenure as FBN chief was shorter than J. Edgar Hoover's reign over the FBI, both men possessed a similar style and media savvy. From the earliest stages of the FBN's evolution, Anslinger had a flair for drama and self-promotion. And like Hoover, he did not start out in law enforcement. While Hoover climbed to the top of the FBI after an early career as a clerk, Anslinger's first exposure to government service was in the US diplomatic corps. A posting to the Bahamas was his first taste of crime fighting. As an important nexus for bootleggers during Prohibition, the island nation was ground zero for efforts to convince Britain and France to assist Washington in its struggle against illicit alcohol. Anslinger became head of the Federal Bureau of Narcotics in part on the recommendation of media giant William Randolph Hearst.

When Herbert Hoover installed Anslinger at the FBN, Europeans were at the forefront of anti-narcotics enforcement. With the creation of the League of Nations in 1920, an Advisory Committee on Traffic in Opium and Other Dangerous Drugs came into being. The mandate of the committee was simple but daunting: regulate the trade of medicinal narcotics use and monitor the flow of all contraband drugs. Overseeing the legal opium trade proved difficult enough. Turkey, a major source of opium production, initially refused calls to co-ordinate with the League. Then there was the question of enforcement. Implementing the League's will was left up to its members, a stipulation that made monitoring opium trafficking in weak states such as China and Iran a fiction. The inter-war period produced some League personalities known for combatting drug trafficking. Thomas Russell, better known as Russell Pasha, made a name for himself as the redoubtable chief of the Egyptian national police. Even though Cairo wrestled its independence away from Great Britain in 1919, Russell Pasha stayed on and succeeded in expelling hundreds of traffickers and suspected white slavers.[42] For a time at least, though, it does not appear that he was aware of the activities of the decade's most celebrated drug baron, Elie Eliopoulos.

Eliopoulos' career in narcotics was born of his own travails and that of his native Greece. He was raised in Piraeus, the main port servicing Athens on the Mediterranean. As the son of a prosperous family, he was educated at Robert College, Istanbul's prestigious American-run preparatory school. He initially made his living providing arms and other provisions to the Greek army during the First World War. Greece's defeat in its war against Turkey in 1922, as well as political instability at home, sent Eliopoulos's business into decline. Smuggling opium revived his family's fortunes. He entered the trade around 1927 through a host of international contacts, particularly fellow Greeks. By 1931, his network of traders and shippers spanned both the Atlantic and the Pacific. It was about this time that he began dispatching heroin to the United States. Anslinger later identified his chief contact, 'Little Augie' Del Gracio, as the supposed supplier of heroin to Lucky Luciano.

After an initial foray into the Chinese opium market, Eliopoulos turned to Istanbul as a source of refined morphine and heroin. Istanbul in the late 1920s was a city much transformed since its days as capital of the Ottoman Empire. After the dissolution of the Ottoman monarchy in 1922, the city lost much of its imperial lustre. With the banishment of the royal family and the flight of its Christian population, many of its grand old palaces and mansions fell into disuse (save for one imperial residence that briefly became a casino). As the country's largest port and commercial hub, Istanbul remained the heart of the Turkish Republic's economy but the complexion of Istanbul's workers and consumers changed with the empire's fall. Intense rounds of fighting, going back to the First Balkan War in 1912, induced hundreds of thousands to find sanctuary in the city. Its neighbourhoods, both new and ancient, possessed a hodgepodge of Muslim peoples. Many came from the former empire's far western and eastern periphery, particularly the Balkans and the Caucasus. Its historic Greek and Armenian communities, which officially comprised a third of Istanbul's residents in 1918, dwindled as a consequence of the Great War. Yet most of the main industries, including the international sale of opium, remained in the hands of native Christians and Jews. Typical among the commercial patriarchs of Istanbul was Leon Taranto and his brother. As one of the city's more prominent Jewish families, the Tarantos tied themselves to the opium trade at the turn of the century. They also distinguished themselves through their support of the new regime of Mustafa Kemal Atatürk. Leon especially boasted close relations with high positioned 'friends' close to Atatürk.[43] For a time, the heroin Eliopoulos shipped westward came from factories run by Leon and his brothers.

The main weigh station for the morphine and heroin Eliopoulos purchased in Turkey was the city of Marseille. France's southernmost harbour also endured dramatic changes in the wake of the First World War. The staggering losses the country incurred by 1918 hit the city and its workforce especially hard. As with Istanbul, a post-war wave of migrants and refugees was instrumental to Marseille's repopulation and growth. Thousands of newcomers from Corsica and southern Italy flocked to the port, amplifying the size of already large migrant communities. They were joined by thousands more from Algeria, West Africa, Tunisia and southern Spain as well as Armenians displaced by the 1915 genocide in the Ottoman Empire. Marseille's swelling population of largely poor workers benefited from the growth of trade in and out of town. The post-war decline of shipping out of Germany and Italy was to the city's benefit. As early as 1919, Marseille resumed its place as an important entrepôt for British mail to India and commodities from Indochina. Its repute as a hive of criminal activity often overshadowed the city's good fortune. Its docks and central thoroughfares were well-known for pickpockets and surly pimps. An unhealthy throng of lowlifes frequented its many gambling dens. Among the tonnage that passed through town was contraband of different sorts. Its diversity helped sustain all kinds of illicit trade. Elie Eliopoulos likely found a warm welcome among the city's Greek residents. 'The Greeks are the overlords of Marseille,' one visitor commented. 'Some of them will sell you grilled almonds but that does not prevent them from being high financiers.'[44] Many seemed to have a hand in all kinds of commerce.

It was Corsicans, and not Greeks, who helped sire the city's most notorious criminal force. Le Milieu, as it came to be known, was less an organisation than a subculture identified with the criminal careers of two men, Paul Carbone and François Spirito. Carbone arrived in Marseille well before the war broke out in 1914. Hailing from a village on Corsica's southwestern coast, Carbone shared in the misery many migrants encountered on the streets of Panier, one of the city's most impoverished neighbourhoods. He joined the army and distinguished himself in the war. After 1918 he became a wild man of some repute. He amassed an impressive number of tattoos, including one above his penis that read, 'for the pleasure of the ladies'.[45] Running prostitutes in Marseille was his gateway to a wider world of crime. In 1924 Russell Pasha expelled him from Egypt on charges of participating in white slavery. Sometime after his return to France he made the acquaintance of his future partner in crime. François Spirito was also a transplant to Marseille, having been born in Naples before the turn of the century. Like Carbone, childhood poverty put him on the path of becoming a pimp at early age. His toughness and acumen brought him to the attention of one of the bosses, or *caïd*s, of prostitution in the city, Antoine La Rocca. Under the tutelage of his new patron, Spirito graduated to armed robbery. After a series of paranoid killing sprees, La Rocca fled Marseille. His absence allowed Spirito and Carbone to branch out and tighten their grip over the city.[46] In addition to gambling, prostitution and extortion, Spirito and Carbone smuggled arms to Spain after civil war broke out in 1936. The two men also staked a large claim over the drugs arriving into the city. By the early 1930s, Carbone conducted business with the likes of Leon Taranto in Istanbul and established processing plants capable of turning morphine into heroin. Drug trafficking also took them to

Paris where they developed relations with Louis Lyon, the capital's most prominent dealer. Their criminal powers climaxed with the election of leftist politician, Simon Sabiani. As a fellow Corsican and a veteran who served alongside Carbone's brother in the war, Sabiani shielded the two bosses from harm. In exchange, they meted out beatings to Sabiani's rivals. When they stood accused of murdering and mutilating the body of a former judge in Paris, the then-deputy mayor plastered posters on walls throughout Marseille proclaiming that 'Carbone and Spirito are my friends'.[47] A court placed Marseille's fearsome caïds under arrest, but they eventually went free on the lack of evidence.

The proliferation of traffickers such as Taranto, Eliopoulos and Carbone compelled the League of Nations to compose a blacklist of the most flagrant smugglers of illicit opiates. By 1937, the list totalled thirty-seven individuals, the lion's share coming from Turkey and the Balkans.[48] With his appointment to head the FBN in 1930, Harry Anslinger aspired to do more than catch violators – he wanted to change the behaviour of states that harboured them. During the 1930s he corresponded with law enforcement agencies throughout the world in the hope of sharing information and securing arrests for known traffickers. He often failed to bring anyone to justice. Nevertheless, both he and Russell Pasha excelled at trying suspects in the court of public opinion. William Randolph Hearst's media empire proved essential in providing readers with salacious reports on the activities of Elie Eliopoulos, Louis Lyon and their customers in New York.[49] Long before anyone declared a 'war on drugs', Anslinger grabbed headlines, established a compelling narrative and terrified the public.

His efforts in international diplomacy were far more impressive. Together with Fiorello La Guardia, then a New York congressman, Anslinger initiated a campaign to shutter factories suspected of having produced heroin smuggled into the United States. He compelled the American government to renew its pressure on

Turkey to join the 1912 Hague Convention. The US ambassador to Ankara co-ordinated with Anslinger and insinuated to the country's foreign minister that information existed of 'people in authority in Turkey [who] were financially benefiting' from drug trafficking.[50] Whether out of fear of further embarrassment, or a genuine desire to comply with the will of the Western-led order, Atatürk declared on Christmas Day 1932 that Turkey would accede to the Hague Convention and establish a national monopoly on opium cultivation. Yet, as the Second World War approached, Anslinger became more mindful of international politics. He minimised the connections between Chiang Kai-shek's Nationalists and Du Yuesheng's Green Gang. In Asia, he pointed the finger at Washington's more hostile rival, the empire of Japan, as the main purveyor of opiates.

Anslinger made bigger waves at home. In 1936, he lent his bureau's credibility to the B-rated picture, *Reefer Madness,* as part of an effort to outlaw the use and cultivation of marijuana. Few saw *Reefer Madness* in theatres, but its absurdist depiction of smoking pot helped seal the criminalisation of the drug for decades to come. A year later, Anslinger opened an investigation into the Hip Sing Tong and their various lodges in the United States. A countrywide manhunt nabbed over thirty suspects in what was described as a transnational ring that dealt in opium, morphine and heroin. Though some of the opiates came from Chinese sources, Anslinger again insisted the tongs' main supplier was Japan. Accounts of the arrests also noted that individuals close to Lucky Luciano were among those arrested.[51] By this point, Lucky had become the FBN's white whale. Anslinger encouraged the press to emphasise suspected links between Luciano and the drug trade, a trend that continued well after the Second World War. Anslinger raged both privately and publicly over Thomas Dewey's decision to parole Luciano in 1947. In an act of revenge, one FBN agent, likely with Anslinger's knowledge, circulated a rumour that Lucky had paid a

$500,000 bribe to go free.[52] When Dewey ran for president against Harry Truman in 1948, newspapers printed stories claiming the New York governor was planning to let Luciano return home once he won at the polls.[53]

Anslinger's coup de grâce came in 1950. That summer, newspapers announced he had given testimony to US Senate investigators. He declared that it was the Mafia, a 'secret Sicilian "black hand" society', that was the true power behind a nationwide vice and narcotics ring. He personally could name 800 members of this mafia. Each was involved in gambling, white slavery, murder and other crimes. The chairman of the committee, Estes Kefauver, vowed to follow up on Anslinger's claims and determine 'whether the Sicilian terrorist society is the dominant power in the national crime picture'.[54] Within months, 'the Mafia' took centre stage as newspapers and television cameras followed the senate's lead.

For many of the traffickers Anslinger pursued, the fighting across the Atlantic and Pacific was more detrimental to their business. Elie Eliopoulos fled Europe after the Nazis seized Greece in 1941. He settled in New York, only to be indicted for trafficking in 1943. Upon his release from prison, he returned to Greece and continued to broker arms and narcotics deals. Leon Taranto remained resentful after the government closed his heroin factory in the early 1930s. A far more shattering blow came in 1942 when the Turkish government, keen to eliminate the influence of non-Muslims in the economy, levied a punitive 'wealth tax' on the Tarantos. Leon, as well as other prominent Jewish and Christian business leaders, were driven to financial ruin and in some cases imprisoned. François Spirito and Paul Carbone compensated for the Nazi occupation in the ways they knew best. When Simon Sabiani threw his political lot in with the Vichy regime, Spirito and Carbone followed suit. For a time, the two caïds transitioned well. A French Resistance intelligence agent saw no use in seeking their support since the men were 'eager to seize any opportunity to promote their illicit trafficking (tobacco, white slaving, black market, brothels, etc.).'⁵⁵ Collaboration with the Germans eventually bore bitter fruit. Paul Carbone died in a 1943 train derailment caused by a bomb planted by La Résistance. François Spirito followed Sabiani abroad into exile as the Nazis were defeated. Control over 'Marseille-Chicago', as locals referred to the town, fell to Antoine Guérini and his brothers. For much of the inter-war period, the Guérinis maintained a relatively stable relationship with Spirito and Carbone despite being rivals to their prostitution and gambling empire. During the war, however, the Guérini clan chose de Gaulle over the Vichy government. As result, they, as well as other pro-resistance caïds, stayed on after the war and took over.

To say that a mafia reigned over Marseille before the war's end is problematic. Neither the French press nor members of the French underworld used the term. The violence and crime witnessed before 1945 led the public to see affairs in Marseille as something more akin to *'banditisme'*.⁵⁶ Commentators otherwise preferred a simple euphemism, Le Milieu, to characterise the circles associated with the city's best-known criminals.⁵⁷ This absence of any discussion of mafias is typical for the time. Beyond certain key exceptions, such the Green Gang of Shanghai, local observers did not necessarily see criminal conspiracies akin to the mafia in cities beyond Italy or the United States. The same may be said of the drug traffickers and white slavers who flourished during this era. Elie Eliopoulos was no gang leader. From all accounts he and his confederates were bound by discreet business transactions and nothing more. There were no cartels or narco alliances established to regulate the illicit marketplace. The inter-war trade in narcotics was fluid, idiosyncratic and wide open.

In the United States, things were different. The public knew and spoke of established mobs led by 'big shots' and gangsters.

Newspapers consistently informed readers of the gossip going on in the underworld. They reported on historic meetings, such as the 1929 Atlantic City gathering, in real time. Talk of who was 'the boss of bosses' was not uncommon by the time the Second World War began.[58] Movies and other pulp accounts reinforced the diction with which people talked about what had happened through Prohibition and after. People understood that gangsters came in distinct varieties; most were Italians, many were Jewish and there were others who were Irish (although they tended to be on the way out). What had yet to take hold was the notion that syndicates conformed organisationally to a set of rules or to a common design. There is no mention in the inter-war press or government statements of capos, consigliere or established families. Veterans of the underworld later professed that things were not as rigid as people came to believe. 'There's no boss of bosses, never has been,' as one Los Angeles boss described it. 'That's all bullshit. Some bosses, maybe because they are older and wiser, command more respect than others, but that's all.'[59]

How Americans spoke about the underworld changed once the war was over. Events forced this rhetorical shift. In 1938, the Federal Bureau of Narcotics happily reported that drug use in the country was down. According to their statistics, only one in every 3,000 Americans was an addict, a 66 per cent drop from two decades earlier.[60] Those numbers rose as the post-war era began. Powering the escalation in drug use was the development of several complex pipelines carrying narcotics into the United States. Among the first engineers of these networks were gangsters born from the 1920s and '30s: Luciano, Lansky, Spirito and the Guérinis. A host of less famous gangs and gangsters aided them. Fragile patterns of economic and political recovery also enabled the rebirth of older underworlds in Italy, China and Japan. They too participated in this revolution in the drug trade.

PART III

Transformation

The Axis surrender of 1945 marked the beginning of a global renaissance within the history of mafias. Pre-war mafias in Asia and Europe regained their strength and acquired greater vitality with the establishment of new governments and regimes. The rapid growth of the United States and other First World economies created tantalising marketplaces for all sorts of illicit wares and services. Cold War politics amplified mafias' political and social power, and the general public in various countries discovered these truths in striking ways, leading to both scandal and disillusionment. Mafias, more than ever, became a problem transcending continental and cultural divisions.

As leaders of the free world, American officials looked upon this trend with worry. Growing concerns after 1945 pushed Washington to invest large amounts of money and attention in combatting organised crime at home and abroad. Official efforts to raise popular awareness of this crusade arguably constitute the most important legacy of this endeavour. Through a series of televised hearings and testimonials, officials in Washington appeared to pull back the curtain on a secret world defined by corruption, violence and intrigue. As the public's interest peaked, Hollywood distilled these revelations in a way that cemented their significance for all time. *The Godfather*'s release in 1971 saw to it that audiences everywhere came to know what mafias were and how they appeared to wield power. Greater numbers of people soon saw fraternities across the world as iterations of the same phenomenon. As a consequence, many languages adopted the words 'mafia' and 'godfather'.

Ironically, it was at this moment that many of the oldest mafias began to weaken in critical ways. The growing effectiveness of law enforcement hastened their decline. Yet as old godfathers were sent to prison, the universe of mafias continued to grow and diversify. Two dramatic economic developments were responsible: the end of the Second World War and the rapid expansion of the cocaine industry. Both heightened public awareness of an ever-growing list of new and exotic mafias. For observers and critics at the end of the twentieth century, the end of the Cold War and the rise of Latin America's cartels and the new mafias of Eastern Europe heralded a far deadlier phase.

The Revenge of the Peasants by Jacques Callot.
Peasant bandits sack a camp in wartime.

Edward 'Ned' Kelly

Ali Pasha of Ioannina

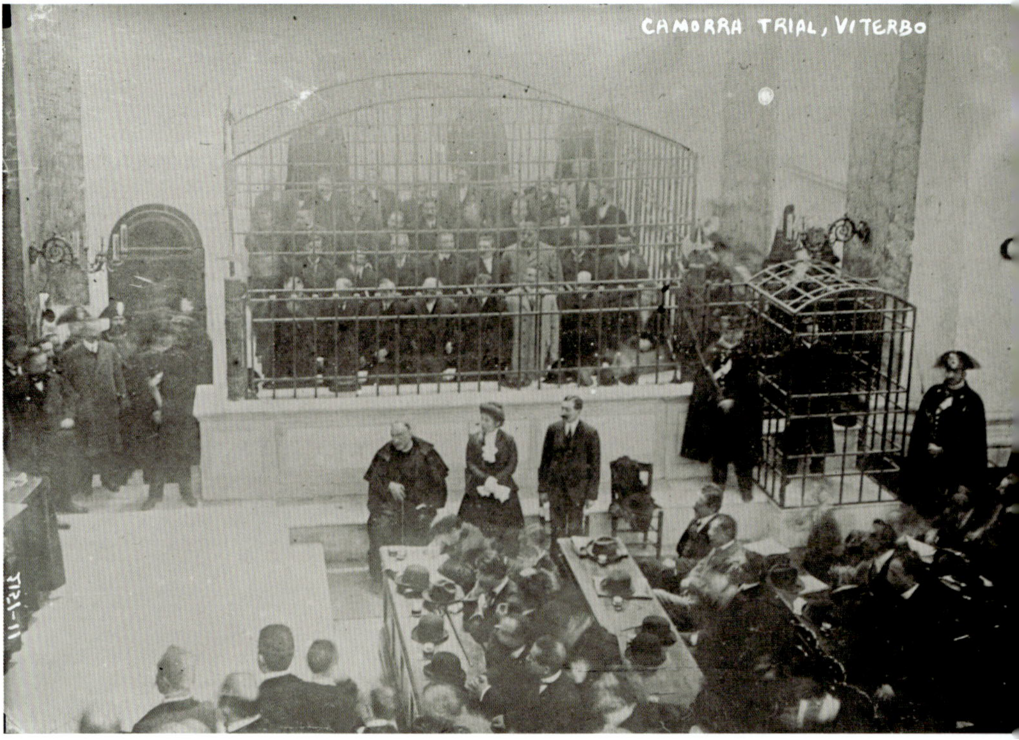

The Camorra on trial in Viterbo, Italy.

Wikimedia Commons

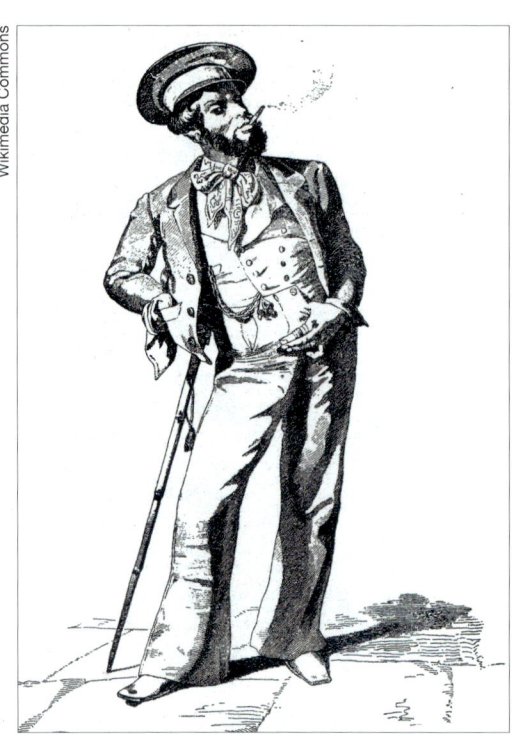

A Camorrista of Naples, *circa* 1866.

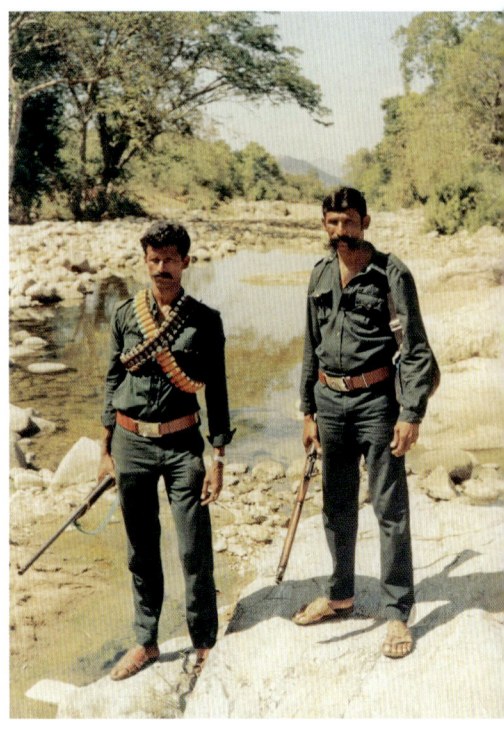

Koose Munisamy Veerappan (right) alongside his younger brother.

Accused 'black hand' extortionists in West Virginia, early twentieth century.

Members of the Hip Sing and On Leong tongs under arrest in New York. In the centre wearing a brimmed hat is Mock Duck, leader of the Hip Sing.

Library of Congress

Yoshio Kodama

'Big-eared Du' Yuesheng as a young man.

Tattooed helper by Suzuki Kinsen is among the earliest depictions of a yakuza in the twentieth century.

Al Capone exiting a federal court, November 1932.

'"I am still the wife of Al Capone and I'll wait for him …" Mae Capone confesses to us', *Paris Soir*, 19 February 1938.

Wikimedia Commons

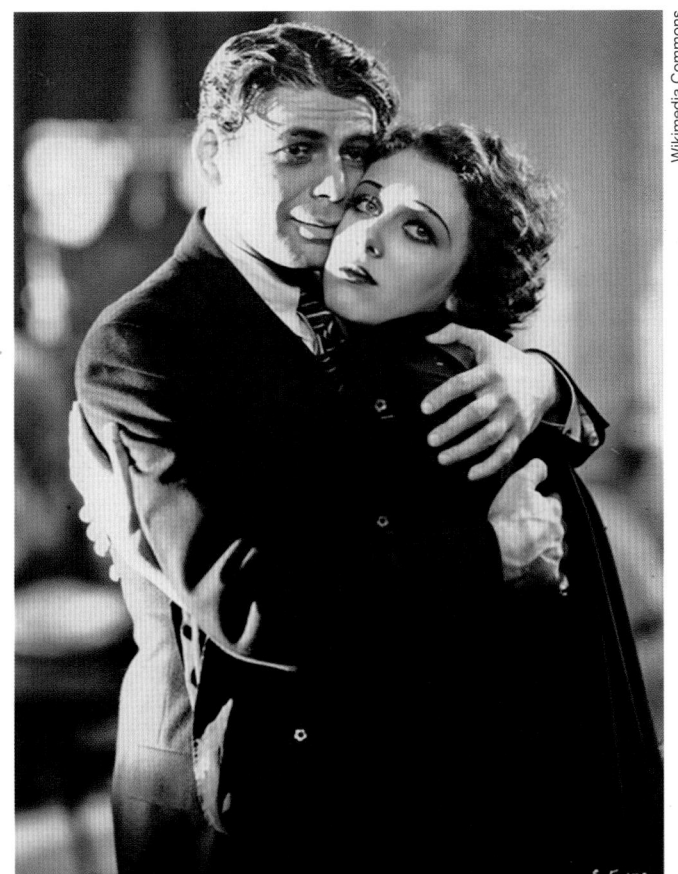

Promotional photograph for the American crime film *Scarface* (1932), starring Paul Muni and Ann Dvorak.

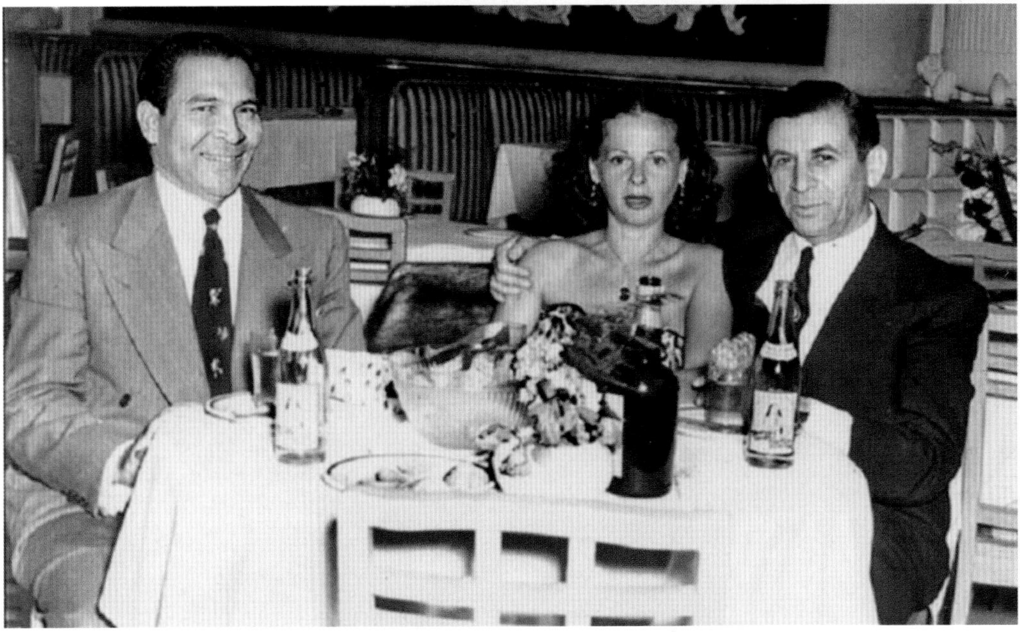

Wikimedia Commons

Meyer Lansky (right) dines with his wife and Fulgencio Batista, former president of Cuba, around 1948.

Where the blame lies by Sackett and Wilhelms Lithograph Co., 4 April 1891. Here Uncle Sam is told that: 'If Immigration was properly Restricted you would no longer be troubled with Anarchy, Socialism, the Mafia and such kindred evils!'

5

Godfathers: The High Tide of Old Mafias

Twins Ronald and Reginald Kray arose from anonymity in the shadow of London's post-war recovery. As the sons of a rag picker, Ronnie and Reg possessed an earthy authenticity that spoke to their early careers as amateur East End boxers. Their path to notoriety was conventional for aspiring gangsters in mid-1950s. They took over nightclubs, profited from extortion and dabbled in random criminal schemes. Fame found them as they began to strike it rich. Their main haunts in the West End brought in movie stars and professional athletes, as well as politicians and artists. Newspapers caught on to the Krays by the early 1960s and transformed them into household names. The celebrities they later claimed to have met or partied with included The Beatles, Joe Louis, Frank Sinatra, Sonny Liston and Judy Garland. The brothers basked in this publicity and were unafraid to let their love of the limelight show.

It was their renown as London's preeminent hard men that brought Ronnie Kray to New York in the early part of 1966. After arriving at Kennedy Airport, a car brought him to a house in Red

Hook, close to the Brooklyn docks. The residence belonged to Joe Gallo and his brothers, arguably the most feared members of New York's Profaci crime family. The early stages of the meeting were awkward. As he awaited his host, a brother of one of the Profaci members, 'an evil-looking midget', hovered menacingly behind him. None of this scared Ron. He was, as he remembered it, decidedly starstruck. 'The atmosphere was electric,' he later revealed. 'I suddenly knew I was in the big league and I'd better make out a good case for being here, otherwise these bastards were liable to chop my balls off.' His patience and fortitude paid off after he elicited a potential deal. Members of the American Mafia were laying claim to casinos in London. What they wanted were local partners to help care for 'big-time American gamblers' coming over to Britain from Las Vegas.[1] Other deals appeared in the offing if their relationship continued. But the outbreak of violent feuds with their South London rivals, the Richardsons, got the better of them. Ron was the to first to land in prison in 1969 after being found guilty at the Old Bailey of murdering a man before a slew of witnesses in an East End pub. Reggie followed him months later after he butchered another man with a kitchen knife. In their old age, they both confessed to being less professional than their counterparts across the Atlantic. One of their biggest mistakes, Reg lamented, was that they had taken the lives of others. 'A Mafia boss would never kill – he'd always get one of his button men to do it for him. [Philadelphia boss] Angelo Bruno once said to us, "Never get shit on your own hands." And he was right.'[2]

Ronnie and Reg did lord over London's underworld, albeit briefly. But unlike the Profaci family, or Angelo Bruno's crews in Philadelphia, their 'firm' of gangsters dissolved once they went to prison. What made the Krays significant was their star power. For the British press, and seemingly for many celebrities, the twins were the closest thing to a homegrown mafia that Britain in the

Swinging Sixties had to offer. Even though their exploits inspired several cinematic tributes, close observers of their time tended to downplay their impact. 'Neither the Krays nor the Richardsons, for all their crimes, ever really came near to the Chicago mobsters they both tried to emulate,' as one journalist noted in 1970. Just how interested the American Mafia was in forming a relationship with the Krays was up for debate. Without much of a drug scene, and a rather robust national gaming board overseeing British gambling establishments, it seemed the American Mafia 'never thought it worth their while' to set up shop in London.[3]

It is tempting to see the Krays as a throwback to a far less dynamic age in the history of crime. Inheritors of the 'delinquent style' of mid-twentieth-century East London, Ronnie and Reg, like other classic East End toughs, got ahead by hook and by crook.[4] Most of the world's thugs and gangs in the mid-1960s were dedicated to similar parochial pursuits: They stole and extorted. Perhaps they ran gambling parlours or whorehouses. Or maybe they were small time peddlers of this or that.

This was certainly the case in Beirut's underworld. In the 1960s, Lebanon's capital still possessed its own brand of neighbourhood strongmen. Unlike the Krays, these *qabaday*, as they were called, constituted a veritable institution that was at least a century old. Thugs of this sort maintained order as much as they exploited their victims. In exchange for a fee, Beirut's qabaday brokered deals, collected debts and regulated the activities of fellow criminals found amongst them. By the 1960s, the Lebanese political system had integrated qabaday into its affairs. As the country drifted towards civil war, Beirut's strongmen served as neighbourhood spies and vote-getters on behalf of political parties and urban patricians.[5] The Krays, for all their power and fame, never enjoyed such connections to Britain's political establishment.

Acknowledging the Krays and the qabaday of Lebanon provides an important point of contrast in looking at the post-war era. In the decades after 1945, the world grew more familiar with the American Mafia on the back of major news events and films. The revived influence of the yakuza, the triads and Italy's mafias were subjects of similar interest for newsprint and television. There was nothing provincial about any of these groups by then. Each seemed invested in illicit trades that were transnational in scope. Each seemed to exert a significant amount of power over politics and culture. All of them together seemed to fit into a common universe of crime.

The American gangsters who sought out the Krays typified trends that were beginning to shape the wider world of mafias. Like those who came of age during Prohibition, mobsters in the United States continued to live in a country largely unaffected by the devastation or upheaval wrought elsewhere by armed conflict. America's post-war prosperity brought about excesses and conveniences mobsters and everyday people embraced with great gusto. Travel across the Atlantic and Pacific was now faster and more regular. Tourism was again flourishing. Commodities and consumer goods were more accessible than they were before the Depression. The average worker, and their children, had more money and leisure time than their parents or grandparents. Before long, a series of 'economic miracles' spread these benefits to various portions of Europe and East Asia.

There were of course those who were left behind by this period of formidable economic growth; impressive upticks in gross national productivity obscured the hardships of people living in neighbourhoods, towns or regions afflicted by endemic poverty. Adding to the silent difficulties of this period were indications that formerly robust industries were beginning to contract and die. Steel output and textile manufacturing continued pre-war patterns of decline in portions of Europe and the Americas. As certain industries faded in the United States, cities resorted to bulldozing an untold number of abandoned factories, workshops and warehouses. These early signs of de-industrialisation begot scenes of degeneration and hopelessness as far back as the 1950s. The most sophisticated of mafias in the New and Old World were cognisant of these developments. In this era of rising economic standards and more stratified consumers, securing niches and inroads into the US and other Western markets became paramount to purveyors of vice and contraband goods. To do this, far more globalised and integrated networks came into being, each aiming to provide illicit commodities and services to both the affluent and the struggling. Of all these increasingly transnational trades, the production, shipment and sale of narcotics proved to be the most profitable.

Global economic changes were not the only forces affecting the development of post-war mafias. Affairs linked to the onset of the Cold War were no less important. The post-war political reconstitution of Japan, Hong Kong, France and Italy breathed new life into criminal syndicates. Throughout the world, anti-communist sentiment helped shape the character of crime syndicates and forge alliances with new political regimes. In the United States, a somewhat contradictory set of conditions shaped both the influence and perception of mafias. On the surface of things, the syndicates that emerged from the post-Prohibition era appeared wealthier and more politically dominant than they were before the war. This collective might, coupled with the secrecy associated with them, openly clashed with an American state that grew even more powerful and intrusive in its reach as the Cold War progressed. This paradox assumed greater importance as issues of crime, drug abuse and corruption gathered greater attention. These conflicting developments led to two opposing narratives. By the 1970s, federal and local law enforcement agencies devoted greater attention and resources to fighting the American Mafia. Washington's anti-mafia offensive took on global dimensions as American agents and officers sought to take their struggle to lands abroad. And yet a series of scandalous revelations during the Cold War seemed to indicate that the American state was more compromised and weaker than at first glance. Washington's efforts at transparency, as well as contributing journalists and academics, helped instil a common belief that mafias were integral to the making of modern politics. More than ever before, film left the most indelible mark on public consciousness when it came to grappling with organised crime and its significance. In this respect, *The Godfather* represents a point of culmination in the global history of mafias.

COLD WARRIORS AND SECRET SOCIETIES: THE RESURGENCE OF THE MAFIAS IN ASIA

Even after the obliteration of Hiroshima and Nagasaki, many Japanese citizens believed they would fight on. For years state propaganda had imbued the nation with a sense of invincibility and destiny despite the losses incurred against the Allies. Emperor Hirohito's decision to surrender shattered what was left of this belief. His historic radio address announcing the war's end on 15 August 1945 marked the first time citizens had heard their monarch's voice. A greater pall of uncertainty soon overshadowed the profundity. An American occupation began almost immediately, leaving much of the population, and women in particular, expecting the very worst. Nurses relieved from government service in one southern Japanese town were sent home with a warning that they would almost certainly be raped by the Americans. 'A doctor gave each of us a syringe filled with poison,' one woman remembered. 'We were to use that before being captured.' Even though no harm came to her, she later admitted that she kept the poison tucked away for years thereafter.[6]

Hirohito's government rightfully shared this same sense of dread. In the early days of the occupation, 1,300 cases of rape were reported in one Japanese prefecture alone. Authorities in

Godfathers

Tokyo soon took greater steps to offset what they believed would be a tsunami of violence targeting the country's women. They approved the creation of 'special comfort stations' and recruited some 70,000 women to staff them. Presiding over this state-run string of brothels was the innocuously named 'Relaxation and Amusement Association'. All conscripted women and girls received a standard payment of roughly one American dollar per visit. The country's centralised sex industry proved immediately popular but lasted no more than six months. American occupation officers were appalled by the government's gross mistreatment of Japanese women. The health of American soldiers also became a matter of concern. With 70 per cent of soldiers in one American unit contracting syphilis, authorities shuttered all the stations and discharged its women with no compensation.[7] Prostitution, naturally, did not disappear. In the absence of government regulation, privately run brothels proliferated. In many cases, gangs of women ran and organised the houses and bars where 'pan pan' girls met and serviced their customers. Each gang had an elder sister, or *anego*, who oversaw their operations. Some even led their girls into hand-to-hand combat against rival houses. Whether these female-run syndicates grew out of pre-war arrangements is not clear. Their brief time at the heart of Japanese vice, however, was typical of the resurgence and reinvention of the yakuza.[8]

The desperation and opportunism that gave birth to anego-led gangs resounded across Japan. The incalculable loss of life and property, coupled with the obliteration of many of the country's cities, begot an economy that depended upon individual initiative and determination. With factories and stores destroyed and families desperate for food, money and work, new jerry-rigged bazaars became the centrepiece of many communities and neighbourhoods. Open-air black markets soon overwhelmed local governments. One of the largest collections of stalls and sellers sat outside the railway station in Shinjuku on the west side of Tokyo. Shinjuku's street dealers peddled whatever wares they found, including contraband goods taken from American or government stores. A system based on extortion and patronage kept the market open and orderly. Formal associations or outright gangs of sellers, gamblers and toughs set the prices and disciplined wayward dealers. Everyone paid a hefty tribute to a local boss, or *oyabun*. Those who rose to the heights of this order tended to be men with violent tendencies. In Osaka, for example, an American enquiry discovered that eighteen out of twenty oyabun had been convicted of murder, assault or acts of intimidation in relation to gambling.[9]

Many chieftains who ran Japan's post-war black market were likely men raised in the yakuza tradition. This was less the case of Shinjuku's upstart boss, Kinosuke Ozu. Life was never kind to Ozu. Abandoned by his mother at the age of two, he was raised by a lecherous father and a prostitute step-mother with a heavy hand. Childhood bullying hardened him further. At fifteen, he bragged, he took a meat cleaver to a boy and nearly sliced him to death. Ozu drifted for a time but eventually became a bodyguard for an assorted set of masters. By his mid-forties, he reckoned he had killed around eighty men, mostly by the point or blade of his sword. It was this reputation that helped him purchase control of the Shinjuku black market. When an American journalist found him in 1947, Ozu was no longer dirtying his hands. He paid his workers good wages. He allied himself with newly formed business conglomerates, or *zaibatsu*, and made himself president of the Street Venders Association. Upon their first meeting, Ozu admitted to his American guest that he thought highly of Al Capone and delighted in being called a gangster. As time went on, he changed his mind and preferred instead to be thought of as a polished gentleman.[10]

Established yakuza in other parts of Japan embraced the

opportunities created by the occupation. The port of Kobe became a critical nexus for trade and resupply for American forces. Most of Kobe's early *gumi*, or gangs, did not survive the war, due to either the fighting itself or concerted government crackdowns. One of the few to re-emerge under the occupation was the Yamaguchi-gumi, comprising just over two dozen members. Its young leader, Kazuo Taoka, initially lacked the gravitas of the gang's founders. Kazuo's wartime imprisonment, and the murders he committed, eventually set him apart from other members. Over the course of three decades, Taoka capitalised on his influence over Kobe's port and clawed away at the interests and rackets of rival gangs. The Yamaguchi grew as it allied itself with some crime families while swallowing others whole. By 1970 it claimed over 10,000 members spread across the central Japanese island of Honshu. Stevedores who owed their allegiances to the Yamaguchi purportedly unloaded 80 per cent of all cargo passing through Kobe harbour, netting Taoka up $17 million dollars a year by the 1960s.[11] Extorting merchant shippers and dockworkers formed only one portion of the gang's proceeds.

The Yamaguchi-gumi led the way among other families in diversifying their interests beyond the realm of vice. During the war, narcotics became a staple among domestic consumers. Government unabashedly supplied workers, soldiers and everyday civilians with stimulants in order to maintain their attentiveness, boost production quotas and suppress hunger. Chief among the drugs dispensed to citizens was methamphetamine, a concoction first distilled by Japanese chemists before the war. The hardships that followed the country's surrender helped sustain addiction rates despite post-war laws forbidding the drug's use and manufacture. Crime surged as methamphetamine consumption and production went underground. In a two-month period in 1954 alone, police in Japan reported that the drug was connected to as many as thirty-one murders.[12] Steady profits encouraged the

Yamaguchi-gumi and other families to assimilate the drug trade into their criminal portfolios. When government investigators first attempted to tabulate the full scope of the yakuza's profits in 1979, it was reported that the production, distribution and sale of stimulants accounted for nearly half of the yakuza's yearly intake, a total sum valued at over ¥100 billion. As the largest of all the yakuza families, the Yamaguchi-gumi netted the lion's share of the total yakuza earnings for this period, an amount totalling an estimated ¥5,383 billion (or just over $900 million in today's money).[13]

Assassinations, arrests and street battles were no less important to the yakuza's post-war boom. Against the backdrop of the American occupation, new or re-established families contended with rival gangs of immigrants from Japan's former empire, often resorting to violence. Taiwanese peddlers cut into the action of Kinosuke Ozu's street dealers in Shinjuku. Taoka's Yamaguchi-gumi faced off against labourers and thugs from Korea. Wars over the fate of local underworlds turned brutal during periods of tension between the 1940s and 1960s. In 1946 an army of roughly a thousand yakuza from Tokyo's Matsuda-gumi took on several hundred Taiwanese street merchants in the district of Shibuya. On another occasion, the mayor of Kobe called upon the Yamaguchi-gumi to march upon a local police station after 300 foreign-born thugs occupied the building. Assistance from Taoka's men earned his family, it was said, a 'long term debt of duty' on the part of the city government.[14]

The anti-foreign sentiments at the hearts of these clashes were among the factors that shaped the yakuza's reemergence as a political force. Under American tutelage, Japan's reformed courts and police services endeavoured to uphold the law with limited staff and few resources. For a time, authorities turned a blind eye to the strong-armed order imposed by the likes of Kinosuke Ozu and Kazuo Taoka. Japan's transition to democratic rule forced a radical change in the historic relationship between the yakuza and the country's elite. The formation of new political parties and intimate ties to the United States widened societal divides. Communist influence flourished briefly as new unions, student groups and other activist groups took shape before being quelled by the occupiers. Native conservatives possessed no special love for the Americans but were far more fearful of surging leftist influence. With American support a reformed Japanese right began to coalesce, an alliance that included large numbers of former imperial officials. Among the earliest figures to define post-war Japanese conservatism was the now ageing cutthroat and fixer, Yoshio Kodama.

Kodama left prison in 1948 despite his designation as a Class A war criminal. By then, Japanese intelligence agents, backed by American funds and support, initiated plans to subvert leftist causes and other threats to the occupation. The CIA did not see Kodama as an asset of great value, reporting, 'He is a professional liar, gangster, charlatan and outright thief.' His ties to the Japanese underworld proved stronger than expected since his favour was often 'sought by weak men in high positions'.[15] Kodama angled his way into becoming a key figure in the Liberal Democratic Party, which remains the cornerstone of Japanese conservativism. His greatest contribution to right-wing causes was his ability to forge consensus and elicit support of yakuza crime families. By the mid-1950s, Kodama convened the first of many events that gathered prominent oyabun alongside business leaders and political stalwarts. Kinosuke Ozu particularly took such overtures to heart. He openly donated to rightist parties and ran unsuccessfully for a seat in the country's National Diet (or legislature). Alongside other bosses, Ozu utilised the legitimacy that came with his political credentials to secure 'advisory' positions within otherwise lawful groups. Before his death, he had joined the Chamber of Commerce, the Tokyo Restaurants Association, the Second Kimono Exchange and the Retail Fish Merchants Association.[16] Party leaders, business interests and state officials also came to count upon the muscle the yakuza could supply. One of the more glaring cases of this arrangement occurred amid a wave of popular protests against the signing of a defensive pact with the United States. Ahead of an official visit by President Dwight Eisenhower in 1960, up to a thousand yakuza armed with spiked bats aided police officers in attacking a march staged by leftist activists. Then-Prime Minister Nobusuke Kishi, a former imperial official and war criminal, purportedly secured yakuza support with the aid of Yoshio Kodama, with whom he had served time.[17]

Legal ambiguities were also critical to the yakuza's rebirth. Before 1964, a gambler or a gambling proprietor were equally subject to arrest. Yet, the law forbade police from apprehending offenders if they were not caught flagrantly in the act of betting or playing. Prostitution was an unregulated industry until 1956. Even then, when finally defined as a crime, lawmakers only proscribed parties from engaging in 'sexual intercourse' for payment, allowing other aspects of the trade to go unpunished.[18] Most importantly, declared membership in the yakuza remained legal. As fundamentally lawful organisations, many with fixed offices in newly built high rises, the absolute numbers of families and self-identified affiliates soared. According to one expansive government report, membership in the yakuza peaked in 1963. By then, there were over 5,100 families in Japan, claiming a total of 184,000 professed followers.[19]

The gangs of the mid-1960s were no longer black-market purveyors; their operations grew more formalised as their equity in vices and services deepened. A system of confederations emerged as powerbrokers such as Yoshio Kodama built unanimity among the leading families. By the 1970s state authorities identified seven large conglomerates made up of gangs with thousands of members. This process of amalgamation was not without periods of upheaval and uncertainty. In 1964, the government tightened gambling laws and cracked down on the yakuza for fear of bad publicity during the staging of the Olympics that year in Tokyo. This increased vigilance whittled down the total number of families, leaving only 2,400 existing gangs by 1980. Intermittent periods of violence also left their mark on the yakuza. A series of wars of expansion rocked Japan as gangs like the Yamaguchi-gumi grew. Compared to other locales, the scale of this violence was relatively limited. Amid the sword and gun battles witnessed in 1970, yakuza fighting resulting in a total of thirty-six men dead and another 147 injured in various parts of Japan.[20]

In 1975, Hollywood served up its first on-screen rendering of Japan's mafia. Coming just three short years after the release of *The Godfather*, *The Yakuza* starred veteran leading man Robert Mitchum in a gumshoe tale of betrayal and revenge set in contemporary Tokyo. Among the screenwriters to take on the film was Robert Towne, who had won an Academy Award the year before for *Chinatown*. Though heavy on blood and action, much of the movie delved into the culture and history of the yakuza as told by its Japanese cast members. Critics panned the picture as slow, convoluted and gratuitously violent. Towne later agreed it was not his best work. Partially to blame, as he saw it, was the nature of the genre itself. The makers of *The Yakuza* wanted the film to capture both American and Japanese aesthetics in its artistry, pacing and storytelling. Yet true yakuza movies, as Towne saw it, were B-rated soap operas, the kind of stories where the characters 'cry and beat their breasts and kill a bunch of people'.[21] Japanese audiences did not need Hollywood to validate their own affection for the yakuza. Beginning in the mid-1960s, a Tokyo film conglomerate, Toei Studios, was churning out dozens of yakuza movies a year. Though screen depictions of the classic bakuto or gambler date back to the silent era, Japan's emerging gangster genre focused on the contemporary world and was deeply sentimental. Toei's yakuza were gallant and selfless and readily fought and killed according to a strict moral code. The antagonists were typically those with power or simply the corrupt. Toei's movies struck a chord with those disaffected by Japan's culture of paternalism and conformity. Living standards had risen dramatically by the 1960s, but as one director remembered it, films about the yakuza captured a sense of despair and defiance among the viewers. For him, true fans of his yakuza pictures were drawn from the working class, people who 'felt virtually at war with the faceless, white-collar, corporate bosses'.[22]

The desire to capitalise on the popularity of *The Godfather* only partially influenced Warner Bros' decision to back production of *The Yakuza*. By the mid-1970s, Japan and its 'economic miracle' had made the country the focus of rarified interest. With the war drifting further into memory, Americans and Europeans increasingly identified the country with technological innovation, industriousness and skyrocketing economic growth. Earlier motion pictures, such as the Bond thriller *You Only Live Twice*, pointed to a growing familiarity and attraction among Western audiences for Japan and its people. *The Yakuza* was also indicative of heightened Western attention to the reach and sophistication of Japan's underworld. By the late 1960s, foreign correspondents were penning larger numbers of curiosity pieces exploring the world of the yakuza. Readers in Sydney, Australia, were treated to an expansive 1971 exposé on the life and notoriety of Kazuo Taoka, who was crowned the 'Mr Big' of all of Japan.[23] The *New York Times* subsequently attained a private interview with Yoshio Kodama, the 'godfather' power broker of the country's political and underworld elite.[24] The oriental mystique of the yakuza also helped draw the gaze of journalists and readers. No enquiry into the world of the Japanese gangster failed to mention their intricate tattoos, the katana swords they often fought with or the severing of their pinkies as acts of contrition.[25]

Godfathers

It took Western observers longer to catch on to the yakuza's growing influence beyond Japan's borders. Two of the earliest foreign markets Japanese gangsters exploited were the sex industries in South Korea and Taiwan. Gangs helped facilitate otherwise public efforts to coax lusty tourists abroad. Japan Airlines promoted junkets in the 1970s that promised opportunities to attend parties where customers could spend a night 'with a consummate Korean girl'. Cheap sex vacations had instant appeal. By 1979, South Korea welcomed more than 520,000 Japanese tourists, over 93 per cent of whom were men.[26] The overlapping interests of the Japanese and Korean underworlds were partially a testament to the influence enjoyed by Hisayuki Machii. Though born in Tokyo, Machii was the son of a Korean factory owner and Japanese mother. His mixed heritage endeared him to thousands of Koreans who remained in Tokyo after the Japanese empire collapsed. Like Yoshio Kodama, his street savvy, toughness and right-wing sensibilities attracted the attention of politicians and intelligence officials. In 1950, he purportedly accompanied Kodama and American Secretary of State John Foster Dulles on an official US visit to Korea's DMZ.[27] While lording over Ginza, Tokyo's premiere entertainment district, Machii reinvigorated Japan's methamphetamine trade. Rapid economic growth in the 1970s, especially in the realms of construction and commerce, helped stimulate the drug's resurgence among overtaxed white-collar and blue-collar workers. To meet demand, Machii and other powerful bosses moved much of their production network to South Korea. Profits from meth sales boomed over the course of the decade, eventually eclipsing more traditional yakuza industries such as gambling and prostitution.

Individual initiative, as opposed to centralised planning, helped reintroduce the yakuza to Hawaii and the west coast of the Americas. Signs of this push across the Pacific were initially episodic. The first inkling of the yakuza's arrival occurred after a car bomb detonated in Honolulu in 1974. The car's owner, Wataru 'Jackson' Inada, escaped the blast. Two years later, gunmen cornered him, sparking a broader investigation into heroin trafficking involving Inada, a soldier in a Tokyo gumi, and Peter Milano, a reputed mafia figure from Los Angeles.[28] The circumstances that brought Milano and Inada together appeared to have been casual and fleeting since no heroin was ever exchanged. Still other cases pointed to far more concerted yakuza efforts to settle abroad. News reports at the end of the 1970s revealed a growing Japanese presence in the vice industries of Hawaii and California. Yakuza interests in prostitution and gambling complemented their expanded involvement in commercial real estate dealings and other industries. Prominent figures sent their children to the United States to study. Mitsuru Taoka, son of the Yamaguchi-gumi's legendary boss, made a name for himself as a producer of yakuza films before he was assassinated in the early 1980s.[29] Increased media attention did not discourage yakuza from flouting their foreign interests. 'We came here first to buy property,' one Yamaguchi boss declared of Hawaii, 'then we buy the people.'[30]

The yakuza's heightened visibility accentuated the return of 'yellow peril' tropes in American media. Among the more racialised topics pursued by journalists were stories of blond, white women lured into brothels in Japan.[31] Revelations of yakuza heroin trafficking and 'white slaving' in the United States tended to blend into a more generalised pattern of coverage that depicted Japan as a threat to American industry and working-class jobs. Hollywood best distilled this interlocking paranoia in such mercilessly racist films as *Black Rain* and *Rising Sun*.

The yakuza were not the only 'oriental' mafia that stoked Western angst. An even larger, more unhinged wave of news coverage swept over Europe and North America with the rediscovery of the triads. As early as the mid-1970s, papers and newscasters warned of a veritable invasion of Chinese gangsters in places such as London, Sydney and San Francisco. Heroin use was now on the rise in these and many other cities. Suspicion reigned that the triads were a likely source of the poison. Journalists often spared few stereotypes in describing what many referred to as the 'Chinese mafia'. Media outlets regularly touted the triads as more violent and unforgiving than the 'Mafia' most people knew from the papers and movies. The Chinese immigrant communities they moved among were rendered complicit, too scared or too insular to help or fight back. Above all, the triads, with their rituals and codes, bore all the mysterious traits of an Asian cult.[32]

Movie studios took their time before weighing in on the paranoia generated by Chinese gangsters. Before the 1980s, Hong Kong pictures buried mafia tropes in far more popular kung fu pictures. American movie makers finally came round to the hype in 1985 with the release of *Year of the Dragon*, a film peppered with predicable amounts of violence, menace and chauvinism. Yet unlike Western interest in the yakuza, the crude breathlessness of this hysteria attached no names or faces to this threat. Officials who spoke confidently of triad involvement in the heroin trade often betrayed little foreknowledge of their activities. To this day, only a small number of accounts of the post-war re-emergence of the triads exist. The story these sources reveal is sketchy at best.

Insight into the influence of the triads first peaked with the publication of a book in 1960. Its author, British police inspector W. P. Morgan, conceived of the work in the aftermath of riots that shook Hong Kong in 1956. An air of crisis gripped the colony that year as fighting in the neighbourhoods of Kowloon left dozens dead and hundreds more injured. Officials were quick to blame 'secret societies' as the source of the disturbance.[33] To raise awareness of the threat posed to the colony, Morgan, as head of the Hong Kong Police Triad Bureau, interviewed sympathetic triad leaders willing to reveal their secret history. The war and its aftermath, as his informants explained, had transformed the power and nature of the triads. Before the Japanese occupation, less than one in ten of Hong Kong's inhabitants belonged to a triad lodge.[34] Britain's retreat from the colony in 1941 empowered many secret societies, particularly those willing to collaborate with the Japanese. Occupation authorities enlisted triad members into the new administration as informants, constables and intelligence assets. More importantly, Japanese officials showed little interest in lodges involved in prostitution, gambling and narcotics use. The chaos that followed Japan's withdrawal from Hong Kong further strengthened the grip of local lodges. Newly restored colonial offices lacked the staff to enforce bans on opium smoking and prostitution, allowing triad factions time to consolidate. The outbreak of civil war in China proper after 1945 made matters more complicated. As a deluge of refugees entered Hong Kong, the number and diversity of secret societies expanded. In addition to the remnants of Shanghai's Green Gang, an entirely new triad surfaced among the displaced. To stem the tide of Mao's advancing Communists, a Nationalist air force general and committed triad by the name of Kot Siu Wong worked to forge an alliance among a variety of secret societies based in the southern city of Canton. This new secret society, which Kot dubbed Hung Fat Shan, only cohered after Mao's forces emerged all but victorious. According to Morgan, few inductees learned the society's true name due to the speed of the Nationalist collapse. Its members instead referred to themselves as devotees of the '14 association', a reference to the street number of the triad's headquarters in Canton. Fealty to Chiang Kai-shek's Nationalists kept portions of Kot's coalition alive in exile after many found a new home in Hong Kong's underworld. The ranks of the 14 swelled to an estimated 80,000 members by 1958 as the society degenerated into a loose confederation of pickpockets, extortionists and drug dealers. At some point, its old Nationalist core improved the society's name. They dubbed their triad '14K' in honour of the finest cut of gold.[35]

Newspapers laid almost exclusive blame upon the 14K Triad for the trouble caused in 1956. Yet upon the release of his book, Morgan warned audiences that Hong Kong's triad problem was far greater. Some 35 per cent of men in the colony, he estimated, belonged to one triad or another, a substantial increase since the pre-war years.[36] Britain's struggle to stem the growth of secret societies contrasted sharply with affairs on the Chinese mainland. Upon taking power in 1949, Mao Tse-tung categorically outlawed all triad lodges, particularly the historic Heaven and Earth Society. Communist authorities imprisoned up to a million suspected triads within a year of the People's Republic's establishment, with an unknown number either executed or assassinated.[37] Other stringent laws, backed by the threat of indiscriminate violence and incarceration, undermined the criminal trades long associated with secret societies. Opium cultivation and use was met with the same harsh treatment at the hands of the Communist government. By 1952, mass arrests swept up over 160,000 individuals suspected of defying the country's new prohibition on trading in drugs.[38] By the late 1950s, prostitution also began to vanish under Mao's harsh authoritarianism. Aiding the government's campaigns against vice and drug use were efforts to mobilise and atomise Chinese society. Large 'floating populations' of itinerate labourers and outcasts, commonplace during the reign of the Qing, disappeared as China's Great Leap Forward began. In Mao's People's Republic, the state saw to it that every citizen, man or woman, remained in their assigned station and place of work.

Beijing's campaign to eradicate the triads and the opium trade mattered little to Harry Anslinger. As the Korean War raged, and the Cold War intensified, agents in his Federal Bureau of Narcotics asserted that Mao's anti-narcotics campaign was just a ruse. Until 1963, the bureau staunchly maintained that opium production in 'Red China' remained vital to the heroin trade.[39] Beijing, Anslinger told the United Nations, was flooding the West with narcotics in order to 'demoralize the free world' and widen its ideological reach.[40] Officials in Hong Kong did not necessarily agree. By the mid-1950s, much of the heroin consumed by addicts in the colony was coming from southeast Asia, not the People's Republic. What prompted opium production in the southeast was a completely separate set of circumstances. In the aftermath of Mao's victory in 1949, opium cultivation boomed along China's frontier with Burma and Thailand. Opium farming assumed acute importance in the Shan States, a former British territory awarded to Burma before the Second World War. Local calls for independence echoed in this remote borderland after 1945. When retreating portions of Chang Kai-shek's Nationalist army settled there at the end of the Chinese Civil War, those calls grew louder. As the Shan independence movement folded into the Nationalist campaign against the Chinese Communist Party, fighters appropriated the local narcotics industry as a necessary evil. Armies needed guns and money, one Nationalist general later explained. And in the mountains of the Shan States, 'the only money is opium'.[41]

Anslinger initially eschewed any connection between anti-Communist forces and the growing opium trade. Red China, he countered, was purposefully moving hundreds of tons worth of the drug via the Thai and Burmese border regions into the Pacific.[42] The FBN began to change its tune in the early 1960s while still refusing to implicate anti-Communist forces in southeast Asia. Anslinger eventually pointed to a very specific source: Hong Kong's triads. American suspicions sharpened with the release of William Morgan's book. Having read Morgan's work, one US Customs representative in Hong Kong grew convinced that the triads had to have a hand in international drug dealing. 'Their size, scope and power,' he argued, 'lead me to believe that they far overshadow the Mafia of Italy.'[43] His senior counterparts in the

FBN came to agree. In a report submitted to the US senate in 1963, Anslinger argued that Hong Kong's triads 'appear to be significant in recent trafficking developments', including the possible forging of new trade routes to West Germany, Spain and Switzerland.[44]

For the remainder of the 1960s, neither Anslinger nor any other American official embellished upon these claims. It was not until 1972 that the world received a detailed account of Asian heroin trafficking and organised crime. Providing these shocking revelations was an intrepid American graduate student from Yale University. Alfred McCoy's *The Politics of Heroin in Southeast Asia* arrived in bookstores amid a raft of news stories detailing rampant drug use among American GIs in Vietnam. The CIA, according to McCoy, bore significant blame for this scandal. Risking life and limb, he had journeyed to Saigon and the mountains of Laos to document the production and transport of opium by Agency assets. American intelligence officers, he insisted, allied with both Sicily's Mafia and the gangs of Marseille, aided in the development and expansion of the post-war heroin market. He admitted it would be difficult for many Americans to believe that the US government was 'in any way implicated in the international narcotics traffic', but the evidence suggested that 'America's heroin plague was its own making'.[45]

An international media firestorm enveloped McCoy's book. Detractors and supporters, however, tended to accept his explanation for how southeast Asian heroin found its way to the West. Responsibility rested with what McCoy called the Chiu Chau syndicates of Thailand and Hong Kong. The Chiu Chau were an ethnic diaspora spread across the Indian Ocean and Pacific rim. Since the 1800s, they had controlled opium trafficking out of Bangkok and coastal China, their ancestral home. Cliques of these Chinese merchants continued to operate through the twentieth century. It was the Chiu Chau who had displaced the Green Gang as the leaders of the Asian heroin market. Curiously,

McCoy drew no connection between this supposed Chiu Chau monopoly and the triads of Hong Kong or southeast Asia. When it came to shipping narcotics to Europe and the Americas, both Hong Kong and American agents believed that Chiu Chau groups worked closely with the 14K Triad. By the late 1970s, branches of the 14K used these ties to wield influence over the distribution of heroin in Amsterdam, New York and London.

Contemporary government reporting echoed many of McCoy's claims. One American diplomat characterised the Teochew, or Zhouzhou as they are referred today, as a 'closed' and 'highly disciplined' people. Teochew networks dominated the heroin trade, he reckoned, in part because they were also 'strongly represented in banking, insurance, pawnbroking, gold and [the] import–export business'.[46] It is not clear whether anyone in the US government challenged the proposition that a diaspora numbering in the millions was responsible for Asia's heroin trade. If not, such suspicions were consistent with earlier views of the American Mafia. Perhaps the Chiu Chau, to some eyes, possessed the same criminal tendencies of Jews or Italians.

Much less is known about American perceptions of the triads in southeast Asia. Native officials in Cold War Bangkok denied even the presence of triads in their city. Some Western officials agreed, expressing only moderate confidence that the triads controlled shipments out of Bangkok. Sceptical observers pointed to the fragmented or diffused nature of Chinese secret societies in explaining their dissent. For one British official posted to Thailand, his experience and instinct left him with one simple, unsophisticated lesson. 'When you get two Englishman together,' he explained to a journalist, 'you've got a club; when you've got two Irishmen together you've got a fight and when you've got two Chinese together, you've got a Triad Society – you've got a secret society anyway.' It was, he concluded, 'the nature of the animal itself'.[47]

*

Godfathers

The connections between older fraternal networks in the Americas and Asia's drug trade are just as murky. By the 1950s, tong wars in the Western Hemisphere had become a thing of the past. Yet in 1959, investigators in San Francisco arrested twenty-one individuals, including the president of the local chapter of the Hip Sing tong, for their involvement in a $100 million dollar heroin ring. Even though the drugs purportedly arrived via Hong Kong, an arresting FBN agent asserted the men were part of a conspiracy hatched in Red China.[48] Harry Anslinger made a point of mentioning the 1959 Hip Sing case during his Senate testimony several years later. Subsequent cases indicated that other tongs possessed Asian heroin ties. One probe in the 1970s pointed to a joint effort by the Hip Sing and On Leong tongs to smuggle 165 pounds of heroin from Thailand into the United States. How this conspiracy came about, let alone what became of the investigation, remains unclear.[49]

The late 1970s marked an inflection point in Western awareness of Chinese organised crime groups. As drug overdoses and street violence became a daily phenomenon on both sides of the Atlantic, journalists treated readers to a steady stream of sensational works detailing the imminent threat of Chinese gangs. The 1979 book *Triangle of Death*, written by an Australian correspondent Frank Robertson, garnered praise from across the English-speaking world for his global account of the carnage reaped by the triads. With decades of experience reporting from Hong Kong, he warned readers not to see Chinese secret societies as a distant or remote threat. Events in places like Amsterdam, London and San Francisco revealed that the tongs were a danger lurking closer to home. Their collective menace was not solely the result of their role in the heroin trade; stories gleaned from various locales suggested they were sadists and butchers of the worst kind. Of some six triad-related murders recorded in Britain and Holland 1976, Robertson avowed that only some victims died quickly. Many met agonising ends under the 'triad penalty of "death by five thousand thunderbolts" and the "flowing of blood from the body's five openings"'.⁵⁰

Anxieties crested further as the tide of migration from Asia to the West rose. The early post-war years featured the resettlement of millions of migrants from Hong Kong, Taiwan and the People's Republic in North America and Europe. Chinese-American communities grew by leaps and bounds, with over a million and a half Chinese migrants arriving in the United States between 1961 and 1998. Yet by the 1970s, social strains grew more visible in many American Chinatowns. Youth delinquency, drug dealing and violence assumed national significance amid a rash of high-profile investigations.⁵¹ Migrant gangs in San Francisco stood accused of at least forty-five murders by the mid-1970s, the most notable occurring in 1977 when gunmen opened fire in a crowded restaurant, killing five and wounding another eleven.⁵² Many youth gangs, such as the Flying Dragons and Ghost Shadows, started as martial arts clubs before becoming wrapped up in petty extortion schemes, prostitution and gambling. The more powerful gangs established ties with historic tongs such as the Hip Sing and On Leong as well as increasingly transnational societies like the 14K.

When the chief detective for the New York Police Department testified before the US Senate in 1984, he admitted that he and his officers knew only so much about the state of organised crime among the city's Chinese residents. Practical challenges made any enquiry daunting. The use of various Chinese dialects made gathering information from wiretaps difficult. Few witnesses ever came forward with information. Officers even uncovered individuals with multiple identification documents, thus muddying connections between known suspects and their supposed crimes. Officers remained certain, however, that the Hip Sing and On Leong ruled over the underworld of New York's Chinatown in conjunction with triads from Hong Kong. Youth gangs were their primary surrogates in extorting legitimate neighbourhood businesses, gambling dens and massage parlours. Officers presented no evidence as to how the triads interacted with the street gangs and old tongs or how the three administered the local drugs trade. Detectives could only say that the triads were in ascendency and that they conformed to 'what the western world would understand to be the traditional "Family" type of organised crime'. More worrisome was the fact that officers understood that the triads commanded the loyalty of some 80,000 'made men' residing in China. It is likely that the 'authoritative source' for this estimate came from William Morgan's research from the late 1950s.[53]

The vague impressions New York police officials imparted to the US Senate are instructive as to the prevailing narrative that enveloped the triads following the Second World War. Among the few things that appear clear is the extent to which triad lodges became more transnational and entrepreneurial. Mass migration from Hong Kong and elsewhere introduced triad societies to a variety of locales abroad. The rapid expansion of the post-war drug trade further incentivised intrepid secret societies to diversify their interests and movements. A far more glaring phenomenon was the shallow depth to which the triads remained understood by the 1980s. The struggles voiced by the New York Police Department were certainly partly to blame; issues of language, organisational secrecy and communal suspicion limited the investigative abilities of Western police officials and enterprising journalists. In the absence of new or more concrete revelations, earlier insights gleaned by William Morgan and Alfred McCoy were recycled year after year. The panic induced by rising rates of drug addiction and crime provided oxygen for much of the hysteria associated with the triads. Circumstances elsewhere influenced how many viewed Chinese gangsters. Cases involving the 'Chinese mafia' appeared to mirror trends in Europe and the Americas. Highlighting the subtle differences between the triads, Chiu Chau networks and the tongs was less than important.

MEXICAN AND FRENCH CONNECTIONS: THE MAFIAS OF THE POST-WAR ATLANTIC WORLD

Harold 'Happy' Meltzer's criminal career was anything but ordinary. At the age of seventeen, Meltzer enjoyed the distinction of being the youngest person in New Jersey's history ever tried for murder.[54] His acquittal on homicide charges in 1927 was not the last time he escaped conviction. After his arrest in 1958 for stabbing a New Jersey man twenty-five times with an ice pick, Meltzer bragged to a reporter that he had beaten three murder raps in total.[55] At some point in between these two cases he engrossed himself in the mob. Police in Los Angeles first encountered him in the 1940s as one of many East Coast gangsters who had migrated west. The LAPD busted him in the company of three other men under suspicion of narcotics trafficking. At the time of his arrest, police uncovered ten unmounted diamonds in his pocket. He was released, it appears, without charge.[56] Meltzer then began to move up in the world. He briefly served as a chief lieutenant for Jack Dragna's feared rival, the famed Hollywood mobster, Mickey Cohen. Later run-ins with the police earned Happy greater media attention and the somewhat buffoonish reputation as one Cohen's 'seven dwarfs'. Hard time in a federal penitentiary did little to set Happy straight. A 1963 FBN report claimed that he remained tied to the drug trade and had engaged in nefarious ventures in Japan, Hong Kong and the Philippines.[57] As late as 1969, FBI informants continued to describe Meltzer as 'the leading Jewish hoodlum' within the Los Angeles underworld and a man with links to powerful mob figures outside of California.[58]

Happy Meltzer's mysterious life took its most dramatic turn in 1951. That year FBN agents implicated him in a vast heroin smuggling network that traversed the Atlantic and North America. According to the indictment, Meltzer oversaw an intricate scheme to import Turkish opium into Mexico. His co-conspirators across the border were then to process the opium into heroin for distribution in the United States. Newspaper accounts of the arrest carefully noted that the ring included known associates of underworld giants such as Meyer Lansky, Frank Costello and Lucky Luciano.[59] For arresting officers, the implication of the Meltzer case was clear – the much-proclaimed narcotics drought that gripped the nation between 1941 and 1945 was over.

Meltzer's arrest resonated with Anslinger's ongoing campaign against trafficking and drug use. Still other trends increased the significance of high-profile drug cases by the early 1950s. Narcotics use gained greater visibility with the growing popularity of modern jazz and other art forms. Fears that music and film pushed young people into drug addiction amplified still greater concerns. As the post-war era commenced, crime and quality of life issues drew increasing amounts of public attention. 'Urban blight', a phrase born out of the visible decline of working-class neighbourhoods in the earlier part of the century, gained new meaning across the United States. Suburban development, as well as the decline of manufacturing, left many cities perceptibly destitute. One post-war study conducted in Baltimore found that 40 per cent of the population lived in neighbourhoods beset by substandard housing, unhealthy environmental conditions and crime.[60] American cities were discernibly more violent places than they were before the war. New York's homicide rate tripled in the six years between 1940 and 1946. Though crime statistics rose and fell over the coming decades, the city's Depression-era lows never returned.[61] Anslinger's bureau played upon these fears, highlighting the corrosive effect narcotics had upon two particularly vulnerable groups: young people and African Americans. Official reporting amplified cases of schoolyard pushers luring children into crime. Health experts and civic reformers affirmed widely held beliefs that narcotics were linked 'to life in slums' across the country.[62] Although official estimates of the number of regular drug users in America were stable between 1950 and 1967,[63] the moral panic inspired by drugs continued to grow.

As in the pre-war period, agents in Washington remained fixated on what they saw as the inherently foreign origins of America's narcotics problem. Transporting and selling drugs, they reasoned, were conspiracies that emanated from individuals and groups abroad. The fight, therefore, had to be taken beyond the country's borders. Officials received the Meltzer case as one of many indicators for where drugs were coming from and who was dealing them. The investigation appeared indicative of trends in Mexico, the point of origin for most opiates dealt in the US during the lean years of the Second World War. Other aspects of the case indicated a revival among older smuggling networks, particularly those based in the Mediterranean. The Meltzer investigation suggested that the scale and complexity of the international heroin trade had changed dramatically. In time, all nuance was lost and anyone who dealt in Turkish heroin was part of what was broadly called the French Connection.

Before his search for willing partners across the Atlantic, Happy Meltzer had cultivated strong relations with opium and heroin smugglers based in Mexico. Yet at the time of his apprehension, one genuinely could not speak of a homegrown Mexican mafia. What instead prevailed was a generally open environment south of the US border, one that made narcotics trafficking both possible and profitable. At the heart of this ecosystem was a historically weak Mexican state. From its days as a Spanish colonial capital, authorities in Mexico City laboured to administer its far-flung territories in a way that was predictable, consistent and just. Undermining the government's efforts was a sordid history of instability. Infighting and invasion between 1821 and 1857 particularly devastated the country, leading to a succession of forty-nine different governments and rulers. Other factors were just as compromising. Inhospitable terrain, long distances and the

Godfathers

lack of money and personnel often compounded Mexico's woes. A testament to these troubles was the enduring problem of banditry. As late as the twentieth century, banal acts of robbery, kidnapping and murder were common on Mexico's main roads and in the countryside. Though rural lawlessness remained a stubborn problem in states close to the capital, violence and crime were conspicuous challenges in Mexico's northern states. Fighting between state-backed militias and indigenous bands such as the Yaqui and Apache plagued the territories of Chihuahua and Sonora as late as the First World War. In each of these provinces, those with access to money and muscle held on to power tightly. The brutality of the state's war against northern native bands, coupled with the prevalence of unruly officials and patricians, bred resentment and bloodshed. A moment of catharsis came in 1910 with the outbreak of the Mexican Revolution. The overthrow of the country's long-serving dictator, Porfirio Díaz, led to a decade's worth of chaos nationwide. As many as 3 million Mexicans died or fled north into exile before the fighting ended in 1920.[64]

Mexico's revolution was almost immediately memorialised as having 'returned forever the people's rights' after years of authoritarianism and abuse.[65] But true liberty and accountability remained elusive, as patterns of misrule returned with a vengeance. Among the most corrupting influence in Mexico's post-revolutionary regime was the onset of Prohibition in the United States. Passage of the Eighteenth Amendment in 1920 transformed the country's border towns into havens for Americans seeking to indulge in alcohol and vice. Politics along the border quickly adapted to the temptations that came with the trans-American sale of alcohol, sex and drugs. In Ciudad Juárez, for example, a large landowning family, the Quevedos, used their political influence to become patrons of the town's underworld. To the west, in the state of Baja California Norte, an upstart cavalry officer named Esteban Cantú seized control of the governor's mansion after the outbreak of the 1910 revolution. Reformist leaders in Mexico City eventually ratified his takeover of the local government and allowed him to reign over the state for almost a decade. Cantú embraced the arrival of American tourists and thrill seekers after 1920. In doing so, he transformed the border town of Tijuana into a gaming oasis. In 1920, an estimated crowd of 65,000 American visitors swarmed into town for a raucous 4th July celebration, overwhelming Tijuana's minuscule population of 1,000 inhabitants.[66] The gambling houses, brothels and dope peddlers who catered to the arriving masses each paid generous bribes to the governor as a price of doing business. Unlike other provincial leaders, Cantú did not simply pocket his ill-begotten gains. He reinvested significant sums of money into education and infrastructure in the state. To this day, street signs and neighbourhoods in various parts of Baja California bear his name.

As Prohibition came and went, increased commerce on the American border prompted its own revolution among drug producers and marketeers. Opium usage first manifested itself in Mexico in the late nineteenth century as a phenomenon generally associated with Chinese immigrants. Like in the United States, nativist sentiment led to both anti-Chinese violence as well as greater government oversight of the drug's consumption. Crackdowns on petty Chinese smugglers and peddlers naturally did little to diminish the Mexican drug economy. Local cultivation of opium poppies, particularly in northern states such as Sinaloa, Durango and Chihuahua, began to take the place of opium imported from Asia before the 1940s. Among this early generation of northern opium farmers and dealers was the father of Ernesto Fonseca Carrillo, one of the founders of Mexico's first reputed drug cartel. Meanwhile, the abatement of maritime traffic during the Second World War compelled American addicts and drug wholesalers to look southward for sources. It was for this reason that Happy Meltzer and Bugsy Siegel journeyed across the border in search of heroin. By the time of his death in 1947, Siegel stood accused of heading a multi-million-dollar drugs ring that ran through Tijuana.[67] Meltzer's links to Mexican heroin dealers cemented his wartime reputation as a premier 'narcotics specialist' loyal to LA gangster Mickey Cohen. That status faded with his imprisonment in the early 1950s.

By the mid-1950s, Mexico's premiere trafficker was neither American nor a man. Ignacia Jasso became the dope queen of Ciudad Juárez by way of marriage. Her husband, 'Pabloté' González, was ten years her senior and had settled in Juárez on the heels of the Mexican Revolution. During the last decade of his life, he made a name for himself as a shootist and all-round supplier of vice and mayhem. Stories implicating him in killings and hold-ups cemented his reputation as 'the terror of Juárez' both north and south of the US border. At the time of his murder in 1930, Ignacia was herself in jail on a narcotics charge. She was then only twenty-seven years old and a mother to six children between the ages of eleven and one.[68] La Nacha, as she was affectionately called, ultimately proved to be more resilient and resourceful than the man she outlived. With the backing of powerful political benefactors such as the Quevedos, she quietly reinvented herself as a general retailer, wholesaler and smuggler of Mexican-produced heroin. She made excellent use of her husband's old suppliers in Mexico City and expanded her base of operations to other states such as Sinaloa and Jalisco. The key to her local operations were women, particularly prostitutes, who worked the bars and brothels of Juárez's red-light district. To evade prison, she bribed judges and politicians who supplied her with legal writs granting her immunity from prosecution. Just as critical to her success was the complicity of her family. By the time of her death in 1982, her children, grandchildren and other blood relatives had served various role in her empire. Just how much money she made from the heroin trade, let alone when she finally ceased her operations, remains fuzzy. What was left of her organisation vanished as larger cartels of traffickers came to dominate cross-border trade. Even though she had helped establish a local orphanage and sponsored other programmes for the poor, she failed to inspire the sort of cult devotion other narcos later enjoyed. Ironically, her husband Pabloté served as the subject of Mexico's first tribute ballad, or *narcocorrido*, ever recorded in honour of a famous drug trafficker. The song, which was released in 1931, only mentions her in passing.[69]

It is possible that La Nacha's reign plateaued just after the Second World War. In the absence of competitors from Europe and Asia, American narcotics officials believed that she possessed customers as far away as Seattle, New York and San Francisco.[70] Her influence receded with the reopening of sea lanes across the Atlantic and Pacific. Other factors minimised both the utility and desirability of Mexican heroin. Price aside, astute addicts and dealers valued Turkish and Asian cuts of dope for its higher morphine content. La Nacha and other Mexican drug traffickers eventually settled for a more modest place in the expanding American market. A CIA assessment from the early 1970s estimated that no more than 15 per cent of the heroin consumed in the United States came from south of the border. Only a portion of this derived from opium harvested in Mexico. Depending on the year and the smugglers involved, a significantly larger percentage of cross-border heroin traffic came from across the Atlantic. By 1970, an estimated 80 per cent of heroin shipped to the US and Europe flowed from Turkey.[71] How Turkish dope arrived in the United States was an infinitely more complex story.

Harry Anslinger and the FBN anticipated a resumption of the transatlantic heroin trade in the very first years after Nazi Germany's defeat. Their attention, however, was fixed on Charles Luciano. Unfounded rumours circulated through early 1946 that

Godfathers

Lucky was in Mexico looking for a way to slip back into the United States.[72] Lucky was indeed anxious to get back into business. His deportation to Italy left him stranded in a country he had not lived in since he was small. 'Italy's dead,' he told one reporter, 'nice, but dead.'[73] In the winter of 1947 he boarded a plane for Havana. There he met a great entourage of well-wishers and longtime friends such as Meyer Lansky, Frank Sinatra, Joe Bonanno and others from New York. Agents in Washington, as well as the American press, caught immediate wind of the conclave, leading to open speculation that the former 'dope king' was hatching something spectacular. By all accounts, the discussions held that winter in Havana touched on a variety of subjects, including the potential resumption of heroin trafficking into the US. Pressure from Washington saw to it that Luciano's sojourn in Havana was short. Within weeks Cuban authorities detained him and shipped him back to Europe aboard a rusty freighter.

The French Connection's genuine moment of conception likely occurred around the same time but much further north in Canada. Post-war Montreal possessed some of Havana's appeal but without the tropical warmth. Prohibition had made Canada's largest city a mecca for rum-runners during the 1920s. Its French persuasion and vibrant club scene drew casual tourists as well as gamblers and lusty johns from both sides of the American border. Yet before 1945, its underworld was parochial and small. Pre-war Montreal, however, did leave a mark upon its most famed gangster. Vincenzo Cotroni arrived in Canada in 1924 as a teenager from Calabria in southern Italy. After abandoning careers as a carpenter and professional wrestler, Cotroni found more gainful employment as a bookmaker. He then parlayed this profession into a decade-long career as a nightclub owner. For a time at least, his underworld status led to his recruitment as a part-time leg-breaker for Quebec's Liberal Party. It was with the help of hoods from much further afield that Cotroni established his own crime family.

At some point around 1947, Cotroni made the acquaintance of a recent immigrant from France by the name of Antoine D'Agostino. French authorities in Algeria and Marseille had arrested D'Agostino before the war for a variety of crimes including rape, prostitution and robbery. After the Nazi invasion, he offered his services to the Gestapo as an informant and enforcer. France's liberation from the German occupation sent D'Agostino into hiding in Canada. It was in Montreal that he reunited with another escaped collaborator, Marseille's former reigning caïd, François Spirito. Both men eventually found their way into Cotroni's orbit. Simultaneously, figures linked to New York's Five Families also made contact with Cotroni. Investigators never fully established how this international alignment was finalised. Only in hindsight did they discover Montreal's importance as a hub for French heroin destined for New York.

As Spirito and D'Agostino settled into their new lives, a much broader pattern of reordering was playing out across the Mediterranean. In Marseille, Spirito and Carbone's former rivals, the Guérini brothers, were successfully consolidating their place as Le Milieu's most prominent bosses. Their ascendency, as they saw it, was justly earned. The oldest of the brothers, Antoine, dutifully answered his nation's call as a conscript in the French army in 1940. For his pains and his reputation, the Vichy government exiled him to Corsica. Meanwhile, Mémé, the younger brother, joined La Résistance and aided in Marseille's liberation in 1944. Their collective service endeared them to the city's long-serving post-war mayor, Gaston Defferre. As heirs to the old Carbone-Spirito duopoly, the Guérinis restored caïd rule over the city's vice industry. The nuts and bolts of their empire, as one intimate remembered it, was 'the world of American [style] bars' that featured 'charming hostesses and nightclubs with well-trained entertainers'.[74] Naturally it was via Marseille's port that their wider influence was felt. With French troops actively combatting insurgents in Indochina (now Vietnam), the two skimmed money off the top of currency shipments dispatched from the colonial capital of Saigon. As in the pre-war era, the Guérinis exercised their interests over the harbour with a co-operative touch. Wartime collaborators living abroad, such as Spirito, were neither ostracised nor ignored. Competing gangs were worked into waterfront schemes. Political favours on behalf of Gaston Defferre did much to maintain a temperate climate within the city's underworld. When far-right militants threatened Defferre in the early 1960s, Mémé saw to it that his men protected him from harm.

The Guérinis likely required little inventiveness in stimulating the inflow of opium into Marseille. Despite the imposition of a ban by the colonial government in 1945, Hmong farmers in northern Indochina continued to produce opium that found its way to France via traffickers in Saigon. Merchant sailors arriving from Turkey, Yugoslavia and Lebanon also cashed in on illicit opium that came into their possession while abroad. By the early 1950s, the caïds of Marseille imposed greater order over the trade. Rather than rely on an uncoordinated flow of opium, gangs established fixed relationships with brokers in Turkey and the Levant. Critical to the forging of these ties were associates and relatives with the links to the eastern Mediterranean. Together, they imbued drug trafficking groups based in Istanbul and Beirut with greater power.

Post-war Istanbul, as one seasoned American narcotics officer put it, was 'the hot spot of the world' when it came to dealing in contraband opium.[75] Purchasing the drug required no more effort than finding a bar or club close to the city's docks. Within a couple of years, a clear pecking order emerged in town in terms of who dispensed the greatest amount of opium or morphine to potential buyers. While handfuls of small-time syndicates passed raw opium to mules who shipped the drugs via Syria and Lebanon, an executive class of *patron*s, or bosses, dealt directly with the

Guérinis and their successors. At the top of this stratum of Istanbul's underworld were two men, Ihsan Sekban and Hüseyin Eminoğlu. Locals referred to both men as being Laz, a small Georgian-speaking minority from Turkey's northwest coast. Like Corsicans in Marseille, Laz migrants came to Istanbul by the tens of thousands over the previous decades in search of work (particularly as sailors and porters). While Eminoğlu may have got his start in the drug business as an errand boy along the docks, Laz Ihsan, as he was commonly known, may have alternately driven a cab or worked as a petty hashish dealer before hitting it big. In contrast to others who formed the French Connection, little else was ever learned about their background or their relationship with Istanbul's Laz underworld. Newspapers rarely mentioned their names, let alone explored the inner workings of their industry. American narcotics officials quickly came to understand that policemen, journalists and politicians protected them. To this day, discussion of Sekban, Eminoğlu and other French Connection notables remains deeply taboo inside Turkey.[76]

By comparison, Lebanon's transformation into a French Connection nexus was far more public and jolting. With its independence from France amid the Second World War, Lebanon reaped the benefits of the peace that followed. The country's reputation as a pro-Western oasis nestled between Nasser's Egypt and Baathist Iraq buoyed its economic prospects. Beirut's tourism industry expanded rapidly through the 1950s as visitors flocked to take in the city's beauty and warmth. Increased international exposure also brought unwelcome repute for other kinds of entertainment available to sightseers. 'Americans would get a bang out of this place,' as one low tourist guide put it. 'Vegas doesn't even start to compare with the frenetic high living, gambling and prostitution of Beirut and its mountain-resort environs.'[77] Beirut's renown as the 'sin city of the Middle East' was predicated upon its earlier history as first an Ottoman and then French imperial entrepôt. As a port welcoming sailors and merchants from all points of the compass, bars, cafés and brothels were longstanding features of the city's landscape. In 1920, Beirut, then a city with just over 100,000 residents, possessed a population of around 1,200 prostitutes, of which at least a third came from Turkey, Greece and France.[78] The city's vice industry grew with the help of its most renowned gangster, Sami al-Khoury.

Born in 1927, al-Khoury came of age in the predominately Christian town of Zahle in the Bekaa Valley. Before ever touching the heroin trade, he grew familiar with narcotics by way of hashish, a staple crop found in the Bekaa. The expansion of Lebanon's tourism industry after the Second World War allowed al-Khoury to grow his criminal repertoire. Through his links to the Lebanese diaspora in Buenos Aires and Rio, he ran a South American network of white slavers tasked with enlisting women into Beirut's commercial sex industry. Together with women trafficked into the country from Europe, Lebanon's capital in the late 1960s reputedly possessed more prostitutes than Paris and Rome combined.[79] Al-Khoury's connections to South America exposed him to the growing trade in cocaine, a rare and highly sought-after commodity in post-war Lebanon. Of all his dealings, it was his status as one of Beirut's largest wholesalers of imported Turkish opium and Syrian morphine that garnered him international renown. Like Ihsan Sekban, his largesse was indebted to his exclusive relationship with Antoine Guérini and other bosses in Marseille. No less valuable to his operation were the politicians and policemen who protected al-Khoury from prosecution and unwanted attention. The freedom with which he went about his business stirred a general feeling of apprehension among narcotics agents from the United States. The extent to which officials abetted drug trafficking by al-Khoury and others led to a consensus within Anslinger's FBN that the Lebanese government was in fact 'in the narcotics business'.[80]

The individuals who transported narcotics sold by Ihsan Sekban and Sami al-Khoury were multinational, adaptable and fluidly linked. Major drug traffickers at times made for strange bedfellows. In the early 1950s, Greeks from Istanbul and Athens negotiated shipments on the behalf of major Turkish traffickers (such as in the case of opium purchased on the behalf of Happy Meltzer's ring in Mexico). Marseille's leading caïds often trusted friends, family members and partners of Armenian descent in securing large shipments from Lebanon and Turkey. Witnesses to these transactions often marvelled at the ease with which historical animosities were set aside. As one middleman understood it, to be an Armenian, even in Turkey, was in itself an advantage since his people 'were a minority without a homeland but were everywhere'.[81] Ties forged by history and diaspora remained important after Turkish opiates were processed into heroin in Marseille. Ships and planes bound for the Americas were met by cohorts of men with diverse pasts. By the early 1950s, Vincenzo Cotroni's outfit in Montreal worked in tandem with the Bonannos, the smallest of New York's Five Families. Cross-border trade was then taken over by Americans such as Carmine Galante, a veteran of the Prohibition era, and Lucien Rivard, a French-Canadian whose miraculous 1965 escape from prison earned him the distinction of being the Canadian Newsmaker of the Year.[82] Before Castro's revolution of 1959, Rivard's interests also extended to Cuba where he colluded with former chemists and smugglers associated with François Spirito and Paul Carbone.

The French Connection's use of Havana and Mexico City as weigh stations proved fleeting. By the 1960s, traffickers out of Marseille looked to Argentina as a more stable base for routing heroin into the American market. Since the late 1940s, Buenos Aires had become the home of former gangsters and Nazi collaborators on the run from French justice. Presiding over the trade in South America was Auguste Ricord, an early apprentice to

François Spirito and a former Gestapo intelligence asset. On his own, Ricord built an impressive empire that spanned the length of the Americas. A smattering of professional smugglers, pilots and merchant seaman from Corsica, Argentina, Chile and Panama funnelled heroin through multiple US ports of entry. Paraguay, then under the brutal dictatorship of Alfredo Stroessner, became an especially dependable base for Ricord's minions. For those who helped build the northern and southern branches of the French Connection, the heroin trade offered a foundation from which gangsters and smugglers expanded into other illicit industries. The wealth the Cotroni family generated from narcotics helped strengthen their hand over illicit gambling and cigarette smuggling in Montreal. Pilots who ferried August Ricord's heroin into the United States at times made as large a killing upon their return trips south. After offloading drugs in Florida, Louisiana and California, smugglers packed their planes with American-made jeans and cigarettes, which sold at three to four times their value on the Latin American black market.[83]

It was in this new environment of trans-Mediterranean and Atlantic trade that the mafias of Italy regained their strength. Their slow road to recovery mirrored the country's broader recuperation after Mussolini's demise. Invading Allied troops found much of southern Italy devastated. Strict food rationing and starvation ravaged the countryside. Banditry reared its head again in Sicily, leaving local authorities outgunned and overwhelmed. British soldiers found the city of Naples so poverty stricken that an estimated 10 per cent of resident women, roughly 40,000 in total, had resorted to prostitution.[84] To arrest the scale of rural lawlessness, as well as restore some measure of political normalcy, the Allied occupation embraced whatever support it could find among more traditional elites. As a post-fascist order took hold, landowners, urban retailers and the scions of old families filled positions of political weight. A good many of these early recruits were men who distinguished themselves as either mafiosi or camorristi. American and British officers were somewhat aware that many of their local collaborators had a chequered past. In Sicily, American intelligence agents understood that many of the translators they hired were provincial capos or American mafiosi who had returned to Italy. By the end of war, at least sixty-five expelled American mobsters took up residence in Sicily.[85] This infusion of US experience, as well as the personal connections that came with it, helped prod the Sicilian Mafia into more expansive directions.

Post-war recovery efforts resuscitated the fortunes of camorristi and mafiosi almost from the start. As in Japan, shortages and the continued rationing of basic needs created a black market ripe for exploitation. The proceeds and power that came from their control of contraband were a critical first stepping stone for capos and camorristi looking to regain strength. The massive influx of funds under the Marshall Plan created even greater opportunities. As reconstruction and modernisation efforts got underway, Mafia and Camorra families positioned themselves as patrons or quiet partners behind the companies bidding for government contracts. This renewed culture of clientelism grew more entrenched as the Italian welfare state came of age. As expanded government offices multiplied, Camorra and Mafia extortionists became the arbitrators of public services, including dolling out jobs and contracts. Illicit profits soared in the 1960s as the Italian economy expanded faster than many of Europe's larger states. New business opportunities, as well as the allure of greater prosperity, permanently altered the country's relationship with its mafias in the south. Rather than seek new lives in the Americas, significant numbers of Sicilian and Neapolitan gangsters resettled in Rome, Milan and other northern cities.

As previously provincial mafiosi made inroads into these virgin territories, yet another 'honoured society' emerged in the public eye. In Calabria, on the toe of the Italian peninsula, crimes authorities had long struggled to contain acts of brigandage and extortion in the countryside. Locals presumed that what confronted them was simply a native variety of Camorra or Mafia. Journalists covering a rash of killings in the mid-1950s discovered otherwise. What they found was a distinct underworld dominated by a group calling itself the 'Ndrangheta. As a culture likely forged in the late 1800s by transplanted camorristi, the 'Ndrangheta embraced similar rituals associated with their counterparts in Naples. As with the Mafia of Sicily, kidnapping and ransom were foundational to the 'Ndrangheta existence. Between 1970 and 1991, more than a third of all kidnappings in Italy were associated with criminals from Calabria.[86] After the close of the Second World War, 'Ndranghetisti equally won over the patronage networks commanding both the country's construction boom and the growth of government services. Opportunities to go north transformed Calabria's mafia into something more than a provincial nuisance. By the 1970s, 'Ndranghetisti purportedly dominated smuggling interests transcending the Italian-Swiss border.[87]

Narcotics trafficking was initially a force very few in Italy anticipated or were prepared for. The very first heroin deals to take place after the war were the product of external pressure and sheer opportunism. While American agents attempted to tie Lucky Luciano to the drug trade, local Italian entrepreneurs struck out on their own, acquiring legally produced heroin or abandoned stocks left over from the war. For a time, chemists in Trieste and other northern cities established morphine and heroin production facilities with an eye towards the transatlantic market. A turning point came in 1957 when Joe Bonanno, overseer of the Montreal-to-New York pipeline, arrived in Sicily at the head of a large American delegation. With the likes of Lucky Luciano and Carmine Galante in tow, Bonanno offered a small coterie of Palermo capos an exceptional opportunity. From then on, they could acquire their own franchise rights to produce and smuggle dope in tandem with brokers and wholesalers out of Marseille. To mitigate any potential strife among cosche who partook in the drug trade, Bonanno suggested that capos on the island form their own governing body akin to the New York-based Commission. Such a ruling council of mafiosi had in fact existed in Sicily for some time, although it may not have wielded much power before the 1950s. What changed after 1957 was the influence narcotics would have over the growth and stability of mafia life on the island. Competition between older and newer cosche increased as new rackets, particularly drug and cigarette smuggling, supplanted older sources of income derived from the Sicilian countryside. The violence that resulted from internal rows fittingly became more grotesque. In 1962, two of Palermo's largest families, the Grecos and LaBarberas, went to war with one another over a disputed heroin deal. In scenes reminiscent of Capone's reign over Chicago, dynamite attacks and targeted killings ushered in a reign of terror. The war culminated in June 1963 when police officers unwittingly detonated a car bomb in Ciaculli, outside Palermo, killing seven of them.[88]

The Ciaculli Massacre, as it was remembered, led to the first major government crackdown on the Mafia in the history of the young Italian republic. Police and carabinieri affected over 1,200 arrests, forcing capos of several powerful families into exile in the Americas.[89] Media scrutiny increased as the parliament in Rome opened its own enquiry into the influence of the Mafia. It took thirteen years for the body to issue a final report. Despite evidence to the contrary, doubts lingered as to whether a criminal fraternity existed in Sicily. Old stereotypes, in many cases, proved more persuasive. One senator insisted that the Mafia was simply a Sicilian state of mind, a product, as he mistakenly put it, of 'a millennium of Muslim domination' on the island.[90] For others, what was witnessed in Sicily was nothing more than *gangsterismo*, an unfortunate artefact imported from the United States.

This hesitancy to recognise Sicily's Mafia, let alone the Camorra or 'Ndrangheta, was echoed in the films of the period. Post-war Italy was the recipient of a number of films set against the backdrop of crime and violence in Naples or on the dry Sicilian landscape. Virtually all of them deal with 'honour societies' with a relatively light touch. Director Francesco Rosi, for example, provided audiences with several dramatic renderings of the Mafia and Camorra, including classics such as *Salvatore Giuliano* and *Hands Over the City*. In neither of these pictures do the characters associated with the Mafia or Camorra take centre stage. The genuine villains of these films were the more abstract forces that governed Italy as a whole. As Rosi described it, *Salvatore Giuliano* was a film dedicated to denouncing 'the links between the power of the state, the power of the institutions and the Mafia'.[91]

Rosi's intensely political treatments of crime in southern Italy resounded among critics of the Italian government. Since the abolition of the Italian monarchy in 1946, electoral politics rendered sharp partisan divisions in various parts of the country. The electoral strength of the Italian Communist Party galvanised backing for the more conservative Christian Democratic Party. In addition to the support of the Catholic Church and prominent commercial interests, Christian Democrats could count upon the assistance of Sicilian capos and their soldiers at election time. Supporting aspiring communist revolutionaries and reformers, let alone revived fascist parties, was out of the question for many in the Mafia. 'While I was in Catania the instructions were to vote only for centrist parties, the "democratic" parties,' one mafioso later confessed. 'The Christian Democrats were a democratic party, truly democratic. They'd share power. The Mafia could get along with that; it would make it possible to do more.'[92] It was also known that the US government and Italy's new NATO allies were equally as enthusiastic to support the continuation of Christian Democrat rule. American diplomats in Rome, however, did not perceive themselves in alliance with the Mafia. In fact, according to one consular official, 'it was impossible to make a definitive judgement' on any party's relationship with Sicily's mafiosi. From his perspective, more rigorous policing and the passage of anti-mafia laws in the early 1960s had made the Mafia into a thing of only 'local importance'.[93]

There were others who also presumed that the government had finally slain the Sicilian Mafia after 1963. Nothing, of course, could be further from the truth. As the dust settled from the Ciaculli Massacre, cosche on the island rebounded and slowly grew in size. By the 1970s the press increasingly spoke of a 'new mafia', one that was more urban, more globalised, more politically connected and less anchored to the provincialism of the past.[94] As heroin trafficking became vital to the livelihoods of historic families like the Grecos, younger leaders came to the fore. When the influence of Marseille's caïds began to wane in the mid-1970s, Sicilian chemists and smugglers with links in the Americas assumed greater importance. According to one estimate, roughly 30 per cent of all heroin consumed in the United States in 1980 was processed or passed through Sicily.[95] Meanwhile, in 1970s Italy, a wave of terrorist attacks and attempted coups by radical leftist and right-wing militants shook the country's political establishment to the core. Long influential clandestine societies, such as the Freemasons and Opus Dei, appeared to be among the forces who controlled Italian politics behind the scenes. Many assumed that Sicily's Mafia, which now operated throughout the country, helped sustain the right's influence at the expense of the public and the state.

More critical voices did not interpret this transformation as a product of the changing economy of crime. In Italy and elsewhere, the politics of the Cold War appeared to favour those who helped engineer the growth of the transatlantic drug trade. Early proponents of this view, such as Alfred McCoy, argued that the French

Connection arose with the tacit support of the United States and its allies. The evidence, as he saw it, was as plain as day. Up until Fidel Castro's seizure of power in 1959, Cuba's pro-American president Fulgencio Batista had given sanctuary to American and French mobsters. In France, Marseille's mayor Gaston Defferre and his Socialist Party enlisted thugs belonging to the Guérini brothers to crush striking workers in 1947. Behind the revival of the old criminal syndicates in both Marseille and Sicily, McCoy argued, were American intelligence officers who employed local mafiosi as agents and toughs. He maintained, however, that the CIA 'did not dabble' in the drug trafficking. Its complicity, whatever it may have been, was instead the 'inadvertent but inevitable consequence' of its role in the Cold War.[96]

Mafias did not need the CIA or the backing of US-led consensus to influence politics. The wealth they began to generate, and the environment in which they operated, provided the basis for the power they enjoyed. In Lebanon, for example, Sami al-Khoury's transnational business dealings attracted the attention of police and spies looking for information. His frequent visits to the famed Casino du Liban, once heralded as a 'cornerstone of the Lebanese economy', put him in contact with drug dealers and money launderers from France as well as elements of the French secret service.[97] In Turkey, Ihsan Sekban and other top traffickers were similarly suspected of ratting out rivals in exchange for police protection. Turkish generals later admitted to American diplomats that Adnan Menderes, winner of the country's first multiparty election, went as far as to harbour officials who 'were involved [in] opium traffic as major violators'.[98] Disclosures such as these left American officials unsettled. Yet the closeness with which criminals and governments often interacted exposed a harsh reality. Mafias did not necessarily undermine the security or stability of states. To the contrary, they were often a part of the reigning establishment.

International attention to the French Connection rose slowly over the course of decades. Isolated arrests of prominent traffickers, such as François Spirito and Sami al-Khoury, brought only intermittent recognition of the complexity of the transatlantic heroin trade through the 1950s. This lack of both public awareness and government urgency troubled Harry Anslinger. By the time of his retirement from public service in 1962, his Federal Bureau of Narcotics still lagged behind J. Edgar Hoover's FBI in terms of funding and popular exposure. Nevertheless, he and his agents remained undaunted in their efforts to bring greater focus to the international drugs trade. Anslinger doggedly pursued the gaze of the American media, as he had before the Second World War. When a committee in the US Senate opened hearings in the early 1950s on organised crime, Anslinger's deputies eagerly presented testimony as to the scope and dangers posed by international traffickers. The narrative that emerged from these senatorial investigations was comprehensive and convincing. Unlike public inquiries in Italy and elsewhere, the Senate's probe into organised crime was tediously dedicated to naming the chief culprits and documenting the trafficking networks that spanned Europe and the Americas. To this day, much of what is known of the French Connection remains grounded in the evidence submitted during these hearings.

The earnestness with which FBN agents attempted to publicise their findings was matched only by the energy with which they sought to bring their foreign partners into line. Since the end of the Second World War, Anslinger's small bureau worked to establish fixed offices in various countries deemed vital to the global fight against narcotics. By 1963, they opened permanent field offices in Bangkok, Mexico City, Paris, Marseille, Rome, Beirut and Istanbul. More significant still were their efforts to provide technical assistance and training to local police forces. FBN agents promoted American investigative techniques, sponsored English classes and counselled partner governments in establishing specialised counternarcotics squads. Much of this work, however, bore scant fruit. Many states, including close American allies, resisted calls for more rigorous controls over native opium cultivation. In Europe and in Asia, agents grew discouraged in the face of local corruption and official complicity in the drug trade. The FBN ultimately had its own problems to contend with. In 1968, the bureau was reorganised and placed under the close supervision of the Department of Justice. Redubbed the Bureau of Narcotics and Dangerous Drugs (BNDD), Anslinger's old organisation drew unwanted scrutiny over what many suspected was a culture of graft and maleficence. After unceremoniously firing dozens of New York-based officers on charges of corruption, the newly expanded BNDD retained only 200 seasoned agents despite a mandate to expand the bureau's size almost eight-fold.[99] After 1970, the new head of the BNDD went as far as to request assistance from the CIA to 'monitor any illegal activities' within his own ranks.[100]

Dramatic changes taking place in Washington partially compensated for the pangs of dejection felt among American narcotics officers. In the winter of 1969, Richard Nixon entered the White House promising to forge an honourable peace in Vietnam. He also vowed action on deepening crises at home. In the aftermath of Martin Luther King's assassination, intense waves of rioting swept across the United States. With hundreds dead and multiple cities in ruin, Nixon framed the unrest as symptomatic of the abysmal state of crime and security in the country. Statistics from America's largest city spoke to the gravity of this challenge. Between 1960 and 1976, the number of robberies in New York had risen an astonishing 1,200 per cent. At the start of this same period, the city also recorded an annual total 390 homicide deaths. That number increased to 1,600 a year within a decade and half.[101] For members of the new administration, rampant drug use was in large measure to blame. And from what they could tell, little headway was being made in stopping the epidemic. According to one CIA study, Turkish opium was abundant to the point that chemists in Marseille were paying 32 per cent less for morphine base than they had a decade earlier.[102] A trafficker could make up to $210,000 inside the United States for selling a kilo of French-refined heroin, some 42 times the going wholesale price.[103] For Nixon, a solution to the American drug epidemic demanded a more vigorous campaign abroad. In a July 1969 message to Congress, the president outlined a ten-point agenda to tackle the nation's narcotics problem. In addition to a host of steps geared towards domestic enforcement and treatment, Nixon promised a robust international effort. 'There are high profits in the illicit market for those who smuggle narcotics and drugs into the United States,' he announced, 'We intend to raise the risks and cost of engaging in this wretched traffic.'[104] It was at this moment that many historians mark the official beginning of America's ongoing War on Drugs.

Nixon's advisors proposed a multi-pronged campaign aimed at stamping out what they believed was the source of 95 per cent of the heroin consumed in the United States. Thousands of narcotics agents and other personnel were to be sent to the Mexican border. Diplomats, along with the president himself, pressed the French government to crack down on illicit heroin labs in the city of Marseille. An equal amount of pressure was heaped upon Turkey, the French Connection's primary opium source. Yet even then, Nixon's men understood there were limits to American influence. Pushing too hard against American allies such as Mexico, they believed, was counter-productive if it led to a breakdown in relations. It also seemed that successful interventions in one or all of these countries could potentially stimulate rises in opium cultivation and heroin trafficking in other parts of the world. Worse still, in southeast Asia, it was assumed that government officials were involved in the trade and were 'expected to hamper suppression efforts'.[105] Nixon and his team soldiered on despite these trepidations. Three years into this offensive, there were signs of success. Mexico did crack down on opium and marijuana cultivation. After some initial tension, Paris complied with American demands, leading to a spectacular series of raids and arrests in the south of France. Ankara also yielded despite objections that banning opium would cause harm to the economy and the lives of farmers.

The phrase 'French Connection' was not a part of the global lexicon at the beginning of Nixon's crusade. Its genesis instead came in the fall of 1971, just after Turkey announced plans to halt all opium cultivation in the country. When reviewers first took in William Friedkin's action movie, *The French Connection*, most drew no connection between the film and the president's antinarcotics campaign. Popular attention instead gravitated to Gene Hackman's relentless performance as Detective Jimmy 'Popeye' Doyle, a ruthless cop who cracks a high-stakes dope case on the streets of New York City. Many critics admired the film for Hackman's unvarnished portrayal of a policeman unencumbered by morality or civility. Popeye, as one *New York Times* columnist saw it, was no 'American fascist'. He was instead an avatar for one of the most 'deprived members of contemporary society', the underpaid cop.[106] Even though the picture opens in Marseille and alludes to the intricacy with which the heroin trade was engineered, Friedkin himself spoke ambivalently about the film's relationship to the actual mafias and crimes it fictionalised.[107] *The French Connection*, like the bestselling book it was based on, was a cop drama immersed in hardboiled action. Nevertheless, the film proved timely. Thereafter, politicians, newspaper reporters and television pundits regularly appropriated the film's title as a catch-all phrase to describe the complexities and personalities associated with transatlantic heroin trafficking.

It is likely that no one who saw *The French Connection* in 1971 imagined that the United States would spend untold billions on anti-narcotics enforcement. Probably fewer still saw Nixon's efforts begetting a proverbial war that continues today. By the time Nixon resigned in disgrace, it was readily apparent that the gains the US had achieved were short-lived. Turkey allowed for the resumption of opium cultivation in 1974. Marcel Francisci, who had taken over the Marseille underworld after the 1967 assassination of Antoine Guérini, remained at large. Worst of all, the drug epidemic remained acute in the United States and was spreading to Europe. French officials estimated in 1978 that were as many as 30,000 heroin addicts in the country, a ten-fold increase in a matter of five years.[108] Similar increases were posted in West Germany, which had up to 80,000 heroin users before the decade was over.[109]

The opening of the War on Drugs is not significant solely for its failure to curb addiction. It was in the aftermath of Nixon's grand offensive that the world witnessed a dramatic metastatis of mafias. From the mid-1970s, reorganised or altogether new criminal syndicates gained strength in Europe and the Americas. The emergence of these new syndicates took advantage of older mafias that grew weaker in the years that followed Nixon's global offensive. Driving this change were two fundamental forces. On the one hand, the slow collapse of communism gave rise to an array of criminal enterprises in countries where the rule of law was beginning to crumble. On the other, narcotics production continued to expand and multiply despite earnest multinational efforts to suppress drug trafficking at its source. A startling number of would-be mafias appeared across Mexico, Colombia, the former Soviet Union, the Balkans and the Sahel. How the world interpreted this more frightening era of crime was, in many ways, the product of a discrete set of preceding events that had transpired in America.

'BIGGER THAN US STEEL': MAFIA POLITICS AND THE GLOBALISATION OF POST-WAR AMERICAN PARANOIA

It took only a few scant minutes for news of Albert Anastasia's death to arrive at the Brooklyn waterfront. Hardened longshoremen purportedly turned white and immediately raced to Manhattan to confirm that indeed the man nicknamed 'the High Executioner' was dead. What they found has since become one of the most iconic images in American Mafia history. Anastasia's corpse was still on the floor of the barbershop of the Park Sheraton Hotel. At twenty minutes past ten o'clock on the morning of 25 October 1957, two gunmen with scarves over their faces fired ten rounds. Only five shots found their mark. Eleven men witnessed the killing, but none moved to prevent Anastasia's death. The New York Police Department announced almost immediately that a hundred detectives were assigned to investigate the murder. No one, however, was ever held to account. Ironically, more than one newspaperman noted that Arnold Rothstein, the man who fixed the 1919 World Series and fostered the careers of Lucky Luciano and Meyer Lansky, was shot outside the same hotel nearly thirty years earlier in 1928. His murderer also went unpunished.[110]

The American public in 1957 did not need a great deal of context to understand the gravity of Albert Anastasia's demise. His name had been circulating in the press for the better part of twenty years. Unlike many of his peers, he was born in Calabria and began his life in the United States as a teenager working the Brooklyn piers. Within two years of his illegal entry into the country, as the *New York Times* put it, he became 'involved in the Mafia criminal society of Sicilians and Calabrians'.[111] His greatest notoriety came with his association with Lepke Buchalter's Murder Inc. At the time of his death, 'the High Executioner' was the head of the Gambino family, one of the city's reputed Five Families. A year earlier, a committee in the US Senate, led by its chief counsel Robert F. Kennedy, called him to testify about his involvement in illicit dealings. Had he lived, Kennedy told the press, he was planning to have Anastasia testify again.

The Senate's peering interest into Anastasia's illegal enterprises reflected a new environment in which officials and everyday citizens understood the Mafia. Print media, particularly in American cities, had never lost interest in criminal 'combinations' and their 'kingpins'. Mob bosses continued to make good copy, a phenomenon drilled home with Lucky Luciano's deportation to Italy in 1946. Rising crime statistics after the war, however, compelled both officials and citizens to reassess the significance of organised crime. The growing belief that a single clandestine organisation controlled vice and narcotics throughout the United States assumed new importance against the backdrop of the Cold War. With fears of Soviet subversion mounting, noted opinionmakers, both high and low, proposed that mobsters and the Red Menace were birds of the same feather. A crisis of morality confronted America, FBI Director J. Edgar Hoover declared in 1956; a crisis that, if left unchecked, would lead to both lawlessness and the unfettered growth of communism.[112] Popular pulp journalists Jack Lait and Lee Mortimer equated the mafia with the perceived ideological and moral threat of the far left. As authors of the popular *Confidential* series, which detailed, often in crude terms, the underworld happenings of various towns across the country, Lait and Mortimer explicitly likened America's Mafia to a 'super-government' whose tentacles extended into the depths of politics and the economy.[113] Mafia cabals, like communist subversives, were inseparable from the modern iniquities of drug use, race mixing or homosexuality.

At a time when issues of crime and corruption were drawing greater amounts of public interest, a new and ambitious member of the US Senate, Estes Kefauver, seized centre stage. Like his more notorious counterpart, Joseph McCarthy, the Tennessee-bred lawyer leveraged the country's mounting anxieties to great effect. He carefully outmanoeuvred McCarthy in first establishing a committee dedicated to exploring the pervasiveness of 'interstate gambling and racketeering activities' (McCarthy accepted this reversal and established his own feared committee dedicated to rooting out communists in public life).[114] Between 1950 and 1951, the Tennessee senator took his investigation on the road, staging hearings in fourteen different cities. Hundreds of witnesses appeared before Kefauver's inquest. Though local municipalities had held similar public enquiries years before, the committee's two-year investigation quickly evolved into a very modern spectacle. Kefauver subpoenaed a veritable who's who of the American underworld to answer questions before his fellow senators. Most, including the likes of Meyer Lansky, Mickey Cohen, Albert Anastasia and other mob luminaries, took shelter under the Fifth Amendment. Frank Costello, heir to Lucky Luciano's New York family, was the only boss to offer direct responses. Costello's appearance before the Kefauver committee topped off what became a tidal wave of mass media interest. In addition to the newspapers and magazines that followed the investigation's every step, it was the new medium of television that brought the issue of the Mafia's rise to power home to average Americans. At its height, anywhere between 17 and 30 million viewers tuned into the Kefauver hearings, a TV audience larger than any that watched the 1951 World Series.[115]

Many readers of the American press were certainly exposed to the notion of the Mafia before 1950. Yet through the power of television, Estes Kefauver saw to it that all Americans recognised and understood its explicit meaning and significance. His committee drew upon several sources in presenting its findings. An early influence on Kefauver's thinking was the surly *Confidential* series written by Jack Lait and Lee Mortimer. The supposed closeness with which the committee echoed the duo's lurid insights drew claims from the authors that the committee's final report was 'practically a plagiarism' of their accounts of crime in Chicago and Washington, DC.[116] Of greater consequence to Kefauver's work was the testimony and insights provided by Harry Anslinger of the Federal Bureau of Narcotics. Anslinger's agents gave the committee hundreds of documents detailing the history, structure and dealings of crime syndicates across the country. Though stopping short of identifying a singular American mafia, the FBN contributed mightily to Kefauver's conclusions. The Mafia, his final report argued, was essential to binding the country's two most dominant criminal syndicates in New York and Chicago together. Lesser gangs followed their lead. 'Wherever the committee has gone,' the report continued, 'it has run into the trail of this elusive, shadowy, and sinister organization.'[117] But what precisely was 'the Mafia'? Kefauver understood it came from Sicily and was brought over to America via thugs who comprised the Black Hand and other groups. The contemporary American Mafia, he cautioned, was no longer 'confined to persons of Sicilian origin'.[118] Though never explicitly stated as such, he and his fellow senators carefully noted the involvement of Jews and, to a lesser extent, Irish and others as well.

For all its hype, the Kefauver Committee drew a range of reactions. A translation of the Senate's final report, *Gangsterismo in America*, as it was titled, sparked little introspection in Italy, despite being the first book to be published on the Mafia since the end of the war.[119] Its publication in Britain under the name *Crime in America* was also met with a degree of indifference and derision. A close reading of Kefauver's investigation, as one reviewer saw it, was that American laws governing vice were 'not only unenforced (which the Senator proves) but unenforceable'.[120] Closer to home, muckraking columnist Walter Winchell mused that American television viewers were likely more envious than indignant after Frank Costello's testimony. How else could 'an average, hardworking, debt-ridden citizen' react after learning Costello could 'swing elections' and kept '$50,000 dollars in cash around the house in spending money'? America, in Winchell's estimation, 'was holding a mirror up to itself'. Those who participated in illegal gambling and other vices were just as complicit in the rackets as Costello.[121] Others were unsettled by Kefauver's intense scrutiny of Italian and Jewish Americans. Pressure from Jewish and Italian interest groups forced the committee to close some of their sessions for fear of drawing accusations of bigotry. Meanwhile, one noted personality remained conspicuously silent. FBI chief J. Edgar Hoover did not endorse Kefauver's findings regarding the Mafia in the press. In speaking before the committee, he placed greater blame on local authorities who failed to enforce the law.[122] In hindsight, Hoover's approbations smack of hypocrisy. It became well-known that he cultivated a close friendship with Clint Murchison Sr, a Texas oil tycoon with extensive ties to mafia figures in New York and elsewhere. Murchison treated Hoover to multiple all-expenses-paid vacations in San Diego where the two enjoyed afternoons betting at the Del Mar Racetrack. 'Murchison owned a piece of Hoover,' one political insider later claimed. 'Rich people always try to put their money with the sheriff, because they're looking for protection ... You can do a lot of illegal things if the head lawman is your buddy.'[123]

Events forced a sudden change in Hoover's attitude towards organised crime. Just weeks after the 1957 assassination of Albert Anastasia, law enforcement officials in rural New York stumbled upon a large gathering of cars and limousines drawn from across the country. Further surveillance revealed a congregation of dozens of well-dressed men at the home of a known former bootlegger. A raid soon followed, leading to the apprehension of fifty-eight suspects. Many of those taken were later charged with obstruction and supplying false statements. Among those known to have attended the fabled meeting in Apalachin,

New York were some of the most notorious figures within the American underworld: New York bosses Vito Genovese and Paul Castellano; Sam Giancana of Chicago; Santo Trafficante from Tampa; and Frank DeSimone, heir to Jack Dragna's crime family in Los Angeles. The meeting, according to later testimony, constituted an emergency session of the fabled Commission first established by Lucky Luciano. In addition to smoothing over internal relations in New York in the wake of Anastasia's killing, attendees at Apalachin also purportedly spoke of the growing importance of the narcotics trade. Regardless of the content of the discussions, the indisputable presence of so many gangsters in one place, let alone in an isolated hamlet 150 miles from New York City, enflamed both the public and the government at large. A sense of embarrassment compelled J. Edgar Hoover to jerry rig a self-styled 'top hoodlum squad' aimed at gathering information on suspected crime bosses. A new round of senate hearings was organised, this time under the leadership of John L. McClellan of Arkansas. The McClellan Committee pursued an even more earnest line of investigation than Kefauver's, dragging in both feared gangsters and the powerful labour leader Jimmy Hoffa, head of the International Brotherhood of Teamsters. It was later, under McClellan's watch, that Anslinger's agents first revealed the details of the French Connection heroin trade. As the 1960s began, much of Washington appeared resolved to take on organised crime in many of its forms.

For all these setbacks, the mood among the country's leading mobsters remained buoyant. The loss of Havana to Castro's revolution compelled the Mafia to deepen its influence in Las Vegas. Control over major illegal gambling networks and wire services remained strong. Alliances with trade unions and local dignitaries provided a variety of crime families with sources of wealth and political protection. When the FBI began wiretapping Meyer Lansky in the early 1960s, agents caught a sense of the ageing gangster's sentiments one night as he watched television with his wife. During a panel discussion, one TV presenter avowed that organised crime was second in size to the American government. Turning to his wife, Lansky rendered his own assessment. 'We're bigger than US Steel,' he told her.[124]

Upon becoming president in 1961, John F. Kennedy embraced the crusade against the Mafia more than any of his predecessors. With the help of his brother Robert, whom he appointed attorney general, Kennedy made his effort to crack down on organised crime a centrepiece of his domestic agenda. Federal authorities intensified their surveillance of prominent crime bosses and sought creative avenues to hold them to account. In 1961, for example, immigration officials deported the reputed head of the New Orleans mob, Carlos Marcello, to Guatemala, the country he listed on his forged birth certificate. Jimmy Hoffa, who had evaded conviction for attempting to bribe a Senate aid in the 1950s, was sent to prison for jury tampering. The greatest of all coups against the American Mafia came in the summer of 1963. That August, news leaked that FBI agents had secured the co-operation of Joseph Valachi, a soldier in New York's Genovese family. Valachi, it was reported, would tell all he knew about Apalachin and the families that held sway over New York and other cities. Above all, he intended to reveal the secret name this constellation of syndicates genuinely went by: La Cosa Nostra.[125] After weeks of media anticipation, Valachi finally sat before John McClellan's committee at the end of September. Like the Kefauver hearings more than a decade earlier, Valachi's testimony garnered a television audience numbering in the millions. Speaking slowly, and at times unartfully, he laid out the history of the American Mafia as he knew it and lived it. He outlined in detail the forbidden rites he witnessed when he was initiated as a soldier in the early 1930s. Each family, he argued, followed the same organisational blueprint that had been passed down to them from

Sicily. It was with the conclusion of the Castellammarese wars, he claimed, that the Commission first came together. Through all this, Valachi named names, described murders and gave credence to the existence of a 'national crime syndicate' that reigned over the whole of America's underworld.

A correspondent for the *Guardian* newspaper in the UK could not help but marvel at the congenial atmosphere that enveloped the Senate's proceedings that fall. His inquisitors 'addressed him as Joe in gentle, understanding tones' and delivered their questions in a more caring manner than those 'fired at witnesses in the test-ban treaty hearings' a month earlier.[126] Yet for all the odd moments of laughter his testimony provided (particularly his description of receiving the 'kiss of death' from his fellow inmate Vito Genovese), the global press absorbed Valachi's revelations with few reservations. The transparency of the hearings, both in its presentation on television as well as in its contents, was without precedent. There was now no denying that an American Mafia existed, that it had a definite history and a hidden culture that gave it life and authority. Critics in the decades that followed, however, would pick apart Valachi's observations and cast doubt on his truthfulness. Ironically, among those to accept the veracity of his testimony were capos and soldiers residing in Sicily. Before Valachi's revelations, no member of Italy's Mafia saw themselves bound to an organisation called Cosa Nostra. After translations of his testimony began to circulate, men in Sicily also began to refer to their 'honoured society' as 'our thing'.[127]

A far more profound crime soon eclipsed the sordid affairs detailed before the McClellan Committee. When John F. Kennedy met his tragic end in Dallas in November 1963, no one in the American press immediately suspected mafia involvement. The apprehension of Lee Harvey Oswald, a man with documented communist proclivities, at first seemed to tell the whole story. Nor did Oswald's murder at the hands of Jack Ruby days later stir public suspicions of a mafia conspiracy. Ruby, as it was revealed, was a local club owner and possessed a seedy reputation dating back to his years living in his hometown of Chicago. This fact, however, bore no weight on the initial judgement of investigators. A year after Kennedy's death, the presidentially appointed Warren Commission declared that Ruby was in no way 'significantly affiliated with organised crime' and that there was no sign of a conspiracy in either his killing of Oswald or the president's murder.[128] Observers in Europe, however, were among the first to express their belief in a mafia plot. Soviet papers speculated from the beginning that any number of actors could have assassinated Kennedy, including Albert Anastasia's long defunct gang, Murder Inc. A prominent French commentator drew inspiration from the testimony of Joseph Valachi and his portrayal of the 'supreme association of crime' present in America. Cosa Nostra, as he understood it, possessed 'deep-rooted political branches' in cities across the country. 'Who says,' he concluded, 'that Dallas is not under its control?'[129]

As Americans were laying their murdered president to rest, Mario Puzo was an obscure author with one modestly successful novel under his belt. His second book, an autobiographical tale of poverty set in Manhattan, had floundered, leaving him with no way to pay off his colossal gambling debts. A 1965 review of his second book sparked his imagination. If it only had a 'little more Mafia stuff in it', the critic suggested, 'maybe the book would have made money'. Puzo took the advice to heart and went to work on a new novel. Though his dismal upbringing was marked by thugs and Prohibition, he had little first-hand knowledge of the mob. Valachi's testimony, which was published as a bound volume, served as his principle point of reference. After Paramount bought the film rights of an early draft in 1968, Puzo embellished his research with trips to Vegas. He coined the remark, 'make him an offer he can't refuse', after hearing how a pit boss convinced a drunk Hollywood actor to vacate the floor of his casino.[130]

Francis Ford Coppola was equally unfamiliar with mafia lore at the time Paramount approached him to direct the dramatisation of *The Godfather*. He had not read Puzo's book, despite it being a bestseller, and had little inclination to make a gangster picture. Like Puzo, however, Coppola needed the money and accepted. What he learned of the Mafia also came from books he read at a local public library near his home north of San Francisco. As production on *The Godfather* began, real mafiosi inserted themselves in the process. Joe Colombo, head of one of New York's Five Families, strongarmed Coppola's team to remove any explicit reference to the Mafia or La Cosa Nostra. Apartments and businesses linked to the mob became sets. The role of Clemenza, Don Corleone's steadfast lieutenant, went to Philip Castellano, a blood relative of Paul Castellano, a successor to Albert Anastasia. For Coppola, however, the connective tissue between his film and New York's underworld was of secondary importance. *The Godfather*, to him, was a morality tale about capitalism and its relationship to American life. Only in the United States, he declared, could 'a Sicilian phenomenon' have flowered. 'Everything the Mafia believed in and was set up to handle – absolute control, the carving out of territories, the rigging of prices and the elimination of competition – everything was here,' he later explained. 'In fact, the corporate philosophy that built our biggest industries and great personal fortunes was a Mafia philosophy.' The Italians who imported Cosa Nostra 'found themselves in the perfect place'.[131]

The film's release immediately touched off fierce debates over the film's depiction of Catholicism and Italian culture. In the lead up to its release, New York boss Joe Colombo organised a campaign denouncing both the media and the government for having unfairly maligned Italian Americans as born criminals and degenerates. Demonstrations staged by his Italian-American

Civil Rights League drew tens of thousands, a fact that compelled Richard Nixon's Justice Department to abandon use of the term 'mafia' in its official pronouncements.[132] The League's contention that the Mafia was a government fabrication lost a degree of credibility after Colombo was shot and seriously wounded in a gangland hit during one of his own rallies.

What was less controversial was *The Godfather*'s general depiction of America's recent past. Unlike most of its predecessors, such as Howard Hawks's *Scarface* of 1932, *The Godfather* was a period piece. Its sequel, which Coppola was initially hesitant to make, delved even further into history. Vito Corleone's journey from Sicily to America, and then from poor immigrant to prosperity, knowingly appealed to a fundamental American experience. Yet in placing the genesis and drama of the Corleone family during an earlier time, Coppola's vision, consciously or not, had an indelible effect upon how audiences came to perceive the history of the United States. Mafias, as *The Godfather* series would have it, were not simply plagues of the present or the product of contemporary moral or political struggles. They reflected elemental facets of the country's founding and the nation's development. Historicising the Mafia through cinema may be the most noteworthy contribution of Coppola's films. *The Godfather* was intended as 'entertainment and not a documentary', yet even as fiction, it undeniably came close to 'some of the realities behind the headlines'.[133] To phrase it another way, *The Godfather* invoked certain truths about the origins and nature of the United States in ways that newspapers or scholarly tomes could not.

The release of Coppola's mafia epics occurred as the mood in the country darkened. Mass demonstrations against the Vietnam War were drawing tens of thousands of participants when the film entered circulation. The rave reviews it received coincided with ongoing talk regarding the secrets hidden in the Pentagon Papers and the assassinations of Martin Luther King and Robert

Kennedy in 1968. *The Godfather* was still playing in theatres when the Watergate scandal erupted in the summer of 1972. Nixon resigned only a few months before the sequel's debut in late December 1974. It was in this climate of scandal and disillusionment that many of the most devastating revelations concerning the American Mafia emerged. In the wake of Watergate, the Senate voted overwhelmingly to establish a committee to investigate acts of government subversion at home and abroad. Headed by Frank Church of Idaho, the Senate enquiry confirmed long-lingering rumours of a pact formed between the CIA and the mob. In the summer of 1975, Johnny Rosselli, who served as the Chicago Outfit's emissary to the West Coast, testified that he had met with a representative from the CIA in 1960 and agreed to help assassinate Fidel Castro. Having lost their casinos in the aftermath of Castro's takeover, the mob appeared to senior American officials to be likely collaborators. The plot, which was first hatched in the summer after the failed Bay of Pigs invasion, admittedly went nowhere. As Rosselli described it to his friend, LA boss Jimmy Fratianno, it was a scam from the start. The CIA also had reached out to Santo Trafficante, the crime boss of Tampa, and Sam Giancana, leader of Chicago's Outfit, but neither committed themselves to killing Castro. 'All these fucking wild schemes the CIA dreamed up never got further than Santo,' Rosselli privately confessed. 'He just sat on it, conned everybody into thinking that guys were risking their lives sneaking into Cuba, having boats shot from under them, all bullshit.'[134] Unbeknown to the Church committee, the secret CIA-Mafia plot went further than Rosselli and the heads of the Chicago and Tampa mobs. Documents released in 1993 revealed that agents had probed the possibility of recruiting other gangsters as a part of an Agency-run hit squad under the operational title, ZR/RIFLE. Among them was Happy Meltzer, the dope dealer extraordinaire from Los Angeles. Meltzer, as one officer described him, possessed the 'background and talent' needed for the operation, given his history of murder and mob activity. It was uncertain, however, 'whether he would be receptive'.[135] ZR/RIFLE, like other CIA-Mafia plots, likely went nowhere after 1961.[136]

A torrent of other terrible secrets followed the opening of the Church Committee. In the winter of 1975, newspapers widely covered the emergence of Judith Exner, who claimed to have been a 'close friend' of John F. Kennedy, Johnny Rosselli and Sam Giancana. Insinuations that she had acted as an intermediary between the Mafia and the president stirred further calls to widen the Senate's enquiry, perhaps even reopen the investigation into the Kennedy assassination.[137] Exner's revelations, coupled with the murders of Rosselli and Giancana in the summer of 1975, pushed suspicions to new heights. Each of these events and more, many assumed, pointed to a grand conspiracy that connected the American underworld to Washington. Congressional investigations into the CIA, the FBI and the Mafia continued through the late 1970s. Parallel admissions and secrets surfaced, such as FBI efforts to wiretap Martin Luther King and undermine the Civil Rights Movement. In 1979, a multi-year congressional investigation into the Kennedy assassination issued a final report declaring the conclusions of the Warren Commission flawed and incomplete. It raised the possibility that the Mafia may have killed the president to avenge the loss of their casinos in Cuba and deter further government encroachment. Its alliance with the CIA, as the 1979 report put it, 'had all the elements necessary for a successful assassination conspiracy – people, motive and means'. However, congressional investigators admitted they were 'ultimately frustrated' in their attempts to 'determine details of those activities that might have led to the assassination'. The report specifically cited the murders of Johnny Rosselli and Sam Giancana as key obstacles in rendering a final judgement.[138]

*

The world media took in these and other conclusions with astonishment. Newspapers and television stations in Europe and elsewhere devoted ample space and airtime to the investigations led by the American Congress. In the Soviet Union, testimony before the Senate and the House of Representatives inspired the popular spy novelist, Youlian Semyonov, to pen his own version of the events that led to Kennedy's death in Dallas. It was China, and not the CIA or Cuban mercenaries, who had the president killed, wrote Semyonov. Yet it was members of the Mafia, as he imagined it, who most probably pulled the trigger.[139] Beneath the surface of this global fixation, events in the United States were leaving a more subtle series of impressions on international observers. By the close of the 1970s, the contemporary language of Hollywood and the American press resounded within the reporting of local affairs elsewhere in the world. Heads of Marseille's crime families were less frequently referred to as caïds, but as godfathers, or *parrain*. Bosses in Mexico also came to be depicted as *padrino*s who led mafias of their own. In Turkey, the absence of any cultural equivalent to a paternal 'godfather' was of little relevance. Major narcotics traffickers, who previously were known simply as bosses or patrons, came to be called *baba*s, or fathers, in honour of the translated titles of Coppola's films. Before *The Godfather*, no one referred to the head of a local cosche as a *padrino*. They were known more affectionately as *compare*, the proper term for any man who becomes a godparent. With time, however, even notorious bosses in Sicily were pictured posing in a manner that mimicked Marlon Brando.[140]

These trends pointed to a new global consensus surrounding the nature and significance of organised crime. From the 1970s on, the term 'mafia' was used everywhere. Often despite the absence of evidence, many assumed mafias existed in their locality. The organisational structure or code described by Joseph Valachi became a near universal point of reference. Events in the United States, in other words, were increasingly internalised and became an instructive base of understanding or comparison. What many learned from Cold War scandals concerning the American Mafia went beyond issues of crime. Governments the world over, it seemed, were the keepers of terrible secrets. Mafias could be a part of a nation's establishment, perhaps in tandem with officials, business leaders and celebrities. Calamities and acts of intrigue took on new relevance in the eyes of critics outside of the United States. What books and newspapers revealed about a country's past or present was progressively looked upon as only part of the story. Great and small states possessed secret histories that only a select few truly knew or understood. Over time, the public everywhere came to suspect that mafias were a part of that history.

One cannot attribute these changes solely to the effect of *The Godfather* or the drama that unfolded after the death of JFK. They were symptomatic of the terror and disbelief generated by the Cold War. Documented cases of mafia influence in politics and crime echoed the Communist conspiracy. Depending how you looked at it, the Mafia and the Red Menace equally emanated from abroad and transcended everyday life. There were those, of course, who doubted all of this. Government crusades against gangsters and communists appeared to many as a ruse meant to obscure more vile plagues, be it militarism, capitalism or simply unadulterated corruption. Coppola himself believed as much. Those who watched *The Godfather* thinking it was solely about the Mafia were mistaken, he argued. The film was about power and the relationship between a self-styled king and his three sons. 'It could have been about the Kennedys. The whole idea of a family living in a compound – that was all based on Hyannisport [the Kennedy family's home in Massachusetts]. Remember, it wasn't a documentary about Mafia chief Vito Genovese. It was Marlon Brando with Kleenex in his mouth.'[141]

Key factors that led to the increasing influence and sophistication of mafias, such as the growth of commerce and the mass movement of peoples, were in continuity with precedents set before the Second World War. Xenophobia remained a lens through which mafias were perceived. The reemergence of the yakuza, the triads and other syndicates rekindled many of the fears spawned by earlier waves of migration to the West. As a successor to the great European empires of the pre-war period, the United States leveraged its strength as a superpower to further combat the crimes that served as the principal sources of mafia wealth. Though often cloaked in the rhetoric and paranoia of the times, Cold War campaigns against organised crime were in continuity with past state efforts that sought to crush mafias (or bandits for that matter). And for all of the might of many post-war states, mafiosi continued to prey upon the contradictions and weakness that stemmed from government efforts meant to destroy them. As in the past, the most successful gangsters and mafias tended to be those who forged alliances with political parties, statesmen and even arms of the state of itself. This proved equally true of weaker countries, particularly those left devastated by war, as well as powerful ones like the United States.

How mafias were perceived also evolved alongside the continued expansion of mass media and the public square. As citizens grew more aware of the world around them, anxieties about the nature of state power grew. As the might of militaries, police forces and intelligence services became more visible and invasive (be it to fight Communism, foreign subversion or popular dissent), popular distrust intensified. Government detractors readily seized upon evidence of official complicity in organised crime as proof of the state's hypocrisy when it came to issues of security. When statesmen in America, Japan and France were found giving sanctuary to gangsters (especially in the name of anti-Communist suppression), journalists and activists justifiably cried foul. Admissions of unlawful government surveillance, let alone acts of subterfuge, appeared even more dubious in light of reports of alliances formed between mafias and arms of the state. Film, television and the popular press hammered these suspicions home. As much as it spoke to the evils of the Mafia, *The Godfather* was an indictment of the state and the powers that be.

6

Between Decline and Revolution: Mafias at Century's End

It was entirely by chance that Jon Roberts's story came to light. For much of his life, public knowledge of how he was involved in the modern cocaine trade was largely confined to court records and local newspaper coverage in Florida. One early autobiographical account mentions him only as a customer of an important Colombian cocaine trafficker and as a person with 'access to the [American] Mafia'.[1] A chance encounter brought Roberts out of obscurity. In 2003, filmmaker Billy Corben was working on his award-winning documentary, *Cocaine Cowboys*. Corben's cousin met Roberts in passing at a Miami pool. After a subsequent lunch meeting, Roberts agreed to be in the film. The story he divulges in *Cocaine Cowboys* is outrageous and larger than life. For nearly a decade, he aided the Medellín Cartel in expanding their foothold in North America. In doing so, he amassed a fortune estimated in the hundreds of millions of dollars. He and his accomplices spurred a monsoon of spending and investment that helped transform south Florida into an epicentre of glitz, tourism and commerce by the early 1980s. He also had no small role in turning the city of Miami, for a brief time, into the murder capital of the world.

The revelations in *Cocaine Cowboys* reflect only a fraction of Roberts's criminal career. He subsequently divulged more to the journalist Evan Wright. He was born Jon Riccobono in June 1948. His father, Nat, was a soldier under a series of redoubtable bosses: Lucky Luciano, Albert Anastasia and, finally, Carlo Gambino. The government deported Nat to Sicily when Jon was nine, but Jon's uncle Joseph, seeing his nephew displaying signs of a tumultuous youth, steered him into the ranks of the Mafia. As a former gunman for Lepke Buchalter and advisor to Carlo Gambino, Joseph Riccobono was among the dozens arrested at Apalachin in 1957.[2] Having survived a brutal tour in Vietnam, Jon plunged into a variety of criminal undertakings. He ran nightclubs, dabbled in drugs and shook down a long list of unsuspecting marks (including one failed attempt at drugging and framing famed television presenter, Ed Sullivan, for rape). By his own account, Jon was nothing like his uncle. He was feral in his instincts and habits. He dressed and lived ostentatiously and consumed massive amounts of drugs. Older mobsters, such as Gambino, were 'like company men at IBM' and he wanted no part of their traditions.[3] After police raided his home under suspicion that he had murdered a corrupt police detective, he escaped to Miami and lived under a new name, Jon Pernell Roberts. Despite arriving nearly penniless, it didn't take long to reinvent himself as a drug dealer. Chance encounters and successful scores led to a string of introductions that expanded his operations and increased his largesse. In 1978, he met Fabito Ochoa, the namesake of Don Fabio Ochoa, patriarch of the Medellín Cartel. It was after that that Jon's dealings entered a new stratosphere of wrongdoing. With his transportation partner Mickey Munday, they innovated an immense series of routes and means of importing cocaine from Colombia. By the time of his arrest in 1986, federal authorities estimated that he and

Munday were responsible for shipping anywhere between $2.3 and $15 billion worth of cocaine into the United States.[4] Through it all, however, Jon's old life in New York remained close behind him. In the late 1970s he was introduced to Meyer Lansky, who, despite his advanced age, was still conspiring and scheming. The American Mafia's senior statesman embraced Jon as the son of a mobster he had known forty years earlier as a close associate of Lucky Luciano. To Jon, he was a 'walking dinosaur like my uncles'. Dressed in a bow tie and suit, Lansky could easily have been mistaken for an appliance salesman.[5]

As extraordinary as Jon Roberts's life may have been, he is but one of many mafiosi to commit their memories to paper. Arguably the first modern gangster memoir was published by Joe Valachi in 1969. The tone of the best-selling *The Valachi Papers* could not be more different from most contemporary mafia chronicles. In relating his experiences to journalist Peter Maas, Valachi clearly intended his recollections to serve as a warning to the public at large. Feelings of social responsibility or regret were far less a factor in bringing Jon Roberts to tell his story. His *American Desperado* is a lurid tale of intrigue, violence and surreal adventure. Roberts's book, though less repentant than others, shares an important trait with many of the mafia memoirs of this time: change. As he grew from a raucous New York nightclub owner to a giant of the drug trade, old men were giving way to younger ones. He and his 'wild Indian' friends cared little for the values and institutions that lay at the heart of what they saw as the American underworld. Roberts betrayed no nostalgia in looking back to his father's generation (he once likened La Cosa Nostra's initiation ceremony to someone receiving an assistant manager's badge at McDonald's).[6]

This was not the case for someone like Tommaso Buscetta. As someone who had helped shepherd Sicily's Mafia through the postwar era, Buscetta looked back wistfully at his father's generation.

Mafiosi of an earlier time, as he saw them, were 'dignified people, gentlemanly and inherently good'.[7] He could remember a better time when capos dressed down, kept a low profile and even rode public transportation. Narcotics trafficking, and the immense profits that came with it, warped and diminished the character of the young who followed him into the life. He later told prosecutors that he foresaw the collapse of Cosa Nostra as early as 1978 due to the extravagance, corruption and violence drugs had brought to Sicily. Buscetta swore to his interrogators he took no part in the trade, even though he admitted to hosting the famed narcotics summit with Joe Bonanno and Lucky Luciano in Palermo in 1957.

Buscetta's prophecy proved half-right. The power of Sicily's Mafia waned considerably as the twentieth century came to a close. The same held true for other older syndicates based in New York, Marseille and Tokyo. Why this happened was only partially linked to the excesses brought about by the expansion of the drug trade. The continued growth and diversification of the narcotics industry led to exorbitant profits that spurred more killing and, in due time, far greater government scrutiny. By the 1990s, La Cosa Nostra, the yakuza and the American Mafia contracted in the face of more rigorous policing, new laws and harsher sentencing. Profound generational divides also served as a source of tension. While their fathers and predecessors may not have been as rarified as they remembered them, Buscetta, Roberts and other younger mafiosi pulled away from the original moorings of their respective secret societies. The allure of making more money was key to this rift. Equally important was the collapse of leadership and the shared alienation they felt towards the past. As the end of the century beckoned, the world was changing rapidly.

An undeniable symptom and driver of this changing world was the sudden rise of the cocaine trade. Unlike opiates, cocaine burst onto the global scene despite significant obstacles. As a crop almost exclusively grown in the Andes, coca was at first a relatively rare commodity. It did not possess the centuries-long appeal that opium enjoyed at the dawn of the modern narcotics trade. Cocaine became a global staple of the drug market by virtue of the ingenuity, vision and the sheer will of a handful of Colombian entrepreneurs.

The architects who conceived of this revolution in Medellín were also the beneficiaries of the acceleration of transoceanic commerce in the late twentieth century. Global commerce had ballooned during the first three decades of the Cold War, rising from $63 billion in 1950 to $2 trillion by 1980. When the century closed, the value of global trade rose to over $6 trillion.[8] Culture too was becoming more globalised, a pattern typified by the ascendency of Michael Jackson, Pizza Hut and Maradona. It was on this wave that Pablo Escobar became one of the richest men in the world and arguably the most notorious. Yet Escobar understood his fame in ways that were different to Al Capone. For Capone, fame was a newer novelty. For Escobar, it was like living out what he had seen in the movies and television.

Escobar's career lasted less than twenty years. Yet in the time of his remarkable rise, the abrupt speed and violence of the cocaine revolution paved the way for more powerful organisations to take shape in Mexico and other places such as Jamaica and Nigeria. The unexpected dissolution of the Second World revealed a myriad of criminal subcultures, none greater than the *vory* of the Soviet Union. Like mafias of the early twentieth century, what many came to call the Russian mafia captured the world's imagination for their exotic traits and merciless dedication to violence. Together with the formation of lesser mafias from the Balkans, their rapid infiltration of American and European markets appeared reminiscent of the perils posed by the supposed Italian and Chinese invasions before them. More than anything, they were received as indications of the corruption and backwardness of the political and economic systems that spawned them. History, in this sense, appeared to be repeating itself but with far greater force and malevolence.

'IT TOOK A HUNDRED YEARS TO PUT THIS TOGETHER': OLD MAFIAS IN RETREAT

Vincent 'the Chin' Gigante first tried out his 'crazy man routine' in the early 1970s. FBI agents who questioned him in 1972 were told by a relative that he suffered from brain damage as a result of his earlier career as a boxer. Witnessing his oblivious state, the agents reported back that there was no need to brace him since he was 'obviously quite disturbed'.[9] The Chin subsequently took his act outdoors. At the end of the 1970s, Gigante was living with his mother on Sullivan Street, south of Bleeker, in the heart of New York's Greenwich Village. As the neighbourhood gentrified, Gigante was seen regularly along Sullivan Street in his bathrobe. Photos of him dishevelled and muttering to himself became a regular staple of New York's tabloid press. There were times when he was caught talking to imaginary pets or even urinating in the street. Yet he remained a free man while other bosses in the city, such as John Gotti, were taken down by the FBI. The law finally came for Gigante in 1996. At trial, his lawyers presented brain scans showing what they argued were definitive signs of Alzheimer's. Brooklyn Judge Jack Weinstein was unmoved. Having read extensively about the disease, he congratulated the Chin's lawyers for being on 'the cutting edge of science'. The problem, as he saw it, was that PET scans could not be used to diagnose Alzheimer's without an autopsy.[10] With that, a jury of his peers found Gigante guilty of racketeering and conspiracy to commit murder. He died in prison in 2005.

The three decades Gigante invested in bringing his crazed persona to life did not necessarily undermine his credibility among those who pledged their loyalty to him. 'Within our family,' one soldier later attested, 'we viewed the Chin as a very, very smart man, a very secretive man, very cunning and very ruthless.'[11] He was of the old school, having first found his footing as a bodyguard for patriarch Vito Genovese. Yet by the time he rose to head the Genovese crime family in 1981, he was the only New York boss to cultivate such a deranged public image. Why he chose to do so remains a mystery. At the time FBI agents first observed his misanthropic behaviour, J. Edgar Hoover was alive and still devoting relatively little of his bureau's resources into apprehending members of the Mafia. The New York Police Department was even more compromised in its disposition towards organised crime. Corruption among the city's police was rife to the point of absurdity. In 1972, authorities accused narcotics detectives of stealing hundreds of pounds of heroin from police evidence lockers, including drugs that had been seized in the investigation that inspired the plot of the film *The French Connection*. In hindsight, Gigante's decision to take on the façade of someone too demented to stand trial appears desperately clairvoyant. By the time the 'Oddfather' finally stood trial, an entire generation of mob leaders had been sent to prison in various parts of the country. The Chin, as one local editor quipped, was the 'Last Last Last Boss'.[12]

The fall of the American Mafia began in the US Congress. By the end of the 1960s, the political climate in Washington was inclined to passing harsher criminal statutes. With federal and state authorities demanding greater resources for investigations into leftist radicals, labour racketeers and common criminals, Congress responded by drafting an omnibus crime bill in 1968. Key to this legislation was an official set of guidelines that now allowed investigators to use wiretapped conversations as evidence at trial. Although civil rights advocates decried the bill as an egregious violation of one's constitutional right to privacy and illicit search and seizure, investigators rejoiced at their new-found powers. Among those to champion the inclusion of the new wiretapping statues was Senator John McClellan, who helped introduce Joe Valachi and La Cosa Nostra to the world in 1963. McClellan empowered his staff to go further in crafting even more restrictive laws targeting organised crime. This bore fruit two years later with the federal adoption of the Racketeer Influenced and Corrupt Organisations (RICO) Act. Passage of this 1970 law is now largely credited to George Robert Blakey, a law professor and former senate investigator. As a one-time staffer in the Justice Department during the 1960s, he saw the FBI's disregard towards mob informants first hand. 'If anyone started talking about the Mafia or using the word, he was told to shut up,' Blakey remembered of the time. 'The Mafia was not [deemed] relevant to the case and we only wanted to hear about the specific crime being investigated.'[13] With the might of John McClellan and the US Congress behind him, Blakey's law made participation in any mob-led conspiracy the axis upon which entire crime families could be indicted. Prosecutors were now at liberty to link bosses to individual acts committed by their subordinates so long as the government could furnish evidence of the crime's relationship to a 'continuing criminal enterprise' (i.e., the Mafia). It is likely Blakey devised the name of the legislation so it could be referred to by its acronym, RICO. As a man with a particular affection for mob films, Blakey's choice was a clear homage to Rico Bandello, the main character in the 1931 classic *Little Caesar*. At the end of the film, he told one crowd of officers, Rico dies unceremoniously in a back alley. His number two, however, survives. 'Nothing happens to Big Boy,' he exclaimed. 'He's still in charge. Nothing has changed. That's the overwhelming value of RICO. It is designed to change the end of the movie.'[14]

Incredibly, it took more than a decade for the FBI and local law enforcement to realise the powers that had been granted to them by Congress. Many sceptical agents found the new wiretapping regulations painstaking. Building a RICO case demanded greater amounts of time and resources than many field offices were willing to expend. In the spring of 1977, *Time* magazine published a lengthy cover story entitled, 'The Mafia: Big, Bad and Booming'. The American Mafia was reportedly 'going through one of its most crucial internal struggles since Prohibition', leading to scores of deaths and the mass takeover of legitimate and illegitimate business both in the east and out west. Despite the country's weakened economic condition, mob families were reaping a windfall in illicit earnings. Law enforcement agencies estimated that the American Mafia was netting $25 billion in annual profits (by contrast, Exxon, then the largest corporation in the United States, cleared $2.6 billion in gains at the end of 1976).[15] When Los Angeles boss Jimmy Fratianno read the story, he could not help but be amused. In his mind, it was as if 'the writer had repeated every lunatic notion ever dreamed up about [our] thing and dumped it into one story'. The notion individual mobsters wielded unquestionable power over places like Las Vegas was downright mindboggling. Attempting to oversee loansharking, drug dealing and prostitution on the Vegas strip was, in his words, like 'trying to control three tidal waves with a machine gun'. He personally was 'hanging by the skin of his teeth' at the time financially. Others he knew in the LA underworld were doing no better.[16]

What editors at *Time* appeared to have gotten right was the general sense of upheaval that appeared to plague crime families from coast to coast. By 1980, virtually all of the founding fathers of the American Mafia had either died or retired. Replacing them were captains and underbosses with no memory of Prohibition or other early events. Their transitions into positions of authority were often violent and unsettling. Chroniclers of the American Mafia have particularly latched on to the life and bloody demise of 'Crazy' Joe Gallo as an early example of this generational shift. The American-born Gallo attained notoriety through the 1960s and '70s for initiating a string of civil wars within the New York underworld. Local newspapers embraced the handsome gangster for his youthful looks and affection for fine art. Crazy Joe made no secret of his support for civil rights and went so far as to recruit African American accomplices in prison. Bob Dylan memorialised him in song, seeing in Gallo a kind of hero 'underdog fighting against the elements'.[17] He was murdered in 1972, supposedly in retaliation for his attempt on the life on Joe Colombo, whose own public campaign against anti-Italian discrimination brought even more unwanted attention to New York's Five Families.

Of all the gangsters who fell in love with the limelight, John Gotti took the mob's star power highest. Gotti was a contemporary of Jon Roberts (Riccobono), who knew him when he was an ordinary 'mad dog' like other young members of the Gambino family.[18] Gotti's dizzying rise to fame began after he murdered Paul Castellano, the courtly boss of the Gambinos, in 1985. Suspicions of his involvement in the killing rapidly led to a string of high-profile trials. The media frenzy around him intensified after he escaped conviction on three separate cases. The camera loved the photogenic Gotti – and Gotti, with his signature silk suits and carefully manicured hair, loved the camera just as much. In 1986, *Time* magazine commissioned Andy Warhol to produce a portrait of him for a cover piece. The media circus he wilfully generated was too much for many of the remaining ageing dons. 'It took a hundred years to put this together,' one boss scolded him, 'and you're ruining it in six months.'[19] A RICO trial in 1992 ended his tenure as the reputed 'Teflon Don'.

Gotti was neither the first nor the last boss to be taken down in a RICO case. After years of being ignored, G. Robert Blakey toured the country and gave seminars at Cornell University preaching the utility of the law he helped craft. His message finally broke through to law enforcement at the very end of the 1970s. Between 1979 and 1984, bosses in Los Angeles, Kansas City and Cleveland were found guilty of RICO conspiracy charges. The mother of all RICO investigations culminated in 1985 with the indictment of each of the sitting bosses of New York's Five Families. At the heart of the government's case against New York's mafia was the contention that the heads of each of family were members of the fabled Commission first formed by Lucky Luciano. Millions of dollars, according to prosecutors, had been extorted and skimmed from the city's construction industry and labour unions at the behest of the Commission. Murder and drug trafficking charges were also amended to the indictment. Four of the five bosses were sentenced to a hundred years in prison.

The trials of the 1980s and '90s brought out other signs of rot inside the American Mafia. In many cases, informant testimony, as opposed to wiretaps, proved vital in attaining convictions. Attaining the co-operation of so many mafiosi sworn to silence set many courtrooms abuzz. Vows of omerta, it seemed, were paper thin. Indeed, personal vendettas and the prospect of decades behind bars compelled a number of prominent hoods to break their oaths. An even more common incentive to offer information to the police and FBI was money. Slews of made men, associates and even bosses became confidential informants in exchange for cash or government promises to look the other way at least for a time. Co-opting hardened criminals for the state's benefit, however, did produce some scandalous results. New England's presiding crime family, the Patriarcas, was brought low in no small measure due to the paid testimony of James 'Whitey' Bulger, leader of Boston's notorious Winter Hill Gang. In exchange for nearly two decades of insider information, his FBI handler knowingly gave Bulger free reign to murder and extort. (The agent who abetted Whitey's duplicity would himself later be convicted on racketeering charges.) Other government dispensations for providing evidence, such as offers of immunity and relocation under the Witness Protection Program, were widely abused. Sammy 'the

Bull' Gravano, whose testimony helped seal John Gotti's 1992 conviction on RICO charges, was arrested for drug trafficking only a few years after assuming a new identity in Arizona. As a former hitman and underboss in the Gambino family, he also published a bestselling memoir detailing his life of murder and theft. Outraged relatives of some his victims took exception to his profiting from their suffering and sued him for $25 million in damages. A judge eventually ordered Gravano to pay plaintiffs just $420,000 in restitution.[20]

Gravano's attempt to capitalise on his old life fed speculation that there was something more to the American Mafia's decline than Washington's growing strength and resolve. As far back as the late 1970s, founding godfather Joe Bonanno perceived a moral deficit at the heart of what he called his 'tradition'. 'Friendship, connections, family ties, trust loyalty, obedience – this was the glue that held us together,' he declared in his autobiography. What now appeared to bind men of his ilk were material things born out of work and money.[21] Decades later, Sammy Gravano appeared to agree.

> 'They say I broke the oath. But it wasn't the oath I thought I was taking,' he avowed. 'I thought it was about honor and brotherhood. I mean, when you took the oath, that honor stuff got you as high as a kite when you were being made. You really believed in it, that it was worth living for and dying for and going to jail for. It was none of that. It was all about greed and power. In reality, it was a total joke.'[22]

Reverence for the Mafia's old code of conduct, let alone any sense of order and discipline, appeared to be vanishing among mobsters in New York. The dictatorial control and loyalty exercised by once venerable families was 'fracturing in the same way that the Soviet Union suddenly collapsed'. 'There is no question,' one investigator quipped, 'the new breed doesn't have the same discipline or loyalties of the previous generation.'[23]

More than any sense of contrition, one cannot help but notice shades of what is often referred to as America's 'national malaise' in accounts of the American Mafia after the 1970s. There is a sense of nostalgia and loss in the words of Gravano and Bonanno. The past was a better and more wholesome place. Institutions were trustworthy and people were made of surer stuff. What brought on this sense of dissonance? Perhaps it was down to, as President Carter famously put it in 1979, 'years that were filled with shocks and tragedy'.[24] For members of the American Mafia, the malaise was likely less the result of the energy crisis, Vietnam or the killing of Martin Luther King than of their changing surroundings. The neighbourhoods that had sired the first crime families, such as the Lower East Side and much of Brooklyn, were vastly different places. Vincent Gigante's Greenwich Village, for example, was approximately 30 per cent Italian when the Chin was a young man.[25] By the time he began tottering around outside his mother's apartment in his bathrobe, it had become far more common to see college students and young bohemians walking along Sullivan Street. Cicero, once the headquarters of Al Capone's empire, experienced an even more dramatic transformation by the end of the twentieth century. Between 1980 and 2000, the Hispanic population of this Chicago suburb jumped from 9 to nearly 75 per cent, a change enabled by the departure of most of the area's long-residing Czech and Italian inhabitants.[26] As white flight emptied other older immigrant quarters, many dons and soldiers moved to anonymous suburbs where their look and culture appeared increasingly out of place. This sense of disconnect lingers in the background of many of the mafia opuses produced by Hollywood from the 1970s forward. Martin Scorsese's *Mean Streets* first captures these unfolding disparities in the very early 1970s. While the young hood played by Harvey Keitel grapples with issues of

Catholic guilt, family obligation and interracial attraction, the world around his home in New York's Little Italy has moved well beyond these hangups. As a group of aspiring soldiers and no-good hoodlums, Keitel and his friends are mere bystanders to changes wrought by the sexual revolution and the city's evolving landscape. While *The Godfather* looks nostalgically at the past, *Mean Streets* portrays the Mafia's men of honour as they appeared in the present day – awkward and out of sync.

When Scorsese released *Mean Streets* in 1973, observers in France did not perceive Marseille's imminent decline. The police raids that smashed the city's many heroin labs wounded but did not kill the city's leading clans. Their power, however, became more diffused as the price of doing business increased. Some leaders, such as Marcel Francisci, relocated to Paris. Others moved to Corsica. The heroin industry was largely relocated to Sicily and Turkey by the end of the decade. As in the United States, those who remained at the helm of Marseille's underworld now tended to be younger, dismissive of the old order and prone to violence. The paragon of this generational shift was Gaëtan 'Tany' Zampa. Tany's pedigree as a gangster was almost ideal. His father, a Neapolitan merchant seaman, was an early confederate of François Spirito and Paul Carbone, a connection that afforded him equally close relations to Le Milieu's earliest patron, the politician-turned-Nazi collaborator Simon Sabiani. It was with these ties that Tany also forged relations with Marseille's long-serving post-war mayor, Gaston Defferre.[27] What Zampa lacked was any inclination for compromise or moderation. After 1973 he went to war with two rival godfathers, Francis the Belgian and Jack the Madman, leaving a trail of murdered soldiers and former associates of the French Connection. The bloodletting continued for years. When the government resumed its attack on Marseille's gangs in the late 1970s, its lead investigator, Judge Pierre Michel, was assassinated (likely on Zampa's orders). Affairs grew even more chaotic after Tany's arrest and prison suicide in 1985. Within a year of his death, as many as thirty-five gangsters died in internecine warfare.[28] 'The thugs, the "men", as they like to call themselves, have lost their minds on the Côte d'Azur,' one commentator lamented. 'They no longer speak, they no longer negotiate, in short, they no longer coexist. They shoot, they shoot each other, they get shot.'[29]

The likes of Jack the Madman and Francis the Belgian narrowly survived Zampa's reign of terror but Marseille was changing for the worse. An enduring housing crisis following the Second World War inspired the government to build massive low-rent estates outside the city centre. Large numbers of people decamped from the once-thriving medieval core to the grim high-rises encircling Marseille. Meanwhile, the region's economy stagnated as port traffic declined. Criminals, including some of the last caïds, found new homes in the city's dystopian suburbs. With the loss of France's colonial holdings in North Africa, hundreds of thousands of expatriated citizens arrived at the city's harbour. The collapse of French rule in Algeria in 1962 brought a flood of some 200,000 refugees, overwhelming the nearly 800,000 inhabitants living in Marseille.[30] Even though immigrants never totalled more than 8.5 per cent of the population, locals perceived a changing of the guard in the city's underworld, with a younger generation of North African gangsters replacing the old Corsican and Neapolitan bosses.[31]

Similar patterns affected Naples. A post-war housing shortage led to an even more intensive government building programme for the city's poor. The hills above Naples gradually became one of the most densely populated districts in Europe, with an average of over 3,000 residents packed into a square mile.[32] It was at the height of Campania's mass suburbanisation that Italy's economy began to flatline. As a region that enjoyed only partial gains from the country's post-war growth, Naples and its environs became ground zero for unemployment. As the ranks of jobless youths swelled among the residents of Naples' overcrowded housing estates, the Camorra found itself reborn through the efforts of a young and charismatic sociopath. Raffaele Cutolo had no history or family ties with Naples' Honour Society before he first entered prison. Yet after repeated violent offences he took it upon himself to organise a select number of his fellow inmates into something that resembled the Camorra of old. Borrowing from what he read in books, as well as the rites of the 'Ndrangheta (in which he was likely inducted), Cutolo fashioned a gang that mimicked the rituals and cruel solemnity of nineteenth-century camorristi. His New Camorra Organisation (*Nuova Camorra Organizzata*), however, was more personality cult than crime fraternity. His studiously maniacal persona garnered a following that branched out beyond the walls of the prison that held him, leading to an empire comprising ex-cons who worked their way into drug trafficking and extortion schemes. By the end of the 1970s, Cutolo's New Camorra was strong enough to challenge traditional camorristi and mafiosi who controlled cigarette smuggling and other vices around Campania. The clash between these new and old forces resulted in a war of extermination. In a five-year period spanning the 1970s and '80s, an estimated 1,000 people were murdered in tit-for-tat assassinations and massacres.[33] Cutolo's bloody defiance of the traditional Camorra, as well as reports of the life of comfort he led behind bars, belatedly prompted government action. In June 1983, over 800 individuals were arrested by a force of 8,000 policemen and carabinieri.[34] The execution of these and other 'maxi-blitzes', as well as Cutolo's transfer to a more secluded state of detention, brought Nuova Camorra's campaign of terror to an end. But Naples would never be the same. With the city recovering from a devastating earthquake in 1980, an unruly admixture of new and old Camorra sank its teeth deeper into the region's economy and politics. 'In areas dominated by the camorra,' as one parliament report put it 1993, 'society, companies and public bodies tend to become dependent on the camorra organization.' Now more than ever the Camorra cemented itself as 'a great mediator' at the intersection of the state, the market and public at large. 'Services, financial resources, votes or the buying and selling of goods: all are subject to camorra mediation,' the report concluded. 'The camorra's activities create a generalised "rule of non-law".'[35]

A more profound crisis was unfolding in Sicily. An uneasy peace held among the island's families in the years that followed the Ciaculli Massacre in 1963. Those conditions changed as the 1970s began. Despite the restoration of an American-style 'Commission', tensions grew among the island's reigning captains. Central to this looming upheaval were simmering levels of discontent within Corleone, the fabled mountain birthplace of Coppola's fictional Godfather. Though historically poorer and more remote than Palermo to the north, Corleone nurtured a younger generation of capos who wished to prove they were not mere 'peasants'.[36] At the head of the Corleonesi push for power was Salvatore 'Toto' Riina. At the age of forty-four, Riina ascended his native clan by way of his reputation for murder and ambition. With the migration of French chemists to Sicily after the crackdown in Marseille, traditional sources of mafia income, such as construction contracts and cigarette smuggling, increasingly paled in comparison to the heroin trade. 'Then,' as one of his allies put it, 'we all became millionaires; suddenly, within a couple of years, thanks to drugs.'[37] By 1982, Sicilian traffickers were supplying heroin users in the northeast of the United States with 80 per cent of their product, netting them in the process a previously unimaginable fortune.[38]

Riina patiently clawed away at the authority of Palermo's principal capos. Between 1972 and 1974, he organised the kidnappings of two high-profile citizens from the town, acts that degraded the standing of Palermo's underworld leaders. Riina's marginalisation of his rivals took another step forward with the expulsion of his main rival from Sicily's Commission, an act that transformed the body into an instrument of Riina's will. In 1981, the Corleonesi unleashed their full wrath with the killing of multiple rival bosses. Topping off the slaughter were the murders of multiple police chiefs and political leaders based in Palermo. Until the outbreak of this 'Second Mafia War', representatives of the Italian state had been immune from violence, but the slaying of the city's prefect, General Carlo Alberto Dalla Chiesa, changed that. Thereafter, denunciations and anger towards the Mafia poured in from various quarters of Italian life, including from the high Catholic clergy (although, tellingly, Pope John Paul II avoided directly condemning the Mafia and its culture of silence during his visit to Palermo in 1982).[39] For officials in Rome, the Mafia posed another daunting challenge to their authority. At the same time the Corleonesi began their war, authorities struggled to put down leftist insurgents led by the Red Brigade. For all the Mafia's past transgressions, the murder of Palermo's most senior administrator was the final straw. Representatives from across Italy's fractured political landscape came together in forming a new 'anti-mafia' parliamentary commission. An even more effective innovation came with the establishment of the first of the so-called 'maxi trials' in 1986. Armed with greater authority and the backing of public opinion, Rome entrusted a Sicilian-bred judge, Giovanni Falcone, to pursue Dalla Chiesa's killers. Falcone took to his calling with vigour and indicted 475 individuals with various mafia-related crimes. An especially designated two-storey bunker, which was surrounded by stone walls and armoured vehicles, served as the main venue for the proceedings against these and hundreds of other offenders that followed.[40]

A central enabler of Falcone's investigation was the nostalgic Palermo boss Tommaso Buscetta, the first of many *pentiti*, or mafia defectors, to co-operate with the Italian government. A series of personal horrors, including the disappearance of two of his children, was instrumental in compelling Buscetta to abandon his blood oath. His rapport with Falcone yielded a treasure trove of revelations that helped initiate criminal indictments against mafiosi in both Italy and the United States. The principal focus of his rage, Toto Riina, remained undaunted. Having lived in hiding from the police since 1970, he and his Corleonesi faction intensified their campaign against the Italian state. Between 1990 and 1993, Italy was torn asunder in mafia violence, with nearly 700 people losing their lives in Sicily alone. The murder epidemic spread to Campania and Calabria, hotbeds of the Camorra and 'Ndrangheta, leading to an additional 1,100 killed in mob warfare.[41] Riina's most startling blow came in May 1992 with a car bombing that killed Giovanni Falcone and his young wife. Riina upped the ante with another bomb attack in Palermo, this one killing a second prominent anti-mafia judge, Paolo Borsellino. The terror the Corleonesi hoped to inspire promptly backfired. In an unprecedented display of local solidarity, tens of thousands of residents in Palermo took to the street in a silent candlelit march to commemorate Falcone's passing. Parliament just as bravely rushed through a series of long-needed reforms. Among the new powers acquired by the government in Rome was the ability to dismiss municipal governments and the creation of an exclusive law enforcement body dedicated to fighting organised crime.

Rome's adoption of more effective measures against the Mafia reflected an even deeper current of discontent building among Italian citizens. Amid the incessant waves of violence sweeping over Italy's south, a series of corruption scandals rocked the capital in the early 1990s. Italy's judiciary responded with a much touted 'clean hands' campaign. Within months, 200 parliamentarians were under investigation for illicit dealings.[42] The perception that the country's most stalwart parties were available for purchase prompted indelible signs of voter outrage at the polls.

Between Decline and Revolution

With the Cold War over, and Europe moving closer towards economic integration, continued electoral defeats forced Italy's most popular parties, the Christian Democrats and the Communist Party, to disband themselves by 1994. Salvatore Riina's surprise apprehension in early 1993 brought only a modest amount of joy among the country's commentariat. 'With the arrest of Riina,' one snarky journalist wrote, 'Italy enters Europe.'[43] For a time, however, the country's troubles continued to deepen. Rather than accept their boss's capture, hardline Corleonesi gangsters launched an even more shocking assault on the Italian mainland. A series of bombings targeting churches, an art gallery and other sites in the country's north left dozens dead or wounded in 1993. Despite reports that officials in Rome sought to negotiate an end to the Mafia's terror campaign, the anti-mafia movement pressed forward in earnest. Between 1991 and 1993, state authorities dissolved forty-two city councils on charges of wrongdoing.[44] Among the politicians caught up in Italy's anti-corruption sweep was former Prime Minister Giulio Andreotti, who stood accused of murder and other crimes by noted pentiti Tommaso Buscetta. Though multiple courts acquitted Andreotti of these charges, testimony of other mafia turncoats cut deeply into the ranks of all of Italy's honour societies. In the twenty years that followed Giovanni Falcone's death, Italy's elite anti-mafia force, the DIA, issued nearly 10,000 arrest warrants for individuals linked to the Cosa Nostra, the Camorra and 'Ndrangheta.[45] Aiding many of these prosecutions were thousands of pentiti who testified on the government's behalf.

By the start of the new millennium, Italy's south was a far safer place than it was at the height of Salvatore Riina's war against Rome. By 2011, Italy's judiciary and police forces had affected a 97 per cent drop in mafia-related murders in Sicily compared to the early 1990s, with similar declines in Campania and Calabria.[46] Improved policing was not the only thing weakening Italy's criminal brotherhoods. Large sections of Italian civil society continued to embrace the anti-mafia movement long after the assassination of Giovanni Falcone. Efforts towards 'cultural re-education' in Sicily led to school programs aimed at pre-empting youth crime and fighting the mafia's code of omerta. Individual and collective campaigns against gang extortion also took hold in Naples and Calabria. Reductions in state investment and contracting had an even more fundamental effect on the economic and institutional influence of Italy's mafias. The contraction of the Italian welfare state, however, had ancillary effects that continued to feed the ranks of local clans and gangs. One study in the 1990s discovered that up to 40 per cent of Sicily's 'at risk youth' abandoned their schooling, a problem that helped sustain the Mafia's ability to recruit and refresh its ranks.[47] As it was in the past, poverty and the limits of government power remained integral to Italy's 'honoured societies'.

Japan experienced nothing like the traumas witnessed in Italy during its tumultuous 'years of lead', but a similar change took hold of the yakuza. As the 1970s drew to close, the Yamaguchi-gumi, Japan's largest criminal confederation, had consolidated control over much of the country's main island. Its steady ascendency was hampered when a gunman nearly snatched the life of its long-serving leader, Kazuo Taoka. Though shot in the neck, Kazuo survived long enough to exact revenge. The brief gang war that followed was as brazen as any under the 65-year-old's tenure as boss. Within a year, Taoka invited the nation's press corps to his home. There, before a crowd of nearly sixty news reporters, his lieutenants read a prepared statement apologising to both the nation and the government for the 'trouble' caused over the preceding months.[48] The hour-long news conference was unprecedented, but pointed to the changes that lay ahead.

In 1981, Kazuo Taoka met his end at the hands of heart disease.

His funeral was no less than a national event. As thousands of mourners assembled before awaiting television cameras and riot police, there was uncertainty as to who would take the reins of the Yamaguchi-gumi. His appointed successor had been thrown in prison and soon succumbed to cirrhosis of the liver. Taoka's remarkable wife, Fumiko, remained the caretaker of his empire for the next three years. Her careful, unspoken leadership could not compensate for lack of consensus over the Yamaguchi's future. Nor could it arrest other tides unfavourable to the yakuza. Japan's mafia could still operate in the open in the early 1980s because the police force was tolerant of its flagrant disregard for order and the safety of average citizens. Yakuza leaders remained at least nominally revered members of the country's elite, but their ranks were beginning to age. In 1966, the number of yakuza members who were over the age of forty was only 14 per cent. By 1986, 36 per cent were either forty years old or older.[49] While the Yamaguchi-gumi wrestled with the question of its leadership, its most powerful benefactor, Yoshio Kodama, was wasting away in hospital. Despite the decades he spent as the Yakuza's principal broker between the country's business and political establishment, Kodama ran into legal trouble towards the end of his life. In 1976, he stood accused of funnelling over $12 million in bribes to politicians on behalf of the American arms contractor, Lockheed.[50] Subsequent police raids on his home added to his woes, leading to charges of tax evasion. With his death in 1984, there was no one left in Japan with his gravitas and pull within Tokyo. Nor was there anyone who could make peace among the yakuza.

Matters worsened when Fumiko Taoka ceremoniously recognised Masahisa Takenaka, a hardnosed veteran of the Yamaguchi, as her husband's rightful successor. A vote among a gathering of 104 minor bosses sealed Takenaka's selection, despite charges of bribery and coercion. His rival for Fumiko's favour, Hiroshi Yamamoto, refused to accept the final tally, leading him and

14,000 other Yamaguchi-gumi members to break away from the clan.[51] Cash pay-offs and other promises persuaded many of those who had recanted their allegiance to return. Yamamoto and others in his newly established Ichiwa-kai clan refused to give up without a fight. Within a year of Takenaka's coronation, Ichiwa-kai hitmen slaughtered the Yamaguchi boss as he visited his mistress's apartment building in Osaka, triggering the most violent of the yakuza wars. For the next five years the Japanese public looked on with morbid fascination as the two sides whittled away at one another. One tabloid paper maintained a daily record of casualties on the front page under the title 'Today's Yama-Ichi War Scorecard'.[52] Yet compared to the hundreds left dead by the Corleonesi push for power, the Yamaguchi civil war was trifling. Of the more than 300 clashes recorded during this period, only twenty-five yakuza died as a result of violence.[53]

The relative lack of bloodletting in the Yamaguchi civil war was not the only difference that set Japan apart from Italy. The decade that produced this conflict was a boom time for the country's corporations and investors. Stock prices quadrupled during a six-year period, topping off at all-time recording on the last day of trading in 1989.[54] Rising corporate earnings and societal prosperity drove a frenzy in the domestic property market (not to mention major building and land acquisitions internationally as well). Japan's bubble years did not escape the attention of the yakuza. While leaders in the old Yamaguchi confederation warred with one another, clans throughout the country exploited the blossoming economy to the best of their abilities. Exorbitant property values incentivised the growth of a yakuza-led industry dedicated to forcing resistant tenants and owners to vacate or sell their homes or parcels of land. Large and small corporations relinquished shares of their profits under the threat of violence or blackmail. Senior clan leaders and larger yakuza confederations were just as likely to legitimately buy into the surging economy.

Banks and brokerage firms abetted the avarice of the yakuza with cheap loans and insider schemes.

The bursting of this boom economy in the early 1990s hurt Japan's underworld in more ways than one. Yakuza clans suffered equally among those with vested stakes in land deals and the stock market. With workers saving more or earning less, yakuza-run bars, clubs, brothels and gambling houses drew fewer customers. Above all, it was the law that would hit the yakuza hardest. After years of news stories featuring yakuza violence and corporate maleficence, the Japanese parliament enacted legislation targeting those involved in organised crime. The 1991 criminal justice reforms did not go as far as outlawing membership in a yakuza clan (a position rejected by many Japanese citizens as against the right of association). It did assign serious penalties to any group identified with the yakuza that engaged in exploitative acts of violence.

Further embellishments of the law added to the scope of yakuza-related crimes and created programs dedicated to pre-empting youth recruitment into local gangs. With yakuza-linked entities and individuals racking up as much 80 per cent of the country's bad loan debt, civil courts became an ever more important venue for those seeking justice and compensation. Yet as one lawyer for the Yamaguchi-gumi publicly declared, others deserved greater blame for the country's economic struggles. The banks, he argued, were like *kashimoto*, or yakuza loan sharks, who ensnare unlucky gamblers. 'It could be said that in the "bubble era", one hundred million people were gamblers, and in this game they used land as the tool for gambling, and the banks played the role of *kashimoto*. I think they are the ones who should be blamed.'[55]

Hong Kong's triads fared much better than the yakuza during the last decades of the twentieth century. Unlike in Japan, British colonial authorities sought no new controls over secret societies. In the 1990s, 4 per cent of all crimes committed in Hong Kong were connected in some way to the triads.[56] What awaited the triads was a far more dramatic change in regime. With British colonial rule ending in 1997, life under the Chinese Communist Party posed new challenges and tantalising prospects. As far back as the mid-1980s, Western journalists were warning of mass flight from Hong Kong. With tens of thousands of residents seeking to depart the colony for fear of Communist rule, many assumed triad gangs would join the exodus.[57] Such predictions proved only partially correct. Rather than leaving the colony for the Americas or Europe, many triads eyed a move to the Chinese mainland. Indications of this development emerged in the wake of economic reforms by Mao's successor, Deng Xiaoping. Deng's decision to ease China into market capitalism in 1978 brought with it impressive economic growth and unrivalled investment opportunities. Previously sleepy towns such as Shenzhen became inundated with workers and foreign entrepreneurs, a cohort that included triads from abroad. As early as 1982, police in the region arrested over six dozen triad members hailing from Hong Kong. A decade later, that number climbed to 338.[58] Yet there were early hints from the heights of the Chinese Communist Party that triad expansion into the People's Republic was acceptable. In a shocking statement issued in 1984, Chairman Deng contended that there were at least some triads that were 'good' and 'patriotic'. As the clock ticked down to 1997, other senior Chinese embellished upon these sentiments. One official speaking after the party's crackdown on pro-democracy demonstrators in Tiananmen Square pointedly invited loyal secret societies to do business in the country. 'As for organisations like the Triads in Hong Kong, as long as these people are patriotic, as long as they are concerned with Hong Kong's prosperity and stability, we should unite with them.'[59]

Events in neighbouring Macau made it clear that there were limits to Beijing's permissive attitude. As a long-neglected outpost of the once mighty Portuguese empire, the city had become a commercial afterthought by the early 1800s. To compensate for its

Between Decline and Revolution

lack of material trade or tax revenue, Portuguese administrators made the fateful decision to turn their enclave into an entrepôt of a different sort. Gambling was legalised in the mid-nineteenth century and eventually became a government monopoly. Yet Macau hardly resembled Monte Carlo. Beyond the Second World War it retained a reputation for drawing in 'the flotsam of the sea, the derelicts, and more shameless, beautiful, savage women'.[60] Having survived the Japanese occupation relatively intact, Macau's gambling industry underwent a slow renaissance in the post-war era. Newer, larger, nicer casinos took root along the city harbour by the mid-1970s.

It was in this environment that Macau's most famous gangster and triad, 'Broken Tooth' Wan, was born. Following a typical trajectory, Wan Kwok Koi was born into poverty and had a youth marred by violence. He got his moniker after losing nine teeth in one of many street fights.[61] By the mid-1980s, Wan's status as a thug for the 14K earned him a place as an overseer of several casino VIP lounges run by his triad. His rise to the top of Macau's underworld culminated in a bloody gang war in the late 1990s. While literally fighting for his life, Wan nonetheless spared his time and money to invest in the production of a film documenting his life story. At the price of nearly $1.7 million, *Casino* was released in Hong Kong in 1998 to middling reviews and ticket sales.[62] The film mattered even less to law enforcement. With dozens left either dead or wounded as a result of gang violence, a Macau court sentenced Wan to fifteen years in prison in 1999. Less than a month later, Chinese troops entered Macau with the expiration of Portugal's lease over the colony. Unlike in Hong Kong two years earlier, Broken Tooth Wan's war moved Macau's citizens to greet the People's Liberation Army's arrival with cheers. Thereafter, blatant displays of triad power and violence were no longer tolerated.

Beijing's raw demonstration of force was in keeping with the times. The end of Wan Kwok Koi's bloody hold over Macau mirrored other counter-offensives targeting organised crime throughout the world. The disjointed retreat of mafias in the United States, France, Japan, Italy and southern China was not a coincidence. It represented the culmination of a global reckoning with organised crime that had begun decades earlier. By the end of the 1990s, world media outlets had grown accustomed to covering the exploits and dangers posed by both native and transnational criminal syndicates. More importantly, governments everywhere understood that mafias were a global problem that demanded a collective response.

As the undisputed victor of the Cold War, the United States again played an outsized role in mapping out a universal plan of action. Passive and active US influence increasingly changed the ways many states were policing mafias through the 1990s. Direct American lobbying, as well as advice on the part of G. Robert Blakey, compelled Canada to adopt RICO-style laws. Other states, particularly in Europe, drew upon American legal models in composing their own anti-organised crime legislation. In 1994, the Clinton administration held an unprecedented international conference called 'Global Organized Crime: The New Empire of Evil'. Attendees at the gathering took in addresses by the heads of the FBI and CIA, who warned the governments of the world that many states were finding 'their authority besieged at home and their foreign policy interests imperiled abroad'.[63] The 1994 Washington summit gave momentum to an even more ambitious push shepherded by the United Nations. By the year 2000, the UN convened a meeting of nations in the city of Palermo. Sicily's principal town delighted in the international spotlight. With the spectre of La Cosa Nostra largely banished from view, Italy's President Carlo Azeglio Ciampi went as far as to kick off the event in Salvatore Riina's old stronghold of Corleone. Under the watchful eye of 10,000 security officials, delegates from 120 nations formally agreed to sign a formal UN Convention Against Transnational Organized Crime that December.[64] As an agreement drafted in the spirit of earlier conventions on the global threats posed by drug trafficking and terrorism, the accord obliged its signatories to recognise the existence of transnational crime syndicates and to amend criminal codes and other mechanisms to punish money laundering and corruption.

The convention's heavy emphasis on the need for greater coordination on the financial aspects of organised crime similarly reflected Washington's influence over the UN Convention. By the year 2000, successful prosecution cases against the American Mafia had led many officials in Washington to tout the importance of pursuing organised crime's ill-gotten gains. In addition to a potential sentence of up to twenty years in prison, conviction under federal RICO statutes allowed judges latitude to seek the forfeiture of all assets acquired as a result of a crime and impose fines of up to twice the amount of the felon's illegal earnings.[65] For many American mobsters, however, the threat of going to court alone was difficult to stomach. Among the snippets of conversation FBI wiretaps gleaned from his headquarters in New York's Little Italy, John Gotti was heard raving against the costs he paid to his lawyers. The thought of paying over $117,000 for printing and photocopying sent him into a rage. 'They're overpriced, overpaid, and–' 'And they underperformed,' one capo chimed in. 'I don't even know,' Gotti spat. 'I don't even know about underperformed. They just can't win, Frank ... They got no fuckin' cohesion. They got no unity. It's like us ...'[66]

Gotti's unknowing admission appears to suggest that the Gambino crime family was less of a financial juggernaut than government prosecutors made it out to be. Given what was known of the Medellín cartel, it is difficult to visualise Pablo Escobar privately lamenting the need to pay tens of thousands of dollars in legal fees. This imagined disparity between Gotti and Escobar, however, strikes at a critical truth about this period of mafia history. The cocaine trade, and the profits that came with it, were altering the scale and gravity of what it meant to be a gangster.

THE COCAINE REVOLUTION: COLOMBIA, MEXICO AND THE PROLIFERATION OF MAFIAS

In a better world, the province of Antioquia could have been the cradle of great wealth. By the mid-twentieth century, it was the central hub of Colombia's coffee industry, then the country's best-known export. It was also home to significant deposits of gold and Colombia's second largest city, Medellín. To this day, Antioqueños nurture a reputation for being industrious and shrewd. History, however, has been unkind to Antioquia and its people. Colombia won independence from Spain in 1810, but political and economic development were hampered by instability in the following decades. As in Mexico, civil conflicts (nine in total) and foreign intervention weakened the growth and maturation of the Colombian state.[67] Advocates for a more decentralised, secular state clashed repeatedly with their more conservative opponents. These tensions reached a boiling point in 1948 with the assassination of a Liberal presidential candidate by a Conservative extremist. Over the next ten years, more than 200,000 Colombians died because of what came to be called 'La Violencia'. Antioquia was among the hardest hit provinces in the country. Approximately 26,000 residents were killed in the region, many in horrible ways. Another 117,000, or approximately 6 per cent of the population, fled their homes for the United States and elsewhere in the Americas.[68] By the 1990s, American cities (led by New York, Miami and Chicago) collectively hosted somewhere between 450,000 and a million Colombian immigrants.[69]

Pablo Escobar was born and raised in this environment. The Liberal leanings of his mother, a schoolteacher assigned to a small village in the southwest of Antioquia, put his family at odds with the overwhelmingly Conservative character of the province. One night when he was a child, a mob of 'Goths', as the Liberals called their opponents, surrounded the school intent on murder. A detachment of soldiers miraculously saved the family from certain death. As they exited the school, Pablo's family discovered one-time friends and neighbours hung from their feet and beheaded with machetes.[70] After that, Pablo and the rest of his relatives relocated to Medellín. 'There are many people who believe that it was Pablo who brought the terrible violence and death to Colombia, but that isn't true,' his brother Roberto later declared. 'Colombia has always been a country of violence. It was part of our heritage.'[71]

Cocaine played no role in fomenting the massacres of La Violencia. At the time in which Pablo Escobar began a new life in Medellín, the drug was still in short supply in the global marketplace. In the years preceding the Second World War, Peru was the centre of the cocaine trade. Even though American agents rarely seized more than five kilograms a year before 1960, pressure from Harry Anslinger's global crusade against narcotics bore down on Lima.[72] By the 1950s, cocaine manufacturing spread to neighbouring Bolivia, though the illicit networks that took root in La Paz and Santa Cruz never attained the size or coherence of the French Connection's heroin trade. Cocaine production and smuggling instead remained a thoroughly 'mom and pop' industry made up of independent operators from across Latin America. US-led, as well as local, investigations regularly flagged the prevalence of traffickers with more exotic migrant backgrounds (particularly Spanish-speaking Arabs and Asians). The trade also attracted well-heeled and respectable patrons, such as the Bolivian smuggler, Blanca Ibáñez de Sánchez. 'Delicia Herrera', as she was known to her customers, forged an intricate yet personalised web of confederates who aided her in muling multi-kilo loads into the

United States. As a fair, well-dressed woman, her appearance regularly dissuaded American customs officials from inspecting her luggage. Blanca did not tether herself to any mafia, nor did she beget any syndicate that continued her work after she was put out of business in the early 1960s. And even though Latin American traders shipped cocaine to various parts of the world through the early Cold War, no one city produced anything like a monopoly. The closest exception was Havana, which served as a key transit point for smugglers heading north to the States or east to Europe. The start of Castro's tenure at the end of the 1950s ended the city's role in the trade after many of its merchants went into exile. Over the next two decades, Cuban traffickers were the prime suspects of multiple distribution rings inside the United States. As with the early influx of Asian opiates into the United States, law enforcement officials initially interpreted Cuban-run smuggling operations as a communist plot meted out by Castro's spiteful government. Cases from the 1970s eventually undermined this presumption. In 1975, for example, US and Mexican agents executed a sting netting forty suspects linked to a 'Cuban mafia' tied to New Orleans mafia boss Santo Trafficante. A main hub of this 'Cuban mafia' was Las Vegas, where they supplied cocaine to the likes of Anthony Spilotro (the mobster who inspired Joe Pesci's role in the film *Casino*). Several Cubans taken into custody had previously worked in American Mafia-run casinos in Havana and were later trained by the CIA as foot soldiers in the failed Bay of Pigs invasion in 1961.[73]

Cocaine attracted only a few enterprising Colombian traffickers before the 1970s. That did not mean that Colombians were unfamiliar with contraband smuggling as an industry. Colombia's black market was historically enormous due to strict government controls and import duties. The bottomless hunger for foreign goods attracted large numbers of people to the smuggling trade, making it a main form of employment in various provinces. As a child, Pablo Escobar was raised on stories about his grandfather, Roberto, who excelled at smuggling contraband. Though the mayor of a small town, Roberto devilishly transported untaxed whisky past government inspection posts in coffins accompanied with a cohort of mourners dressed in black. Under the cover of night, he removed the whisky and injected it into empty eggshells to be sold to local drinkers.[74] Pablo made his own way into the contraband trade as a teenager, smuggling cigarettes, washer-dryers, guns and other things. His willingness to kill and intimidate without remorse anchored his first enterprises. He was already making hundreds of thousands of dollars by the time he was in his early twenties. Pablo's insatiable ambition and expanding opportunities didn't allow him to rest. Among the parcels he came to ship within his contraband convoys was cocaine paste produced in Peru and Ecuador.

Precisely when Pablo had his 'eureka moment' that led to his transformation into a coke exporter is not clear. By the early 1970s, marijuana cultivation was beginning to expand rapidly. Spurred by growing demand in the United States, large landowners along the Colombian coast invested heavily in cannabis farming. Aiding the sudden growth of Colombia's marijuana industry were networks of distributors formed among Colombian migrants living places such as Miami and New York. As individuals born out of La Violencia of the 1940s and 1950s, many of these early traffickers viciously outmuscled rival syndicates made up of Cuban expatriates. American demand for marijuana eventually reached its absolute limit. By 1975, an estimated 27 per cent of all American high school seniors confessed to smoking weed within the previous month (another 6 per cent purportedly was smoking every day).[75] With market saturation and new strains of cannabis cutting into profits, eager Colombian entrepreneurs looked to cocaine as an alternative product for export.

Unlike New York's Commission, no insiders ever penned

an account of the Medellín Cartel's conception. It likely came together serendipitously. Pablo Escobar's extensive contacts in transport and commerce, coupled with his merciless reputation for violence, were crucial for his breakthrough into the coke market, but so were childhood friendships. Jorge Ochoa met Pablo when they were young. The Ochoa surname, however, needed no introduction. Jorge's father, Don Fabio Ochoa Restrepo, was a well-known landowner, restaurateur, horse breeder and entrepreneur in Medellín well before the cocaine craze gathered steam. Don Fabio's various businesses allowed the family entry into high society as well as leverage among the country's contraband dealers. His sons, Jorge and Fabito, traded on the Ochoa name in becoming familiar with the narcotics trade. By the mid-1970s, the boys dabbled in shipping small quantities of coke to Miami but initially lacked the connections and know-how to establish a thriving business. Pablo Escobar served as a valuable ally.

The Ochoas' greatest assets were land and political clout. Various ranches owned by the family served as laboratories where coca leaves were processed into cocaine. The construction of the fabled Tranquilandia, an immense processing plant located in the Colombian jungle, underscored what became the trademark of Medellín Cartel: cocaine production on an industrial scale. An equally ingenious system of transshipment provided the necessary outlets for the Ochoas' cocaine to flow. A key innovator within the Medellín milieu was Carlos Lehder. Though the son of a well-off German immigrant father and beauty queen mother, Lehder spent his early adulthood stealing cars in the United States and selling them to his brother in Colombia. His transformation into a cocaine importer occurred soon after his release from a federal penitentiary. Lehder was among the first to utilise light aircraft to move cocaine across the US border. His greatest coup was the purchase of a deserted Bahamian island, Norman's Cay, some 70 kilometres southeast of Nassau. Under the protection of corrupt authorities, Norman's Cay was transformed into an unlicensed airport that channeled tons upon tons of cocaine into south Florida. It remains difficult to say how much Lehder made from his operations on the island. Investigators projected that he netted a profit of some $300 million in the years between 1979 and 1980 (a sum totalling over $1.1 billion in contemporary dollars). With Lehder purportedly moving thirty plane-loads of cocaine off Norman's Cay during a single day, it's likely that $300 million is a low estimate.[76]

We still don't know how Lehder, Escobar and the Ochoas allied, but perhaps the greatest mystery is why their organisation came to be known as a 'cartel' as opposed to a 'mafia'. After all, much of the Western public had grown accustomed to the existence of mafias elsewhere in the world. It was likely either an American agent, or a Latin American official, who first uttered the word. Official DEA reports featured the phrase as far back as the early 1970s. What may have inspired the term was the distinct composition of cocaine smuggling networks. Rather than a singular organisation, cocaine traffickers were composed of a collection of independent smugglers, distributors and producers. In the shadow of the energy crisis of the early 1970s, these consortiums likely reminded investigators of the ties formed between oil-producing nations in OPEC. It was this correlation that likely led officials to conceive of cocaine networks as 'cartels'.[77]

What powered the construction of the Medellín Cartel was not the desire to monopolise the cocaine trade nor manipulate the price of the drug. More fundamental to its origins was a shared aversion to material risk. With the assistance of the Ochoas and others, the syndicate found sanctuary among complicit political figures, business leaders and landowners. Exponentially rising profits expanded this umbrella of protection, allowing the cartel to pay off ever larger numbers of state officials. In banding together, otherwise rival smugglers sent their shipments in mixed loads northwards, thus defraying the cost of potential losses by interdiction or accident. Together, everyone made money. Still, even for those on the inside, knowing who actually ran the cartel was a matter of speculation or perspective. For Jon Roberts, née Riccobono, his friendship with Fabito Ochoa provided his main window into the internal dynamics of the organisation. Pablo Escobar, as he saw it, was 'a street guy', someone who enforced order and discipline on behalf of the outfit. Meanwhile, Don Ochoa and Jorge sat back and ruled as the organisation's CEO and president. While everyone got their hands dirty, Don Ochoa 'rode his horses and ate great food. He was just like any other fat fucker sitting on top of a big corporation.' Pablo may have been tough, but it was the Ochoas 'who owned the [coca] leaves'.[78]

How Mexico's modern cartels emerged is a far less opaque story. As older heroin empires began to wane in the 1960s, a younger generation of desirous *narcotraficantes* was breaking new ground. In 1975, Mexican authorities arrested Alberto Sicilia Falcon in his palatial home in the border town of Tijuana. DEA officials had tracked Sicilia Falcon's movements as far back as 1971. Before a federal court, American prosecutors argued that he came to generate a weekly income of up to $3.6 million in cross-border drug sales. Alberto's arrest, on the surface of things, accentuated the apparent rise of a 'Cuban mafia' at work in the United States (it was his 'cartel', according to authorities, that had supplied Santo Trafficante and Vegas mobster Anthony Spilotro).[79] Yet unbeknown to authorities in Mexico City and Washington, Sicilia Falcon's operation was an early indicator of events reshaping drug trafficking all along the US border.

Alberto was a refugee from the 1958 Cuban revolution. He was not yet thirty when he settled in San Diego with an eye towards the dope trade. He somehow drew together a cohort of contacts and suppliers with links to marijuana and opium producers in Sinaloa, as well as cocaine dealers from Colombia. According to witness testimony, he brokered deals worth hundreds of tons of marijuana with leftist Mexican insurgents in exchange for American-made weapons.[80] Such revelations did not surprise American officials or their counterparts south of the border. By the mid-1970s, Mexico was a state racked by rebellion. In the wake of a bloody government crackdown on students in the capital in 1968, at least a dozen guerrilla organisations formed across the country.[81] The proliferation of armed groups occurred as Nixon issued his declaration of war against narcotics traffickers along the border. With the backing of American agents and material support, Mexico's empowered military and police services went to war against suspected leftists and drug suppliers throughout the north of country. Operation Condor, as it came to be known, inflicted a terrible toll upon the Mexican landscape. Whole villages were razed as aircraft sprayed herbicides on countless farms and ranches. Troops killed without consequence and rounded up thousands who were then tortured and imprisoned. By 1978, as many as 3,000 Mexican citizens were killed in clashes with soldiers and police, with another 7,000 brutally tortured while in the state's custody.[82]

Among the regions hardest hit by Operation Condor was the northern state of Sinaloa. As the historic centre of Mexico's illicit opium industry, Sinaloa had been home to generations of families with trafficking experience and strong ties to corrupted members of the country's political elite. The destruction of their properties and businesses forced many to leave the state and seek new opportunities in major cities such as Guadalajara, Tijuana and Ciudad Juárez. Blood relations and marriage nonetheless remained a bond through which they continued to consort and do business. By the mid-1970s, the seeds of what became the Guadalajara Cartel began to sprout. At the head of this grand reordering of Mexico's underworld was an unassuming former policeman named Miguel Angel Félix Gallardo. Miguel's ability to straddle the worlds of crime and politics was the talent that put him on the path to great wealth. He learned the drug trade from one of Sinaloa's oldest and most esteemed traffickers, Pedro Avilés Pérez, the reputed 'Lion of the Sierras'. Avilés ranked among the first Mexican smugglers to transport South American cocaine to the US after having made a fortune in opium and marijuana production. Félix Gallardo also married well, becoming closely linked to the upper echelons of Sinaloa's political class. After displacing Avilés, who was assassinated by Mexican police, he hitched his star to an ambitious cadre of traffickers who also had learned at the Lion's feet. There was Ernesto Fonseca and his nephew, Amado Carrillo Fuentes, who both came from families long involved in the cultivation of opium and marijuana. Rafael ('Rafa') Caro Quintero, the final member of the cartel's triumvirate, also served under Avilés and was the third generation within his family to work as a dope smuggler. Filial ties solidified connections to other fledgling narcotraficantes, such as the Arellano Félix brothers in Tijuana on the American border.[83] A regular schedule of handsome payoffs to Mexico's security service allowed Miguel to utilise Guadalajara, Mexico's second largest city, as the seat of power for the alliance formed among each of these otherwise dubious individuals. As in Medellín, Félix Gallardo's Guadalajara Cartel was an organisation that offered security and predictability for all who signed on. Their collective came to dominate the flow of narcotics across the multiple ports of entry that spanned between San Diego and El Paso. By the early 1980s, their success attracted the attention of surrogates with direct links to Colombia. As American authorities grew more aware of Medellín's influence over the flow of cocaine into Florida, Pablo Escobar and others looked to Guadalajara and the land routes they controlled as a viable alternative for transporting coke into the US. Miguel Félix Gallardo's emergence as the Medellín Cartel's indispensable middleman netted him and his compatriots fortunes estimated in the hundreds of millions of dollars.

Between Decline and Revolution

The cartels of Guadalajara and Medellín differed from old mafias in distinct ways. Neither organisation was born out of an instinctual desire to monopolise vice in its various forms; through to their demise, they remained steadfastly tied to cocaine as their main source of wealth and influence. Though as compact and as easily shipped as heroin, coke initially lacked the stigma of opiates among interested consumers. Its relative scarcity made it even more attractive to its distributors. The immense profit margins that accompanied the mass production and sale of the drug resulted in the rapid expansion of both syndicates. As time passed, even relatively small wholesalers and street dealers were making money beyond their wildest imaginations. Collectively, their cocaine fortunes transformed economies of various sizes. By 1988, drug trafficking accounted for 5 per cent of Colombia's national economy. Narcotics sales in the United States likely registered less than a per cent of America's GDP during the same year but nevertheless weighed in at a projected $100 billion in proceeds.[84] By the start of the new millennium, the drug trade's importance in the United States increased. One Mexican government study projected that the US economy would shrink by as much as 22 per cent if the narcotics trade suddenly vanished. In the case of Mexico, the country's economy would contract by as much as two-thirds.[85] All of these figures, of course, were based upon educated projections. Yet if they were even close to true, they speak to the awesome grip the cocaine trade had upon much of the Americas.

It was at the most local of levels that people tended to perceive cocaine's most outrageous effects. As ground zero for the Medellín Cartel's infiltration of America, Miami generated the greatest amount of attention. In spite of an early history as a sleepy vacation and retirement mecca, the city evolved during the early 1980s into a Xanadu for fashion, entertainment and good looks. By the end of the 1980s, local journalists discovered that Miami's consumers engaged in more cash transactions on cars, real estate, jewellery and legal services than anywhere in the state (and perhaps most places in the country).[86] Evidence of this spending spree was visible through the towering growth of Miami's skyline as well as the mushrooming of shopping plazas, glitzy nightclubs and luxury housing. As early as 1979, federal investigators took note of the increased deposits of what they suspected was drug money in various banks in the Miami area. Over the next decade, the Miami branch of the Federal Reserve boasted surpluses ranging between $4 and $6 billion. The closest comparison to such excessive holdings was the federal bank in Los Angeles, whose own surplus jumped from $165,000 to $3.8 billion between 1985 and 1988.[87]

But in making cocaine more accessible than ever before, Mexican and Colombian traffickers were forced to confront several unanticipated difficulties. 'The more successful we were in smuggling, the less money they made per kilo. That was the twist of it,' Jon Roberts remembered. With the price of a kilo dropping from $50,000 to $6,000 between the late 1970s and early 1980s, traffickers were compelled to sell more cocaine to more buyers in order maintain their original profit margins.[88] This increased competition often led to violence and disorder. The advent of crack in the mid-1980s brought even greater unwanted exposure. Though smoking coca base had gained popularity throughout South America through 1970s, the popularisation of rock cocaine among American addicts ushered in an onslaught of media hysteria and political handwringing. Rising homicide rates across urban centres, as well as gut-wrenching images of addicted 'crack babies', came to be seen as evils that could be directly traced to the cartels of Mexico and Colombia. For all of its outward glamour, Miami appeared to embody the darkest elements of the cocaine revolution. In 1975, the city's metro area was the scene of some fifty killings. By 1981, that number had climbed to 600.[89] Other factors, such as the availability of firearms, exacerbated the problem. Of all the murders committed in Miami in 1980, roughly 23 per cent were committed with a machine gun. Commentators and politicians also saw the violence as an outgrowth of immigration. Since the mid-century, the city had welcomed in thousands of Cubans and other newcomers from Latin America. Amid the exponential rise in violence in south Florida, a second great wave of migrants hit the city as tens of thousands of Cuban and Haitian refugees arrived from across the sea. The belief that many of the Cubans were former inmates expelled by Fidel Castro induced an increase in hostility towards the city's Latin American residents. In a demonstration of their discontent with the changing environment, Miami voters turned out in droves to pass an ordinance in 1980 forbidding the city to spend public funds on programs promoting bilingualism.[90]

Personal observations, as well as accounts drawn from the press, led large numbers of officials to assume that the cartels bore many of the characteristics of more familiar mafias. They appeared to have the look of an American, Italian or Japanese crime family with their respective bosses, capos and soldiers. As in Prohibition, cocaine trafficking inspired a highly corporatised and rational ethos within the business dealings of various syndicates. These similarities appeared to cease, however, when officials reckoned with their exaggerated propensity for violence. By the 1980s, the 'Colombian necktie', a gruesome punishment meted out by the cartels, became common parlance among crime reporters assigned to tackle the drug wars.[91] The assertion that the Medellín Cartel made the Mafia look like 'Sunday school kids' was one that filtered through much of the American and European media. 'Unlike the Mafia,' one US paper warned, 'cocaine traffickers may wipe out the entire family of a rival or transgressor. Wives, husbands, children and even in-laws are considered fair game.'[92]

It is hard to say whether Pablo Escobar or Miguel Félix

Gallardo would have agreed with this assessment. Aspects of their lives, however, left little doubt that they saw the organisations they built as being cut from the same cloth as the American Mafia. Félix Gallardo referred to his organisation as the 'family', not a cartel. Heads of major distribution points in Culiacán, Tijuana and elsewhere were referred to as captains. Their underlings were their soldiers.[93] Pablo exuded an especially unbridled affection for real and imaginary gangsters. He loved *The Untouchables*, a 1960s television series celebrating the exploits of Eliot Ness. He purportedly watched all 120 episodes of the show at least three times. In his interactions with others, he consciously mimicked the 'slow manners and long silences' of Marlon Brando's performance as Vito Corleone.[94] In addition to his private zoo stocked with exotic animals, his estate at Hacienda Nápoles featured a bullet-ridden automobile that he bragged belonged to Bonnie and Clyde and a classic Pontiac supposedly owned by Al Capone. 'The Bonnie and Clyde car had been sold to him by our friend in the United States who introduced us to Frank Sinatra,' his brother Roberto remembered. 'Frank Sinatra was real; I wasn't so certain about those cars.'[95]

One can easily fathom why mafia movies and mob lore imprinted themselves upon Escobar and others who joined the cocaine cartels of the era. Despite early efforts by migrant mafiosi in places such as Argentina during the nineteenth century, La Cosa Nostra never became an engrained force in South America.[96] More than anything, Escobar and others likely saw *The Godfather* as instructional. To this day, recruits in one Mexican cartel are required to watch Coppola's complete trilogy as a necessary tutorial in the meaning of loyalty and family values.[97] Hollywood also internalised the rise of the cartels and projected upon it its own interpretation of their place within history and popular consciousness. Brian De Palma's 1983 remake of *Scarface* reiterated key themes from Howard Hawks's original film, especially

America's tortured relationship with violence and material excess. It also placated the anti-drug sentiments of the American government, with federal prosecutors going as far as to share their files with the film's producers while the picture was in development.[98] Yet as in the case of *The Godfather*, some interpreted De Palma's decision to reimagine the film's main characters as Cuban as an indictment of Latin American immigrants in the country. 'We filmed in Los Angeles because the Cuban community chased us out of Miami,' screenwriter Oliver Stone later declared. 'And unfortunately, once again some of the media portrayed the film as racist. But you have to be very careful, too; every community tends to be very sensitive.'[99]

Song, as well as ritual, initially popularised the exploits of cartels to a far greater degree. As the offspring of families from rural Sinaloa, the founders of the Guadalajara Cartel were raised on ballads and folk traditions that lionised outlaws. Chief among the most revered bandits of Sinaloa was Jesús Malverde. Like the medieval Robin Hood, Malverde likely is an amalgamation of genuine and fictitious brigands who avenged the poor and punished the rich during the nineteenth century. Ballads celebrating his life depict him as a righteous man driven to crime. For his sins, the state executed him and left his body unburied. Whether true or not, Malverde's mythos earned him a shrine in the state's capital of Culiacán. By the advent of the Guadalajara Cartel, his status as a folk saint attained new heights when a chapel was erected near to his supposed resting place. Although never christened by the Catholic Church, the site drew large numbers of devout pilgrims as the cocaine trade grew to gargantuan proportions. Ernesto Fonseca, founder and eldest member of the cartel, is said to have aided in the construction of the chapel.[100] Malverde's growing identification as the patron saint of *los narcos* lent new significance to the songs that celebrated his life. It inspired more contemporary artists to offer the same tribute to Mexico's emerging pantheon of godfathers. By the time he landed in prison, Miguel Félix Gallardo was touted as the 'boss of bosses' in one popular tune. Rafa Caro Quintero received even earlier plaudits as a 'boss of bosses', a man who 'formed a great empire that is giving to this day' (in the words of the popular group, Los Invasores de Nuevo León).

Before Pablo Escobar's heyday, ballads of this sort were unheard of in Colombia. Rumour has it that the narcocorrido made its way into the country after one ranking member of the cartel visited Culiacán on business.[101] Escobar eventually attained his own songs of tribute, but an even greater honour awaited him after his death. Like Malverde, his tomb became a site of pilgrimage for curiosity seekers, well-wishers and desperate visitors hoping to obtain his blessings from beyond the grave. Years after his passing, at least some locals maintained that Escobar was a good Catholic deserving of such reverence. He was a murderer and drug trafficker, one councilman admitted. 'Of course,' he added, 'and this will sound ugly to say, but if it were not for the fact that he opened the doors to the drug market, Colombia would be a poor country like Haiti.'[102]

In life, Pablo Escobar aspired to be something more than a narco saint. With a vast fortune at his disposal, he imagined himself ascending to Colombia's presidency by the early 1980s. 'At no time did he believe his business would prevent him from having a political career,' his brother Roberto observed. 'Even in America it was well known that the father of the beloved JFK had made a fortune from the sale of illegal alcohol.' What Pablo and the Kennedys had in common was the necessary power, financial or otherwise, to realise their political goals.[103] It was with this in mind that he stood for election to Colombia's Chamber of Representatives. A self-serving populism, tinged with anti-American nationalism, was his platform as a Liberal Party candidate. He declared his intention to build a thousand housing units on the north side of Medellín on land formerly used as a landfill. His vision of a 'Medellín without slums' also embraced plans to construct schools, hospitals, roller rinks and soccer fields catering to the poor. Assisting Pablo were hired publicists who lauded his good works through his own radio show and personal newspaper.[104]

Winning a term in office did not endear him to the country's political establishment. Senior Liberal leaders seized upon press reporting of Escobar's earlier arrest as a drug trafficker and successfully expelled him from the party within a year of his election. Yet for all his apparent iniquities, Pablo Escobar and the Medellín Cartel did not yet rank as a clear threat to Colombian sovereignty and security. At the time of his brief political career, Bogotá was in the grip of a far more dangerous struggle with leftist guerrillas. The most dominant group, the Armed Revolutionary Forces of Colombia (or FARC), eventually took control of 40 per cent of the country's territory by the late 1990s.[105] At first, the Medellín Cartel was not immune to leftist violence. In 1981, militants seized the daughter of Don Fabio Ochoa for ransom, an act that led to a swift and indelible response. After forging an agreement with fellow traffickers, business leaders and landowners, the cartel's patriarch helped form a counter paramilitary group aptly named Death to Kidnappers (better known by its Spanish acronym, MAS). MAS's brutal offensive set a serious of vicious precedents. Bogotá's fragile hold over law and order worsened as private anti-guerrilla armies akin to MAS proliferated. Rather than escalate their war against the cartel, leftist guerrillas eventually made their peace with both the drug trade and the cartels. In the hopes of boosting their material strength, the FARC, as well as other militant organisations, turned to cocaine as a revenue source. The kidnappers who had offended Don Ochoa went to greater lengths to compromise with Escobar and the Cartel. When the government sought to finalise an extradition treaty with the United States in 1985, scores of fighters attacked the country's Palace of Justice. By the time Colombian security forces regained control of the building, half of the country's supreme court lay dead. Though never categorically proven, it is generally believed that Escobar helped engineer the assault.

The attack on the Palace of Justice punctuated a period of growing uncertainty for the Medellín Cartel. Awareness of the scale of illegal cocaine production peaked with the discovery of Tranquilandia, the cartel's massive conversion laboratory. With American technical assistance in hand, elite Colombian troops seized the immense compound in March 1984. The destruction of metric tons of unrefined coca paste was a transgression neither Pablo nor other cartel members could forgive or forget. Though he managed to cow the government into quashing a warrant issued against him, Escobar ordered the assassination of the country's justice minister, Rodrigo Lara Bonilla. Ongoing fears of apprehension and extradition intensified the cartel's fury. The war Escobar and his associates waged against the Colombian state left a death toll that exceeded the worst years of Salvatore Riina's campaign against Rome. Some 200 judges and 700 police officers died combatting the Medellín Cartel over the next decade. Perhaps thousands more, most of them innocent bystanders, were also claimed by the fighting.[106] Despite the threat of death and the temptation of enormous cash payoffs, members of Colombia's security establishment doggedly pursued the cartel's principal leaders. The state's persistence eventually paid off. Carlos Lehder was ingloriously captured and sent to the US for trial in 1987. Facing arrest, Fabio Ochoa's sons reluctantly turned themselves in in 1991 (the don himself, however, never faced arrest or trial). A guarantee to serve out his sentence on Colombian soil also enticed Escobar to come in from the cold. For more than a year, Escobar was housed in La Catedral, a cavernous prison he built for himself. His stay there could hardly be called incarceration;

Wikimedia Commons

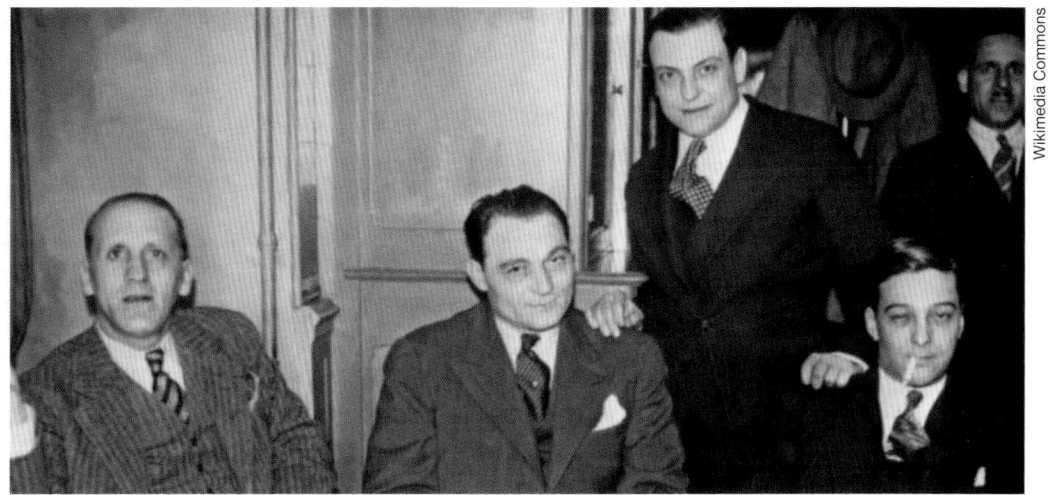

Seated, left to right: Simon Sabiani, Paul Carbone and François Spirito.

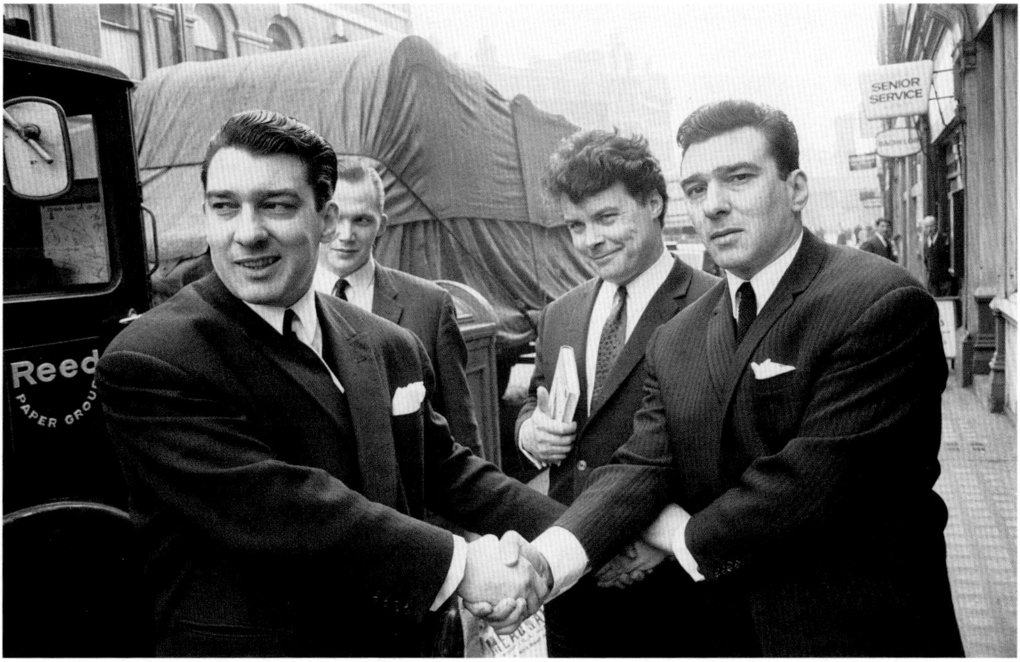

© Trinity Mirror / Mirrorpix / Alamy

The Kray twins celebrate their acquittal on extortion charges in April 1965.

Men stand over the body of Salvatore Giuliano in Castelvetrano, Sicily in 1950.

Joe Valachi (seated on the right) testifies before the US Senate. Against the wall are organisation charts of the Profaci, Bonanno, Gambino, Lucchese and Genovese crime families of New York.

Gambino leader John Gotti

Harry Anslinger, the first commissioner of the US Treasury Department's Federal Bureau of Narcotics.

FBI director William Webster (left) and Rudolph Giuliani during a press conference on mob arrests in February 1985 at the Federal Plaza in Manhattan.

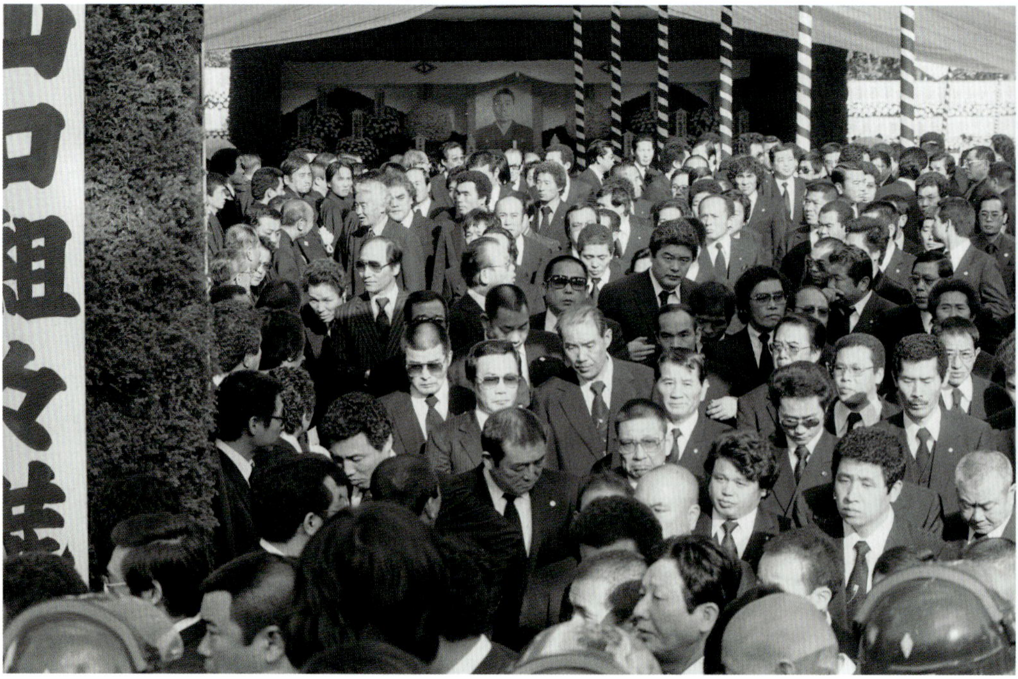

Funeral of Yamaguchi-gumi leader Kazuo Taoka.

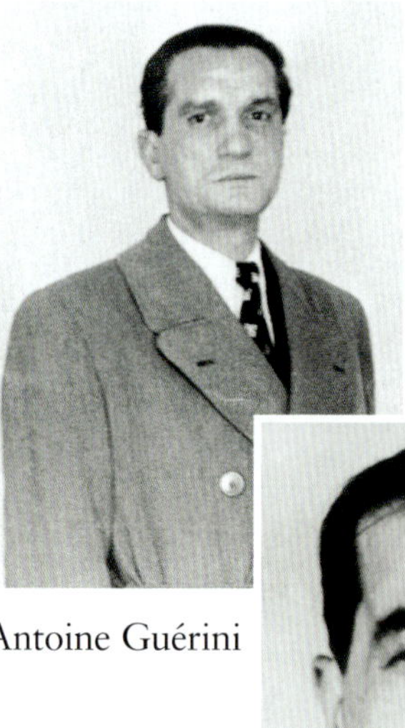

Antoine Guérini

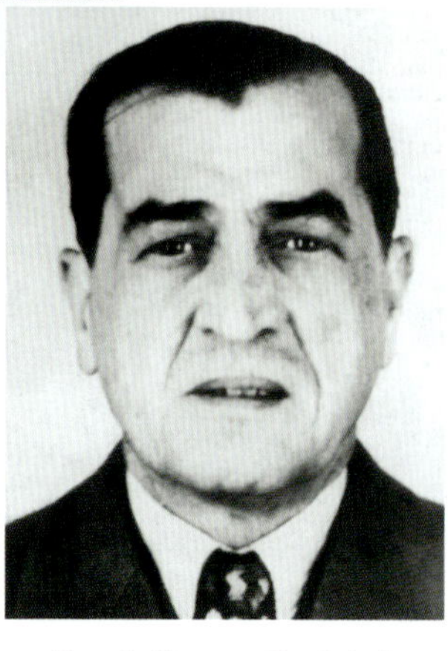

Barthélemy Guérini

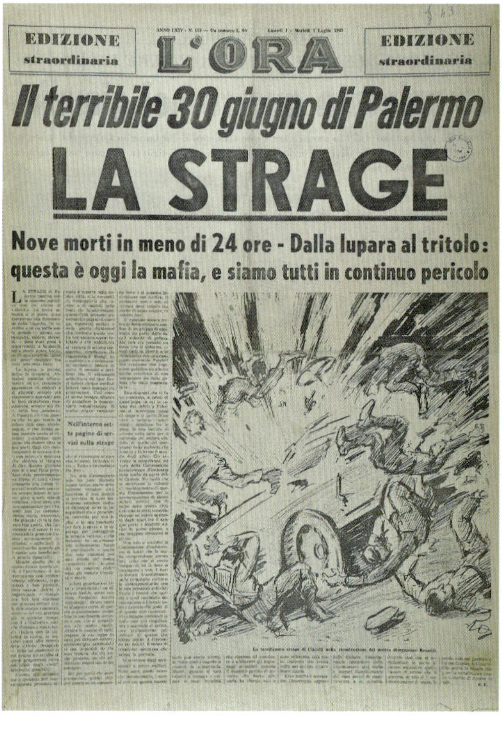

EDIZIONE straordinaria

L'ORA

EDIZIONE straordinaria

Il terribile 30 giugno di Palermo

LA STRAGE

Nove morti in meno di 24 ore - Dalla lupara al tritolo: questa è oggi la mafia, e siamo tutti in continuo pericolo

Nell'interno sei pagine di servizi sulla strage

'The Massacre': front page coverage of the Ciaculli Massacre by Palermo newspaper *L'Ora*, 1 July 1963.

Nigel Burgher / Flickr

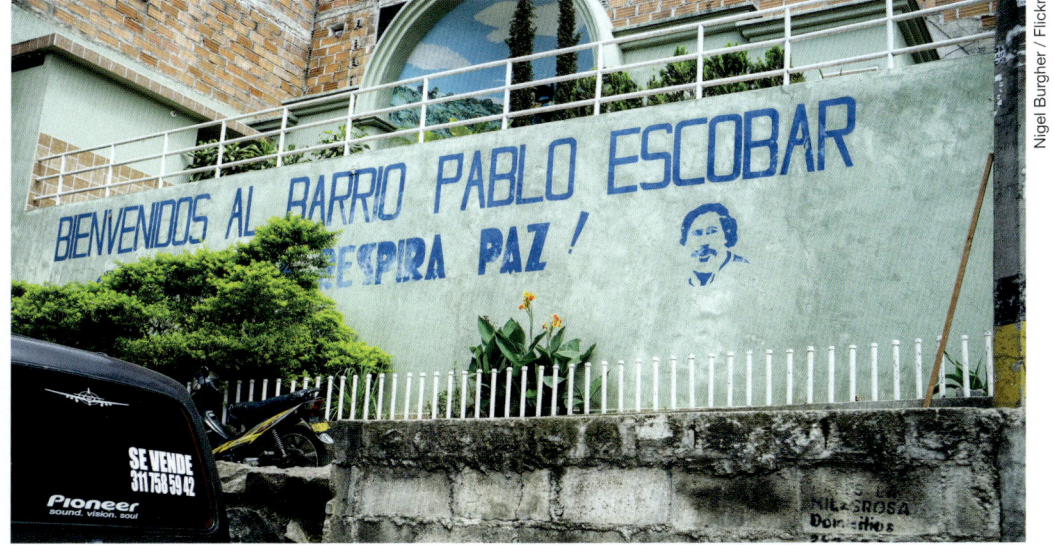

A mural in Medellín, Colombia reads: 'Welcome to Barrio Pablo Escobar. You can feel the peace!'

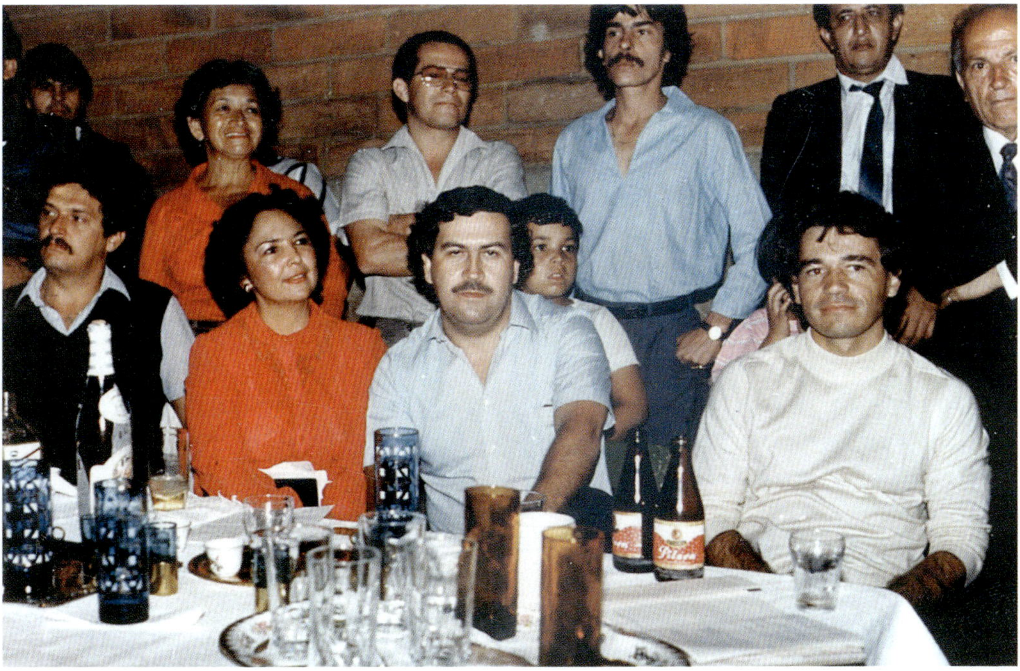

© Abaca Press / Alamy Stock Photo

Pablo Escobar (middle) seated next to Carlos Lehder (front right).

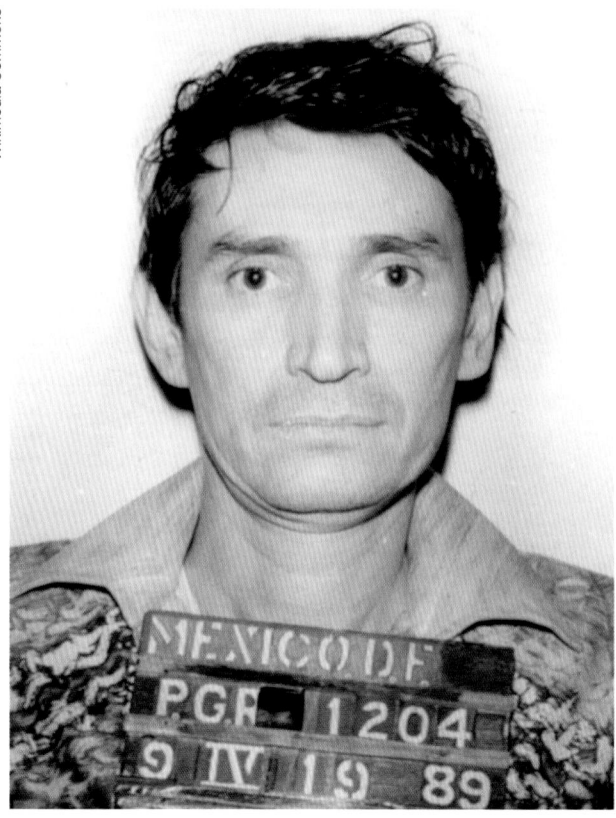

Miguel Félix Gallardo

Young men display gang signs in front of Crip graffiti.

Vyacheslav Ivankov

Promotional image of MS-13 members from the film *Sin Nombre*.

Dawood Ibrahim

Mario Puzo, author of the *The Godfather*, and Francis Ford Coppola.

'Mob's Greatest Hits': a display in the Mob Museum, Las Vegas.

with amenities such as hot tubs, a gym, a fully stocked bar and entertainment systems, Escobar lived well and continued to oversee his empire. His wanton exploitation of Bogotá's goodwill came to an end when he ordered the execution of several of his lieutenants on the grounds of his own prison. He managed to elude authorities who sought to transfer him to a state prison but remained on the run for the rest of his life. When an elite Colombian detachment caught up with him in December 1993, rival cartels and vengeful victims were also on his trail. Only one lightly armed bodyguard was at his side when he died in a hail of gunfire.

Officials in Washington were no less jubilant than their Colombian counterparts at the news of Escobar's death. For the United States, it marked a hopeful turning point in America's now decades-long war on drugs. Much had changed, however, in the time that had passed between Nixon's commencement of this struggle and the closing stages of the Medellín Cartel. At the time of Ronald Reagan's election in 1980, counternarcotics enforcement was not a priority. At the outset of his term, Reagan's team went as far as to consider cutting the size of the Justice Department. Narcotics use, from many accounts, appeared to have stabilised. Cocaine, as one article in *Time* declared, was seen as 'no more harmful than equally moderate doses of alcohol and marijuana, and infinitely less so than heroin'.[107] Events around the country and within the White House changed the administration's approach before the end of Reagan's first year in office. Outrageous acts of street violence, particularly in cities such as Miami, sharpened calls for a harder-nosed approach towards drug trafficking. Powerful voices in the president's cabinet echoed these sentiments, leading to the rapid expansion of the FBI and DEA budgets. The US Congress joined in the crusade, passing harsher federal sentencing guidelines for drug possession, distribution and smuggling in 1984. And as chaos raged in Colombia, Reagan directed military and intelligence officials to take a more direct role in fighting narcotics trafficking abroad. The drug threat, the president announced in 1986, was 'every bit as much a threat to the United States as enemy planes and missiles'.[108] Evidence of cocaine's growing power over Latin America also played to Washington's enthusiasm in combatting the expansion of Soviet influence. With Nicaragua in the hands of the Moscow-backed Sandinista regime, Pablo Escobar and other cartel leaders reached out to Managua in the hopes of establishing a new airbridge to North America, one similar to Norman's Cay. Escobar's alliances with other Latin American governments also extended to Manuel Noriega, generalissimo of Panama, who allowed the cartels to deposit their funds in local Panamanian banks.

Escobar's influence over Central America was a godsend for the Reagan administration. The president took to the airwaves in March 1986 to reveal evidence demonstrating that top Nicaraguan government officials were 'deeply involved in drug trafficking'. Validating Reagan's claims were photographs depicting Pablo Escobar in the company of Nicaraguan soldiers loading 1,200 pounds of cocaine onto an awaiting aircraft.[109] Unbeknown to the American public, US-supported anti-communists and the Medellín Cartel had formed their own alliances. A plane crash in 1988 revealed that anti-Sandinista forces had received American weapons from a front company headed by Juan Matta Ballesteros, one of Miguel Félix Gallardo's early coke connections. DEA representatives later characterised him as an individual 'at the same level as the rulers of the Medellín and Cali Cartels'.[110] By far the worst offender was Manuel Noriega, who traded secrets and arms to both Communist and anti-Communist forces in Latin America. With the conclusion of Washington's Contra Wars against Nicaragua, an army of 20,000 American troops invaded Panama. After cornering him at the Papal diplomatic residence in Panama City, American officers rendered Noriega back to Miami to stand trial for drug trafficking and other charges. One of the witnesses who helped send him to prison was Carlos Lehder, who testified at length as to Noriega's dealings with the Medellín Cartel.[111]

Equally uncomfortable contradictions coloured the end of the Guadalajara Cartel. Mexican state complicity in the drugs trade was a well-known fact well before Reagan took office. The depths of this collaboration, however, became painfully clear with the kidnapping and murder of DEA agent, Enrique 'Kiki' Camarena. In February 1985, Camarena disappeared after being accosted by several men in front of the US consulate in Guadalajara. His whereabouts remained unknown during the month that followed. Dithering on the part of Mexican authorities incurred Washington's fury, leading to a punitive slowdown of Mexican traffic across the US border. His body eventually appeared hundreds of miles away alongside a pilot who assisted the DEA in counternarcotics operations. Camarena's remains were in an advanced stage of decomposition and exhibited horrific signs of torture that had likely lasted days. News reports circulated that police officers were likely involved in the kidnapping. Before the body was even found, US officials took custody of audio recordings of Camarena's torture, which pointed to possible links between drug traffickers and Mexico's security services. Before long Mexican officials indicted and secured the capture of Rafael Caro Quintero, who had gone into hiding in Costa Rica. Quintero's arraignment did little to quiet the storm. Hearings held before the US Senate led to accusations that individuals close to Mexican president Miguel de la Madrid were involved in the drug trade and possibly Camarena's disappearance. Suspicion mounted that the DFS, Mexico's intelligence service, was critical to the workings of the Guadalajara Cartel. 'They are a very, very big problem,' one US investigator told the *New York Times*. 'Every time we grab someone, they're carrying a card from the DFS. A lot of people have been issued badges who are not really on the payroll.'[112] The dissolution of the DFS shortly after Camarena's death pointed to a reshuffling of Mexican drug politics but not a complete transformation. By the early 1990s, it was estimated that cartels were spending $500 million on government bribes. Confirmation of the scale of a pay-to-play system in the country seemed all but certain when the wife of Raúl Salinas, brother of President Carlos Salinas de Gortari, was arrested in Switzerland attempting to withdraw $84 million from one of her accounts. A subsequent investigation uncovered a total of $250 million stashed away in 289 separate Swiss accounts linked to Raúl Salinas.[113]

There is no agreement as to whether Miguel Félix Gallardo approved of Kiki Camarena's abduction and killing. Yet it became abundantly clear that Félix understood the gravity of the crime. The arrest of Caro Quintero, as well as Ernesto Fonseca, left him alone at the top of the Guadalajara Cartel. His position, however, became more tenuous as Americans applied more attention and resources to policing drug trafficking on the Mexican border. His arrest in April 1989 came without warning (supposedly, it is claimed, at the direct order of newly elected President Carlos Salinas). Shortly after his apprehension, he organised one last meeting of the cartel's main figures. Power thereafter devolved into the hands of regional bosses based in Tijuana, Culiacán, Ciudad Juárez, Tecate and Mexicali. Gallardo's fall by no means ended drug trafficking across the border. Nor did it minimise the potential for violence. In the decade that followed, a more contentious, and often more chaotic, arena of competition took shape among the successors of the Guadalajara Cartel. Between 1993 and 2001, an estimated 2,800 people were the victims of murder, rape or abduction in Ciudad Juárez alone. Lawlessness in the city was so profound during this period that experts and officials struggled to pinpoint what percentage of these crimes were attributed to drug violence.[114] The spectre of government patronage grew even more visible with the dissolution of Gallardo's empire. In 1997, Jose de Jesús Gutiérrez Rebollo, the general in charge of Mexico's counternarcotics operations, was arrested months into the job on charges of abetting the operations of Juárez boss, Amado Carrillo Fuentes. According to American intelligence sources, Rebollo organised meetings between Fuentes and other senior military officers, tipping him off to both American and Mexican investigations. Rebollo's effort to crush the Juárez Cartel's main rivals, however, brought him into conflict with other generals accused of patronising Arellano Félix's organisation in Tijuana. At the time of his arrest, informants claimed General Rebollo and other officers were finalising negotiations over a $60 million bribe from Fuentes.[115]

Colombia witnessed a similar pattern of fragmentation and state collusion after the demise of Pablo Escobar. The arrest and death of other prominent Medellín bosses splintered what remained of the country's largest cartel, thus creating new avenues for growth among Colombia's remaining syndicates. Stepping into the breach was an extensive network of producers and distributors based in the southwestern city of Cali. Mystery still obscures the origins of the Cali Cartel. Formed in the mid-1970s, its most prominent founders, Gilberto and Miguel Rodríguez Orejuela, worked as drug store clerks at a young age before turning to crime. At a time when marijuana and coca paste were flowing freely across Colombia, the brothers and their partners enlisted as many as ninety-two cousins and relatives in building a drug pipeline into New York and other American cities.[116] While Pablo Escobar and Carlos Lehder played to the public, the Rodríguez brothers scorned the attention of the media. Their methods of violence and intimidation were equally unassuming. Bodies of those kidnapped and murdered often disappeared or were found without identifying features. Their willingness to kill also extended to cleansing Cali of populations that hindered 'the requirements of progress', such as the homeless, prostitutes and homosexuals.[117]

A concerted campaign to buy political support and security cemented the cartel's standing among Cali's elite. A 1994 police and judiciary investigation uncovered evidence that the Cali Cartel had paid off at least twelve generals and more than two dozen senior officials in the city. The cartel's influence also extended over most of Cali's police force and virtually all of the security staff at the local airport.[118] Public attention to the cartel's power reached fever pitch when newspapers revealed that Ernesto Samper, winner of Colombia's 1994 presidential contest, had accepted drug money from Cali. Accusations of corruption soon rippled across Bogotá, leading to several high-profile resignations from the government. Samper, however, remained defiant. One year later, he oversaw the arrest of Gilberto and Miguel Rodríguez Orejuela. The full decapitation of the Cali Cartel's leadership crippled the organisation for good.

As in Mexico, the Colombian state, however corrupt, proved its resilience. But in striking down large organisations, a hydra-like system of smaller groups took their place. Older geographic epicentres, such as Medellín and Cali, mattered less as *cartelitos*, or mini-cartels, took shape in areas previously at the periphery of the cocaine trade. More striking was how quickly these new groups branched out abroad. Less than two years after the Cali Cartel's demise, officials in neighbouring Panama were reporting that at least twenty Colombian cartelitos were operating in the country.[119]

The afterlife of the word 'cartel' speaks to more than just the impact the syndicates of Medellín and Guadalajara had upon popular consciousness. Why cartels prevailed as institutions partially reflected the historical continuities that brought them to life. The cornerstones of Escobar's and Félix Gallardo's empires were networks of druggists, shippers, smugglers and wholesalers with roots dating back a generation or more. Veterans of the French Connection played a noticeable role in both Mexico and Colombia. Had he not been arrested in 1972, Marseille's most notorious underworld chemist, Joseph Cesari, admitted to his jailers that he would have headed to Colombia to build a series of labs.[120] One French Connection chemist, Laurent Fiocconi, did manage to evade arrest and settle in Colombia. With the help of old and new acquaintances, he operated labs on behalf of both the Cali and Medellín Cartels. Natives who worked in his jungle lab dubbed him 'the Magician' after he began trebling their rate of cocaine production. When one group of Medellín distributors sought to test his skills, he happily transformed ten kilos of cocaine base into eleven kilos of powder ready for sale. 'When they saw this, they fell on their asses,' Fiocconi remembers. '*El Mago* [The Magician]!'[121]

Some of the groups that enabled the cocaine revolution to flourish were indeed long in the tooth. The Camorra, the yakuza, Sicily's La Cosa Nostra and the American Mafia all took advantage of the cocaine trade. Other crime factions, however, appeared to emerge seemingly from nowhere. Observers especially saw this being the case in countries such as Jamaica and Nigeria. Both states possessed a history of cliques or gangs engaged in various crimes before large amounts of cocaine arrived on their shores. Yet as they became stopovers for smugglers transiting to North America and Europe, both nations witnessed the radical rise of their own local mafias.

When Jamaica gained its independence from Great Britain in 1962, it did so as a state with few lucrative resources or sustainable commodities. Old colonial exports such as sugar and bananas, together with bauxite mining and tourism, left large numbers of people in poverty. Bitter questions over economic development and relations with London put in place a contentious two-party system well before independence was finally attained. Both parties eagerly sought out the support of the lower classes, creating an environment marked by both political patronage and electoral intimidation. Bands of party-linked 'rudeboys', some of them armed with guns, became frequent sights in the capital of Kingston as early as the 1960s.[122] Crime proliferated under these conditions. In 1970, the Jamaican government announced that 12,900 violent crimes had been committed that year (the political opposition, meanwhile, estimated that the true figure was probably north of 30,000).[123] Tensions within Jamaica soared with the election of Michael Manley as prime minister in 1972. As an advocate of radical socialist policies, Manley drew the support of Cuba and the ire of the United States. Despite noted peacemaking efforts by Bob Marley, far and away the country's most famous citizen, Manley's standoff against his most prominent rival, Edward Seaga, continued through much of the decade (Marley himself was nearly assassinated when he announced a concert in Manley's honour). The drugs trade added to the lethality and global impact of Jamaica's political woes. Marijuana cultivation and usage was commonplace on the island well before independence. With the American market beckoning, a new contraband industry took form as the pot boom took off in the early 1970s. Cocaine and heroin trafficking assumed even greater appeal in advance of Kingston's decision to adopt a US-backed marijuana eradication programme in the mid-'80s. Soft drugs, as one American diplomat put it, had always been a 'major element of [the] narcotics problem' in Jamaica. Yet it was already apparent in 1972 that the country was 'being used as [a] transit point for hard narcotics for [the] US [market]'. As evidence, the diplomat pointed to the seizure of 460 pounds of heroin and ten pounds of cocaine within a three-year period, all from Latin America.[124]

Who precisely were the trailblazers of this trade is not clear. American investigators in the mid-1970s contended that young Americans 'unconnected to traditional sources of organised crime' may have been among the first actors to cart large amounts of marijuana across the Caribbean.[125] A far more structured and indigenous brand of Jamaican trafficker clearly emerged after the 1980 election. With Michael Manley up for re-election that year, political violence spiralled out of control. By the time his long-time rival, Edward Seaga, claimed victory, an estimated 800 people were killed in party-backed gang violence.[126] Large numbers of Jamaicans left the country in the wake of the election, a group that included individuals connected to urban gangs. With cocaine now gushing across the Caribbean, cliques of 'posses' and 'yardies' served as retailers and smugglers for dealers based in Latin America. This was the case of Errol Codling, Britain's reputed 'Godfather of the Yardies'. As a reggae artist known as Ranking Dread, he achieved fleeting celebrity in the early 1980s for his minor hit, 'Fattie Boom Boom' (not to be confused with the more popular reggae single 'Hey Fatty Bum-Bum' by Carl Malcolm). At some point, however, he left Jamaica for London and, by all reports, entered the drugs trade. Before 1990, authorities in the United States, Canada and Britain prosecuted and deported Codling for a variety of crimes including drug possession, prostitution, carrying illegal firearms and rape. Newspapers also accused him of complicity in as many as thirty murders for which he was neither tried nor imprisoned.[127] Most shockingly, investigators in the United Kingdom leaked revelations that the Irish Republican Army hired Codling to assassinate Prime Minister Margaret Thatcher in 1987. Detectives believed he got cold feet after seeing the extensive security cordon that surrounded Downing Street and the Houses of Parliament.[128]

Back in Jamaica, cocaine dealing supplemented the power of politically influential gangs such as the Shower Posse. Based in the poor neighbourhood of Tivoli Gardens, the Shower Posse first assumed notoriety as the militant arm of Edward Seaga's Jamaica Labour Party. Cocaine dealing, and their connections to Jamaican migrant communities in Toronto, Miami, New York and London, made them a force beyond politics. The press on both sides of the Atlantic depicted the Shower Posse and other Jamaican gangs as a 'Black mafia' that killed wantonly and without remorse. By the early 1990s, British, Canadian and American law enforcement warned that posses and yardies had cornered the crack cocaine market in several cities. What made them most feared was their reliance on heavy weaponry such as Uzis and other automatic weapons.[129] 'Not since the Mafia emerged to rule organised crime during the 1920s have authorities faced such a threat,' one Florida journalist surmised.[130]

Crime emanating from Nigeria produced somewhat less hysteria during the 1980s and '90s. Yet in a world that seemed increasingly awash in new and exotic mafias, observers looked upon the rise of organised crime in West Africa as emblematic of cocaine's contagious reach. Nigeria attained its independence two years before Jamaica. Yet unlike Jamaica, forging a coherent nation remained an elusive task. Civil war broke out in the country seven years after colonial administrators departed the capital of Lagos. Nigeria's union was restored in 1970, but deep fractures remained among the country's three largest ethnic groups. A succession of six military governments came and went after the war was finished, thus begetting a culture of coups and uncurbed authority in both the capital and the countryside. What sustained some degree of continuity between regimes was a shared understanding among elites when it came to the 'national cake'.[131] Fleecing of the state treasury, as well as the splitting of oil revenues and other natural resources, helped sustain peace among the powerful. Little, however, was set aside for Nigeria's rapidly growing population. Large numbers of Nigerians opted to leave the country rather than face unemployment, poverty and, at times, rampant violence. By 1991, there were 47,000 Nigerian citizens living in the UK and another 100,000 claiming residence in the United States.[132]

It was not this diaspora that necessarily initiated Nigeria's entrance into the global narcotics market. As early as the 1950s

American narcotics agents uncovered a ring of Lebanese smugglers that had used Nigeria as a transit point in shipping heroin from the Levant to New York. This pattern of trade appeared to endure into the 1990s when French authorities busted Lebanese traffickers passing through Paris. By then cocaine had arrived on the scene.[133] Exactly when Nigerians living at home and abroad entered the cocaine market remains murky. Stories concerning enterprising exchange students, or perhaps navy officers operating out of India, are among the few anecdotes pointing to the development of a 'Nigerian Connection' within the drugs trade. By the time the Medellín Cartel was in its death throes, significant numbers of Nigerians were participating in the cocaine trade. In 1991, officials in Lagos admitted more than 15,000 of its citizens were held in jails worldwide on drug charges.[134]

Who or what controlled cocaine trafficking out of Nigeria was a subject foreigners could only guess at during the 1980s and '90s. Some surmised that cocaine came into the country via Brazil, which was then transported by mules to Europe and North America. The scale and sophistication of the trade led European and American observers to assume that there was nothing random or haphazard about these networks. 'These are people working for very organised groups,' one American report declared in 1994, 'which we have felt is with the protection of Government officials.'[135] Rampant corruption in and beyond the division of Nigeria's 'national cake' encouraged these suspicions. The world of politics and crime blurred with reports that Nigeria was in fact ruled by a 'Kaduna mafia' during this era. Though admittedly bearing no genuine resemblance to La Cosa Nostra, the Kaduna mafia comprised a secretive clique of elite figures from Nigeria's predominately Muslim north. It was this cabal of generals, business leaders and provincial notables that many saw as the true source of power in the country. Cases involving the Kaduna elite's links to the drugs trade produced rare moments of embarrassment. In 1985, the son of one of the country's wealthiest families was arrested in Lagos for what was characterised as his role in an international cocaine and heroin smuggling ring. Then-ruling General Muhammed Buhari scrambled to account for the network's existence, especially since the penalty for drug trafficking was death by firing squad. The mystery deepened when a 'well dressed' woman accused of assisting the ring threatened to out the 'big men' who really sat atop the gang. She purportedly died of food poisoning while in police custody.[136]

Unlike groups hailing from Jamaica, there is limited evidence that Nigerian traffickers retailed their wares on the streets of European or American cities. Who actually dispensed their drugs to Western users was a question many in the Atlantic world simply assumed away. This ambivalence, in historical terms, is illustrative of a common blind spot among state investigators. In Washington, federal and congressional agents invested most of their energy and resources in tracking major wholesalers. When it came to the evolution of street dealing and regional distribution, their interest was less pronounced. When the Federal Bureau of Narcotics presented a 1965 presidential commission with a national survey of organised crime, agents directed little attention to the groups or individuals who sold addicts their drugs. In places such as Boston, Philadelphia, Detroit and Washington, DC, blame was simply placed on disorganised 'negro violators' and 'peddlers' who either worked directly for major mafia families or who somehow acquired the drugs independently.[137] Drug dealing by outlaw motorcycle gangs, for example, received none of the attention La Cosa Nostra attained on the part of US Congress (despite the fact that groups like the Hell's Angels were known for retailing mass shipments of marijuana from Mexico as early as the 1960s).[138]

By the early 1970s, a handful of African American kingpins attained fleeting stardom. It arguably took authorities almost a decade to catch on to the network built by Frank Matthews, whose dope-dealing empire stretched across the mid-Atlantic and the Midwest. Despite his humble roots in North Carolina, Matthews turned a $20,000 heroin deal with a Cuban fugitive into a steady drug pipeline linked to French Connection smugglers based in Venezuela. From his home in New York City, he joined forces with a string of citywide heroin retailers who came to dominate markets in Baltimore, Washington, Detroit and Atlanta.[139] When police apprehended him in 1973, federal authorities estimated that his drug profits from the previous year likely exceeded $10 million.[140] After jumping bail, Matthews disappeared without a trace. Matthews's fall was followed by the arraignment of other prominent African American gangsters, most notably Frank Lucas and Nicky Barnes, Harlem's reputed 'Mr Untouchable'. By the end of the 1970s, the American press was generally in agreement that a Black mafia had been met and defeated in various parts of the country.

The growth of the cocaine trade, more than any major drug epidemic before it, begged more serious enquiries as to who was selling consumers their drugs. Understanding who the dealers were was not simply a matter of public health. By the mid-1980s, stories of mass shootings and indiscriminate killings inundated newspaper and television reporting from coast to coast. Youth gangs were habitually the chief culprits. Popular culture picked up on this trend almost immediately, integrating it into movies and music almost effortlessly. It was in this environment that LA gangs the Bloods and Crips were held up as the poster children for the scourge of drug dealing and violence. Though they were not mafias in a traditional sense, their sophistication and pervasiveness drew frequent comparisons to more established crime groups.

Concern over youth gangs grew independently of America's rising interest in mafias. For much of the post-war years, experts tended to agree that societal ills, not organised crime, were what drew young men to band together and behave violently. Gangs plagued Los Angeles no more than any other place in the United States in the 1950s. The young African American men who formed post-war gangs such as the Slausons, the Gladiators, the Farmers and the Businessmen often came from working-class families. Police and reformers initially construed them as social delinquents in one sense or another. When they clashed, they did so out of a spirit of neighbourhood solidarity and petty differences. Racial animosities also played a role in the spread of gangs in Los Angeles. As the first signs of white flight were observed in neighbourhoods south of LA's downtown in the 1950s, Black gangs did battle against a band of white teenagers calling themselves the Spook Hunters.[141]

Raymond Washington, founder of the Crips, turned to gangs for protection, identity and a sense of belonging. The politics of the time inspired him to think beyond himself and his surroundings. Though born in Texas, he came of age in south Los Angeles amid the Civil Rights Movement. He was twelve when intensifying police violence touched off the infamous Watts Riots of 1965. Inspired by the nationalist militancy and chic appeal of the Black Panther Party, Washington founded the Crips at some point around 1970. The origin of the name is a matter of dispute. Though it was possibly a reference to the stylised 'crippled' walk the members adopted, Washington and other leaders touted the gang's name as an expression of their ideological leanings (one early member believed Crip was an acronym for 'Continuous Revolution in Progress').[142] The adoption of a Crip constitution, one that echoed the Black nationalist principles of the Black Panther Party, added to the unique character of the gang. Remarkably, satellite chapters of the Crips sprang up through much of south Los Angeles within months of its formation. Long-standing neighbourhood animosities, as well as Washington's own propensity for violence, prompted a counter-coalition to form among the disaffected. The proliferation of gangs calling themselves 'Bloods' reflected a shared affinity for Black nationalism. Yet older personal and neighbourhood tensions persisted. Internecine warfare between the two gangs became endemic to south Los Angeles as early as 1971 (with as many as twenty-nine young people killed as a result of gang feuds during this early period).[143] Popular culture, likely brought on by *The Godfather* and other films of the genre, prompted many Bloods and Crips to see themselves as a more bona fide class of criminal. By the end of the decade, Crip graffiti spraypainted on neighbourhood walls spoke of gangs 'identifying themselves as mobsters, gangsters and mafia[s]'.[144]

By the time a drive-by shooting took the life of Raymond Washington in 1979, the cocaine trade in Los Angeles had already begun to gather steam, with Colombian-linked retailers dealing in thousands of kilos of the drug. During this early surge of cocaine sales in the city, the reputed 'godfather of drugs' in south Los Angeles, Thomas 'Tootie' Reese, had built a mini-cocaine empire without the aid of either the Bloods or Crips.[145] It required the slow popularisation of cheaper crack and freebase cocaine for factions of the two gangs to be drawn into the drug trade. By the mid-1980s, federal officials were warning that the combination of Colombian trafficking and gang street dealing had a created a threat 'far more menacing than the traditional Mafia network'.[146] An orgy of gang violence in south Los Angeles appeared to confirm the harrowing state of affairs. By 1990, the annual number of gun-related homicides in Los Angeles County soared to 1554, nearly a four-fold increase from two decades earlier, with a third connected to gang warfare.[147]

Hollywood, as well as early hip-hop pioneers like NWA and Ice-T, brought the terror associated with the Bloods and Crips to audiences far beyond the California coast. The year 1988 featured the release of NWA's *Straight Outta Compton* and the blood-drenched gang opus, *Colours*. Both works sparked a firestorm of controversy amid news reports of record boycotts and shootouts between Bloods and Crips at local multiplexes. Gangsta rap's sudden popularity also underscored what was becoming the genuine dissemination of LA gang culture across the country. Police investigations and local media outlets tracked a steady outmigration of California gangsters to scores of towns and cities during the late 1980s. Expanding the crack trade to virgin territory prompted at least some out of Los Angeles. 'Everywhere you go ... you're going to see some people from LA,' one Crip dealer professed. 'If they got, you know, a dope house out there or a dope street out there ... you'll run into somebody on that street from LA.'[148] A great many other gangsters carried the culture further still to Latin America as a result of their deportation as illegal migrants. The undeniable mystique of the Bloods and Crips, with their telltale dress and slang, eventually inspired copycats in Europe. For observers abroad, the diffusion of LA gang culture, and seemingly the drug trade with it, appeared in keeping with the times. 'It's official,' one British observer declared in 1989. 'The Mafia does not run organised crime in America.'[149]

Just how integral the Bloods and Crips were to the distribution of cocaine within Los Angeles, let alone the United States, stirred some debate from the start of the crack epidemic. Media panic, as well as dire pronouncements by law enforcement officials, tended to blur or inflate the correlation between the rise in gang activity and the spread of cocaine in America. It was true, one USC research team contended in 1986, that street gangs engaged in drug sales. But the data suggested that they did not monopolise it. Most gangs, they believed, were too incohesive and unruly to 'take on Mafia characteristics'.[150]

The nuances that separated Bloods and Crips from the American Mafia tended to be lost on those who saw them as equally terrible expressions of the same phenomenon. Within popular media and in government circles, a new narrative took shape and became more fixed as time went on. Old syndicates, such as La Cosa Nostra, were dying off. More terrifying ones, such as the Crips, were taking their place. Other factors beyond the cocaine revolution fostered this emerging point of view. After the fall of the Berlin Wall, a series of new mafias arose in Eastern Europe and the old Soviet Union. The sudden proliferation of these mafias caught many by surprise, even though their development was many years in the making.

THIEVES AND BANDITS: THE RISE OF MAFIAS IN EUROPE'S EAST

The travails that have shaped the modern city of Dnipro encapsulate the larger saga of empire within much of Eastern Europe. Until the mid-eighteenth century, the land that it sits on today boasted no history of urban development. Located on the Dnieper River in what is now Ukraine, it was at the crossroads of several competing states. It had been the scene of intermittent warfare between Cossacks and Tatars, as well as Poland, the Ottoman Empire and Russia for decades on end. Something like an extended era of peace came about with Russia's conquest of the Crimea in 1774. Soon after, what was once a fledgling military encampment on the Dnieper was transformed into a settlement dubbed Yekaterinoslav, so named in honour of the reigning tsarina, Catherine the Great. Within a century the town became a showplace for Imperial Russia's earnest attempts at industrialisation. As the 'Manchester of the South', Yekaterinoslav boomed into a metropolis dotted with heavy smokestacks, blast furnaces and brick-laden factories. Its population spiked to over 200,000 by the First World War and boasted communities speaking Russian, Ukrainian, Yiddish, Polish, German and Belorussian.[151] The outbreak of the Great War ended its early epoch of prosperity and ushered in a sorrowful series of events that transformed and decimated the town and its people.

Russia's October Revolution of 1917 inaugurated a new regime and a change to the city's name and character. It now came to be known as Dnipropetrovsk in a tribute to a local Bolshevik activist who served as a minister in the formation of the Soviet Union. The name change was emblematic of a profound cultural shift. Dnipropetrovsk became a leading industrial centre in the Soviet Republic of Ukraine – a new state reflecting Lenin's desire to liberate and uplift the Ukrainian national majority living on the old empire's western periphery. Stalin upheld Ukraine's national sovereignty but earnestly sought to crush and atomise its population. The period between the world wars was a time of great hardship for the residents of Dnipropetrovsk, one marked by the cruelties of forced collectivisation and famine. Hitler's invasion of the Soviet Union in 1941 led to still greater injuries. In 1939, 18 per cent of the city's residents identified themselves as Jewish. By the end of the German occupation, virtually all 90,000 of them had either fled or been murdered in the Holocaust. Another 30,000 civilians were executed for various crimes. More than double that number was shipped westward as slave labourers.[152] Much of Dnipropetrovsk was destroyed when Stalin's army reclaimed the region in 1944.

By the time Mikhail Gorbachev took power in 1986, Dnipropetrovsk had been reborn as a city of secrets. After the war it resumed its place as an important industrial centre despite the scars left by the Nazi invasion. Yet with the onset of the Cold War, Soviet authorities incorporated the city into its expansive defence sector with the establishment of a massive automotive factory and a ballistic missile facility. Dnipropetrovsk thereafter became off-limits to foreign visitors and the press was forbidden from mentioning its main industries. Published photographs taken from within the city were strictly censored. When Vitali Vitaliev visited Dnipropetrovsk in the wake of Gorbachev's ascendency, none of these traits particularly interested him. For years Vitaliev had made a name for himself as one of the Soviet Union's most prolific foreign correspondents. The advent of *glasnost* and the loosening of press restrictions added to his fame with his pursuit of stories about state corruption and the hardships of daily life in the Soviet Union. On a train home to Kharkiv, in eastern Ukraine, a fan of his work suggested he go to Dnipropetrovsk to explore the existence of what he called 'the Soviet Mafia'. Vitali claimed to have never heard of such a thing. After first poking around Moscow for answers, he returned to Ukraine and slowly uncovered an incredible story. The city, it seemed, had previously been under the sway of a gangster mysteriously known as 'the Sailor'. Born Alexander Milchenko, the Sailor grew up in Amur, a neighbourhood possessing a storied reputation for crime and violence. Why Amur cultivated this distinction puzzled Vitaliev. Perhaps, he reasoned, it was 'the hot temper of the locals, typical southerners, or may be in the cheap and plentiful local wine – no one knows exactly'.[153] Whatever the case, Amur eventually got the better of Milchenko. After a failed attempt at playing competitive soccer, he and other local toughs dabbled in theft, robbery and eventually extortion. It was his decision to host crooked card games that really set his criminal career in motion. Even though gambling was illegal in the Soviet Union, the Sailor and his men soon amassed large amounts of money. The Sailor's gang took another giant step forward when it allied itself with black marketeers and the producers of illegally produced wares. Through bribes and the threat of violence, Milchenko protected Dnipropetrovsk's underground economy and bought off much of the city's police and officials. Local authorities repeatedly thwarted attempts at investigating and arresting the Sailor through the late 1970s and early 1980s. When Vitaliev published his exposé in the popular satirical magazine *Krokodil* in the summer of 1987, officials in

Dnipropetrovsk prevented the magazine's distribution to local vendors.

There was an undeniable hunger for stories such as this among the Soviet public during this late stage of the Cold War. But, as Vitaliev later insisted, people in the country lacked the context to truly understand what was happening in central Ukraine. 'Back in 1987,' he remembered, 'I had to explain to my readers what "mafia" and "racket" meant in general and what was special about their Soviet versions.'[154] Within months, however, things changed rapidly. By the time the Berlin Wall fell, the Soviet press, along with the international media, was awash in reports of an expansive Soviet mafia. An even more ominous monsoon of stories of gangland violence swept over the USSR. How and why this crime wave first took shape soon became the subject of an expansive number of articles and books. At the heart of this search for answers was an obvious yet disturbing set of questions: how did such a crisis emerge so quickly within such an authoritarian system? And what precisely was this thing people were now calling the Soviet mafia?

Contrary to Vitaliev's insistence, the concept of the mafia was not unknown in the Soviet Union. Nineteenth-century news reports from Sicily likely provided readers in the Russian Empire their first exposure to the word. Senior Bolsheviks were certainly aware of its meaning and existence. From his home in exile in Mexico City in the late 1930s, Leon Trotsky published a collection of articles he entitled *Stalin's Gangsters*. Two years before his assassination, he decried the Soviet secret police as a 'centralised Mafia of terrorists' bent upon murdering dissidents at home and abroad.[155] How the notion seeped into popular consciousness remains obscured by the nature of the Soviet system. A stringent regime of censorship, as well as the harsh penalties that came with blatantly criticising rule from Moscow, made it almost impossible for average citizens to explore the meaning of the term as it applied to their own lives. Soviet media, however, were unabashed in talking about the mafias abroad. The national encyclopaedia defined organised crime as 'a form of criminal activity carried on in bourgeois countries, primarily the US'.[156] It was in this spirit that a redacted version of Mario Puzo's *The Godfather* was first translated into Russian and other Soviet languages in the late 1970s.[157] Despite the chasm that set the East apart from the West, the nature of the Soviet system in the 1970s did in fact give critics sufficient context to understand Puzo's novel as a window into the nature of power in the country.

By the time Coppola's two films exited theatres, evidence of Premier Leonid Brezhnev's deteriorating health was becoming visible. He began slurring his words in televised addresses and walked without ease in his public appearances. The jokes that circulated at his expense were symbolic of his hold over the ship of state. One popular joke placed him on a train alongside Stalin and Khrushchev. When the train suddenly stopped, all three premiers jumped out. 'Shoot the engineer,' Stalin roared. 'No,' Khrushchev counselled, 'we'll raise his wages.' 'I know what we'll do,' Brezhnev concluded. 'We'll climb on board, we'll pull down the blinds and we'll pretend the train is moving.'[158] For many Soviet citizens, the train had definitely ground to a halt. Under Brezhnev's watch, the economy stagnated. The Soviet Union's immense oil wealth eased some of the pain in the form of massive subsidies. Between 1973 and 1985, as much as 80 per cent of the Soviet Union's hard currency earnings came from petroleum exports.[159]

Unfortunately, the wealth was unevenly distributed and most of the money went into the pockets of state officials, reflecting the solidification of a political hierarchy centred on party elites and their dependents. In each state and autonomous region forming the Soviet Union, a rigid system of personalised rule formed around cliques of high officials drawn from ethnic majorities and dependable lackies. No one with ambition ascended far without cadre approval. Those who successfully ingratiated themselves into the *apparat* enjoyed the benefits of receiving cars, apartments and rationed goods earlier or more often than the average citizen. Before Brezhnev's death, it was becoming difficult to deny the hypocrisies at the heart of the Soviet system. In 1981, a play entitled *We, the Undersigned* debuted in Moscow. It featured the story of a young idealist hoping to save a rural construction project from the incompetence and venality of his bosses. In one key scene, the protagonist sought to rally his supervisor to his side by appealing to his senses. 'We have a real Mafia here, do you understand?' he declares. 'Not a Mafia that murders people, like in Sicily. But to trample a man underfoot when he's in the way – they'll do it without blinking an eye.' Much to the chagrin of the authorities, these and other bold reflections upon life in the Soviet Union regularly drew the applause of Moscow audiences.[160]

Mikhail Gorbachev came to power in 1986 intent upon saving the Soviet system from itself. In doing so, he helped speed its demise. In announcing a reformist effort bracketed by restructuring (*perestroika*) and openness (*glasnost*), Gorbachev willed the country to adopt elements of Western entrepreneurialism and adaptiveness. Other fundamental features of the Soviet one-party state remained untouched. Under the guise of this new age of reform, Vitaliev's dispatches from Dnipropetrovsk gained both relevance and acclaim. Before long the Soviet press was filled with stories outing the exploitation of 'mafias' throughout the country. Brezhnev's reign was particularly singled out as the genesis moment for a wide variety of clans and conspiratorial groups who lorded over towns, districts and members states belonging to the USSR. Western journalists visiting the Soviet Union devoured these stories with a bottomless appetite. Soviet newspapers, after all, seemed to be filled with 'lurid tales of mobsters and hit men, mass murder, central Asian extortion rings, sexual deviance and other ripe nastiness'.[161]

Between Decline and Revolution

The tenor of reporting grew more morose as Communist regimes in Eastern Europe began to dissolve and upheaval racked the periphery of the USSR. Increasingly stories of mass corruption gave way to ominous reports of gangland killings in the streets of major cities like Leningrad and Moscow. With Moscow's grip over its constituent lands unravelling, 'Soviet mafias' appeared to be the true source of authority everywhere. Despite his defection and resettlement in Australia, Vitali Vitaliev continued to decry the plight of citizens in his former homeland. He concurred with those who asserted that the Communist Party was itself something akin to a mafia. Yet Vitaliev cautioned Westerners who took delight in seeing the Bolshevik system's implosion. Was it possible, he posed, that the Soviet mafia could 'grow into an international criminal organisation similar to the infamous Cosa Nostra?' According to some gangsters who spoke to Vitaliev in 1990, many indeed desired to 'migrate to the West'.[162]

The contagion of Soviet criminality was spreading but it would take a bit more time for Vitali Vitaliev's prophecy to resonate with observers outside of the USSR. Amid the Soviet Union's dissolution, many journalists and analysts tended to ignore the internal complexity and diversity within the much heralded 'Soviet mafia'. As many suspected, the Communist Party apparatus had helped to shape criminal conspiracies in various parts of the country. But as the end of the Cold War heralded the rise of post-Soviet oligarchs and their conspiratorial accomplices, an even older force that few outside the Soviet Union fully comprehended came into view: the 'world of thieves' – Russia's historic criminal fraternity.

When Stalin and Lenin devised the notion of the Soviet Union, they undoubtedly never imagined that it would form the basis of deeply-rooted culture of corruption. Creating a union of socialist republics from the lands of the old Russian Empire was conceived as a means of compensating for the country's history of colonial oppression. The Union of Soviet Socialist Republics was designed to civilise and empower 'small peoples' and nationalities, thus speeding their journey down the road to socialism. In the years that followed the 1917 Revolution, Moscow cultivated handpicked cadres to serve as regional leaders based on their fidelity to the Communist Party and, in many cases, their ethnic identification. By the post-war era, the ruling classes of this 'affirmative action empire' had taken on a life of its own. Younger generations of local and national party offices were not simply distinguished by their loyalty but at times by their personal or filial connections to their patrons. Leonid Brezhnev did much to nurture and perpetuate the clannishness of the Soviet provincial politics. It was under his watch that a system of favours and material privileges kicked into high gear. From the very top down, appointments to positions of authority, the awarding of contracts and the dispensation of personal luxuries were indelibly tied to one's personal relationship to the state apparatus. In time, critical sectors of the state and its economy became private fiefdoms. There were the likes of Haydar Aliyev, the long-serving first secretary of the state of Azerbaijan. For *Washington Post* correspondent David Remnick, Aliyev governed his stately domain no differently from the way 'the Gambino family ran the port of New York'. Under him were mini-mafias run by party retainers and Aliyev's own relatives who paid him tribute. Men close to Aliyev exploited numerous sectors of the Azeri economy: the caviar trade on the Caspian Sea, oil extraction, the transport industry and the distribution of fruits, vegetables and cotton. Aliyev's patronage network encroached upon academia, with members of his extended family staffing universities and scholarly institutes. Taken together, Remnick understood that each of these mafias 'reported to him, enriched him, worshiped him' just like any New York don.[163]

The dissolution of the USSR enshrined this system of extraction and abuse among the successor states born in the winter of 1991. In Ukraine, the humble city of Dnipropetrovsk maintained these continuities from the Soviet past. Locals still remember Leonid Brezhnev as the originator of the country's enduring power structure. Having served as Dnipropetrovsk's general secretary, Brezhnev left the city alongside a small coterie of retainers who accompanied him to Moscow. Thereafter, influential men and women from Dnipropetrovsk assumed positions of power both in Ukraine and beyond it. Though renamed Dnipro after the country's independence in 1991, the city and its outlying districts remain a breeding ground for Ukraine's clannish elite. Multiple ruling figures, including presidents such as Leonid Kuchma and Volodymyr Zelenskyy, were born or worked within the city or its environs before making it big. The patronage networks of operatives that launched the careers of Kuchma, Zelenskyy and others inspire many to believe that a 'Dnipro mafia' still exercises inordinate power over the Ukrainian state.[164]

High party cliques like those surrounding Haydar Aliyev did not necessarily devise the means by which the Soviet state was exploited or bled of its resources. In the years that followed the Second World War, an 'economy of shadows' slowly manifested itself within the many nooks of the USSR's vast state economy.[165] Its origins were simple and intuitive. Factory directors and distributors found ways of diverting goods or watering down their products to produce a private profit. Skilled labourers licensed themselves off the books for a fee. Truly daring entrepreneurs worked off hours in their own workshops to produce black market goods. In Soviet parlance, they were cryptically labelled *tsekhoviki*, or workshop employees, who misused government property or services.[166] By the 1970s, the fleecing of the state became more aligned with party power blocks or cliques. There was the case of Otari Lazishvili, who began life as a chauffeur and economics student before reinventing himself a black marketeer. Heralded as a 'Soviet version of *The Godfather*' in the Western press, Lazishvili devised a system of skimming state-manufactured goods by falsely declaring them damaged or broken. He generated obscene amounts of wealth at a time when most citizens struggled for essential goods. He flew to Moscow to watch his favourite football team, bet thousands of rubles on sporting events and owned two villas with swimming pools. What made Lazishvili's rise possible was his relationship to Georgia's first secretary, Vasil Mzhavanadze. A 1973 anti-corruption campaign ended both his career and that of his patron. Their brief time in the sun, however, foretold of worse cases to come.[167]

Tsekhoviki continued to plague various corners of Soviet society as the 1980s began. It was with the commencement of Gorbachev's reforms that it assumed even more ominous implications. The slow introduction of semi-private co-operatives allowed formerly shadowy figures to corner the market on key goods. Stocks at state retail stores dwindled to perilous levels, forcing consumers to either wait in excruciatingly long lines or pay the exorbitant prices demanded by this new class of petty capitalist. A select few took advantage of privatisation in ways that were far more ambitious and impactful. Boris Abramovich Berezovsky could hardly be called a *tsekhovik* when he first went into business. With a doctorate in mathematics, he spent years working in the Soviet National Academy of Sciences developing computer systems aimed at improving economic production. For his efforts he was paid a meagre salary of roughly 500 rubles a month. In 1989 he conceived of a bold plan that took him out of the world of academia. Having worked on the computerisation of the state's automotive industry, Berezovsky approached the heads of the country's largest car manufacturer, Avtovaz, with a proposal to open a private joint venture with a foreign company in the hopes of improving production and maximising profits. He found that partner in Logo, an automation firm based in Italy. As general director of the newly established Logovaz, Berezovsky reaped a fortune as the company quickly transitioned from computerisation to domestic auto sales.[168] With the Soviet Union's dissolution and the full abandonment of state Communism, he moved rapidly to invest in other sectors previously owned by the government. By 1994 he took over what once was the premiere television station, Soviet Channel One. Berezovsky went on to buy oil refineries and acquire a major stake in Aeroflot, the country's national airline. Each of these later accomplishments came with the blessing of Russia's newly elected president, Boris Yeltsin.

On the surface of things, there was nothing illegal about Berezovsky's emergence as one of Russia's first oligarchs. Yet what counted as the law, let alone law enforcement, was often blurry or negotiable. As states left the Soviet Union, dire economic conditions made many things possible. Bribe-taking was ubiquitous. Yeltsin's former bodyguard claimed that Berezovsky funnelled millions to Russia's president on the behalf of other oligarchs who sought to pillage the state economy, though the funds were declared to be profits from Yeltsin's memoir, which Berezovsky also helped to publish.[169] Policemen, judges, local officials and media personalities were bought off with far less. In an environment in which the arms of the state were at the mercy of anyone rich enough to pay for protection, the marketplace often devolved into a free-fire zone. Business rivals could just as easily be killed as intimidated, bought out or outhustled. Boris Berezovsky himself discovered as much in 1994 when he nearly lost his life in a car bomb attack. In the absence of impartial courts and state security services, gangsters and mobs frequently became the arbiters of the marketplace.

The gangs of the post-Soviet era were the descendants of criminal fraternities dating back a century or more. As in the case of Europe before the French Revolution, cities such as Moscow developed their own underworld cultures of thieves, beggars and other petty deviants. Some developed their own cant, internal laws and rituals no different from that of criminal collectives formed in

London or Amsterdam. Perhaps the most dominant institution uniting common criminals was a system of guilds or *artely* made up of men and women with specific skills. Like most European guilds, Russian pickpockets, horse thieves and robbers became bound to an *artel* for their sake of their own protection and the good of their trade. Artely regulated its members through a harsh system of discipline and secrecy. And like outlaws everywhere, the exploits of legendary gangs were a source of inspiration for a unique genre of poems and prison songs known in this context as *blatniye*.[170]

By the end of the Romanov dynasty, the artel system began to evolve under the weight of profound change. The abolition of serfdom in 1861 sent a wave of peasants into the empire's cities, leading to a dramatic expansion of local underworlds. The tsar's government responded in kind through more rigorous forms of law enforcement and the enlargement of the state's prisons. What counted as law and order utterly collapsed with the Russian Revolution. As civil war engulfed the whole of the now dead Russian Empire, crime and urban violence spiked to extreme levels. It was estimated that there were as many as ten to fifteen times the number of robberies and murders committed in the country in the year 1918 alone. Lenin's consolidation of Bolshevik rule by 1922 returned some manner of peace to various parts of the new Soviet state.

Yet with the imposition of Communist orthodoxy and bitter discipline, the prison system of the former tsars took on more ominous dimensions. Individuals convicted of political crimes, as well as those found guilty of more pedantic transgressions, were sent to even larger, far harsher labour camps in some of the most remote parts of the Soviet Union. Between 1934 and 1952, an estimated 18 million Soviet citizens were interned in the country's massive gulag system.[171] It was within the confines of the gulags that the 'world of thieves' took on uniformly hardened traits. The first accounts of what became known as the *vory-v-zakone*, or thieves-in-law, come from a handful of witnesses who survived their internment. Like the case of the Camorra and the Sicilian Mafia, prison life created conditions that allowed for the amalgamation of time-honoured artely traditions into a culture centred on loyalty, secrecy and sacred rites. A *vor*, or thief, bore distinctive tattoos marking them as a member. Inductees were sworn to cut all ties to the state, be it in the form of military services, court testimony or work on the part of government administration. A real vor vowed to 'live only on what he has stolen, seized, acquired by deception, [or] won at cards ...'[172] Those who broke any of these codes often found themselves before a court of their peers, called a *skhodka*. Like the USSR as a whole, the Russian language, or at least some derivative of it, served as the thieves' main idiom. Eastern orthodoxy was privileged as the dominant religion of the *vory* (in large measure as a sign of defiance of the Soviet system). Yet over time, as people from throughout the former Russian empire arrived in the camps, the 'world of thieves' became a truly multinational collective.

Stalinist oppression, as well as the Nazi invasion in 1941, eventually opened a chasm within the world of thieves. Many vory were tempted into serving their jailers as snitches and unofficial foremen on prison work sites. Others broke with their fellow thieves for the sake of ethnic solidarity. 'The code is important,' one Chechen gangster later testified, 'but blood is everything.'[173] Stalwarts labelled these turncoats the 'unconverted' or, more commonly, 'bitches'. As the Second World War drew to a close, the camps swelled with ever larger numbers of inmates more willing to collaborate with the state than abide by the internal rule of the thieves-in-law. Likely at Moscow's behest, prison officials finally sought to finish off the vory once and for all. Beginning in 1948, a brutal wave of massacres swept over the Soviet gulag system. Unknown hundreds died in what later was remembered as 'the

Bitches' War' (*suchya voina*). When the killing ended, much of the thieves' world was eradicated. Yet like the post-war Mafia in Sicily, those who survived the Bitches' War maintained elements of the old tradition yet were transformed by the violence. Most reconciled themselves to the undeniable power of the Soviet state. Collaboration with the police and other officials was no longer an infraction that could lead to expulsion or death at the hands of one's fellow vory.

Until the 1980s, those who claimed any part in the thieves' traditions largely disappeared within the cracks of Soviet society. Evidence of their influence or vibrancy is at best fragmentary during the years Khrushchev and Brezhnev reigned over the USSR. It is very possible that most citizens or officials forgot their existence altogether. Gangs such as the one organised by the Sailor in Dnipropetrovsk may have been completely unaware of the vory's rites and rituals. Or it may be the case that Vitali Vitaliev was simply ignorant of the traditions the Sailor may have represented. Nevertheless, there are at least fragmentary signs that a new generation of thieves did integrate themselves into the growing culture of state corruption during the Brezhnev era. In 1972, police uncovered an extensive extortion ring organised by an unabashed vor dubbed 'the Mongol'. Gennady Karkov earned this nickname on account of his Asiatic features. After having served six years in prison for theft, he assembled a gang of thirty men and proceeded to extract hefty sums from black marketeers under the pain of torture. Karkov had the run of his Moscow fiefdom for over a decade until his imprisonment in 1972.[174] He set an example for the kind of power unabashed gangsters would have over the Soviet Union's burgeoning shadow economy.

A rapid decline in living standards in the 1980s provided the context for the vory's increased visibility in the Soviet Union. Gorbachev's policy of perestroika led to a proliferation of large and small entrepreneurs who were ripe for exploitation. The ranks of potential thieves grew in tandem with the return of thousands of broken and desperate men coming home from the fighting in Afghanistan. Meanwhile, the impoverishment of the Soviet state weakened all efforts at maintaining a well-run marketplace. Police officers and petty officials who earned a mere pittance in wages were now even more corruptible than at any time in the past. Crime of various types skyrocketed as conditions worsened. In 1986, there were 1,100 extortion cases in Russia; three years later, that number rose to over 4,000. New records were set following the dissolution of the Soviet Union, with extortion cases topping off at over 17,000 in 1996.[175]

As a system of economic oligarchs arose after 1991, violence became endemic among Russia's newly minted patricians. Allying oneself to a street gang or a distinguished vor became an essential part of doing business. Chechen gangsters, for example, served as security guards for Boris Berezovsky. Despite their growing exposure, very few thieves-in-law became members of the post-Soviet elite. One noted exception was Otari Kvantrishvili, or Kvazho to his closest associates. Born in rural Georgia but raised in Moscow, Kvazho was a sports, gambling and wrestling enthusiast as a young man. He also possessed a violent streak, leading to his conviction for gang rape in 1966.[176] Inducted as a proper member of the vory, Kvazho solidified his place in the Moscow underworld as a member of Gennady Karkov's gang. He papered over his early career as an extortionist and criminal savant as the USSR dissolved. He established a charitable organisation and joint stock companies that thinly masked his dealings in smuggled goods and illicit currency trading. He entered uncharted waters with the election of Boris Yeltsin. Whether attending tennis matches as a part of the president's greater entourage, or hobnobbing with famous singers, Kvantrishvili went far beyond the realm of the traditional vor in all respects. It ultimately proved his undoing. After he declared his intention to enter politics, which included the founding of his own party, his fellow vory in Moscow passed a death sentence upon him. The notion that a traditional thief, let alone a Georgian, desired such power was an anathema. 'Moscow,' one informant declared, 'is not Sicily.'[177] Foreign journalists who picked up on his assassination in 1994 saw his death as emblematic of the grim state of post-Soviet society. Moscow that year, as one British reporter saw it, was now the world's crime capital, a place with 'more mafia victims per week than in the worst days of Chicago, more casinos than Las Vegas per head of population, [and] more prostitutes and massage parlours than anywhere else' on the globe.[178]

Another scion of the Mongol's gang left Moscow and went west. Vyacheslav Ivankov had joined Gennady Karkov's gang in the early 1970s. Yet with his arrest on firearms and narcotics charges, he missed much of the early days of the vory's resurgence during the last years of Gorbachev's rule. With his release from prison in 1991, he allied himself with the Solntsevo, an expanding gang from the capital's southwestern suburbs. Ivankov, known as 'the Jap' in criminal circles, took to the gang even though its leaders were not inducted members of the thieves' world. Rather than make his way in an already hotly contested environment, Ivankov accepted an assignment to move to the United States. By the early 1990s, American cities had welcomed in hundreds of thousands of Soviet émigrés. A significant number of migrants came as refugees in the 1970s. Most were Jews who were allowed to leave the USSR, who settled en masse in New York City and south Florida. By the early 1980s, some 20,000 were clustered in the neighbourhood of Brighton Beach on the southern shores of Brooklyn.[179] A second larger wave of émigrés arrived in the waning days of Communist rule. By the early 1990s, Hollywood, in the heart of Los Angeles, boasted an Armenian population of 45,000, the majority comprising recent refugees from the Soviet Caucasus.[180] Ivankov clearly arrived with a plan to exploit the growth of these communities and prosper from his ill-gotten gains. In 1995, police arrested him in New York on charges of extorting $3.5 million from two Manhattan businessmen.[181] His reputation as the 'Russian godfather' in the US was well established in the international press even before he was sent away to prison that year.

FBI Director Louis Freeh had declared in 1994 that Russian mobsters were 'rapidly networking' with the likes of La Cosa Nostra, the triads, the yakuza and the Colombian cartels,[182] and cases from around the world appeared to validate his alarm. The murder of a low-level Russian mobster in the small Colombian town of Melgar in 1998 highlighted a sudden increase in cocaine trafficking from Latin America to the former USSR. With former Soviet citizens paying as much as four times the normal rate in the United States, experts estimated that up to fifty tons of coke was arriving in Russia for local consumption and redistribution to Europe.[183] News reports from Sri Lanka, Thailand, Israel and Japan spoke of sophisticated Russian networks trading in women lured abroad to work as prostitutes.[184] Other sensational stories told of Russian mobsters co-opting willing and unwilling sports stars in various schemes. Many of these cases included players drawn from the National Hockey League. US investigators alleged in the late '90s that Slava Fetisov, a legendary member of the Red Army team and Detroit Red Wings, was once president of a company Vyacheslav Ivankov used to launder money. Fetisov denied ever knowing Ivankov but admitted that he was once acquainted with the celebrity vor, Otari Kvantrishvili. 'Yes,' Fetisov told one reporter, 'we know each other but I never knew what he's been doing. I never get [into] any business with those people, never.'[185]

As pervasive as the notion of the 'Russian mafia' became during the 1990s, it was widely understood that gangsters from the former Soviet Union formed no national whole. Russian news outlets, as well as the press abroad, took great pains to emphasise the specific threat of vory and thugs from the Caucasus. Of all the old Soviet nationalities to inspire fear in and beyond Russia, Chechens struck the most resounding chord. Outsiders who tracked the rise of organised crime in the late Soviet Union at first took note of Chechen gangsters as one of many ethnic groups operating in major cities such as Moscow. 'The Soviet mafia is run, to a large extent, along ethnic lines,' one British journalist projected in 1989. 'Go to the Uzbekistan restaurant in Moscow to find the Ossetian mob from the Caucasus or to the "Baku" to see the Chechen godfathers ensconced, having ousted the boys from Saratov in a shoot-out six months ago.'[186] It required the breakup of the USSR, and the declaration of an independent state in Chechnya, for many outsiders to appreciate the terrible gravity of Chechen history. As a region conquered by the Romanovs in the mid-nineteenth century, Chechens distinguished themselves for their fierce defiance of Russian rule. Neither the tsar's armies, nor Stalin's efforts at collectivisation, fully broke Chechen resistance. Under the pretext of the Nazi invasion, Moscow intensified its campaign of oppression in the Caucasus. In 1944, Stalin sanctioned efforts to expel nearly 500,000 Chechens from their homes. Most were transported to Kazakhstan and other locations in Central Asia. Soviet officials estimated that at least a quarter of the deportees died or disappeared as a result of the deportations.[187] Even while in exile, local administrators maligned Chechens as innate bandits inclined towards theft and non-compliance.

Only a portion of the deportees returned to Chechnya after their term of exile was lifted in 1957. Many stayed on in Kazakhstan. Others relocated to major cities in the Soviet Union, including Moscow. An official census in 2002 estimated, for example, that 20,000 Chechens lived in Russia's capital. The real number, others guessed, was likely close to 100,000.[188] At least some Chechens reconciled themselves to the Soviet state and integrated themselves into various elements of the Communist administration. Far greater numbers remained disillusioned and aggrieved, especially among those who lived in urban settings outside of Chechnya. Though small handfuls may have been inducted into the ranks of the thieves' world, Chechens who drifted into crime tended to band together on the basis of blood and national solidarity. Gangsters in the 1980s and '90s tended to refer to themselves as members of a brotherhood (*bratva*) as opposed to any mafia.[189] With the proliferation of the extortion trade at the end of the Gorbachev era, Chechen gangs made a name for themselves for their violence as well as their distinct look. 'They got their style – zoot suits, slick hair – from Western mafia movies, even though they had plenty of money to buy modern clothing,' one police inspector observed. In noting their clannishness and distrust of outsides, they seemed to him 'very similar to the Sicilian mafia'.[190]

The outbreak of war in Chechnya in 1994 further elevated the stature of Chechen criminals. As guerrillas battled Russian forces in the Chechen countryside and the country's newly declared capital in Grozny, Russian media accentuated their role within the Moscow underworld. The time-honoured trope that Chechens were nothing more than inborn bandits and Muslim fanatics became an inescapable part of how both citizens and officials interpreted the nature of Chechen criminality. This enmity helped inspire the plot of Russia's first mafia blockbuster, *Brother*, which was released in 1997. Taking its cues in part from the daily headlines, the film featured a young Russian veteran of the Chechen war who drifts into the Moscow underworld. His chief antagonists, naturally, are Chechens.

Precisely when and how Chechen brotherhoods came to be involved in transnational crime is not clear. Yet as early as 1991, their presence beyond the borders of the Soviet Union became undeniable. A string of drug trafficking, money laundering and murder cases pointed to the spread of Chechen gang influence in cities such as Frankfurt and London. Like the 'Russian mafia', the 'Chechen mafia' became a brand name that inspired dread among both the public as well as rival criminals.[191] Gangs from the former Soviet Union, however, were by no means the only mafias to cast a shadow from the old Communist east. Against the backdrop of the civil war in Yugoslavia in the early '90s, the increased presence and influence of Albanian criminals assumed even greater significance in cities throughout Western Europe and the United States. Like Chechens and the mysterious vory, Albanian gangsters appeared to be a force cloaked in mystery. As a people associated with the most mountainous and remote portions of the Balkans, Western observers tended to depict them as clannish, backward and prone to blood feuds. How and why Albanians first came to be associated with mafias, however, had very little to do with these crude stereotypes. What many euphemistically would call the Albanian mafia possessed a concrete history that dated back to before the fall of the Berlin Wall.

As in other cases, the development of Albanian syndicates cannot be understood without appreciating the makings of the modern Albanian diaspora. Like the global community of Irish people and their descendants, there are many times more Albanians living outside their ancestral lands than on them. The formation of a worldwide Albanian community is rooted in a series of terrible events in the twentieth century. The Balkan Wars of 1912–13, as well as Yugoslav campaigns to expel Muslims from the south of the country, drove hundreds of thousands of Albanians from their lands before 1945. Patterns of abuse continued to force Albanians out of Yugoslavia during the Communist period, with tens of thousands leaving for Turkey and the West before the breakup of the country in 1991. The fall of Enver Hoxha's brutal Communist regime unleashed an even larger deluge of refugees flowing out of Albania. By 2001, it was estimated that up to 800,000 citizens of Albania departed their homes for Greece, Italy and points beyond.¹⁹² Despite the scale of these migration waves, indications of Albanian involvement in organised crime were limited before the outbreak of Yugoslavia's civil wars. New York City was among the first locations where the activities of Albanian gangsters came into public view. In 1984, federal prosecutors arrested four men as a part of a loose network of traffickers who had funnelled 110 pounds of heroin from Turkey to the US via Yugoslavia. This lesser known 'Albanian Connection', as one narcotics agent put it, constituted a new avenue for the drug's distribution within the United States, amounting, it was believed, to as much as 40 per cent of heroin imported into the country during that time.¹⁹³

Albanian linkages within the heroin trade drew far greater attention as fighting raged in the western Balkans. Belgrade's heightened oppression of Albanians continued as war consumed neighbouring Bosnia, a campaign which culminated with the outbreak of war in Kosovo in 1999. By the end of that year, a final flood of refugees swept into Western Europe and the United States. By the year 2000, Albanians constituted 6 per cent of the population of Switzerland.¹⁹⁴ The sudden, shocking appearance of so many of these migrants in various corners of Europe coloured early reporting of Albanian drug networks in the 1990s. Years before the start of the war in Kosovo, policy experts warned of a continentally active 'Albanian mafia' that rivalled or surpassed the influence of gangs from the former Soviet Union. Remote villages and towns such as Veliki Trnovac (the supposed 'Medellín of the Balkans') acquired reputations as hubs of the European heroin trade.¹⁹⁵ At first, no face, gang, family or clan was associated with the rapid increase in Albanian-linked narcotics cases. Many assumed their collective strength and success stemmed from their culture. 'They are relics of an archaic tribal society,' one German exposé posed. Their clannishness, amorality and brutality were what gave them a 'competitive advantage' in 'infiltrating Western civilization'.¹⁹⁶ American officials, however, suspected early on that at least some Albanian traffickers possessed links to militants seeking to free Kosovo from Yugoslav rule. On the day NATO began its bombardment of Serbia in March 1999, officials from the European Union convened an emergency session dedicated to what they called the 'Kosovar Narcotics Trafficking Networks'. Among the more serious elements of these networks was the Kosovo Liberation Army, which was then fighting for its life with the assistance of NATO warplanes.[197]

Though officials and experts possessed only vague ideas as to the history and innerworkings the 'Albanian mafia', most were certain that Turkey played a central role in its origins. By the end of the twentieth century, Turkish syndicates operating in Europe bore only a passing resemblance to the gangs that had aided the French Connection. Though some major traffickers, such as İhsan Sekban and Hüseyin Eminoğlu, remained active as the Marseille mafia was coming apart, a new generation of traffickers and gangsters had begun to make their presence known back in the 1970s. Their roots, however, were far more eclectic and fractious than their predecessors. At least some fancied themselves as *kabadayı*. Like their counterparts in Lebanon and other portions of the Middle East, this class of Turkish strongmen presented themselves as caretakers of the Istanbul and Ankara underworlds. As the supposed descendants of Ottoman-era street thugs, they derived most of their infamy from their role as gambling magnates and extortionists. A select few augmented their wealth through heroin smuggling and the illicit arms trade.

A parallel, and at times overlapping, component of Turkey's changing underworld was the growing visibility of Kurdish traffickers and gangsters. Though it is possible to find evidence of some Kurdish involvement in the heroin trade earlier in the century, the breakdown of the French Connection allowed many Kurds an opportunity to capitalise on their strategic advantages. With much of Turkey's Kurdish population residing on the country's southern and eastern frontier, many aspiring smugglers possessed easy access to cheap sources of opium coming from Afghanistan, Pakistan and Iran. As local opium production came under increased government oversight, Kurds joined other Turkish citizens in building heroin refinement and distribution networks catering to European consumers.

Other forces caused the character of the Turkish underworld to change. Since the 1960s, Turkish citizens were among hundreds of thousands of immigrants invited to settle in Western Europe as guest workers. These numbers grew through the 1970s and '80s as thousands, particularly Kurds, leftists and religious minorities, fled the country due to acts of government oppression. Many of those who came during this latter period were instrumental in aiding the growth of Turkey's most notorious terrorist organisation, the Kurdish Workers' Party (better known as the PKK). Among the more influential émigré groups known for supporting the PKK were drug smugglers. Behçet Cantürk, perhaps the most famous Kurdish trafficker of the 1970s, actively financed Kurdish militants in both Iraq and Turkey in conjunction with arms dealers and heroin retailers based in Europe. Right-wing activists, as well as well-known kabadayı, were no less drawn to the narcotics industry. Newspapers in the 1970s and 1980s frequently featured underworld gossip concerning drug dealing kabadayı bosses and their links to political radicals. Emblematic of this trend was gambling magnate İsmail Hacısüleymanoğlu, who, in addition to his role as a patron of Istanbul's underworld, was a financial backer of Turkey's most ardent nationalist party, the Nationalist Action Party.[198] After his apprehension by Turkish authorities, Behçet Cantürk charged Hacısüleymanoğlu with monopolising Turkish heroin smuggling into Holland during the 1980s.[199]

This complex interplay of politics, migration and crime became the stuff of scandal by the 1980s and '90s. In the spring of 1981, a Turkish national, Mehmet Ali Ağca, came within inches of taking the life of Pope John Paul II. Ağca's deranged ravings did little to mask what seemed like a conspiracy involving both Turkey and Communist Bulgaria. Years earlier, he had been arrested for murdering one of Turkey's most renown investigative journalists. The killing, investigators concluded, was in retaliation for a series of newspaper articles detailing crimes linked to the right-wing Nationalist Action Party. After escaping from prison with the help of other extremists, Ağca found sanctuary in Bulgaria among a cohort of Turkish heroin traffickers, a group which included İsmail Hacısüleymanoğlu. Newspapers and former officials in Turkey added to the scandal claiming that several activists and traffickers associated with Ağca were in fact agents of the Turkish intelligence service.[200]

Events in the fall of 1996 confirmed that the Turkish state was in league with the Turkish underworld. That November, emergency crews responded to a terrible car crash involving four passengers in the small town of Susurluk, south and east of Istanbul. Only one passenger survived. Among the dead were an Istanbul police captain and one of the most wanted men in Turkey, Abdullah Çatlı. In the late 1970s, Çatlı had murdered seven leftist students in Ankara and assisted Mehmet Ali Ağca in escaping from prison. He had been on the move in more recent years after his own prison escape in Switzerland where he was being held for heroin trafficking. In the mangled car investigators also found guns, drugs and a diplomatic passport signed by the Minister of the Interior (the alias printed on the passport was previously employed by Mehmet Ali Ağca). Adding further suspicions was the one surviving passenger, a member of parliament and the head of a pro-government Kurdish militia. A firestorm of outrage and disbelief followed what is now remembered as the 'Susurluk incident'. After a string of enquiries and reports, government ministers admitted that they had employed Çatlı as a hitman to target suspected militants and sympathisers linked to the PKK.

This brazen alliance between the Turkish state and what many in the local press referred to as the Turkish mafia led to the coining of a new phrase among commentators: the deep state (*derin devlet*). Though its origins are somewhat obscure, one prominent journalist speculated it was first uttered before Susurluk.[201] At first, the deep state referred to a general culture of subterfuge within the government. Over time, it assumed other connotations. It could mean the bonds and interests shared by the country's civilian elite, its military and the underworld. It could stand for secret cabals or organisations. Or it could constitute a transnational conspiracy involving plotters inside of Turkey and backers found abroad. As the new century began, many Turks increasingly saw their tortured history as a product of the deep state.

European commentators tended to interpret the implications of the Susurluk scandal as a testament to Turkey's ramshackle state.[202] By the end of the 1990s, the country's economy was sputtering. The government's efforts to crush the PKK had left tens of thousands dead and hundreds of thousands displaced. People of all walks of life were fleeing the country in record numbers. In 1972 there were only 600,000 Turkish citizens living Europe as immigrants or asylum seekers. Thirty years later, this population had grown more than fourfold. Perhaps more striking, 800,000 of these newcomers attained citizenship in their host countries.[203] With the signing of the Treaty of Maastricht, many living in the newly christened European Union wrestled with the implications of so many Turkish workers and naturalised citizens. As tensions over the influence of Turkish migration escalated, many critics pointed to the rising influence of Turkish syndicates operating across the continent. It was widely believed that it was Turkish godfathers who supplied Albanian drug smugglers and dealers with the heroin they sold in cities such as Hamburg and Zurich. Amid stories of the Turkey's war against the PKK, European officials cast greater attention to Kurdish gangs at work in Holland

and the UK. In 1998, police arrested Hüseyin Baybaşın, head of one of the largest heroin smuggling rings in European history. Dubbed the 'Pablo Escobar of heroin', Baybaşın and his brother had worked their way up from petty dealers of cigarettes and other contraband in Turkey to multi-ton drug importers by the 1970s.[204] Once Dutch authorities sentenced him to prison for life in 2001, Hüseyin Baybaşın spun tales for the press that were incredible in scope. He had, like Behçet Cantürk before him, supported the PKK financially. Yet he also insisted that his career had been aided by the Turkish state from its start. Half the money from every deal he made, he claimed, went to the government in Ankara. 'To us, it was a kind of tax, in exchange for which we received protection in all aspects. If the money was confiscated or we were arrested, then our contacts with the government came to fetch us and said that we worked for the state. They even protected us in Europe.'[205] In addition to unofficially financing Turkish cultural centres in Europe, Baybaşın swore he had received training as an intelligence agent. He went on to claim he received requests for assistance in various intelligence matters from a number of European governments. His jailhouse revelations suggested that Turkey's deep state was a force with international reach.[206]

The deep state was still not yet global parlance at the time Baybaşın went away to prison. That moment came decades later thanks to Donald Trump's popularisation of the phrase. Nonetheless, many in the world could comprehend the essence of Baybaşın's claims by the 1980s and '90s. Revelations from Latin America and the old Soviet Union suggested that the rise of 'new' mafias was indicative of a number of post-Cold War trends and appeared symptomatic of a more unstable world. Due to organised crime, as well as terrorism and ethnic conflict, many who hoped the world had earned a peace dividend became quickly disillusioned. The troubles gripping Russia, as one observer noted, had particularly 'dampened the triumphant mood' in the West.[207]

Yes, mafias had been a part of global affairs long before the Iron Curtain came down. Yet La Cosa Nostra, both in America and Italy, as well as the triads and the yakuza, were often depicted as parasites, discrete anomalies embedded within regions or cities in otherwise stable or reasonably well-governed countries. What appeared to make the Russian, Nigerian, Balkan, Mexican and Turkish mafias different was their relationship to the states that nurtured them. New mafias, at their worst, were expressions, or perhaps quite literal extensions, of innately flawed states. At a time that featured the troubling rise of 'failed' or 'failing' states, new mafias represented threats that went beyond the banal challenges of law enforcement. They constituted grave threats to a world order no longer defined by superpower competition. 'The end of the Cold War,' as President Bill Clinton summarised it, 'fundamentally changed America's security imperatives. The central challenge – the threat of communist expansion – is gone. The dangers we face today are more diverse.' Maintaining global peace now demanded international co-ordination on countering menaces deriving from civil wars, weak states and rogue nations. Together with tackling problems such as the nuclear proliferation, peacekeeping and terrorism, combatting mafias reflected the new political realities of a more integrated and globalised world.[208]

When describing events during the final decades of the twentieth century, commentators tended to dispense with certain nuances in talking of the new mafias of the post-Cold War. Unlike Italy or the United States during the 1950s and '60s, no government held extensive public enquiries bent upon forensically documenting or proving the existence of mighty crime families. The presumed collective dangers posed by Nigerian, Jamaican, Colombian, Mexican, Russian and Chechen criminals were enough to openly indict them as expressions of the era's emerging mafias. Virtually no one, for example, spoke of Turkish syndicates possessing rigid systems of rank or ritual. Albanian gangs may have been bound by blood (or *gyak*) and organised by authoritative chiefs (or *kryetar*).[209] Yet the identities of these chieftains, as well as who was among the first pioneers of Albanian or Turkish organised crime, remained completely unknown. Authorities asserted that Albanian gangs abided by a system of medieval law known as the Kanun of Lekë Dukagjini. As a series of prescriptions governing family relations as well as blood feuds, many assumed that the Kanun functioned as an Albanian version of the Mafia's omerta in Sicily. In truth, according to polls conducting in the mid-2000, only 23 per cent of Albanians living in the Balkans had ever read the code, let alone fully grasped its particulars.[210] Arguably for many journalists, officials and readers, the full history of the supposed mafias of Nigeria, Turkey and Kosovo was somewhat irrelevant. The threat they embodied was immediate and perhaps emblematic of far more daunting domestic issues such as immigration, economic inequality and generational discontent. Moreover, they were taken as examples of what seemed like an ever-growing list of mafias now inundating the Western world. In this sense, the notion of the mafia was becoming more diluted. The threshold for what constituted a mafia, at least outside the realm of academia or public policy, was minimised. More than ever, mafias were not perceived as entities solely brought to life by gangsters and professional criminals. The public everywhere grew more accustomed to seeing terrorists, bankers, lawyers, business leaders and politicians as equal contributors to the inner workings of organised crime. As a new millennium progressed, talk of 'deep states' or de facto 'mafia states' became commonplace.

Still, it is hard not to hear echoes of the past in accounts from the 1990s. For many, what made these mafia terrifying were the cultures and personages they represented. From the perspective of the West, gangsters still tended to be foreigners from lands so often deemed exotic and backward looking. Or, at the very least, they came from ethnic or racial groups long perceived as troublesome or disposed towards crime. A new decorum generally prevented many journalists and officials from speaking explicitly of new racial or national perils. Yet the xenophobia that inspired earlier views of mafias, triads and yakuza remained very much present.

CONCLUSION

The Great Dilution: Making Sense of the Twenty-First Century

When we first meet Tony Soprano, we find him reluctantly revealing his very private sense of foreboding. 'It's good to be in something from the ground floor,' he cryptically tells his therapist. 'I came too late for that, I know. But lately I'm getting the feeling I might be in at the end. That the best is over.' 'Many Americans, I think, feel that way,' Dr Melfi assures him. 'I think about my father,' he continues. 'He never reached the heights like me. But in a lot of ways, he had it better. He had his people. They had their standards. They had pride. Today, what do we got?'

From the start, the viewer is to understand the duality of Tony's fears. When *The Sopranos* debuted in January 1999, it was touted as a mafia show with a twist. Viewers, however, likely knew that the American Mafia had become a shadow of its former self. Subsequent scenes, be it with Tony's nephew Christopher or his Uncle Junior, appear to affirm this fact. Yet as we watch Tony plodding down his driveway to pick up his newspaper, the greater context of his anxieties is displayed subtly on the screen.

Conclusion

The front-page headline of his local paper reads, 'Clinton Warns Medicare May Be Bust In Yr. 2000'. Scene notes on the original script of this premiere episode tells us that the headline's placement was deliberate.[1] America, we are led to believe, is also on the wane.

Both tropes, the parallel decline of the Mafia and the United States, wind their way through the full run of the show's six long seasons. In shaping the narrative arc of *The Sopranos*, David Chase, the show's creator, drew upon current events. The shadow of doom, he told one interviewer, grew darker for Tony Soprano in the wake of September 11th. 'I think it changed the whole show,' he recalled of 9/11. The series, and its main character, 'became a little more melancholy after that', abandoning much of its early light-heartedness and humour. Chase acknowledged that it may seem unrealistic to some that the Mafia would be so affected by the collapse of the Twin Towers. However, he had heard from 'FBI guys' that actual mobsters 'were volunteering to finger Islamic radicals' in the aftermath of the attacks.[2]

In the real world, American officials openly expressed doubts about the American Mafia's loyalty. 'They will deal with anybody if they can make a buck,' one senior FBI official declared in 2006. 'They will sell to a terrorist just as easily as they would sell to an order of Franciscan monks ... If the mob has explosives and a terrorist wants them and they have the money, they could become instant friends.'[3] Indeed, the horror of 9/11 almost immediately begot greater examination of Al-Qaeda's links to organised crime. With Washington poised to strike at Osama bin Laden's bases in Afghanistan in the fall of 2001, news outlets frequently highlighted the country's links to the global heroin trade. In truth, there was nothing new or novel about Afghanistan's relationship with narcotics trafficking. International concern over the extent of illicit opium production in Afghanistan dated back to at least the 1950s. As Turkey began to implement greater controls over its own crop in the mid-1970s, Afghani opium cultivators expanded production to meet foreign demand. Opium smuggling continued through to the end of the century despite the 1979 Soviet invasion and the outbreak of civil war thereafter. As the United States laid the groundwork for its offensive against Al-Qaeda in late 2001, some journalists noted ironically Afghanistan's ruling Taliban had effectively banned opium farming under UN supervision the year previously.[4] Other reports from the region were more dubious. Days before the first US warplanes began targeting Al-Qaeda's camps, it was revealed that Osama bin Laden previously had attempted to concoct a higher potency variant of heroin in the hopes of producing 'greater addiction and havoc than drugs available in Western cities'. His plans for a 'super heroin' assault on the West failed, despite purportedly attempting to recruit chemists for the job.[5]

Narcotics remained at the forefront of the news as the War against Terror progressed. Reporting from the Caucasus suggested that Chechen guerillas with links to Al-Qaeda relied heavily on heroin trafficking to fund their operations against Russia and the West.[6] Meanwhile, NATO troops found themselves pitted against Afghani fighters who relied upon illicit opium sales to fund their insurgency. As time passed, international forces had to find ways to fight the resistance and wean farmers away from growing poppies. Both tasks proved difficult. One Washington thinktank declared in 2010 that Afghanistan was in the grips of a 'narco-jihad' that was succeeding despite the coalition's efforts.[7] Other experts posed that the drug trade was only a marginal source of financing for the Taliban and other fighters. Supporters gleaned funds through robberies and kidnappings for ransoms in Pakistan. Other forms of contraband financing were no less important, including such things as the sale of stolen cars and illicit logging undertaken by the elusive 'timber mafias' of Afghanistan and Pakistan.[8] Each of these industries continued to thrive after

Conclusion

the withdrawal of US troops from Kabul in the summer of 2021. Meanwhile opium production surged after the American departure, accounting for approximately 14 per cent of Afghanistan's gross domestic product in 2022. A post-war ban on poppy cultivation by the Taliban did much to suppress the importance of Afghan opium but little to hinder the growth and diversification of the country's narcotics industry.[9] According to statistics gathered by the UN, nearly thirty tons worth of methamphetamine was seized in 2021, constituting a twelve-fold increase over the previous five years. Afghanistan currently ranks second only to Myanmar for meth production globally.[10]

Afghanistan's transformation into a hothouse of illicit doings is symptomatic of trends in our age. Conventional or 'traditional' mafias no longer appear to monopolise the business of organised crime. Official studies and journalistic investigations on various continents show ongoing patterns of terrorist involvement in drugs and other lucrative crimes, revealing that 'non-traditional' actors have supplanted gangsters as the main purveyors of vice. Meanwhile, multiple governments today stand accused of promoting organised criminal activities within their borders and beyond them. The existence of such 'mafia states' is worrying, as are the court cases levied against prominent corporations and banks that show business leaders and major industries act as extensions of the world of organised crime.

Reports from Afghanistan and elsewhere have not necessarily denigrated or minimised the importance of so-called 'classic mafias'. Far from it. The introduction of digital trading, internet commerce and other contemporary industries have provided many historic crime groups with a second wind. Court cases and headlines from across the world confirm this. An even more dramatic transformation has gripped the drugs trade. The steady popularisation of new synthetic drugs has reshaped the global consumer market and created new addiction epidemics and difficulties for law enforcement. Amid all of this, news stories and films set in Tokyo, New York and Naples offer frequent reminders that the mafias of old are still very much with us.

For much of their notional history, mafias were depicted as collectives and conspiracies born from without. Gangsters and mafiosi often appeared or were portrayed as foreigners, minorities or the product of strange or exotic cultures. The gangs, societies and families they formed were seen as alien, or better yet parasitic, in relation to the nations, states and economies that hosted them. More recent events undermine that supposition. Twenty-first century mafias are not necessarily separate or distinguishable from the 'establishment' or the 'mainstream'. What, after all, do you call a state or corporation engaged in organised criminal activity? And what is so special about mafiosi when so many politicians, businessmen and terrorists are seen as behaving no differently?

THE TERROR-MAFIA NEXUS IN PERSPECTIVE

Precisely when Sami al-Khoury departed this world remains unknown. As Lebanon's foremost contributor to the French Connection, it is likely he retired before his country's dissolution into anarchy. If he did live to see the start of the Lebanese civil war, it was very likely he stood to make a profit. The outbreak of fighting in 1975 compelled multiple factions to engage in illicit commerce to finance their movements and secure territory. Smuggling operations thrived along the coast, creating lucrative markets for stolen cars, contraband cigarettes and other illicit wares. Drug trafficking boomed as farmers expanded production and dabbled in new crops. Sami al-Khoury's birthplace, the rough Bekaa Valley, assumed greater importance as the beating heart of Lebanon's drug economy. In addition to hashish, long a staple of the region, locals planted opium poppies and opened

Conclusion

small conversion laboratories for the purpose of exporting morphine and heroin. By 1978, Lebanon was exporting an estimated 10,000 tons of hash annually.[11] Drugs not produced locally were often transhipped from abroad. Shipments of Afghan-sourced heroin, some estimated in the tons, passed through Lebanese ports between 1975 and 2000. Lebanon's immense global diaspora was integral to many of the crimes hatched during the civil war. Conspirators of Lebanese descent were identified as complicit in shady deals and money laundering spanning Australia, West Africa, the Americas and Europe. Meanwhile, leading political figures in Lebanon accrued shockingly large fortunes during the growth of organised crime. Members of the prominent Gemayel family, which oversaw numerous Christian militias in the civil war, netted annual income of $1 to $5 billion off the sale of hashish and other smuggled goods entering and exiting the ports they controlled.[12]

Hezbollah, the Shia Islamist group, was established amid the hashish industry's renaissance in the Bekaa Valley. From its origins in the early 1980s, many of its earliest members heralded from villages and towns where hemp and poppy fields dotted the landscape. Awakened and mobilised with the help of Syrian and Iranian agents, Hezbollah's fighters threw themselves into combat, attacking Israeli occupation forces and foreign peacekeepers. Their greatest coup came in 1983 with the detonation of a truck bomb that claimed the lives of over 300 American and French soldiers. With Ronald Reagan's War on Drugs in full swing, American commentators keyed in on the connection between the group and the narcotics trade emanating from their main base in the Bekaa. Even though definitive links were not established during this early stage of Hezbollah's existence, the fact that an Islamic resistance group, backed by the defiantly revolutionary government in Iran, was associated with drugs was an irony few observers could pass up. Ayatollah Khomeinei, one prominent critic wrote in 1988, sanctioned the trade since it 'served the dual purpose of debilitating the Great Satan and paying the bills' on behalf its fighters in Lebanon.[13]

Hezbollah emerged from the Lebanese Civil War stronger than many of its rivals within the country. In forming a veritable state within a state in Lebanon's south, its leadership gradually oversaw the expansion of its criminal enterprises. Through the assistance of supporters and confederates in various states throughout the world, Hezbollah developed an intricate web of companies and charities that helped it launder money and finance its activities. A critical source of these funds was narcotics. Connections forged through the Lebanese diaspora brought Hezbollah into contact with cocaine producers in Latin America. Its brokers brought it into contact with other militant groups such as the FARC in Colombia, as well as newly established cartels such as the Zetas of Mexico.[14] Syria's own collapse into civil war led Hezbollah to branch out beyond more 'traditional' narcotics. The rapidly growing field of synthetic drugs found a home in territories claimed by Syrian dictator Bashar al-Assad. Among the new narcotics to hit the market was Captagon, an amphetamine admixture. Though Hezbollah's supreme leader, Hassan Nasrallah, denied any ties to the trade before his death, press reporting and expert analysis from the Levant suggests that Hezbollah engaged in the Captagon market as a regulator and exporter of the drug to various states in the region.[15]

Revelations that Hezbollah profited from drugs were fodder for those who have heralded the rise of narcoterrorism across the world. Lebanon's premiere militant group, however, was only one of many to inspire this realisation. The term was first used by the President of Peru, Belaúnde Terry, in 1983. For him, the brutal campaign waged by the Shining Path on counternarcotics officers and the country's military was nothing short of *narcoterrorismo*.[16] Evidence from other warzones and states under

Conclusion

siege made the concept of narcoterrorism globally applicable. The FARC collaborated with Colombia's cartels. Chechen rebels and fighters loyal to the PKK taxed drug smugglers operating within their respective territories. There was also the case of the Kosovo Liberation Army, whose links to heroin trafficking prompted Serb officials to insist that they were fighting 'bandit-terrorist activity' in their country.[17]

Talk of a 'terror-crime nexus' assumed new dimensions with the opening of the War on Terror. Western officials and journalists openly speculated that Al-Qaeda stood poised to exploit local underworlds for their own potential gain. News editors and commentators mused over various nightmare scenarios, including joint plots that would see Al-Qaeda acquire nuclear material. Meanwhile, clear patterns of evidence suggested that guerrillas in Afghanistan and Iraq were making the most of the aid provided by money launderers and illicit traffickers. It was estimated in 2006 that anti-coalition fighters in Iraq were generating anywhere between $70 and $200 million annually in financing through a variety of illicit trades, including kidnapping, counterfeiting and oil smuggling. If such estimates were correct, one US report declared, 'terrorist and insurgent groups in Iraq may have surplus funds with which to support other terrorist organisations outside of Iraq'.[18]

Terrorists, in truth, have always drawn strength from what may generally be called organised crime. Radical groups plaguing the West in the nineteenth century relied heavily upon smuggling and other schemes to attain arms and money. The proliferation of resistance groups fighting Ottoman rule in the Balkans, for example, gave birth to a vibrant gun-running industry that endured beyond the First World War. In addition to smuggling second-hand and stolen arms, Balkan traffickers dabbled in illicit tobacco sales as a secondary source of income.[19] The growth of the Palestine Liberation Organisation was certainly indebted to financial donations offered by Saudi Arabia and other Gulf states, yet after Yasser Arafat's organisation settled in Beirut before the Lebanese Civil War, it too became engrossed in criminal activity: alongside Turkish extremists like Abdullah Çatlı and Mehmet Ali Ağca, PLO agents found sanctuary in Bulgaria and partook in the country's thriving heroin trade.[20]

Despite these trends, terrorism's rise through the second half of the twentieth century tended to be seen as distinct from the world of mafias. Nevertheless, the realisation that terrorists behaved like gangsters provided a welcome pretext to attack and delegitimise the movements they represented. In the wake of the Good Friday Agreement in Northern Ireland, official accusations that members of the Provisional Irish Republican Army had a controlling interest in Belfast's drug trade aroused the ire of news commentators in the United Kingdom.[21] The tenor of this rage grew louder in 2002 when former IRA militants were arrested in Colombia for assisting the FARC in its campaign against the government in Bogotá. Even though the men were not charged with drug trafficking, one British commentator surmised that the IRA possessed 'an ambiguous attitude to hard drugs as it does not want it to be condemned for corrupting young people'.[22] Former leaders of the IRA, as well as some scholars, have consistently cast doubt on the group's involvement in narcotics.

There were still other cases where the line between terrorism and organised crime genuinely blurred to the absolute point of ambiguity. A particularly glaring example of the fuzzy divide between mafias and political extremism can be found in the life of Dawood Ibrahim Kaskar. Ibrahim, like so many gangsters before him, was a product of inauspicious beginnings. He was born in Mumbai in 1955 to a poor Muslim family from the north of India. From the outset of his life, little separated him from the millions who eked out a living in the city. Dawood's father, who attained a job as a policeman, was among the lucky ones. Mumbai's culture

Conclusion

of gangs and kingpins pulled Ibrahim in the opposite direction. In his youth, he thrived among the networks of pickpockets and smugglers who organised themselves according to neighbourhood or along regional, confessional or ethnic lines. Success brought him into the orbit of a powerful syndicate led by Pathan migrants from the north. The Pathans introduced Dawood to far more lucrative trades such as moneylending, gambling and, above all, gold smuggling. In time, he and his own small gang of followers graduated from petty extortion and theft to bank robbery.

At the age of twenty-five he muscled his way into the gold trade, an industry that brought him to markets beyond India. In the early 1970s he developed contacts in Dubai willing to buy gold and other wares. Business and real estate opportunities were rife in this burgeoning eastern metropolis of the newly independent United Arab Emirates, and Ibrahim seized them. With some 85 per cent of its population made up of immigrants, many of whom hailed from south Asia, Dubai's historic and economic ties to India gave Dawood a base from which he continued to grow his interests and influence.[23] He eventually expanded his operations into narcotics trafficking and sports fixing on a grand scale. To this day, a fully comprehensive accounting of Ibrahim's many business dealings, be it lawful or otherwise, remains elusive. Whatever the case may be, notoriety, as well as his purported support for India's film industry, brought Ibrahim into the most elite circles of south Asian life.

As he entered middle age, Dawood Ibrahim's career assumed monstrous dimensions. In December 1992, communal tensions in Mumbai spiked with the demolition of a historic mosque by Hindu nationalists. Months later a string of bombings exploded across the city, leaving 257 dead and hundreds more wounded.[24] Mass arrests quickly prompted Indian authorities to assert that Dawood Ibrahim organised the attack as an act of vengeance. Indian officials further maintained the bombings succeeded with the aid of the Pakistani intelligence service, ISI. Demands for his extradition from Dubai purportedly compelled Ibrahim to relocate to Pakistan, where he may or may not continue to live. His disrepute grew by leaps and bounds a decade later when US officials implicated him in assisting in the terror attacks of September 11th. The precise role he played in the 9/11 conspiracy is not clear. An American congressional report from 2003 simply stated that Ibrahim had 'found common cause with Al-Qaeda' and shared 'smuggling routes with the terror syndicate'.[25] Pakistan has consistently denied connections to the Mumbai bombings in 1993 and asserts it has not given Dawood Ibrahim sanctuary of any kind.

Mumbai's most powerful gangster remains confoundingly understudied and underappreciated outside the subcontinent. His obscurity endures despite receiving the distinction of having been named one of the richest gangsters in history by *Forbes* (Pablo Escobar, according to the magazine, still retains the top spot).[26] Western bias may have a lot to do with his anonymity in much of the world. After all, there is little direct evidence that Dawood's influence extends deeply into Europe and North America. His alleged involvement in illegal gambling and match fixing, for example, has been confined to domestic and international cricket events concerning India and Pakistan. The extent to which Ibrahim's malfeasance does register beyond south Asia has largely concerned his supposed acts of terrorism. To this day, he shoulders the reputation of being India's version of Osama bin Laden.

An uncomfortable truth may be at the heart of Dawood Ibrahim's lack of recognition. Mafias, by and large, are creatures of the Western imagination. Why the world came to care about Capone, Escobar, and other mafia luminaries is the collective fear and intrigue they once inspired among Western officials and everyday citizens. The case of Dawood Ibrahim may reveal something about the extent to which terrorism has usurped the place of mafias within modern Western consciousness. Mafias, at various

Conclusion

points, represented imminent mortal dangers to the integrity of states, economies and societies in West. The 9/11 attacks abruptly displaced this anxiety as Washington and its allies went to war with violent political extremism in various parts of the world. As a smuggler, racketeer and altogether thug, Dawood Ibrahim initially failed to register in the Atlantic world. It was instead as an ally of Al-Qaeda and as an instrument of Muslim extremism in India that he made his presence felt within Washington and other Western capitals. Here and in other cases, the extent to which a terrorist can be distinguished from a gangster may simply be a matter of perspective. That perspective tends to be from the vantage point of the West.

The concept of the mafia, one must remember, first entered popular consciousness during a far earlier age of violent extremism. Nineteenth-century news reports of the political upheaval in Sicily introduced the term into Western parlance. Italy's original mafiosi were similarly treated as expressions of political terror, not just crime. Their resonance as a symptom of the times grew in scope in parallel with other examples from separate parts of the world. By the end of the First World War, commentators perceived mafia-like traits among militants from the Irish Republican Army, Armenia's Dashnaktsutyun and other groups. What altered the notion of the mafia at first derived from the meteoric growth of the global contraband trade, be it in alcohol or narcotics. The United States, more than any other force at work, shifted popular attention away from the early comparisons many made between Sicily's honoured society and political radicals. As the world collected itself in the aftermath of the Axis defeat, mafias became almost exclusively associated with discrete criminal enterprises devoid of any revolutionary goals. Syndicates like La Cosa Nostra (on both sides of the Atlantic), the Camorra, Marseille's Milieu, and the yakuza tended to favour the powers that be. Subsequent groups, such as the Cali Cartel, Jamaica's Shower Posse or the ubiquitous

'Russian mafia' also tended to favour political stability as opposed to revolutionary change.

What, then, changed? Has the world simply regressed or returned to the notion that there is no difference between terrorism and gangsterism? There may be some truth to this rhetorical question. What clearly has changed is the political economy that now envelopes many radical movements. The breadth of the illicit marketplace has grown since the nineteenth century. The narcotics trade, more than any form of commerce, has become a vital resource for would-be militants. Why terrorists involve themselves in illicit trades may not be a pure reflection of choice or utility. Hezbollah did not elect to become involved in drugs because of its attractive profit margins. It instead grew out of the illicit economic environment in which it was founded. The same may be said of the FARC, the PKK and the Taliban. This fact is indicative of how mafias are changing (or at least how they are viewed). Involvement in organised crime does not require excessive effort. The global prevalence of illicit commerce makes it both enticing and accessible for peoples and interests of various walks of life.

MAFIA CAPITALISM: REASSESSING THE BUSINESS OF ORGANISED CRIME

In the late twentieth century, Seagram's was a corporate colossus. From its earliest years as a Montreal-based distiller of spirits, it grew into a multinational conglomerate with holdings stretching across multiple sectors. Its portfolio at one time included stakes in household brands such as Dupont and Universal. Seagram's dramatic rise is inexorably linked to the fortune amassed by Sam Bronfman. He and the rest of his family first found prosperity as hotel owners on the Canadian prairies during the early decades of the twentieth century. A young Sam, however, thought bigger, seeing still greater opportunity in alcohol distribution. With the

Conclusion

advent of Prohibition south of the border, he and his brother established themselves in mail order alcohol shipments and the mixing of spirits for resale. This venture brought the family new revenue streams but also unwanted attention. In 1922, bootleggers murdered Sam's brother-in-law in a Canadian border town just across from North Dakota. Unfazed, Sam relocated to Montreal and dedicated himself to the more lucrative distilling industry. Without a background in alcohol production, he relied on the expertise of others. He incorporated the Seagram's name after acquiring a family-run string of whisky distillers in Quebec and Ontario. The location of his operations granted Sam Bronfman an advantage in supplying bootleggers across the American northeast. Later in life, he steadfastly defended the origins of his extensive wealth. 'Of course we knew where [our alcohol] went,' he told one interviewer, 'but we had no legal proof. And I never went on the other side of the border to count the empty Seagram's bottles.'[27] To this day, the Bronfmans enjoy a distinct place within contemporary Canadian life. As a family of philanthropists and magnates, the Bronfman name adorns university buildings and Jewish education centres across North America.

Mafias likely contributed to the birth of the Seagram's empire but this did not mean that Sam Bronfman was a mafioso. Seagram's early history, however, reveals something important about the nature of mafias. Organised crime, as it was originally conceived by reformers, was not simply an expression of human frailties. Gambling and vice were industries. Those who operated these industries, as American critics first saw them, were not simply lowbrow toughs. They were saloon keepers, club owners, boarding house matrons and the people of influence who protected them. Indeed, regimes of prohibition enabled the ascendency of syndicates, gangs and mafias who shipped contraband wares or oversaw the distribution of illicit goods or services. There were also those like the Bronfmans who were just as essential to the evolution of this underground economy. In the case of the bootlegging trade, otherwise legitimate businesses followed Seagram's lead in knowingly selling to the American market. The Bronfmans were not alone in capitalising on their ill-gotten gains. Legitimate businesses, be they manufacturers, distributors, shippers or bankers, have long played a role in enabling the rise of mafias.

More recent history serves as a reminder that the opposite may also be true: mafias may serve as allies or enablers of otherwise legitimate businesses. News reports in the 1990s engendered an oft-used cliché that a kind of 'wild west' capitalism had replaced Communism through much of the former Soviet Union.[28] In the absence of honest lawmen, gangsters became the guarantors and protectors of aspiring entrepreneurs and conglomerates. Extreme circumstances have not always been necessary for alliances to form between mafias and industry. An honest account of Hollywood's ascendency as a global force is not possible without considering the roles played by mafia-backed fixers and executives. It is a story that is almost singularly embodied in the silent career of one of the most powerful lawyers ever to ply his trade in the United States: Sidney Korshak.

Korshak's first practice was in Chicago in the early 1930s. As a young defence lawyer, he distinguished himself in the service of racketeers and bootleggers linked to Al Capone. The legal aid he gave Chicago's Outfit became a platform from which he expanded his list of clients. He became a dealmaker and advocate in labour disputes and real estate purchases, all the while deepening his ties to gangsters in Chicago, Las Vegas and Los Angeles. Among the friends he made along the way was Lew Wasserman, a talent agent who helped transform the MCA company into a multimedia powerhouse. By the end of the Second World War Korshak was well ensconced among the Hollywood elite and associated leaders of industry. 'He calls himself a labour-relations expert but he's really a fixer,' his friend Johnny Rosselli recalled. 'A union cooks

Conclusion

up a strike and Sid arbitrates it. Instead of a payoff under the table he gets a real big fee, pays taxes on it and cuts it up. All nice and clean.' In addition to Hollywood studios, his client list included several businesses with links to Chicago's Outfit, including the Del Mar Racetrack, Madison Square Garden and Las Vegas's Desert Inn.[29] FBI agents in Los Angeles explicitly expressed apprehension in targeting Korshak despite what they knew about his relations with the American underworld. Senior administrators in Washington concurred that Korshak was a 'prominent lawyer' and issued specific instructions to pursue an investigation only if it could be done 'in a circumspect manner'.[30] Korshak's closest brush with justice was an in-depth series of articles in the *New York Times* in 1976. In addition to detailing a lengthy list of his celebrity clients, such as Lew Wasserman and *Godfather* producer Robert Evans, the series told of his decades-long relationship with top Chicago mobsters such as Tony Accardo and Sam Giancana. A federal investigator told the *Times* that he was the one individual who 'could blow organized crime wide open in Chicago, Las Vegas, New York and California' if he were ever convicted and granted immunity.[31] That day never came. Lew Wasserman's reign as one of the great mandarins of Tinseltown was similarly muddied by the *Times* scandal. Further embarrassment followed when it was discovered that MCA had hired a Gambino-connected heroin trafficker to run a portion of its music department despite having no experience in the entertainment industry. An FBI agent who sought to dig deeper into potential wrongdoing at MCA was purportedly prevented from doing so by his superiors on account of the controversy it would cause.[32]

The radical expansion of the narcotics industry in the 1980s altered much of the landscape that shaped interactions between mafias and legitimate businesses. As mafias and cartels reaped enormous profits from cocaine sales, massive sums of money flowed into various legal enterprises. Even though tax-related crimes had brought down mafia dons since the time of Al Capone, 'money laundering' as a concept and a crime was in its infancy at the start of the cocaine revolution. It was only in the context of the Watergate scandal in 1973 that the phrase first came into existence. And it was not until 1986 that the US Congress passed its first legislation criminalising financial transactions derived from unlawful activity. Nevertheless, other states and national legislatures followed suit. Washington furthered the internationalisation of its fight against money laundering by helping to establish the Financial Action Task Force. As an institution formed with the consent of the G7 in 1989, the FATF was conceived as a monitoring body geared towards overseeing the implementation of money laundering legislation in countries around the world. The FATF's relevance has only grown since then. In the early 2000s, the International Monetary Fund estimated that between 2 and 5 per cent of the world's gross domestic product was born out of illegal activity (a sum that was at least the equivalent of Spain's national economy).[33] Major banks and corporations have since been ensnared in startling acts of financial malfeasance. In 2012, US and Mexican investigators accused HSBC of gross complicity in laundering up to $881 million in narcotics proceeds on behalf of cartels in Mexico and Colombia. Traffickers grew so accustomed to dealing with HSBC branches that they manufactured their own 'specially shaped boxes' that specifically fitted through the teller windows of banks in Mexico. The British financial giant settled with investigators after agreeing to pay what was then a record $1.92 billion fine.[34]

There is no evidence that Sidney Korshak was a 'made man'. Nor is there evidence that executives at HSBC were directly linked to any mafia of any kind. Yet there are other noted business leaders whose successes were at least partially indebted to their mafia ties. Allegations of mafia collusion dogged Silvio Berlusconi from his early days as a construction and media mogul. Fearing that he may fall victim to the 'Ndrangheta's kidnapping campaign in the 1970s, Berlusconi hired the services of a Sicilian gangster who purportedly guaranteed his safety on behalf of the Cosa Nostra. One state judge later found that the mobster's employment was part of a 'complex strategy destined to make an approach to the entrepreneur Berlusconi and link him more closely to the criminal organisation'.[35] Berlusconi's entrance into Italian politics intensified public scrutiny of his business practices and his attitude towards organised crime. As Italy's three-time prime minister, he raised eyebrows when he watered down anti-mafia laws and declared magistrates who fought organised crime mentally disturbed. One 'Ndrangheta boss publicly stated in 1994 that he and others like him 'all vote for Berlusconi'.[36] In 2013, a judicial report definitively declared that his mafia-linked allies helped 'pour millions of Berlusconi's money into the Mafia's coffers' in exchange for protection and help with his business empire.[37] Epic stories of Berlusconi's corruption and ties to organised crime became crucial elements of his political epitaph after his death in 2023.[38] The controversies concerning Berlusconi have not necessarily tarred Italy's reputation as a place to do business; the Berlin-based NGO Transparency International rates Italy less corrupt than Poland, Greece and Slovakia.[39] Another international research group, the EU-backed Global Initiative against Transnational Organised Crime, similarly characterises Italy as among the more 'resilient' of the globe's governments when it comes to their ability to counteract or blunt organised criminal activities.[40] The same cannot be said for a great many other nations. Events since the end of the Cold War leave no doubt that there are countries where mafias thrive at the expense of lawful business enterprises. Paying bribes or the siphoning of capital and commerce is a reality confronting investors and companies in many parts of the world. So too is the prospect that unscrupulous actors exploit the weaknesses of local administrations in extracting natural resources or selling tainted products. Perhaps even more common is the general lack of state capacity or interest in overseeing financial transactions that may aid criminals hoping to launder their profits.

Closing loopholes and overcoming administrative inertia is a worldwide challenge. It is long been suspected that international money launderers have found a ready sanctuary in the London housing market. According to one 2013 study, overseas investors purchased 90 per cent of all luxury properties in the city. What fraction of these acquisitions were paid for with illicit funds is unclear. Nevertheless, official estimates for that year alone projected that property purchases helped wash £57 billion in dirty money.[41] The Russian invasion of Ukraine in 2022 led to more concerted attempts at tightening the UK legal codes. As of yet, new restrictions only modestly hinder property buyers looking to spend their ill-gotten gains. Gaps in the law still allow most purchasers to remain anonymous.[42]

Globalisation's ceaseless pace, coupled with new innovations, make it even more difficult to disentangle lawful commerce from organised criminal enterprises. The increased digitisation and speed of financial transactions have particularly provided old mafias with a new lease on life. Investigations in the early twenty-first century suggest that groups like the yakuza and the 14K Triad have utilised the cryptocurrency trade as an avenue to launder billions of dollars in illicit profits.[43] Roberto Saviano's fearless investigation into many contemporary business interests of the Camorra underscores the multiplicity of ways clans in Campagna have maintained their vibrancy. On both the page and on screen, the disturbing insights of his chilling book *Gomorrah* reveal the extent to which camorristi have attained global influence through sweatshop work, capital investment and more casual crime. The arrest and imprisonment of mafia chieftains like Toto Riina, he contends, masked a Camorra that was perhaps three to four times larger than all the other criminal groups of Italy.[44] As a decentralised collective of rival bosses and cliques, the Camorra's reach now

Conclusion

stretches to all continents through interlinking weapons dealing, money laundering, construction fixing and drug trafficking enterprises. One mighty clan, the Casalesi, forged a dizzying number of international connections as illicit waste dealers. From Latin America to Europe to Africa, camorristi aided in disposing pollutants of various types with the aid or at the behest of multiple local governments. When a tsunami wiped out communities across the Indian Ocean in 2004, many in the Casalesi clan 'turned pale, as if each of them had a wife, lover or a child in danger'. 'In truth,' Saviano declared, 'something much more precious was at risk: their business.' What the terrible waves revealed was 'hundreds of drums of hazardous or radioactive waste' on the beaches of the east African coast.[45]

Among the lessons imparted by *Gomorrah* is the extent to which the Camorra remains embedded within Neapolitan society. Its enterprises abroad also affirm that its continued relevance is indebted to the complicity of elites elsewhere in the world. This, of course, should come as no surprise given the evolution of mafias through history. What has changed, perhaps, is the extent to which states are compromised by mafiosi of various sorts. Or, perhaps more worryingly, it is the degree to which states themselves outwardly behave as de facto organised criminal enterprises.

COMING FULL CIRCLE:
MAFIAS AND STATES IN OUR TIME

Felipe Calderón assumed the presidency of Mexico in late 2006 under a shadow of doubt. His opponent, Andrés Manuel López Obrador, contested the results, claiming irregularities and vote-rigging had tipped the contest in Calderón's favour. Mass protests and court challenges marred the transition of power in the months that followed the election. In his inaugural address, Calderón acknowledged this discontent and pleaded with the opposition to unite in the name of Mexico. Setting aside partisan differences was essential, he asserted, in tackling the most profound challenge confronting the nation: crime. His first act as president would be to direct his cabinet to come up with a plan to 'renew the mechanisms of prosecution and delivery of justice'. The armed forces, Calderón ordered, were to 'redouble their efforts to guarantee national security above any other interest'. Victory was assured, he said. Yet he also asked for patience. 'I know that restoring security will not be easy or fast, that it will take time, that it will cost a lot of money, and even, and unfortunately, human lives.'[46] With that, Mexico went to war with its cartels.

Much had changed in the country since Miguel Félix Gallardo presided over the country's narcotics industry in the late 1980s. By the time Calderón was elected president, all of the Guadalajara Cartel's original leaders had passed on or were in prison. Other groups assumed power in areas previously considered to be liminal to the main axes of the Mexican drug trade. In the northeast, northbound narcotics traffic fell under the Gulf Cartel. Its founder, Juan Guerra Cárdenas, initially enjoyed less media exposure despite having a smuggling career that dated back to the first half of the twentieth century. One factor that added to the Gulf Cartel's power was the recruitment of soldiers and officers formerly trained as elite anti-narcotics agents. Conflicts with other cartels elevated the importance of these defectors, who renamed themselves Los Zetas in honour of the unit they previously served in in the Mexican army. Their knack for brutality became their trademark in dealing with their opponents, a trait likely acquired under the influence of former military advisers deployed to Guatemala. As the new millennium progressed, beheadings and public mutilations became frequent sights in the Gulf states of Tamaulipas and Monterrey. The ranks of the Zetas swelled. With the group now numbering in the thousands, the Zetas broke away from the Gulf Cartel and expanded nationally and abroad. Among their first international partners was Italy's 'Ndrangheta.⁴⁷

Meanwhile, an even more extraordinary group emerged in the country's heartland. The state of Michoacán, north and west of Mexico City, had long possessed a reputation for its agricultural diversity and richness. In earlier times, local traffickers and drug producers went into business with Colombian cartels trading in heroin and marijuana. The new century brought increased competition from cartels inside Mexico and introduced new sources of revenue, such as the production of methamphetamines. One local faction in Michoacán seized upon these expanding business opportunities and allied themselves with the Zetas, a relationship that brought with it paramilitary training and support from the Gulf Cartel. Dubbing themselves La Familia Michoacána, they too showed a propensity towards cruelty (in one noted incident in 2006, Familia members entered a disco and hurled multiple decapitated heads on the dance floor). Distinguishing themselves further was their invocation of evangelical Christianity in their public statements and iconography. Taking their cues from the American bestseller *Wild at Heart*, a self-help tome preaching a hypermasculine devotion to Christ, La Familia proclaimed it was 'divine justice' whenever they 'killed who needed to be killed'.⁴⁸

Each of these groups complemented the terror invoked by the one man who loomed over Mexico at the start of the century. El Chapo, Joaquín Guzmán Loera, possessed an upbringing that was commonplace among traffickers from the mountains of Sinaloa. When he was a boy, Guzmán's family harvested marijuana and opium. Carting both commodities to market was his first taste of the trade. Legend has it that El Chapo's initial brush with good fortune came after he entered the ranks of the Sinaloa state police. It was then that the young man met Miguel Félix Gallardo, a one-time officer himself, who coaxed Guzmán into his nascent cartel of Sinaloan traffickers. El Chapo drew the Mexican public's attention after his arrest in the killing of a Catholic cardinal in 1993. He presented himself to prosecutors as a simple farmer and father of four who had never gone to school past the third grade.[49] Prison spared him some of the bloodletting that ensued after the breakdown of the old Guadalajara Cartel. As he amassed power over other confederates based in Sinaloa, he catapulted himself into mafia superstardom when he miraculously escaped incarceration in 2001. By Calderón's inauguration, he had moved to consolidate control over much of the country's cross-border drug traffic. Clashes between El Chapo's men and those of his rivals were claiming thousands of lives as Mexico's president issued his declaration of war. The Mexican Armed Forces' intervention in this conflict resulted in an orgy of violence unlike anything the country had seen since the revolution of 1910. Pitched gun battles between army detachments and heavily armed narcos broke out in major cities such as Tijuana, Culiacán and Ciudad Juarez. The death toll left by the fighting was staggering. During Calderón's six years in office, anywhere between 50,000 to 120,000 people were killed. At least half of these estimated casualties were the result of 'narco-executions'.

Calderón's successor, Enrique Peña Nieto, fared no better. Between 2012 and 2015, Mexico witnessed another 63,000 drug-related killings.[50] Despite extensive financial and material backing from Washington, foreign observers could not help but conclude that the country was on the verge of collapse. 'It gives one the sense,' Uruguay's president told one journalist in 2014, that Mexico 'is a kind of failed state, in which public authorities have completely lost control. They have been devoured from the inside.'[51] Officials in Mexico City rejected such comparisons and took pride in killing or capturing a number of wanted kingpins during this bloody decade. In addition to the heads of the Zetas and Gulf Cartels, Chapo himself was apprehended. His imprisonment again proved brief after he tunnelled his way to freedom

Conclusion

in 2015. Guzmán's third and final capture a year later put an end to his reign but hardly dented the power of his Sinaloa cartel. In the fall of 2019, elements of the Mexican military and police raided a residence in Culiacán, seizing one of El Chapo's young sons. The cartel responded swiftly, surrounding the government detachment and holding them hostage. After a day of heavy fighting, authorities released Ovidio Guzmán and withdrew from the city completely. The government remained silent throughout the 'Battle of Culiacán', leaving most Mexicans to learn the truth of the events through social media. The disaster, one reporter lamented, 'offered a terrifying vision of the power exercised by organised crime in Mexico, distilling in a single eight-hour stretch the extent to which the nation is captive by criminal networks'. The government's surreal defeat was as if it was conjured up 'by a too enthusiastic screenwriter, pushing the limits of credibility'.[52]

To look solely at Mexico's struggles is to ignore far more positive elements of its most recent history. Since the start of the new century, the country accrued gains in its economic development despite the scale of the violence. In 2000, voters ended seventy years of one-party rule over Mexico under the Institutional Revolutionary Party. Eighteen years later, they made history again in electing leftist candidate Andrés Manuel López Obrador to the presidency. On the other hand, the enduring strength of the cartels also suggests there is more continuity between these recent regimes and those of the past. After Felipe Calderón left office, his former Secretary of Public Security was arrested in Texas for accepting millions of dollars in bribes from the Sinaloa Cartel. Subsequent criminal proceedings in the United States featured testimony from former government officials stating that Calderón had waged his war on drugs as an effort to support Joaquin Guzman's own campaign against the Gulf Cartel and other adversaries.[53] Such accusations leave many to wonder just how much political progress Mexico has made as a state in the last hundred years.

Other countries in the Western Hemisphere evinced similar signs of instability. In 2010, authorities in Jamaica attempted to arrest Christopher 'Dudus' Coke, heir to the founder of the country's notorious Shower Posse. Residents and gangsters in the heart of the capital defied the police, setting up barricades and shooting at police entering the Kingston neighbourhood of Tivoli Gardens. International media coverage of the clashes dredged up revelations that Coke and his gang were long-time supporters of Edward Seaga, whose Liberal Party then held power. More striking was the apparent enthusiasm with which many in the capital appeared to champion Coke as a hero and true patron of the poor. Amid the fighting, protestors demanded the police end their assault on Tivoli Gardens, with one dissident holding a placard reading, 'Jesus died for us so we will for Dudus'.[54] Coke's eventual surrender restored order in Jamaica's capital, but at the expense of some seventy-six civilian deaths.[55]

More scandalous still have been affairs in El Salvador, a country where gangs possess an even tighter grip on power. Central to this trend has been the exponential growth of La Mara Salvatrucha. MS-13, as it also known, is not a purely native expression of Salvadorian life. Like the Bloods and Crips, La Mara was conceived on the meaner streets of Los Angeles. Its original members came of age in the turbulent 1980s on the city's eastside, an area historically associated with deeply entrenched gangs of Chicano natives. Purportedly many of the first Maras were young 'stoners' who bonded over their love of drugs and heavy metal. At a time of increased gang activity throughout Southern California, MS-13 drew ever larger numbers of young Salvadorian men from families displaced by the civil war in their home country. As with other LA gangs, their distinct look and culture spread quickly beyond Los Angeles. With close to a million Salvadorian refugees living in communities between California and Washington DC, cliques identifying with MS-13 were found in every state except

Conclusion

West Virginia and South Dakota by 2008. Its deep ties with other Latino gangs were cemented when the gang adopted the number thirteen in its name, a token reference to the letter M, the thirteenth letter of the alphabet, and a shorthand expression used by the prison gang, the Mexican Mafia. With many MS-13 members living in the US as undocumented migrants, law enforcement officials enthusiastically began to deport large numbers of accused gangsters by the early 2000s. It was later estimated that American authorities had expelled 8,000 gang members a year before the end of the millennium's first decade. The deportations were a disaster for the weak states of Central America.[56] Crime rates in El Salvador, Honduras and Guatemala soared as news outlets spread accounts of massacres, machete attacks and wanton killings across the region. Like the Zetas in Mexico, MS-13 embraced inhuman acts of cruelty as integral to their identity and approach towards crime. 'Wherever the Mara Salvatrucha is,' read one leaked letter between gang leaders, '[we are] going to kill, control and rape again. We are super crazy.'[57] To combat the spread of gangs, successive governments in Central America have resorted to extreme measures. Most recently, El Salvador's young president, Nayib Bukele, endorsed a policy of round-ups and mass incarceration to deal with the problem of gangs. As of 2023, it is estimated that 1 per cent of the country's population is behind bars, many without any charge.[58]

It is tempting to interpret these trends in Latin America as reminiscent of the plight of much older states and empires. One could draw parallels between the threat of gangs and cartels in the present and the dangers posed by powerful bandits at various points in history. There is some value in making such comparisons. Banditry's historical prevalence often was indicative of a state's fragility. In looking at modern-day Mexico or El Salvador, institutional limitations cannot be ignored when it comes to their abilities to fight crime. Yet in all fairness, both San Salvador and

Mexico City are combatting forces that are significantly stronger than any bandit gang found in their collective histories. Incidents such as the so-called Battle of Culiacán testify to the relative parity between national militaries and criminal groups when it comes to arms, communications and other logistical capabilities. It is difficult to imagine a bandit of the early modern age possessing the sort of financial clout enjoyed by the mafias and cartels of the present day. No amount of highway robbery or kidnapping could match the lucrative proceeds of the contemporary drugs trade. It is the ability to pay off or co-opt the highest-ranking members of a country's political elite that allows many modern kingpins to remain free from prosecution. Yet as seen in the case of El Chapo, the force of arms or vast sums of bribe money does not keep the state at bay forever.

Yet as powerful as many mafias prove to be today, few desire the power to rule. Neither the Sinaloa Cartel nor the Maras possess an ideology or political agenda. Nor have they sought to supplant the governments that oppose them. Pablo Escobar's brief populist political career aside, it is hard to imagine any contemporary godfather wanting to assume responsibility over such banal functions as supplying the public with schools, hospitals or other services. By no means, however, are mafias typically divorced from politics. Particularly powerful syndicates and kingpins often show a willingness to act in the interest of political leaders and state enterprises. At one extreme, one may point to the consolidation of Slobodan Milošević's power in Belgrade in the early stages of his rule over Yugoslavia.[59] More recent events have exposed the willingness of some gangsters to act as conspiratorial agents in the service of the government. Beijing's crackdown on democratic institutions in Hong Kong was greatly aided by triad thugs who beat protesting dissidents with total impunity.[60] Numerous cases emanating from Putin's Russia appear to underscore an enduring 'spook–gangster nexus' wherein elements of the underworld

Conclusion

actively contribute to espionage and other covert Russian actions abroad.[61]

More common still is the extent to which criminal syndicates, both now and in the past, have participated in electoral politics. One striking contemporary case is that of Sedat Peker of Turkey. Peker is one of the country's most influential figures on the Turkish far right. As far back as the 1980s, he made a name for himself as an extortionist with close ties to right-wing militants and extremists. His notoriety grew in the 1990s when it was revealed he had intimidated players and fixed football matches on the behalf of prominent clubs such as Fenerbahçe.[62] Like other right-wing thugs, Peker cultivated close ties with state officials and allegedly served as a gun-for-hire by the Turkish clandestine service. Despite his imprisonment for his role in an alleged coup plot against Recep Tayyip Erdoğan's government in the mid-2000s, Turkey's current president reconciled with Peker after the two were photographed warmly conversing with one another at a wedding. Erdoğan's favour prompted Peker to lend his support to the government during a heated election campaign in 2015. Before one roaring crowd, he assured Erdoğan's voters that 'blood will flow in streams' with the impending defeat of the government's opponents.[63] Formal efforts to prosecute Peker for incitement came to naught.

Erdoğan's tightening grip over the Turkish government ultimately left this political marriage of convenience high and dry. In 2020, Peker mysteriously fled into exile. He re-emerged one year later, this time through a series of widely viewed videos posted to YouTube. Millions tuned into his broadcasts after he promised to reveal details of various illicit dealings involving Erdoğan's government. He did not disappoint. Over the spring of 2021, he went on at length as to how one former prime minister helped import five tons of cocaine into the country from Venezuela. On other occasions, he expounded on crimes supposedly committed by another official, who he claimed covered up a variety of heinous acts including incidents of murder and rape.[64] Even though Peker failed to fault Erdoğan by name, Turkey's opposition press, not to mention tens of millions of anti-Erdoğan voters, delighted in the revelations.

States that are poorer, institutionally weaker or more unstable surely are more typical settings for strong relations between mafiosi and their social or political betters. Yet even a cursory inspection of American history eliminates any suspicion that strong states are more immune to the influence of mafias. What euphemistically may be called 'Chicago-style politics', be it under Al Capone or after, was not abnormal nor unprecedented at various times and places in the United States. As vote getters, personal fixers, police informers and would-be secret agents, mafiosi in the United States cultivated relations with politicians and officials.

Insights gleaned from present-day China add to this body of evidence. Western law enforcement officials maintain that traditional crime groups like the triads have played a role in promoting China's interests abroad. In addition to their own criminal enterprises, Chinese crime syndicates have aided Beijing in monitoring the activities of Chinese nationals abroad.[65] This alliance, however, has come with certain costs. Despite the invasiveness of the state's governing institutions, China struggles to limit the administrative influence enjoyed by the triads and other crime groups. A culture of clientelism, often referred to as *guanxi*, provides a venue for gangsters to secure contracts and influence decisions on promotion in provincial government. Above all, ostensibly illegal activities often become joint ventures that bind state officials to members of local underworlds. All available evidence suggests that there is nothing organised or monolithic about this pattern of corruption. Nor do triads and other secret societies necessarily lie at the heart of these relationships. To the contrary, altogether new constellations of regional and national mafias continue to grow and diversify throughout China.⁶⁶ What is generally known about the Chinese underworld, however, remains relatively obscure and underexplored.

Trends in the new millennium have compelled many to ponder an even more profound phenomenon: states that overtly exploit illicit industries for political and economic gain. Beginning with the reign of Hugo Chávez, the government of Venezuela garnered exorbitant attention for allegedly condoning, and perhaps promoting, the outflow of cocaine from the country. American efforts to document the regime's activities continue to glean evidence of a systemic relationship between drug traffickers and the Venezuelan state.⁶⁷ More shocking is the North Korean government's involvement in organised crime. Evidence of Pyongyang's complicity dates as far back as the 1970s after several North Korean diplomats were apprehended abroad under suspicion of drug trafficking. In 1995, American officials estimated the Democratic People's Republic was producing forty tons of opium a year, a sum analogous to Mexico's projected output of the drug. Officials and defectors later claimed that farmers, many of them often starving, were compelled to cultivate opium at the behest of the regime. North Korea's desperate need for foreign currency led the government to branch out into other illegal industries, such as methamphetamine production and illegal arms shipments.⁶⁸ At least some of the proceeds, according to regime insiders, went directly to the country's long-serving dictator, Kim Jong-il. 'To help you understand,' one defector explained, 'all the money in North Korea belongs to the North Korean leader,' he says. 'With that money, he'd build villas, buy cars, buy food, get clothes and enjoy luxuries.'⁶⁹

It is likely that the earliest advocates of prohibitionist laws governing narcotics never imagined the advent of durable 'mafia states' such as Venezuela and North Korea. With the adoption of the Hague Convention in 1912, it was generally assumed that the emerging global consensus on drug use, coupled with international pressure, would force wayward governments into complying with the new order of things. More than a century on, the flaws of this logic are clear. Why it has failed cannot be attributed to the power or persuasion of individual gangsters or syndicates. Mafia states exist due to the undeniable allure of illicit industries. There is now no doubt that profit from organised crime is the engine that drives the perpetuation of gangster enterprises. The history of mafias is testament to the fact that punitive policing, no matter how robust, at best addresses the symptoms of the problem. A lasting solution to the challenge posed by mafia syndicates and regimes likely requires a complete reassessment of laws and norms that engender organised criminal industries. Arriving at a new global consensus on narcotics, let alone on other proscribed commodities or services, would be daunting to say the least. It appears far more likely that mafias, regardless of their contours, are here to stay.

NEITHER A PLAQUE, SIGNPOST NOR STATUE: DEALING WITH MAFIAS AS HISTORY

Michael Corleone confronts Hyman Roth at a critical juncture before the climax of *Godfather II*'s second act. Hyman knowingly stands at the threshold of makings one final deal aimed at turning Havana into a mafia sanctuary; Michael, and the viewer, know the venture is doomed. Sensing his partner's hesitation, Lee Strasberg, playing the role of a very thinly veiled Meyer Lansky, waxes fondly about a man Michael had killed years previously:

> There was this kid that I grew up with; he was a couple years younger than me, and sort of looked up to me, you know. We did our first work together, worked our way out of the street. Things were good and we made the most of it. During prohibition, we ran molasses up to Canada and made a fortune; your

father too. I guess as much as anyone, I loved him and trusted him. Later on he had an idea to make a city out of a desert stopover for GIs on the way to the West Coast. That kid's name was Moe Greene, and the city he invented was Las Vegas. This was a great man; a man with vision and guts; and there isn't even a plaque or a signpost or a statue of him in that town.

Coppola never allowed Moe Greene the honour of getting a plaque. Yet in the real world, Las Vegas made sure that Bugsy Siegel received his. His memorial sits in a park where his original Flamingo Hotel stood until 1993. What surrounds this monument today is a more contemporary version of his resort, one that frankly sits somewhat modestly across from the ultra-luxurious Bellagio Hotel and Casino. Departing the park northwards along Las Vegas Boulevard, the glitz of the Strip begins to dull after several blocks. The foot traffic thins and the businesses, hotels and casinos become more down market. As one enters the city centre, the buildings and the landscape look increasingly nondescript. What constitutes the administrative core of Las Vegas resembles any number of major urban areas west of the Mississippi.

It is in this less lively part of Las Vegas that one finds the National Museum of Organised Crime and Law Enforcement. 'The Mob Museum', as it is far more affectionately known, was a signature initiative of the administration of Mayor Oscar Goodman. Goodman's long career in politics was in no small part due to his earlier distinction as a defence lawyer for a variety of luminous mafia clients (men such as Meyer Lansky and Anthony Spilotro). The museum is housed in the city's old courthouse, where Estes Kefauver once held a hearing in 1950 on the scourge of organised crime in Las Vegas. Exhibits include guns used by both gangsters and police and a portion of the wall against which shooters massacred seven of Al Capone's rivals on Valentine's Day in 1929. Visitors of age can finish their tour with a Prohibition-era drink in a mock speakeasy in the basement. The museum's proprietors champion their work as an attempt to educate the public on the dangers of organised crime and the accomplishments of American law enforcement. Critics, however, decried the city's decision to use public funds that otherwise could have been spent on revitalising downtown Las Vegas. Oscar Goodman, who is featured prominently in the museum, rejected such calls. 'I am annoyed at the people who are criticizing us for using redevelopment money for this,' he told one Vegas newspaper. 'What do they want me to use it for? A sewer?'[70]

The Mob Museum welcomes hundreds of thousands of visitors a year, making it among the most popular tourist attractions in Las Vegas. It is not the only one of its kind. Hot Springs, Arkansas, a time-honoured vacation destination located just west of the Mississippi, boasts its own Gangster Museum of America. Premised on the region's lively history as a playground for Prohibition-era gamblers and bootleggers, the museum offers a small collection of trinkets and memorabilia from the country's mafia past. A far more earnest and sombre attempt at distilling history can be found at the No Mafia Memorial in Palermo, Sicily. Unlike the Mob Museum, visitors who enter the memorial pay no admission fee. Located in a nineteenth-century palazzo in the city's core, the museum displays no guns or evocative trappings of mafia life. Its pictures and displays are intended to incite pathos and reflection rather than excitement. Here the mafia is rendered as the source of genuine grief and shame.

Far across the world in Medellín, there was once a museum dedicated to the life of Pablo Escobar. Owned by his brother Roberto, the former residence featured exhibits that paid far greater tribute to the gaudy materialism and outrageous exploits of the man and his cartel. Medellín's local government, citing zoning violations, ordered the home to be demolished in the summer of 2023. Supporters of the closure heralded the move as

Conclusion

a blow against unwanted 'narco-tourism' which had flourished in the wake of the Netflix bio-series featuring Escobar. It was better, as one proponent insisted, that Medellín be recognised as 'an example of innovation and social inclusion', not the one-time capital of the cocaine trade.[71] Other locals were less sure. 'The place raised so many doubts,' one local journalist said, particularly since the museum 'twisted the history of the Medellín Cartel and narco-terrorism for tourists.' And yet, he continued, 'It's hard to believe that Medellín still doesn't have a place to share its complex story about our narco past.' Increasingly, the city government appeared more likely to 'destroy [the remnants of] this history instead of creating collaborative public processes to help Medellín truly grasp its present, past, and future'.[72]

The predicament facing Colombia is one shared by citizens in various parts of the world. Depending on where you are, mafias are deeply woven into the fabric of history. And yet so few governments or societies appear willing to deal with them publicly. Why this is the case is understandable. In many instances, be it Latin America, Asia or Europe, mafias are not purely expressions of the past; they remain fixtures of present-day politics, economy and society. There are also practical issues to consider. Honestly documenting a mafia's history, or displaying its material remnants, may be beset by the loss or inaccessibility of testimony, public records or physical artefacts. Above all, it is easy to imagine the well-placed fears many would have in considering the opening of a museum, memorial or archive dedicated to gangsters. While tourists may delight in mafia lore, others who live in the shadow of such a venture may see it as an unwanted tribute to the pain and disgrace of the past.

Most people of course do not experience the history of mafias by way of a trip to Medellín, New York or Palermo. On-screen adaptations provide the most common window into this element of the past. The ever-growing number of movies and television series featuring historic mobs and gangsters is testament to this global phenomenon. In this regard, the more conventional historian has an opportunity, or perhaps an obligation, to play a greater role. Fiction, as ironic as it sounds, has done the most to capture the historical relevance of mafias. Many cinematic depictions of the mafia are indeed crude in their glorification of the violence and wanton impulses of gangsters. Still other screen adaptations of mafia life have given audiences accessible, and at times very thoughtful, lessons about the past. Here *The Godfather* set the standard. Since 1971, the world has come to embrace the mafia as a lens through which they may see history in a newer, more genuine light. The development of a vibrant community of mafia historians may help augment this sense of discovery among students and audiences. There is a great deal more to be learned from archives and libraries in various parts of the world. There are still countries, cities and regions whose mafias have yet to be documented. Understanding the past, to again paraphrase James Ellroy, should be an effort to recapture events and individuals ranging from the gutters to the stars. Bringing mafias into the light may be painful, but at a time in which more people find themselves persuaded to believe in the existence of 'deep states' and other conspiracies, the good it may do would be its own reward.

NOTES

Introduction

1. Robert Evans, *The Kid Stays in the Picture* (New York: New Millennium Press, 2002), p. 225.
2. Ibid., p. 226.
3. Jean de Baroncelli, 'La Mafia du "Parrain"', *Le Monde*, 19 October 1972.
4. 'Nixon's Triumphant Return', *Los Angeles Times*, 11 August 1969.
5. Jill Jonnes, *Hep-cats, Narcs and Pipe Dreams: A History of America's Romance with Illegal Drugs* (Baltimore, MD: Johns Hopkins University Press, 1999), pp. 262–3.
6. 'Mafya'ya Bakiyor: Baba', *Cumhuriyet*, 16 November 1973.
7. James Ellroy, *American Tabloid* (New York: Knopf Doubleday Publishing Group, 2011), p. 1.

1. The Long Scourge: Banditry and the Pre-History of Mafias

1. John Cam Hobhouse, Baron Broughton, *Travels in Albania and Other Provinces of Turkey in 1809 & 1810* (London: John Murray, 1855), p. 49.
2. For a great discussion of the life and significance of Ali Pasha, see Katherine Elizabeth Fleming, *The Muslim Bonaparte: Diplomacy and Orientalism in Ali Pasha's Greece* (Princeton: Princeton University Press, 1999); Noel Malcolm, 'Ali Pasha and Great Britain during the Napoleonic Wars', in *Rebels, Believers, Survivors: Studies in the History of the Albanians* (Oxford: Oxford University Press, 2020), pp. 149–244.
3. Timothy Reuter, 'Plunder and Tribute in the Carolingian Empire', *Transactions of the Royal Historical Society* (vol. 35, 1985), pp. 75–94.

4   Matthew Restall, *Seven Myths of the Spanish Conquest* (Oxford: Oxford University Press, 2003), pp. 27–43.
5   Charles Tilly, 'War Making and State Making as Organized Crime', in Peter Evans, et al. (eds), *Bringing the State Back In* (Cambridge: Cambridge University Press, 1985), p. 173.
6   Hans van Wees, 'The Mafia of Early Greece: Violent Exploitation in the Seventh and Sixth Centuries BC', in Keith Hopwood (ed.), *Organised Crime in Antiquity* (London: Duckworth, 1999), pp. 1–51.
7   Thomas Grünewald, *Bandits in the Roman Empire: Myth and Reality* (London: Routledge, 1999), p. 16.
8   Ibid., p. 118.
9   Morten Oxenboell, *Akutō and Rural Conflict in Medieval Japan* (Honolulu: University of Hawai`i Press, 2018).
10 Julius Ruff, *Violence in Early Modern Europe* (Cambridge: Cambridge University Press, 2001), p. 236.
11 Katrin Lange, '"Many a Lord is Guilty, Indeed for Many a Poor Man's Dishonest Deed": Gangs of Robbers in Early Modern Germany', in Cyrille Fijnaut and Letizia Paoli (eds), *Organised Crime in Europe: Concepts, Patterns and Control Policies in the European Union and Beyond* (Dordrecht: Springer Netherlands, 2004), p. 129.
12 Chris Frazer, *Bandit Nation: A History of Outlaws and Cultural Struggle in Mexico, 1810–1920* (Lincoln, University of Nebraska Press, 2006).
13 See Fredrick Anscombe, 'Albanians and "Mountain Bandits"', in Fredrick Anscombe (ed.), *The Ottoman Balkans 1750–1830* (Princeton: Markus Wiener Publishers, 2006), pp. 87–113.
14 David M. Robinson, 'Banditry and the Subversion of State Authority in China: The Capital Region during the Middle Ming Period (1450–1525)', *Journal of Social History*, 33.3, (2000), pp. 527–63.
15 J. L. Anderson, 'Piracy and World History: An Economic Perspective on Maritime Predation', *Journal of World History*, vol. 6, no. 2, 1995, pp. 175–99.
16 Patricia Risso, 'Cross-Cultural Perceptions of Piracy: Maritime Violence in the Western Indian Ocean and Persian Gulf Region during a Long Eighteenth Century', *Journal of World History*, vol. 12, no. 2, 2001, pp. 293–319.
17 James H. McClintock, *Arizona, Prehistoric, Aboriginal, Pioneer, Modern: The Nation's Youngest Commonwealth Within a Land of Ancient Culture* (Chicago: S. J. Clarke Publishing Company, 1916), p. 18.
18 Anton Blok, 'The Peasant and the Brigand: Social Banditry Reconsidered', *Comparative Studies in Society and History*, vol. 14, no. 4, (1972), p. 500.
19 For further examples of this discussion, see Anton Blok, 'Rams and

Billy-Goats: A Key to the Mediterranean Code of Honour', *Man* (1981), pp. 427–40; Catherine Wendy Bracewell, *The Uskoks of Senj: Piracy, Banditry, and Holy War in the Sixteenth-Century Adriatic* (Ithaca, NY: Cornell University Press, 2015); Başak Tuğ, *Politics of Honor in Ottoman Anatolia: Sexual Violence and Socio-Legal Surveillance in the Eighteenth Century* (Leiden: Brill, 2017); Stephen Wilson, *Feuding, Conflict and Banditry in Nineteenth-Century Corsica* (Cambridge: Cambridge University Press, 2003).

20 'Illustrations of the History and Practices of the Thugs', *The Times*, 13 January 1838.

21 Kim Wagner (ed.), *Stranglers and Bandits: A Historical Anthology of Thuggee* (Oxford: Oxford University Press, 2009), p. 32.

22 Eric J. Hobsbawm, *Primitive Rebels: Studies in Archaic Forms of Social Movements in the 19th and 20th Centuries* (New York: W. W. Norton, 1959), p. 41.

23 Fikret Adanir, 'Heiduckentum und osmanische Herrschaft. Sozialgeschichtliche Aspekte der Diskussion um das frühneuzeitliche Räuberwesen in Südosteuropa', *Südost-Forschungen*, 41 (1982), pp. 43–116.

24 Lenard J. Cohen, 'Political Violence and Organized Crime in Serbia', in William Crotty (ed.), *Democratic Development and Political Terrorism: The Global Perspective* (Boston: Northeastern University Press, 2005), pp. 396–419.

25 Richard White, 'Outlaw Gangs of the Middle Border: American Social Bandits', *The Western Historical Quarterly* 12.4 (1981), p. 396.

26 T. J. Stiles, *Jesse James: Last Rebel of the Civil War* (New York: Knopf Doubleday, 2010).

27 James Clarke Holt, *Robin Hood* (London: Thames and Hudson, 1982), p. 16.

28 James Clarke Holt, 'The Origins and Audience of the Ballads of Robin Hood', *Past & Present* 18 (1960), p. 91.

29 Stephanie Barczewski, *Myth and National Identity in Nineteenth-Century Britain: The Legends of King Arthur and Robin Hood* (Oxford: Oxford University Press, 2000), p. 21.

30 Laura Basu, 'Remembering an Iron Outlaw: The Cultural Memory of Ned Kelly and the Development of Australian Identities', PhD Dissertation: Utrecht University, 2010, p. 33.

31 Kenneth Morgan, *Australia: A Very Short Introduction* (Oxford: Oxford University Press, 2012), p. 44.

32 C. M. Law, 'The Growth of Urban Population in England and Wales, 1801-1911,' *Transactions of the Institute of British Geographers*, 41 (1967), p. 126.

33 Malcolm Gaskill, 'The Displacement of Providence: Policing and

Prosecution in Seventeenth- and Eighteenth-Century England', *Continuity and Change*, 11.3 (1996), pp. 341–74; Joan Kent, 'The English Village Constable, 1580–1642: The Nature and Dilemmas of the Office', *Journal of British Studies*, 20.2 (1981), pp. 26–49.

34 Mark Galeotti, 'The world of the lower depths: crime and punishment in Russian history' in Mark Galeotti (ed.), *Organised Crime in History* (London: Routledge, 2009), p. 86.

35 Clive Emsley, *Gendarmes and the State in Nineteenth-Century Europe* (Oxford: Oxford University Press, 1999), p. 3.

36 Clive Emsley, 'Policing the Empire/Policing the Metropole: Some Thoughts on Models and Types', *Crime, History and Societies* 18.2 (2014), pp. 43–54.

37 Gillian Spraggs, *Outlaws and Highwaymen: The Cult of the Robber in England from the Middle Ages to the Nineteenth Century* (London: Pimlico, 2001), p. 234.

38 Roger Wells, 'Popular Protest and Social Crime: The Evidence of Criminal Gangs in Rural Southern England, 1790–1860', *Southern History* 13 (1991), pp. 32–81.

39 Ahmed Emin Yalman, *Turkey in the World War* (New Haven: Yale University Press, 1930), p. 262.

40 George L. Simpson, 'Frontier Banditry and the Colonial Decision-Making Process: The East Africa Protectorate's Northern Borderland Prior to the First World War', *The International Journal of African Historical Studies*, 29.2 (1996), pp. 279–308.

41 Nicholas Werth, 'The "Chechen Problem": Handling an Awkward Legacy, 1918–1958', *Contemporary European History*, 15.3 (2006), pp. 347–66.

42 'Le bandit Spada affronte le jury', *Le Petit Parisien*, 5 March 1935.

43 Rhys Blakely, 'Where macho men are proud to fire blanks', *The Times*, 21 March 2008.

44 Catherine Philip, 'India's Bandit King Betrayed', *The Times*, 20 October 2004

45 '"All the big secrets are gone with him"', *Guardian*, 21 October 2004 (www.theguardian.com/world/2004/oct/21/india.theeditorpressreview, consulted 2 October 2022).

46 Suketu Mehta, 'Outback Outlaw', *New York Times*, 26 December 2004.

47 Fred A. McKenzie, 'The Worst Street in London', *Daily Mail*, 16 July 1901 (reprinted in https://www.casebook.org/victorian_london/the-worst-street-in-london.html, consulted 25 April 2023).

48 For further reading see Judith R. Walkowitz, *City of Dreadful Delight: Narratives of Sexual Danger in Late Victorian London* (Chicago: University of Chicago Press, 1992), pp. 191–228.

Notes

2. Love and Relaxation for Sale: Vice and the Roots of Organised Crime

1. Gray Brechin, *Imperial San Francisco: Urban Power, Earthly Ruin* (Berkeley, CA: University of California Press, 2006), pp. 245–6.
2. 'A School of Vice: Children Trained Amid Shame and Crime', *San Francisco Chronicle*, 10 February 1888.
3. Herbert Asbury, *The Barbary Coast: An Informal History of the San Francisco Underworld* (New York: Basic Books, 2002), p. 238.
4. 'City's Morals Improved is Jury's Finding', *San Francisco Chronicle*, 2 December 1921.
5. Nils Johan Ringdal, *Love for Sale: A World History of Prostitution* (New York: Grove Press, 2007), pp. 21–23.
6. Hanan Hammad, and Francesca Biancani, 'Prostitution in Cairo', in Magaly Rodriquez Garcia, et al. (eds.), *Selling Sex in the City: A Global History of Prostitution, 1600s–2000s* (Leiden: Brill, 2017), p. 238.
7. Ibid., p. 240.
8. 'Antiquarian Intelligence', *The Journal of the British Archeological Association*, 46 (1890), p. 250.
9. John Towner, 'The Master of Ceremonies: Beau Nash and the Rise of Bath, 1700–1750', in Richard Butler and Roslyn Russell (eds.), *Giants of Tourism* (Wallingford: CIBA, 2010), pp. 18–31.
10. David Schwartz, *Roll the Bones: The History of Gambling* (New York: Gotham Books, 2006), pp. 130–4.
11. Philip Ethington, *The Public City: The Political Construction of Urban Life in San Francisco, 1850–1900* (Cambridge: Cambridge University Press, 1994), p. 425.
12. 'Ten Cent Lodgings', *San Francisco Chronicle*, 5 October 1890.
13. Pablo Piccato, *City of Suspects: Crime in Mexico City, 1900–1931* (Durham: Duke University Press, 2001), p. 27.
14. David Dixon, *From Prohibition to Regulation: Bookmaking, Anti-Gambling and the Law* (Oxford: Oxford University Press, 1991), p. 48.
15. Schwartz, p. 301.
16. Susan Conner, 'The Paradoxes and Contradictions of Prostitution in Paris', in Magaly Rodriquez Garcia, et al. (eds.), *Selling Sex in the City*, p. 190.
17. Clive Emsley, 'Introduction: Political Police and the European Nation-State in the Nineteenth Century', in Mark Mazower (ed.), *The Policing of Politics in the Twentieth Century* (Providence, RI: Berghan Books, 1997), pp. 1–25.
18. Mark Finnane, 'The Origins of "Modern" Policing,' in Paul Knepper and Anja Johansen (eds.), *The Oxford Handbook of the History of*

Crime and Criminal Justice (Oxford: Oxford University Press, 2016), pp. 456–73.

19 Haia Shpayer-Makov, 'Detectives and Forensic Science: The Professionalization of Police Detection', in Paul Knepper and Anja Johansen (eds.), *The Oxford Handbook of the History of Crime and Criminal Justice* (Oxford: Oxford University Press, 2016), pp. 474–96.

20 Donald Thomas, *The Victorian Underworld* (New York: New York University Press, 1998), pp. 308–21.

21 Simon Cole, *Suspect Identities: A History of Fingerprinting and Criminal Identification* (Cambridge, MA: Harvard University Press, 2009), p. 132.

22 Peter D'Agostino, 'Craniums, Criminals, and the "Cursed Race": Italian Anthropology in American Racial Thought, 1861–1924', *Comparative Studies in Society and History*, 44.2 (2002), p. 323.

23 Neil Larry Shumsky and Larry M. Springer, 'San Francisco's Zone of Prostitution, 1880–1934', *Journal of Historical Geography* 7.1 (1981), p. 77.

24 See for example: 'Paid Chinese Gambling Den: Police Arrest 130 Orientals for Playing Fantan and Pi Gow', *San Francisco Chronicle*, 28 December, 1908.

25 'Chinese Vice Found Unhampered', *San Francisco Chronicle*, 2 February 1901.

26 'Police Ban on Slumming in Barbary Coast', *San Francisco Chronicle*, 9 October 1921.

27 Ashwini Tambe, *Codes of Misconduct: Regulating Prostitution in Late Colonial Bombay* (Minneapolis: University of Minnesota Press, 2009), pp. 52–8.

28 Julia Laite, 'Traffickers and Pimps in the Era of White Slavery', *Past and Present*, 237 (November 2017), p. 244.

29 Michael Woodiwiss, *Organized Crime and American Power* (Toronto: University of Toronto Press, 2001), p. 174.

30 Charles Van Onselen, *The Fox and the Flies* (New York: Walker & Company, 2007), p. 150.

31 Schwartz, p. 344.

32 Mark Haller, *Illegal Enterprise: The Work of Historian Mark Haller* (Lanham, MD: University Press of America, 2013), pp. 150–1; Gus Russo, *The Outfit: The Role of Chicago's Underworld in the Shaping of Modern America* (New York: Bloomsbury, 2001), p. 197.

33 'The Excise Cases', *New York Times*, 29 June 1888.

34 Woodiwiss, p. 179.

35 Martin Booth, *Opium: A History* (New York: St. Martin's Press, 1999), p. 39.

36 Ibid., p. 36.

Notes

37 Thomas De Quincey, *Confessions of an English Opium-Eater* (New York: John B. Alden, 1885), p. 1.
38 Martin Nesvig, 'Forbidden Drugs in Colonial America', in Paul Gootenberg (ed.), *The Oxford Handbook of Global Drug History* (Oxford: Oxford University Press, 2022), pp. 156–160.
39 Rod Phillips, *Alcohol: A History* (Chapel Hill, NC: University of North Carolina Press, 2014), p. 124.
40 Yengwen Zheng, 'The Cultural Biography of Opium in China', in Paul Gootenberg (ed.), *The Oxford Handbook of Global Drug History* (Oxford: Oxford University Press, 2022), pp. 274–5.
41 Booth, p. 73.
42 Richard Davenport-Hines, *The Pursuit of Oblivion: A Global History of Narcotics* (New York: W. W. Norton Company, 2004), p. 155.
43 James Nicholls, *The Politics of Alcohol: A History of the Drink Question in England* (Manchester: Manchester University Press, 2009), p. 38.
44 Davenport-Hines, p. 170.
45 'L'Vice de la Opium', *Le Temps*, 7 September 1889.
46 Edward Huntington Williams, 'Negro cocaine "fiends" are a New Southern Menace', *New York Times*, 19 February 1914.
47 Dominic Streatfield, *Cocaine: A Definitive History* (London: Virgin Books, 2002), 149.
48 John Jennings, *The Opium Empire: Japanese Imperialism and Drug Trafficking in Asia, 1895–1945* (Westport, CT: Praeger, 1997), p. 8.
49 Anne L. Foster, 'Prohibiting Opium in the Philippines and the United States: The Creation of an Interventionist State', in Alfred W. McCoy and Francisco A. Scarano (eds), *Colonial Crucible: Empire in the Making of the Modern American State* (Madison: University of Wisconsin Press, 2009), p. 99.
50 Peter Andreas and Ethan Nadelmann, *Policing the Globe: Criminalization and Crime Control in International Relations* (Oxford: Oxford University Press, 2006), p. 27.

3. Origins: Mafias of the Early Twentieth Century

1 William Trollope, 'Naples: Its "Fondaci", its Brigandage and its "Camorra"', *The Gentleman's Magazine*, Volume CCXLI, July to December 1877 (London: Chatto & Windus, Piccadilly, 1877), p. 349.
2 William Trollope, 'The "Mafia" and "Omerta" in Sicily', ibid., p. 159.
3 Frederick Edwyn Forbes, *Five Years in China: From 1842 to 1847* (London: R. Bentley, 1848), p. 51.
4 Florike Egmond, 'Multiple underworlds in the Dutch Republic of

the Seventeenth and Eighteenth Centuries', in Fijnaut and Paoli, pp. 77–107.
5   John L. McMullan, 'Criminal Organization in Sixteenth and Seventeenth Century London', *Social Problems* 29.3 (1982): pp. 311–23.
6   Robert Jütte, *Poverty and Deviance in Early Modern Europe* (Cambridge University Press, 1994), pp. 182–5.
7   'The Pope's Encyclical Letter on Freemasonry', *Clevedon Mercury and Courier*, 28 June 1884.
8   See John Dickie, *The Craft: How the Freemasons Made the Modern World* (New York: Public Affairs, 2020).
9   Ibid., pp. 121–49.
10 James Walston, 'See Naples and Die: Organized Crime in Campania', in Robert Kelly (ed.), *Organized Crime: A Global Perspective* (Totawa, NJ: Rowman & Littlefield, 1986), pp. 134–58.
11 Tom Behan, *The Camorra: Political Criminality in Italy* (London: Routledge, 1995), p. 13.
12 John Dickie, *Blood Brotherhoods: A History of Italy's Three Mafias* (New York: Public Affairs, 2014), p. 41.
13 John Dickie, *Cosa Nostra: A History of the Sicilian Mafia* (London: Hodder and Stoughton, 2004), pp. 34–8.
14 Henner Hess, *Mafia and Mafiosi: The Structure of Power* (Lexington, MA: Lexington Books, 1977), pp. 1–2.
15 Salvatore Lupo, *History of the Mafia* (New York: Columbia University Press, 2009), pp. 31–6.
16 Anton Blok, *The Mafia of a Sicilian Village, 1860–1960: A Study of Violent Peasant Entrepreneurs* (Prospect Heights, IL: Waveland Press, 1988), p. 95.
17 James Fentress, *Rebels and Mafiosi: Death in a Sicilian Landscape* (Ithaca, NY: Cornell University Press, 2000), p. 156.
18 Dickie, *Blood Brotherhoods*, p. 33.
19 Behan, p. 22.
20 Trollope, 'Naples', pp. 349, 363.
21 Lupo, p. 83.
22 Dickie, *Cosa Nostra*, p. 49.
23 Diego Gambetta, *The Sicilian Mafia: The Business of Private Protection* (Cambridge, MA: Harvard University Press, 1996), p. 101.
24 Gianluca Fulvetti, 'The Mafia and the "Problem of the Mafia": Organised Crime in Italy, 1820–1970', in Fijnaut and Paoli (eds.), *Organised Crime in Europe*, p. 53.
25 Dickie, *Blood Brotherhoods*, p. 66.
26 Dickie, *Cosa Nostra*, pp. 55–6.
27 D'Agostino, p. 326.
28 Alexander Rumpelt, *Sicilien Und Die Sicilianer* (Berlin: Allgemeiner Verein für deutsche Literatur, 1902), p. 128.

29 'Murders by the Armenian Mafia', *Manchester Guardian*, 15 September 1903.
30 'Naši Dopici: Kičevska Anarahja', *Stara Srbija*, 26 May 1921.
31 'The Cork Mystery', *Bristol Times and Mirror*, 23 March 1920.
32 Behan, pp. 23–4.
33 Dickie, *Blood Brotherhoods*, pp. 189–220.
34 Jack Reece, 'Fascism, the Mafia, and the Emergence of Sicilian Separatism (1919–43)', *The Journal of Modern History*, 45.2 (1973), pp. 268–9.
35 Dickie, *Blood Brotherhoods*, pp. 225–6.
36 Ibid., p. 258.
37 Dickie, *Cosa Nostra*, p. 176.
38 'The Camorra's Methods', *Manchester Guardian*, 12 July 1911.
39 Tai Hsuan-Chih and Ronald Suleski, 'Origin of the Heaven and Earth Society', *Modern Asian Studies*, 11.3 (1977), pp. 405–25.
40 Details of the FBI's investigation into the Wu Tang Clan can be found in documents released under the US Freedom of Information Act. No charges were filed as a result of the FBI's inquiry. See for example: https://vault.fbi.gov/russell-tyrone-jones (consulted 28 June 2023).
41 Jean Chesneaux, 'Secret Societies in China's Historical Evolution', in Jean Chesneaux (ed.), *Secret Societies in China in the Nineteenth and Twentieth Centuries*, (Stanford: Stanford University Press, 1972), p. 18.
42 Charlton M. Lewis, 'Some Notes on the Ko-lao in Late Ch'ing China' in Chesneaux, *Secret Societies in China in the Nineteenth and Twentieth Centuries*, pp. 97–112.
43 See Phil Billingsley, 'Bandits, bosses, and bare sticks: beneath the surface of local control in early Republican China', *Modern China* 7.3 (1981), pp. 235–88.
44 Lucien Bianco, 'Secret Societies and Peasant Self-Defense, 1921–1933', in Chesneaux, 217.
45 Brian Martin, *The Shanghai Green Gang: Politics and Organized Crime, 1919–1937* (Berkeley, CA: University of California Press, 1996), pp. 9–43.
46 Frederic Wakeman, *Policing Shanghai, 1927–1937* (Berkeley, CA: University of California Press, 1995), pp. 9–13.
47 Martin, pp. 40–3.
48 Wakeman, p. 14.
49 Kathryn Meyer and Terry Parssinen, *Web of Smoke: Smugglers, Warlords, Spies and the History of the International Drug Trade* (Lanham, MD: Rowman and Littlefield Publishers, 1998), pp. 152–3.
50 Marin, p. 146.
51 'China Deals With Racketeers In Way All Her Own', *Victoria Daily Times*, 6 July 1935.

52 William P. Morgan, *Triad Societies in Hong Kong* (Hong Kong: Government Press, 1960), p. 78.
53 Eiko Maruko Siniawer, 'Befitting Bedfellows: Yakuza and the State in Modern Japan', *Journal of Social History*, 45.3 (2012), p. 625.
54 Hiroaki Iwai, 'Organised Crime in Japan', in Robert Kelly (ed.), *Organised Crime: A Global Perspective* (Totawa, NJ: Rowman & Littlefield, 1986), pp. 208–15.
55 Eiko Maruko Siniawer, *Ruffians, Yakuza, Nationalists: The Violent Politics of Modern Japan, 1860–1960* (Ithaca, NY: Cornell University Press, 2008), pp. 20–5.
56 Sir Archibald Clark Kerr to Viscount Halifax, 31 August 1938, in *The Opium Trade, 1910–1941: Volume 5 – 1927–1941* (Wilmington, DE: Scholarly Resources, Inc., 1974).
57 Junichi Saga, *Confessions of a Yakuza* (Tokyo: Kodansha International, 1991), pp. 77–8.
58 Ibid., p. 195.
59 James Haley, *Captive Paradise: A History of Hawaii* (New York: St. Martin's Press, 2014), p. 334.
60 'Japanese Gamblers Are Class Apart', *The Pacific Commercial Advertiser*, 18 November 1905.
61 'The Japanese Procurers', *Pacific Commercial Advertiser*, 22 May 1900
62 Bill Mihalopoulos, *Sex in Japan's Globalization, 1870–1930: Prostitutes, Emigration and Nation-Building* (London: Routledge, 2016), p. 48.
63 'Japanese Gambler Jailed By Police', *Fresno Morning Republic*, 17 November 1913; 'Japs Engage in Deadly Conflict', *Santa Cruz Sentinel*, 9 November 1909; 'Sumida Hunted Trouble', *Spokane Chronicle*, 18 April 1908; 'Will Deport Jap Procurer', *The Missoulian*, 25 October 1907.
64 Eve Armentrout-Ma, 'Urban Chinese at the Sinitic Frontier: Social Organizations in United States' Chinatowns, 1849–1898', *Modern Asian Studies*, 17.1 (1983), pp. 107–35.
65 'Chink Masons to Make Merry', *Pittsburg Press*, 9 July 1905.
66 Asbury, *Barbary Coast*, p. 184; 'Peace to Reign: Warring Chinese Tongs Bridge the Bloody Chasm Permanently', *Marysville Appeal-Democrat*, 30 January 1901.
67 Lucie Cheng Hirata, 'Free, indentured, enslaved: Chinese prostitutes in nineteenth-century America', *Signs: Journal of Women in Culture and Society* 5.1 (1979), pp. 3–9.
68 'Chinese Tong War Revealed in Court', *The Ottawa Journal*, 30 July 1924; 'Four Killed, Score Injured as Mexico Tong War Begins', *The Bulletin* (Pomona, CA), 24 September 1924.
69 Richard Dillon, *The Hatchet Men: The Story of the Tong Wars in San Francisco's Chinatown* (Sausalito, CA: Comstock, 1962), p. 21.

Notes

70 Scott Seligman, *Tong Wars: The Untold Story of Vice, Money, and Murder in New York's Chinatown* (New York: Viking, 2016), p. 120.
71 Dillon, p. 140.
72 Seligman, p. 66.
73 Herbert Asbury, *The French Quarter: An Informal History of the New Orleans Underworld* (New York: Alfred A. Knopf, 2003), pp. 406–22.
74 Patrizia Salvetti, *Rope and Soap: Lynchings of Italians in the United States* (New York: Bordighera Press, 2017), p. xviii.
75 David Critchley, *The Origin of Organized Crime in America: The New York City Mafia, 1891–1931* (New York: Routledge, 2009), p. 14.
76 Ibid., pp. 37–60.
77 Robert Lombardo, *The Black Hand: Terror by Letter in Chicago* (Champaign, IL, University of Illinois Press, 2010), pp. 27–9.
78 'Pittsburg Black Hand', *Kansas City Kansas Globe*, 30 July 1906.
79 'Alien Group Crimes', *Daily Herald* (Biloxi, MS), 15 September 1925.
80 'The Black Hand (Wallace McCutcheon, 1906)', YouTube (https://www.youtube.com/watch?v=AzyuKxrHG0M, consulted 2 July 2023).
81 Joanne Ruvoli, '"Most Thrilling Subjects": D.W. Griffith and the Biograph Revenge Films', in Dana Renga (ed.), *Mafia Movies: A Reader* (Toronto: University of Toronto Press, 2011), pp. 59–67.

4. From Booze to Dope: The Advent of Global Mafias

1 Joseph McBride, *Hawks on Hawks* (Berkeley: University of California Press, 1982) pp. 48–9.
2 Scott Breivold (ed.), *Howard Hawks: Interviews* (Jackson: University of Mississippi Press, 2006), p. 110
3 N800.114 N 16 Eliopoulos, Elie/27, 19 November 1932, RG 59; General Records of the Department of State, USNA.
4 'Paul Kelly to Tell His Woes to Mayor', *New York Times*, 8 May 1912.
5 Tyler Anbinder, *Five Points: The Nineteenth-Century New York City Neighborhood* (New York: Free Press, 2012), p. 437; Herbert Asbury, *Gangs of New York* (New York: Thunder Mouth Press, 2001), p. 252.
6 Neil Hanson, *Monk Eastman: The Gangster Who Became a War Hero* (New York: Knopf Doubleday, 2010), pp. 105–8.
7 Daniel Czitrom, 'Underworlds and Underdogs: Big Tim Sullivan and Metropolitan Politics in New York, 1889–1913', *The Journal of American History*, 78.2 (September 1991), p. 550.
8 Robert Lacey, *Little Man: Meyer Lansky and the Gangster Life* (Boston: Little, Brown and Company, 1991), p. 46.
9 Woodiwiss, p. 176.
10 Lisa McGirr, *The War on Alcohol: Prohibition and the Rise of the American State* (New York: W. W. Norton, 2015), p. 52.

11 David Pietrusza, *Rothstein: The Life, Times, and Murder of the Criminal Genius Who Fixed the 1919 World Series* (New York: Basic Books, 2010), 195.
12 Dennis Eissenburg, *Meyer Lansky: Mogul of the Mob (*New York: Paddington Press, 1979), pp. 105–6.
13 Critchley, pp. 140–2.
14 'Detroit: Fourth in the U.S.; Fourteenth in World,' *Detroit Free Press*, 22 June 1930.
15 'Gangs Toll 21 Since June 1st', *Detroit Free Press*, 29 September 1930.
16 Rufus Schatzburg and Robert Kelly, *African American Organized Crime: A Social History* (New Brunswick, NJ: Rutgers University Press, 1996), pp. 91–3, 96.
17 'Police Follow Scant Clues to Murder of "Joe the Boss"', *The Union Standard*, 17 April 1931.
18 Critchley, p. 180.
19 Joseph Bonanno with Sergio Lalli, *Man of Honor: The Autobiography of Joseph Bonanno* (New York: Simon & Schuster, 1983), pp. 150, 161.
20 Chris Smith, *Syndicate Women: Gender and Networks in Chicago Organized Crime* (Berkeley: University of California Press, 2019), p. 56.
21 Russo, p. 27.
22 'Does She Hold the Key to the Dreaded Mafia Mysteries?' *St. Louis Star and Times*, 11 September 1921.
23 Robert Schoenberg, *Mr. Capone* (London: Robson Books, 1995), p. 128.
24 'Brundridge Sees Capone About Lingle Killing', *Chicago Tribune*, 19 July 1930.
25 Russo, p. 25.
26 Fred D. Pasley, *Al Capone: A Biography of a Self-Made Man* (Garden City, NY: Garden City Publishing Company, 1930), p. 11.
27 'New Films in London', *The Times*, 27 June 1932.
28 'Von Sass bis Diamond', *Westdeutsche Landeszeitung*, 7 September 1930.
29 Jacques Boulenger, '"Gangsters"', *Le Temps*, 30 October 1931.
30 'Akıllara hayret verıcı bir hadise: Şikago Haydutları kıralı Amerika hükümetine bir muahede aktını teklif ediyor!' *Vakit*, 2 December 1930.
31 'Capone Convicted of Tax Dodging', *New York Times*, 18 October 1931.
32 McGirr, p. 69.
33 Chales Rappleye and Ed Becker, *All-American Mafioso: The Johnny Rosselli Story* (New York: Doubleday, 1991), p. 53.

Notes

34 Lacey, p. 152.
35 Bob Thomas, 'Las Vegas is Called New Barbary Coast', *Oakland Tribune*, 30 December 1946.
36 Rosalie Schwartz, *Pleasure Island: Tourism and Temptation in Cuba* (Lincoln: University of Nebraska Press, 1997), p. 97.
37 Eisenburg, p. 174.
38 Tim Newark, *Lucky Luciano: The Real and the Fake Gangster* (New York: St. Martin's Press, 2010), p. 159.
39 'Luciano War Aid Called Ordinary', *New York Times*, 27 February 1947.
40 'California Tentacles of Luciano's Dope Ring, Mafia Bared by the U.S.', *San Francisco Examiner*, 26 February 1947.
41 Harry J. Anslinger and Will Oursler, *The Murderers: The Story of the Narcotics Gang* (New York: Farrar, Straus and Cudahy, 1961), pp. 9–10.
42 Thomas Russell Pasha, *The Egyptian Service 1902–1946* (London: John Murray, 1949), p. 228.
43 'Joseph Grew to Secretary of State', 18 November 1931, 1930–34; FBN Files, 1916–70; DEA Records; RG 170, USNA.
44 Nicholas Hewitt, *Wicked City: The Many Cultures of Marseille* (London: Hurst, 2019), p. 103.
45 Simon Kitson, *Police and Politics in Marseille, 1936–1945* (Leiden: Brill, 2014), p. 39.
46 Derick Goodman, *Villainy Unlimited: The Truth About the French Underworld Today* (London: Elek Books, 1957), p. 79.
47 Kitson, p. 14.
48 Alan Block, 'European Drug Traffic and Traffickers between the Wars: The Policy of Suppression and its Consequences', *Journal of Social History* 23.2 (Winter 1989), pp. 321–3.
49 'Drug Barons and China', *The North China Herald*, 7 June 1933; 'Report Bares World "Dope" Ring Activities', *San Francisco Examiner*, 7 May 1933.
50 'Charles E. Sherrill to Secretary of State', 1 November 1932, 1930–34; FBN Files, 1916–70; DEA Records; RG 170, USNA.
51 '30 in 5 Cities Nabbed as U.S. Hits Dope Ring', *Brooklyn Daily Eagle*, 21 November 1937.
52 John McWilliams and Alan Block, 'All the Commissioner's Men: The Federal Bureau of Narcotics and the Dewey–Luciano Affair, 1947–54', *Intelligence and National Security* 5.1 (1990), pp. 177–8.
53 '1948 Election Victor? Luciano Says He Is', *Daily News* (New York), 21 May 1948.
54 'Mafia Called Power in Vast Crime Ring', *Brooklyn Daily Eagle*, 12 June 1950.
55 Paul Jankowski, *Communism and Collaboration: Simon Sabiani and*

    Politics in Marseille, 1919–1944 (New Haven, CT: Yale University Press, 1989), p. 116.
56 'Nouvel Acte de Banditisme à Marseille', *Le Radical de Marseille*, 11 November 1943.
57 'Deux Policiers Impliqués à Marseille dans un Traffic d'Armes au Profit du "Milieu"', *Le Monde*, 15 November 1976.
58 J. Richard (Dixie) Davis, 'Boss of the Underworld', *St. Louis Post-Dispatch*, 15 September 1939.
59 Ovid Demaris, *The Last Mafioso* (Bronx, NY: Ishi Press International, 2010), p. 18
60 *Traffic in Opium and Other Dangerous Drugs for the Year Ended December 31, 1941* (Washington DC: US Treasury Department, Bureau of Narcotics, 1942), p. 4.

5. Godfathers: The High Tide of Old Mafias

1 Reg and Ron Kray with Fred Dineage, *Our Story* (London: Pan Books, 1989), p. 50.
2 Ibid., p. 55.
3 Julian Norridge, 'The Krays and the Richardsons – why they were bound to fail', *Evening Standard*, 24 March 1970.
4 Dick Hobbs, *Doing the Business: Entrepreneurship, Detectives and the Working Class in the East End of London* (Oxford: Clarendon Press, 1988), p. 125.
5 Michael Johnson, 'Popular movements and primordial loyalties in Beirut', *The Middle East* (1983), pp. 178–94.
6 Edgar Porter, *Japanese Reflections on World War II and the American Occupation* (Amsterdam: Amsterdam University Press, 2007), p. 170.
7 John Dower, *Embracing Defeat: Japan in the Wake of World War II* (New York: W. W. Norton, 2000), p. 130–1; Stephen Mansfield, *Tokyo: A Biography* (Tokyo: Tuttle Publishing, 2016), p. 140.
8 Holly Sanders, '*Panpan*: Streetwalking in Occupied Japan', *Pacific Historical Review*, 81.3, (2012), pp. 404–31.
9 Christopher Aldous, *The Police in Occupation Japan: Control, Corruption and Resistance to Reform* (London: Routledge, 2014), p. 109.
10 Darrell Berrigan, 'Tokyo's Own Al Capone', *Saturday Evening Post*, 10 October 1947.
11 David E. Kaplan and Alec Dubro, *Yakuza: Japan's Criminal Underworld* (Berkeley, CA: University of California Press, 2003), pp. 74–5.
12 Miriam Kingsberg, *Moral Nation: Modern Japan and Narcotics in Global History* (Berkeley, CA: University of California Press, 2014), p. 183.

Notes

13 Iwai, pp. 210–11.
14 H. Richard Friman, 'The Impact of the Occupation on Crime in Japan', in Mark Caprio and Yoneyuki Sugita, (eds.), *Democracy in Occupied Japan: The US Occupation and Japanese Politics and Society* (London: Routledge, 2007), p. 105.
15 Siniawer, *Ruffians, Yakuza, Nationalists*, p. 155.
16 Berrigan, 'Tokyo's Own Al Capone'.
17 Siniawer, pp. 162–3.
18 Peter Hill, *The Japanese Mafia: Yakuza, Law and the State* (Oxford: Oxford University Press, 2010), p. 114.
19 Iwai, p. 209.
20 Max Suich, 'Nippon Crime Incorporated', *Sydney Morning Herald*, 21 April 1971.
21 George Stevens (ed.), *Conversations at the American Film Institute with the Great Moviemakers: The Next Generation* (New York: Knopf, 2012), p. 667.
22 Federico Varese, *Mafia Life: Love, Death, and Money at the Heart of Organised Crime* (Oxford: Oxford University Press, 2018), p. 144.
23 Max Suich, 'Mr. Big of Japan', *Sydney Morning Herald*, 23 April 1971.
24 Richard Halloran, 'Little Known Japanese Wields Vast Power', *New York Times*, 2 July 1974.
25 Donald Kirk, 'Yakuza Flourish in Modern Japan', *Honolulu Star-Bulletin*, 15 December 1975.
26 Kaplan and Dubro, pp. 234–5.
27 Robert Whiting, *Tokyo Underworld* (New York: Vintage, 2000), p. 86
28 James Dooley, 'The role here is small – for now', *Honolulu Advertiser*, 22 March 1978.
29 Tom Emch, 'Bad News for Organized Crime', *San Francisco Examiner*, 27 January 1980; 'Yakuza does business here in three ways', *Honolulu Advertiser*, 30 January 1980.
30 Kaplan and Dubro, p. 287.
31 'Linda Deutsch, 'U.S. entertainers lured into Japanese prostitution', *San Francisco Examiner*, 11 April 1982; Scot Winukar, 'Tough Times for Bay Area Hookers', *San Francisco Examiner,* 10 August 1983.
32 T. S. Monks, 'More Powerful than the Mafia It's ... The Chinese Connection', *Sydney Morning Herald*, 7 August 1976; Peter Gladstone Smith, 'Triad Invasion of London Feared', *Sunday Telegraph*, 21 November 1976; Gerald Waring, 'Illegal Immigration Racket Linked to China "Mafia"', *Vancouver Sun*, 28 July 1960.
33 'Riots Caused by "Secret Societies"', *Daily Telegraph*, 13 October 1956.
34 Morgan, p. 67.

35 Ibid., p. 82.
36 'Triads will exist for many years', *South China Morning Post*, 7 April 1961.
37 Peng Weng, *The Chinese Mafia: Organized Crime, Corruption and Extra-Legal Protection* (Oxford: Oxford University Press, 2017), pp. 51–2.
38 Zhou Yongming, 'Nationalism, Identity and the State-Building: The Antidrug Crusade in the People's Republic, 1949–1952', in Timothy Brook and Bob Tadashi Wakabayashi (eds.), *Opium Regimes: China, Britain and Japan, 1839–1952* (Berkeley: University of California Press, 2000), p. 387.
39 *Traffic in Opium and Other Dangerous Drugs for the Year Ended December 31, 1962* (Washington DC: US Treasury Department, Bureau of Narcotics, 1963), 25; *Traffic in Opium and Other Dangerous Drugs for the Year Ended December 31, 1963* (Washington DC: US Treasury Department, Bureau of Narcotics, 1964), p. 34.
40 'U.S. Charges China Spurs Drug Habit', *New York Times*, 5 May 1954.
41 Bertil Lintner, 'The Shans and the Shan State of Burma', *Contemporary Southeast Asia*, 5.4 (1984), p. 410.
42 William O. Walker III, *Opium and Foreign Policy: The Anglo-American Search for Order in Asia, 1912–1954* (Chapel Hill: University of North Carolina Press, 1991), p. 206.
43 'Frank Long to C. A. Emerick', 13 April 1961, Hong Kong, 1958–December 1961, FBN Files, 1916–70; DEA Records; RG 170, USNA.
44 U.S. Senate Permanent Subcommittee on Investigations, *Organized Crime and Illicit Traffic in Narcotics, Part 5* (Washington DC: US Government Printing Office, 1964), 1358.
45 Alfred McCoy, *The Politics of Heroin in Southeast Asia* (New York: Harper & Row, 1972), p. 14.
46 'State to Bangkok, Canberra et. al.', 16 April 1973, SOC 11-5 Far East, Subject-Numeric File, RG 59; General Records of the Department of State, USNA. Also see Melissa Macauley, 'Entangled States: The Translocal Repercussions of Rural Pacification in China, 1869–1873', *The American Historical Review* 121.3 (June 2016), pp. 755–79.
47 Fenton Bresler, *The Chinese Mafia* (New York: Stein and Day, 1981), p. 78.
48 Bill O'Brien, 'Big Red China Dope Ring on Coast Broken', *San Francisco Examiner*, 15 January 1959.
49 Douglas Valentine, *Strength of the Pack: The Personalities, Politics and Espionage Intrigues that Shaped the DEA* (Waterville, OR: Trine Day, 2009), p. 263.

Notes

50 Frank Robertson, 'Triad makes the Mafia look like Amateurs', *Daily Telegraph*, 27 May 1976.
51 Erika Lee, *The Making of Asian America: A History* (New York: Simon & Schuster, 2015), p. 288.
52 Gordon Lew, 'New Dragons Clash in the "Gilded Ghetto"', *Los Angeles Times*, 18 September 1977.
53 United States Senate, Hearings before the Committee of the Judiciary, *Organized Crime in America* (Washington, DC: US Government Printing Office, 1984), pp. 119, 159, 259–60
54 'Jersey's Youngest Murder Defendant Claims Alibi', *Daily News*, 21 December 1927.
55 'Yanowsky Case Open Despite Last Clue', *The Morning Call*, 22 November 1958.
56 'Crack dope ring, jail 5 gangster suspects in L.A.', *Daily News*, 22 October 1946.
57 US Senate, Permanent Subcommittee on Investigations, *Organized Crime and Illicit Traffic in Narcotics, Part 3* (Washington DC: US Government Printing Office, 1964), p. 781.
58 See for example: SAC, San Diego to Director, FBI, 8 November 1969, in JFK Assassination Collection, NARA Record Number: 124-10280-10162, see Mary Ferrell Foundation https://www.maryferrell.org/showDoc.html?docId=79236#relPageId=2&search=happy_meltzer
59 '3 Suspects Seized in Narcotics Case', *New York Times*, 7 March 1951.
60 'Back Streets of Baltimore', *Baltimore Sun*, 12 September 1954.
61 Eric Schneider, *Vampires, Dragons and Egyptian Kings: Youth Gangs in Post-war New York* (Princeton: Princeton University Press, 1999), p. 75.
62 'Narcotics Linked to Life in Slums', *New York Times*, 15 June 1953.
63 *Traffic in Opium and Other Dangerous Drugs for the Year Ended December 31, 1954* (Washington DC: US Treasury Department, Bureau of Narcotics, 1955), 31; *Traffic in Opium and Other Dangerous Drugs for the Year Ended December 31, 1965* (Washington DC: US Treasury Department, Bureau of Narcotics, 1965), 19; *Traffic in Opium and Other Dangerous Drugs for the Year Ended December 31, 1967* (Washington DC: US Treasury Department, Bureau of Narcotics, 1968), p. 23.
64 Robert McCaa, 'Missing Millions: The Demographic Costs of the Mexican Revolution', *Mexican Studies/Estudios Mexicanos*, 19.2, (2003), pp. 367–400.
65 Thomas Benjamin, *La Revolución: Mexico's Great Revolution as Memory, Myth, and History* (Austin: University of Texas Press, 2000), p. 44.
66 Dennis Merrill, *Negotiating Paradise U.S. Tourism and Empire in*

67 *Twentieth-Century Latin America* (Durham: University of North Carolina Press, 2009), p. 37.
67 'Smuggling by Plane: 66 Million in Dope Traffic', *The Press Democrat*, 29 June 1947.
68 '"El Pablote" Shot, Killed', *El Paso Times*, 12 October 1930.
69 Juan Carlos Ramirez Pimienta, '"El Pablote": una nueva mirada al primer corrido dedicado a un traficante de Drogas', *Mitologías Hoy* 14 (2016), pp. 41–56.
70 US House of Representatives, *Treasury Department Appropriation Bill for 1944* (Washington: US Government Printing Office, 1942), p. 482.
71 'The World Opium Situation', October 1970, CIA-RDP73B00296R000300060031-9, CIA Records Search Tool (CREST), USNA.
72 Frank Holeman, 'Luciano Skips; May be in Mexico, Headed Here', *Daily News*, 3 September 1946.
73 Newark, p. 180.
74 Marie Paoleschi, *Le Milieu et Moi* (Paris: Fanval, 1987), p. 217.
75 George White to Harry Anslinger, 10 June 1948; George H. White Papers, Box 1, Folder 7, Special Collections Department, Stanford University.
76 See Ryan Gingeras, *Heroin, Organized Crime and the Making of Modern Turkey* (Oxford: Oxford University Press, 2014).
77 Lee Mortimer, *Around the World Confidential* (New York: G. P. Putnam's Sons, 1956), p. 198.
78 Jens Hanssen, *Fin de Siècle Beirut: The Making of an Ottoman Provincial Capital* (Oxford: Oxford University Press, 2005), p. 210.
79 Sean O'Callaghan, *Damaged Baggage: The White Slave Trade and Narcotics Trafficking in the Americas* (New York: Roy Publishers, 1970), p. 43.
80 Jonathan Marshall, *The Lebanese Connection: Corruption, Civil War and the International Narcotics Traffic* (Palo Alto, CA: Stanford University Press, 2012), p. 38.
81 Alvin Moscow, *Merchants of Heroin: An In-Depth Portrayal of Business in the Underworld* (New York: Dial Press, 1968), p. 4.
82 André Cédilot and André Noël, *Mafia Inc.: The Long, Bloody Reign of Canada's Sicilian Clan* (Toronto: Vintage Books Canada, 2012), p. 64.
83 Pierre Galante and Louis Sapin, *The Marseilles Mafia: The Truth Behind the World of Drug Trafficking* (London: W. H. Allen, 1979), p. 101.
84 Dickie, *Blood Brotherhood*, p. 277.
85 Salvatore Lupo, 'The Allies and the Mafia', *Journal of Modern Italian Studies*, 2.1 (1997), p. 31.

86 Gianluigi Nuzzi, *Blood Ties: The 'Ndrangheta: Italy's New Mafia* (London: Pan Books, 2012), p. 84.
87 James Walston, 'Italian is not spoken here', *Guardian*, 17 July 1976.
88 Lupo, *History of the Mafia*, p. 205.
89 Jane Schneider and Peter Schneider, *Reversible Destiny: Mafia, Antimafia and the Struggle for Palermo* (Berkeley: University of California Press, 2003), p. 66.
90 Dickie, *Blood Brotherhood*, p. 385.
91 Peter Cowie, *Revolution!: The Explosion of World Cinema in the 60s*, (London: Faber and Faber, 2004), p. 79.
92 Varese, *Mafia Life*, p. 171.
93 'American Consul in Palermo to Department of State', 27 August 1965, SOC-11 Italy, Subject-Numeric File, RG 59: General Records of the Department of State, USNA.
94 Allusions to a 'new mafia' in Sicily can be found through much of the post-war English-speaking press. It was particularly after the Ciaculli massacre that the phrase became more widely used. See for example, 'Italians to Probe Menace of the New Mafia Mobs', *Daily Mirror*, 21 May 1962.
95 Schneider and Schneider, p. 69.
96 McCoy, p. 8.
97 Marshall, *Lebanese Connection*, p. 47.
98 American Embassy Paris to American Embassy Ankara, 13 June 1970, Paris 7764, Subject Numeric Files, 1970–73, RG 59: General Records of the Department of State, US National Archives.
99 Newsday, *The Heroin Trail* (New York: New American Library, 1973), p. 221.
100 Matthew R. Pembleton, *Containing Addiction: The Federal Bureau of Narcotics and the Origins of America's Global Drug War* (Amherst: University of Massachusetts Press, 2017), 283.
101 Eric Schneider, *Smack: Heroin and the American City* (Philadelphia: University of Pennsylvania Press, 2008), pp. 117–22.
102 Critical Collection Problems Committee, 'Intelligence Activities Against Narcotics and Dangerous Drugs', October 1972, CIA-RDP88B00365R000200050042-6, CIA Records, USNA.
103 Edward Jay Epstein, *Agency of Fear: Opiates and Political Power in America* (New York: G. P. Putnam's Sons, 1977), p. 108.
104 'Text of Nixon's Message to Congress Proposing 10 Steps in Fighting Narcotics', *New York Times*, 15 July 1969.
105 Memorandum for the President, 20 October 1969, Box 30; White House Special Files, Staff Member and Office Files: Egil Krogh, 1969–73; Richard Nixon Presidential Library and Museum, Yorba Linda, California.
106 Stephen Farber, 'Movies', *New York Times*, 27 November 1971.

107 Louis Marcorelles, 'Hollywood sans Hollywood', *Le Monde*, 1 February 1972.
108 Embassy Paris to Secretary of State, Telegram 41546, 20 December 1978, 1978PARIS41546, Central Foreign Policy Files, 1973–79/ Electronic Telegrams, RG 59: General Records of the Department of State, USNA.
109 DEA, 'Threat Assessment: Middle East Heroin', 6 December 1979, Subject Files of Attorney General Epstein, Southwest Asian Heroin, RG 60, USNA.
110 Meyer Berger, 'Anastasia Slain in Hotel Here; Led Murder Inc.', *New York Times*, 26 October 1957.
111 Ira Henry Freeman, 'Anastasia Rose in Stormy Ranks', *New York Times*, 26 October 1957.
112 Lee Bernstein, *The Greatest Menace: Organized Crime and the Cold War* (Amhurst, MA: University of Massachusetts Press, 2002), p. 47.
113 Jack Lait and Lee Mortimer, *Chicago Confidential* (New York: Dell Publishing House, 1950), pp. 184, 204.
114 William Moore, *The Kefauver Committee and the Politics of Crime, 1950–1952* (Columbia, MO: University of Missouri Press, 1974), p. 49.
115 Berstein, p. 62.
116 Woodiwiss, p. 246.
117 Estes Kefauver, *The Kefauver Committee Report on Organized Crime* (New York: Didier, 1951), p. 128.
118 Ibid., p. 175.
119 Dickie, *Blood Brothers*, p. 324.
120 Colin Welch, 'America's Crime Syndicate', *Daily Telegraph*, 27 February 1952.
121 Walter Winchell, 'Reactions more envy than indignation', *Birmingham News*, 29 March 1951.
122 'Keep Up Crime Hunt, Chief Says', *St. Louis Globe-Democrat*, 27 March 1951.
123 Jonathan Marshall, *Dark Quadrant: Organized Crime, Big Business, and the Corruption of American Democracy* (Lanham, MD: Rowman and Littlefield, 2021), p. 149.
124 Selwyn Raab, *Five Families: The Rise, Decline and Resurgence of America's Most Powerful Mafia Empires* (New York: St. Martins Griffin, 2006), p. 156.
125 James Cary, 'FBI Hides Key Underworld Figure Who Names Genovese as Crime Chief', *Washington Post*, 8 August 1963.
126 Richard Scott, 'Gang leader ordered murder from gaol', *Guardian*, 28 September 1963.
127 Dickie, *Blood Brotherhood*, p. 132.
128 Earl Warren, *Report of the President's Commission on the*

Assassination of President John F. Kennedy (Washington, DC: US Government Printing Office, 1964), p. 790.
129 Robert H. Estabrook, 'Europeans Skeptical on Kennedy's Death', *Washington Post*, 17 December 1963.
130 Mark Seal, *Leave the Gun, Take the Cannoli: The Epic Story of the Making of The Godfather* (New York: Gallery Books, 2021), p. 62.
131 Gene D. Philips and Rodney Hill (eds), *Francis Ford Coppola: Interviews* (Jackson, MS: University Press of Mississippi, 2004), pp. 26–7.
132 Raab, p. 189.
133 Charles Champlin, '"Godfather": The Gangster Film Moves Uptown', *Los Angeles Times*, 19 March 1972.
134 Demaris, p. 193.
135 'Happy Meltzer with Aliases', 19 December 1960, HSCA Segregated CIA Collection, Box 7, Mary Ferrell Foundation, (https://www.maryferrell.org/showDoc.html?docId=57644#relPageId=1&search=happy_meltzer%20background%20and%20talent, consulted 17 August 2023).
136 See United States Senate, *Alleged Assassination Plots Involving Foreign Leaders* (Washington DC: US Government Printing Office, 1975), pp. 181–90.
137 John M. Crewdson, 'Kennedy Friend Denies Plot Role', *New York Times*, 18 December 1975.
138 US House of Representatives, *Final Report of the Select Committee on Assassinations of the U.S. House of Representatives* (Washington DC: US Government Printing Office, 1979), p. 115.
139 Daniel Vernet, 'Politique-fiction à Moscou', *Le Monde*, 25 September 1978.
140 Roberto Saviano, *Gomorrah* (New York: Farrar, Straus and Giroux, 2007), p. 250.
141 Philips and Hill, p. 28.

6. Between Decline and Revolution: Mafias at Century's End

1 Max Mermelstein, *The Man Who Made It Snow* (New York: Simon & Schuster, 1990), p. 197.
2 State of New York, *Report of the New York State Joint Legislative Committee on Crime, Its Causes, Control & Effect on Society* (1970), p. 244.
3 Jon Roberts, and Evan Wright. *American Desperado: My Life – From Mafia Soldier to Cocaine Cowboy to Secret Government Asset* (New York: Crown, 2011), p. 43.
4 Ibid., p. 525.

5   Ibid., pp. 245–6.
6   My thanks to Evan Wright for sharing this personal anecdote with me.
7   Tim Shawcross, *Men of Honour: The Confessions of Tommaso Buscetta* (London: Collins, 1987), p. 42.
8   'Evolution of trade under the WTO: handy statistics', World Trade Organization (https://www.wto.org/english/res_e/statis_e/trade_evolution_e/evolution_trade_wto_e.htm, consulted 14 July 2025).
9   Larry McShane, *Chin: The Life and Crimes of Mafia Boss Vincent Gigante* (New York: Pinnacle Books, 2016), p. 100.
10 Jimmy Breslin, 'The End of the Mob', in *The Playboy Book of True Crime* (Vermont, CA: Playboy Press, 2007), p. 367.
11 McShane, p. 11.
12 Mark Kriegel, 'Trial puts fox in henhouse', *Daily News*, 26 June 1997.
13 Raab, *Five Families*, p. 172.
14 Ibid., p. 216.
15 'The Mafia: Big Bad and Booming', *Time*, 16 May 1977.
16 Demaris, p. 349.
17 Tom Folsom, *The Made Ones: Crazy Joe Gallo and the Revolution at the Edge of the Underworld* (New York: Weinstein Books, 2008), p. 3.
18 Roberts and Wright, p. 103.
19 Jimmy Breslin, *The Good Rat: A True Story* (New York: Ecco, 2008), p. 198.
20 John Marzulli, 'She's killing them "over & over again"', *Daily News*, 10 February 2012; Dennis Wagner, 'Mobster reveals life in the Valley', *Arizona Republic*, 18 July 1999.
21 Bonnano, p. 404.
22 Peter Maas, *Underboss: Sammy the Bull Gravano's story of life in the Mafia* (New York: HarperCollins, 1997), p. 300.
23 Selwyn Raab, 'In the Mafia, Too, a Decline in Standards', *New York Times*, 19 January 1992.
24 Kevin Mattson, *What the Heck Are You Up To, Mr. President?: Jimmy Carter, America's 'Malaise', and the Speech that Should Have Changed the Country* (New York: Bloomsbury, 2009), p. 211.
25 McShane, p. 16.
26 Raad Cawthorn, 'In Cicero, it's a time of a major changes', *Philadelphia Inquirer*, 20 June 1998.
27 Jérôme Pierrat, *Une Histoire du Milieu: Grand banditisme et haute pègre en France, de 1850 à nos jours* (Paris: Denoël, 2003), p. 333.
28 Jean Contrucci, 'Deux nouveaux règlements de comptes à Marseille', *Le Monde*, 22 October 1985.
29 Pierre Georges, 'L'interminable "guerre de la limonade"', *Le Monde*, 2 October 1985.

Notes

30 Hewitt, p. 201.
31 Ibid., p. 209.
32 Tom Behan, *See Naples and Die*, p. 69.
33 Dickie, *Blood Brotherhood*, p. 471.
34 Behan, p. 82.
35 Dickie, p. 547.
36 Alexander Stille, *Excellent Cadavers: The Mafia and the Death of the First Italian Republic* (New York: Vintage, 1996), p. 106.
37 Schneider and Schneider, p. 66.
38 Lupo, *History of the Mafia*, p. 241.
39 Henry Kamm, 'Pope Reproves Mafia Obliquely in Sicily', *New York Times*, 22 November 1982.
40 Schneider and Schneider, p. 139.
41 Letizia Paoli, 'The Italian Mafia', in Letitizia Paoli (ed.), *The Oxford Handbook of Organized Crime* (Oxford: Oxford University Press, 2014), p. 137.
42 Dickie, *Blood Brotherhood*, p. 581.
43 Stille, p. 388.
44 Letizia Paoli, *Mafia Brotherhoods: Organized Crime, Italian Style* (Oxford: Oxford University Press, 2003), p. 206.
45 Paoli, 'The Italian Mafia', p. 135.
46 Ibid., p. 137.
47 Jane Schneider and Peter Schneider, 'Civil Society and Transnational Organized Crime: The Case of the Italian Antimafia Movement', in Felia Allum and Stan Gilmour (eds), *Routledge Handbook of Transnational Organized Crime* (London: Routledge, 2014), p. 361.
48 Kaplan and Dubro, p. 113.
49 Hill, p. 51.
50 Lintner, *Blood Brothers*, p. 173.
51 Kaplan and Dubro, p. 120.
52 Misha Glenny, *McMafia: A Journey through the Global Underworld* (New York: Knopf, 2008), p. 290.
53 Hill, p. 50.
54 Takatoshi Ito and Takeo Hoshi, *The Japanese Economy* (Cambridge, MA: MIT Press, 2020), 97.
55 David Holley, 'Japan Mob Muddies Loan Crisis', *Los Angeles Times*, 24 February 1996.
56 Yiu Kong Chu, 'Hong Kong triads after 1997', *Trends in Organized Crime* 8.3 (2005), p. 6.
57 Luke Hunt, 'Triad exodus poses new drug threat', *The Age*, 11 May 1997.
58 Federico Varese, *Mafias on the Move: How Organized Crime Conquers New Territories* (Princeton: Princeton University Press, 2011), p. 150.

59 Bertil Lintner, 'Chinese Organised Crime,' in Mark Galeotti (ed.), *Global Crime Today: The Changing Face of Organised Crime* (London: Routledge, 2005), p. 90.
60 Schwartz, p. 223.
61 Lintner, *Blood Brothers*, p. 75.
62 Varese, *Mafia Life*, p. 138.
63 Woodiwiss, *Organized Crime and American Power*, p. 382.
64 Alessandra Stanley, 'Palermo Shows Off as a Cleaned-Up Mafia Capital', *New York Times*, 13 December 2000.
65 James B. Jacobs and Elizabeth Dondlinger Wyman, 'Organized Crime Control in the United States of America', in Letizia Paoli (ed.), *The Oxford Handbook of Organized Crime* (Oxford: Oxford University Press, 2014), p. 538.
66 Woodiwiss, pp. 288–9.
67 Francisco Thoumi, 'Colombian organized crime: From drug trafficking to parastatal bands and widespread corruption', *Traditional Organized Crime in the Modern World: Responses to Socioeconomic Change* (New York: Springer, 2012), p. 132.
68 Mary Roldán, *Blood and Fire: La Violencia in Antioquia, Colombia, 1946–1953* (Durham, NC: Duke University Press, 2002), p. 5.
69 Patrick Clawson and Rensselaer Lee, *The Andean Cocaine Industry* (New York: Palgrave Macmillan, 1996), p. 22.
70 Alonso Salazar, *Pablo Escobar, El Patrón del Mal* (Doral, FL: Aguilar, 2012), 42.
71 Roberto Escobar Gaviria, *The Accountant's Story: Inside the Violent World of the Medellín Cartel* (New York: Grand Central, 2009), pp. 5–8.
72 Paul Gootenberg, *Andean Cocaine: The Making of a Global Drug* (Durham, NC: University of North Carolina, 2006), p. 336.
73 Mark Olva, '"Cuban Mafia" cocaine trail to Vegas ambushed', *Reno Gazette-Journal*, 2 August 1975.
74 Salazar, p. 37.
75 Streatfield, p. 240.
76 Ibid., p. 233.
77 Francisco Thoumi, *Political Economy and Illegal Drugs in Colombia* (Boulder, CO: Lynne Rienner, 1995), p. 142.
78 Roberts and Wright, p. 299.
79 United States Senate, *Federal Drug Enforcement: Hearings Before the Permanent Subcommittee on Investigations of the Committee on Government Operations* (Washington: US Government Printing Office, 1975), 1454. DEA officials specifically referred to Sicilia's ring as a cartel, marking one of the earliest instances the term was used.
80 Benjamin Smith, *The Dope: The Real History of the Mexican Drug Trade* (New York: W. W. Norton and Co, 2021), p. 291.
81 Carlos Hernandez, 'Narcomundo: How Narcotraficantes Gained

Control of Northern Mexico and Beyond, 1945–1985', PhD Dissertation: University of California Los Angeles, 2015, p. 212.
82 Smith, *The Dope*, p. 300.
83 Guillermo Valdés Castellanos, Historia del narcotráfico en México (Mexico City: Aguilar, 2013), p. 179.
84 Robert Rast, 'Drugs and the US Economy', *San Francisco Examiner*, 8 September 1989.
85 Charles Bowden, *Down by the River: Drugs, Money, Murder and Family* (New York: Simon & Schuster 2002), p. 3.
86 'A Decade of Dirty Money', *Miami Herald*, 11 February 1990.
87 Justin Gillis and Stephen Doig, 'Drug trade may add billions to Dade economy, experts say', *Miami Herald*, 11 February 1990.
88 Roberts and Wright, p. 456.
89 Ibid., p. 339.
90 James Kelly, 'South Florida: Trouble in Paradise', *Time*, 23 November 1981.
91 Bob Drury, 'A Supply and Demand of Violence: As Gangs Proliferate, So Does Unchecked Murder', *Newsday*, 3 September 1987.
92 'Agents say 1 arrest won't stop vicious cocaine cartel', *El Paso Times*, 10 February 1987.
93 Jesus Blancornelas, *El Cártel: Los Arellano Félix: la mafia más poderosa de la historia de América Latina* (Mexico City: Debolsillo, 2004), p. 54.
94 Salazar, p. 27.
95 Escobar Gaviria, p. 95.
96 Varese, *Mafias on the Move*, pp. 101–45.
97 Ioan Grillo, *El Narco: Inside Mexico's Criminal Insurgency* (New York: Bloomsbury Publishing, 2011), p. 200.
98 Steven Prigge, *Movie Moguls Speak: Interviews with Top Film Producers* (Jefferson, NC: McFarland and Company, 2004), p. 121
99 Charles Silet (ed.), *Oliver Stone: Interviews* (Jackson: University of Mississippi Press, 2001), p. 48
100 James Creechan and Jorge de la Herran Garcia, 'Without God or Law: Narcoculture and Belief in Jesus Malverde', *Religious Studies and Theology* 24.2 (2005), p. 23.
101 Luis Astorga, 'Los Corridos de Traficantes de Drogas En México y Colombia', *Revista Mexicana de Sociología*, 59.4 (1997), p. 254.
102 Raphael Croda, 'Pablo Escobar: Un capo de culto', *Proceso*, 8 December 2013.
103 Escobar Gaviria, p. 98.
104 Guy Gugliotta, *Kings of Cocaine: Inside the Medellín Cartel* (New York: Simon & Schuster, 1989), p. 97.
105 Larry Rohter, 'With U.S. Training, Colombia Melds War on Rebels and Drugs', *New York Times*, 29 July 1999.

106 Angélica Durán-Martínez, *The Politics of Drug Violence: Criminals, Cops and Politicians in Colombia and Mexico* (Oxford: Oxford University Press, 2017), 118.
107 Dan Baum, *Smoke and Mirrors: The War on Drugs and the Politics of Failure* (Boston: Little, Brown, 1996), p. 142.
108 'Remarks on Signing the Just Say No To Drugs Week Proclamation', (https://www.reaganlibrary.gov/archives/speech/remarks-signing-just-say-no-drugs-week-proclamation#:~:text=By%201980%20illegal%20drugs%20were,losing%20its%20future%20by%20default, consulted 1 December 2023).
109 Alexander Cockburn and Jeffrey St. Clair, *Whiteout: the CIA, Drugs, and the Press* (New York: Verso, 1998), pp. 323–5.
110 Jonathan Marshall, *Drug Wars: Corruption, Counterinsurgency and Covert Operations in the Third World* (Forestville, CA: Cohan & Cohan Publishers, 1991), p. 44.
111 Streatfield pp. 494–5.
112 Richard Meislin, 'The Campaign against Corruption has a Long Way to Go', *New York Times*, 21 April 1985.
113 Smith, pp. 372–3.
114 Bowden, p. 4.
115 Tim Golden, 'U.S. Officials Say Mexican Military Aids Drug Traffic', *New York Times*, 26 March 1998.
116 Gootenberg, *Andean Cocaine*, pp. 304–5.
117 Durán-Martínez, p. 154.
118 Clawson and Lee, p. 170.
119 Hermes Sucre Serrano, 'PTJ denuncia proliferation de "cartelitos"', *La Prensa*, 6 October 1997.
120 Alexandre Marchant, 'The French Connection as an Illicit Trade Network', in Paul Gootenberg (ed.), *The Oxford Handbook of Global Drug History* (Oxford, Oxford University Press, 2022), p. 511.
121 Laurent Fiocconi and Jerome Pierrat, *Le Colombien: Des parrains corses au cartels de la coke* (Paris: Toucan Noir, 2009), pp. 198, 220.
122 Colin Clarke, 'Politics, Violence and Drugs in Kingston, Jamaica', *Bulletin of Latin American Research*, 25.3 (2006), pp. 423, 425.
123 NARA, American Embassy Kingston to Department of State, August 20, 1971, Subject-Numeric File, RG 59: General Records of the Department of State, US National Archives.
124 Ibid., 6 October 1972.
125 Ron Sachs, 'There's Almost No Stopping Smuggled Pot from Jamaica', *Miami Herald*, 8 September 1974.
126 Enrique Desmond Arias, 'Latin American and Caribbean Drug Trafficking Groups', in Paul Gootenberg (ed.), *The Oxford Handbook of Global Drug History* (Oxford. Oxford University Press, 2022), p. 524.

Notes

127 Michael Hanlon, '"Yardie" gangs leave trail of murder, coke in United Kingdom', *Toronto Star*, 13 November 1988; John Steven, 'Godfather of Yardies Deported', *Evening Standard*, 8 November 1988.

128 Jayne Howarth, 'Yardie "in IRA plot to kill Thatcher"', *Birmingham Post*, 3 March 1997.

129 Neil Darbyshire, 'Why the Yard Fears the Yardies,' *Daily Telegraph*, 13 October 1988; Philip Mascoll, 'Murderous posses gain Metro foothold', *Toronto Star*, 25 February 1990.

130 Amy Stromberg and Renee Krause, 'Agents arrest "posses"', *South Florida Sentinel*, 14 October 1988.

131 Obi N. I. Ebbe, 'The Political-Criminal Nexus: The Nigerian Case', *Trends in Organized Crime*, 4.3 (Springer, 1999), pp. 32–3.

132 Stephen Ellis, *The Present Darkness: A History of Nigerian Organised Crime* (Oxford: Oxford University Press, 2016), p. 120.

133 Jude Oboh, *Cocaine Hoppers: Nigerian International Cocaine Trafficking* (London: Rowman & Littlefield, 2021), p. 24.

134 Ellis, p. 123.

135 Elaine Sciolino, 'State Dept. Report Labels Nigeria Major Trafficker of Drugs to U.S.', *New York Times*, 5 April 1994.

136 Richard Hall, 'Buhari Challenge to Drug Barons', *Observer*, 30 June 1985.

137 'Working Papers for the Report on Organized Crime and Corruption – December 1965 for President's Commission on Enforcement and Administration of Justice', FBN Files, 1916–70; DEA Records; RG 170, USNA.

138 See for example: 'U.S. Agent Links Hell's Angels to Narcotics Ring', *St. Louis Dispatch-Post*, 7 November 1965.

139 Donald Goddard, *Easy Money* (London: Panther, 1980), p. 115.

140 Frank Faso and Paul Mesil, 'The New Mafia: From Rags to a Rolls – the Story of No. 1', *Daily News*, 11 June 1974.

141 'Spook Hunters Only Rumor to County Council', *California Eagle*, 24 December 1959.

142 Mike Davis, *City of Quartz: Excavating the Future of Los Angeles* (London: Verso, 2006), p. 299.

143 George Percy Barganier, 'Fanon's Children: The Black Panther Party and the Rise of the Crips and Bloods in Los Angeles', PhD Dissertation: University of California Los Angeles, 2011, p. 81.

144 Phil Garlington, 'Graffiti Tells Story About Teen-Age Street Gangs in San Diego', *Los Angeles Times*, 18 June 1978.

145 Jesse Katz, 'Tracking the Genesis of the Crack Trade', *Los Angeles Times*, 20 October 1996.

146 Scott Harris, 'Study Cites Menace of Drug-Crime Networks', *Los Angeles Times*, 23 July 1986.

147 David Freed, 'L.A. Found Armed, Dangerous', *Los Angeles Times*, 17 May 1992.
148 Gary Webb, *Dark Alliance: The CIA, the Contras and the Crack Cocaine Explosion* (New York: Seven Stories Press, 1998), p. 353.
149 Michael Woodiwiss, 'Mafia pushed aside', *Observer*, 26 March 1989.
150 Davis, p. 313.
151 Andrii Portnov, *Dnipro: An Entangled History of a European City* (Boston: Academic Studies Press, 2022), pp. 73–4.
152 Ibid., pp. 230–5, 252.
153 Vitali Vitaliev, *Special Correspondent: Investigating in the Soviet Union* (London: Hutchinson, 1990), p. 107.
154 Ibid., p. 101.
155 'Trotsky Charges Soviet Has "Mafia"', *New York Times*, 14 April 1938.
156 Scott Shane, 'Russian Godfather meets a stylish Socialist end', *Manchester Guardian*, 23 July 1988.
157 Vitaliev, *Special Correspondent*, p. 116.
158 My special thanks to Bob Edelman who told me this joke as his student back in 1996. I've repeated it many times since.
159 Stephen Kotkin, *Armageddon Averted: The Soviet Collapse 1970–2000* (Oxford: Oxford University Press, 2008), p. 15.
160 Anthony Austin, 'Soviet Writer Rebuked for Deviation in Hit Play', *New York Times*, 12 May 1981.
161 David Remnick, 'The Soviet Mob Blotter: Lurid Accounts of Murder, Mayhem & Mafia Fill the Press', *Washington Post*, 23 March 1988.
162 Vitali Vitaliev, 'Comrade Godfather: The mafia in the Soviet Union', *Sydney Morning Herald*, 11 August 1990.
163 David Remnick, *Lenin's Tomb: The Last Days of the Soviet Empire* (New York: Random House, 1993), p. 181.
164 See for example: Daryna Shevchenko, 'Dnipro, city with a Soviet soul', *Kyiv Post*, 27 July 2013 (https://www.kyivpost.com/post/8290, consulted 19 December 2023).
165 Katya Vladimirov, 'Red Buccaneers: Soviet Criminal Enterprises, 1950s', *Canadian-American Slavic Studies* 35.2-3 (2001), p. 268.
166 Gilles Favarel-Garrigues, *Policing Economic Crime in Russia: From Soviet Planned economy to Privatisation* (London: Hurst, 2011), p. 34.
167 Mark Galeotti, *The Vory: Russia's Super Mafia* (New Haven: Yale University Press, 2018), 94; 'Wheeling, dealing Soviet gets 15 years in prison', *Vancouver Sun*, 10 February 1973.
168 Paul Klebnikov, *Godfather of the Kremlin: Boris Berezovsky and the Looting of Russia* (New York: Harcourt, 2000), pp. 52–4.
169 Ibid., pp. 118–9.
170 Yakov Gilinskiy and Yakov Kostjukovsky, 'From thievish artel to

criminal corporation: the history of organised crime in Russia', in Cyrille Fijnaut and Letizia Paoli (eds), *Organised Crime in Europe: Concepts, Patterns and Control Policies in the European Union and Beyond* (Dordrecht: Springer Netherlands, 2004), pp. 184–8.
171 Federico Varese, *The Russian Mafia: Private Protection in a New Market Economy* (Oxford: Oxford University Press, 2001), p. 164.
172 Ibid., p. 151.
173 Galeotti, *The Vory*, p. 56.
174 Ibid. pp. 81–2.
175 Volkov, p. 2.
176 Steve Erlanger, 'A Slaying Puts Russian Underworld on Parade', *New York Times*, 14 April 1994.
177 Galeotti, *The Vory*, pp. 109–11.
178 David Hearst, 'Don't tell Russians that size doesn't matter', *Guardian*, 18 April 1994.
179 Joyce Wadler, 'By the Sea, a Bit of Russia Blossoms Here', *Washington Post*, 4 April 1982.
180 Herman Wong, 'Armenians Save Their Culture', *Los Angeles Times*, 20 April 1990.
181 Karen Ball, 'He swipes at extort rap', *Daily News*, 11 June 1995.
182 Hugh Davis, 'Russian mobs stealing American dream', *Sunday Telegraph*, 20 November 1994.
183 Tim Johnson, 'Russians muscle into the drug trade', *Miami Herald*, 3 July 1998.
184 Michael Specter, 'Traffickers' New Cargo: Naive Slavic Women', *New York Times*, 11 January 1998; Julian West, 'Russia's mafia exports vice to Sri Lanka', *Sunday Telegraph*, 11 January 1998.
185 *Frontline*: Interview with Vyacheslav Fetisov (https://www.pbs.org/wgbh/pages/frontline/shows/hockey/interviews/fetisov.html, consulted 4 January 2024); Tom Gulitti, 'A look at NHL, organized crime ties', *The Record* (Hackensack, New Jersey), 12 October 1999.
186 Helen Womack, 'The Moscow Mafia', *Independent*, 21 October 1989.
187 Werth, pp. 356–7.
188 Mairbek Vatchagaev, 'Who's Who in the Moscow Chechen Community', *The Jamestown Foundation*, 3 July 2008 (https://jamestown.org/program/whos-who-in-the-moscow-chechen-community/, consulted 5 January 2024).
189 Mark Galeotti, '"Brotherhoods" and "Associates": Chechen Networks of Crime and Resistance', in Robert Bunker (ed.), *Networks, Terrorism and Global Insurgency* (London: Routledge, 2014), p. 174.
190 Stephen Handelman, *Comrade Criminal: Russia's New Mafiya* (New Haven: Yale University Press, 1995), p. 50.

191 Mark Galeotti and Clive H. Schofield, *Cross-Border Crime in the Former Soviet Union* (Durham: International Boundaries Research Unit, University of Durham, 1995), 20; Glenny, p. 62.
192 Jana Arsovska, *Decoding Albanian Organized Crime: Culture, Politics and Globalization* (Berkeley: University of California Press, 2015), p. 91.
193 D. J. Saunders and Mike Santangelo, 'Feds targeted for hits', *Daily News*, 18 September 1985; 'Heroin's new traders', *Daily News*, September 18, 1985.
194 Arsovska, p. 91.
195 Yigal Chazan, 'Albanian drug barons find their way around the war', *Guardian*, 1 November 1994.
196 Ariane von Barth et al., 'Sprache der Morde', *Der Spiegel*, 2 August 1999.
197 Frank Viviano, 'KLA Linked to Enormous Heroin Trade', *San Francisco Chronicle*, 5 May 1999.
198 Metin İnan, 'Babalar Dünyası'nda bir dönemin sonu!', *Milliyet*, 24 December 2015.
199 Soner Yalçın, *Behçet Cantürk'ün Anıları* (Istanbul: Doğan Kitapçılık, 2007), p. 118.
200 'Eymür'den "Şok" Metkup', *Milliyet*, 27 July 2001; Soner Yalçin and Doğan Yurdakul, *Bay Pipo* (Istanbul: Doğan Kitapçılık, 2003), p. 394.
201 Mehmet Özkök, 'Derin devlet sözünün mucidi', *Hürriyet*, 25 November 1997.
202 See for example: Nicole Pope, 'Les scandales de corruption déstabilisent l'Etat turc', *Le Monde*, 23 November 1996.
203 Kemal Kirişci, 'Turkey: A Country of Transition from Emigration to Immigration', Mediterranean Politics, 12:1 (2007), p. 92.
204 Tony Thompson, 'Heroin "emperor" brings terror to UK streets', *Observer*, 17 November 2002.
205 Frank Bovenkerk and Yücel Yeşilgöz, *The Turkish Mafia: A History of the Heroin Godfathers* (Lancs, United Kingdom: Milo Books Ltd., 2007), pp. 235–6.
206 See for example: Soner Yalçın and Doğan Yudakul, *Reis: Gladio'nun Türk Tetikçisi* (Istanbul: Doğan Kitapcılık, 2007), p. 154.
207 Stephen Handelman, 'Russian Mafiya', *Foreign Affairs*, 73.2 (March/April 1994), 83–96.
208 'A National Security Strategy of Engagement and Enlargement', The White House, 1994 (https://history.defense.gov/Portals/70/Documents/nss/nss1994.pdf, consulted 12 January 2024).
209 Petrit Korça, 'The Albanian Cartel: Filling the Crime Void', *Jane's Intelligence Review*, 1 November 1995.
210 Arsovska, pp. 65–6.

Conclusion. The Great Dilution: Making Sense of the Twenty-First Century

1. See: https://assets.scriptslug.com/live/pdf/scripts/the-sopranos-101-piot-1999.pdf (consulted 18 January 2024).
2. See David Chase Interview: https://interviews.televisionacademy.com/interviews/david-chase?clip=25254 (consulted 18 January 2024).
3. 'Feds worry that terrorists, mobsters might collaborate', *Denver Post*, 1 October 2006.
4. Luke Harding, 'Drug war: Edict reverses policy that wiped out crop', *Guardian*, 25 September 2001.
5. Barry Meier, '"Super" Heroin Was Planned By bin Laden, Reports Say', *New York Times*, 4 October 2001.
6. Julian Borger, 'Pentagon outlines plans to take war on terror to Georgia', *Guardian*, 28 February 2002.
7. Vanda Felbab-Brown, 'Narco-Jihad: Drug Trafficking and Security in Afghanistan and Pakistan', (https://www.brookings.edu/articles/narco-jihad-drug-trafficking-and-security-in-afghanistan-and-pakistan/, consulted 15 January 2024).
8. Max Bearack, 'Pakistan's plan for tackling deforestation: A billion trees', *Washington Post*, 16 May 2016; Antonin Sabot, 'Le dialogue avec les talibans aurait dû être engagé dès 2001', *Le Monde*, 29 May 2009
9. 'Afghanistan Opium Survey 2023', UNODC Research Brief (November 2023).
10. Jacques Follorou, 'Methamphetamine takes over from heroin in Afghanistan', *Le Monde*, 14 September 2023.
11. Robert Fisk, *Pity the Nation: Lebanon at War* (Oxford: Oxford University Press, 1991), p. 122.
12. Marshall, *Lebanese Connection*, 85.
13. Jack Anderson and Dale Van Atta, 'Khomeini's Drug Trade', *Washington Post*, 3 April 1988.
14. Mahmut Cengiz and Camilo Pardo-Herrera, 'Hezbollah's Global Networks and Latin American Cocaine', *Small Wars Journal*, 25 April 2023 (https://smallwarsjournal.com/jrnl/art/hezbollahs-global-networks-and-latin-american-cocaine-trade, consulted 26 January 2024).
15. Caroline Rose and Alexander Söderholm, 'The Captagon Threat: A Profile of Illicit Trade, Consumption and Regional Realities', *New Lines Institute for Strategy and Policy*, April 2022 (https://newlinesinstitute.org/wp-content/uploads/20220404-Captagon_Report-NLISAP-final-.pdf, consulted 26 January 2024).
16. Peter A. Lupsha, 'Towards an Etimology of Drug Trafficking and Insurgent Relations: The Phenomenon of Narco-Terrorism',

International Journal of Comparative and Applied Criminal Justice 13:2 (1989), p. 62.
17 Jovana Gec, Serbia ends crackdown on Albanian rebels in Kosovo', *Atlanta Constitution*, 28 September 1998.
18 John F. Burns and Kirk Semple, 'U.S. Finds Iraq Insurgency Has Funds to Sustain Itself', *New York Times*, 26 November 2006.
19 Ramazan Hakkı Öztan, 'Tools of Revolution: Global Military Surplus, Arms Dealers and Smugglers in the Late Ottoman Balkans, 1878–1908', *Past & Present*, 237 (November 2017), pp. 167–95.
20 Barry Rubin, *Revolution Until Victory? The Politics and History of the PLO* (Cambridge, MA: Harvard University Press, 1994), p. 52.
21 Colin Randall, 'Terrorist "hypocrites" ply deadly trade', *Daily Telegraph*, 3 January 1996.
22 Martin Hodgson and Rosie Cowan, 'Provos pool know-how at school of terror', *Guardian*, 15 August 2001.
23 Hussain Zaidi, *Dongri to Dubai: Six Decades of the Mumbai Mafia* (New Delhi: Lotus Collection, 2012), p. 181.
24 Ibid., p. 229.
25 US House of Representatives, Committee on International Relations, 'The Challenge of Terrorism in Asia and the Pacific' (Washington, DC: U.S. Government Printing Office, 2003), pp. 80–1.
26 'Dawood Ibrahim is 2nd richest gangster of all time; 10 things about most wanted global terrorist', *India Today*, 25 May 2017.
27 Michael Marrus, *Mr. Sam: The Life and Times of Samuel Bronfman* (New York: Viking Press, 1991), 135.
28 See for example: Charles Hanley, 'Rubles, not scruples, count for new capitalist merchants', *Miami Herald*, June 20, 1993; Nick Rouse, 'Sport is not immune to the Wild West of Modern Russia', *Sunday Telegraph*, 27 February 1994.
29 Marshall, *Dark Quadrant*, pp. 164–5.
30 SA, Las Vegas to Director, FBI, SUBJECT: SIDNEY KORSHAK, 18 April 1963 (see: https://vault.fbi.gov/Sidney%20Korshak/Sidney%20Korshak%20Part%201%20of%203/view, consulted 8 February 2024).
31 Seymour Hersh, 'Korshak Again the Target of a Federal Investigation', *New York Times*, 30 June 1976. An internal FBI report refuted Hersh's assertation. However, it was not clear who within the FBI spoke to the *New York Times* claiming that such an investigation existed. See To Mr. Fehl from [redacted], SUBJECT; SIDNEY R. KORSHAK, INFORMATION CONCERNING (https://vault.fbi.gov/Sidney%20Korshak/Sidney%20Korshak%20Part%202%20of%203/view, consulted 8 February 2024).
32 William Knoedelseder, *Stiffed: A True Story of MCA, the Music and the Mafia* (New York: Harper Collins, 1994), pp. 350–1.

33 Jay S. Albanese, *Transnational Crime and the 21st Century* (Oxford: Oxford University Press, 2011), pp. 110–11.
34 Carrick Mollenkamp, 'HSBC became bank to drug cartels, pays big for lapses', *Reuters*, 11 December 2012.
35 Dickie, *Blood Brotherhood*, pp. 421–2.
36 Ibid., p. 594.
37 Michael Day, 'Berlusconi "paid Mafia bosses millions of euros in pact lasting decades"', *Independent*, September 2013.
38 Jason Horowitz and Rachel Donadio, 'Silvio Berlusconi, a Showman Who Upended Italian Politics and Culture, Dies at 86', *New York Times*, 12 June 2023; 'Silvio Berlusconi, Italy's scandalous celebrity PM, dies at 86', *The Times*, 12 June 2023.
39 'Corruption Perception Index 2023', *Transparency International* (January 2024), 2.
40 'Global Organized Crime Index 2023', *Global Initiative against Transnational Organized Crime* (Geneva, 2024), p. 128.
41 Cole Moreton, 'How can you tell a multinational from the Mafia? You can't', *Independent*, 31 January 2016.
42 Jasper Jolly, 'Owners of 100,000 properties held by foreign shell companies unknown despite new UK laws', *Guardian*, 3 September 2023.
43 Elizabeth Shim, 'Report: Japan's Yakuza laundered $270M through crypto exchange', *UPI*, 14 May 2018; Tom Wilson, 'Thai-based China trade group says man named in crypto scam report no longer a board member', *Reuters*, 6 December 2023.
44 Saviano, p. 45.
45 Ibid., p. 294.
46 'Calderón plantea paquete de reformas con un fuerte acento lopezobradorista', *La Jornada*, 2 December 2006.
47 Anabel Hernandez, *Narcoland: The Mexican Drug Lords and Their Godfathers* (London: Verso, 2013), pp. 203–4.
48 Salvador Maldonado Aranda, 'Drogas, violencia y militarización en el México rural: El caso de Michoacán', *Revista Mexicana de Sociología* 74.1 (January–March 2012), pp. 28–30.
49 Anabel Hernandez, *Los Señores del Narco* (Mexico City, Grijalbo, 2011), pp. 56–62.
50 Jonathan Rosen and Roberto Zepeda, *Organized Crime, Drug Trafficking, and Violence in Mexico: The Transition from Felipe Calderón to Enrique Peña Nieto* (London: Lexington Books, 2016), pp. 53, 69.
51 Uki Goni, 'Uruguay president José Mujica apologises for calling Mexico a "failed state"', *Guardian*, 24 November 2014.
52 Azam Ahmad, 'Con escape del hijo del "Chapo", México sufre una derrota impresionante', *Proceso*, 18 October 2019. Originally printed

as Azam Ahamd, 'The Stunning Escape of El Chapo's Son: It's Like "a Bad Netflix Show"', *New York Times,* 18 October 2019.
53 Alan Feuer and Maria Abi-Habib, 'Former Mexican President Accused of Supporting Sinaloa Cartel', *New York Times,* 7 February 2023.
54 Tom Leonard, 'Drug Battle Triggers State of Emergency', *National Post,* 25 May 2010.
55 'Ex-PM Testifies About Deadly Raid', *Miami Herald,* 10 February 2015.
56 Al Valdez, 'The Origins of Southern California Latino Gangs', in Thomas Bruneau, et al., *Maras: Gang Violence and Security in Central America* (Austin, TX: University of Texas Press, 2011), pp. 23–42.
57 Chris Kraul, et al., 'L.A. Violence Crosses the Line', *Los Angeles Times,* 15 May 2005.
58 Megan Janetsky, 'El Salvador's president jailed 1% of the population. Their children are paying the price', *Associated Press,* 19 February 2024.
59 Danilo Mandić, *Gangsters and Other Statesmen: Mafias, Separatists, and Torn States in a Globalized World* (Princeton: Princeton University Press, 2021).
60 Gerry Shih, 'China's backers and "triad" gangs have a history of common foes. Hong Kong protesters fear they are next', *Washington Post,* 23 July 2019.
61 Galeotti, *Vory,* p. 242.
62 Patrick Keddie, *The Passion: Football and the Story of Modern Turkey* (London: IB Tauris, 2018), p. 91.
63 'Sedat Peker'in "oluk oluk kan akacak" sözleri sosyal medyanın gündeminde', *Cumhuriyet,* 10 October 2015.
64 'Mehmet Ağar ve Tolga Ağar hakkında suç duyurusu', *Cumhuriyet,* 12 May 2021; 'Sedat Peker'den 7. video: Yeni uyuşturucu hattını kurmak için Venezuela'ya Erkam Yıldırım gitti', *Gazete Duvar,* 25 May 2021.
65 Vanda Felbab-Brown, et al., 'Chinese crime and geopolitics in 2024', *Brookings Institute,* 29 January 2024.
66 See Peng Wang, *The Chinese Mafia: Organized Crime, Corruption and Extra-Legal Protection* (Oxford: Oxford University Press, 2017).
67 Antonio Maria Delgado and Valentina Lares, 'Leak offers new proof of how Venezuela has turned into narco-state', *Miami Herald,* 8 November 2023; Joshua Goodman and Jim Mustian, 'Secret US spying program targeted Venezuelan officials, flouting international law', *Associated Press,* 1 February 2024.
68 Raphael Perl, State Crime: 'The North Korean Drug Trade', in Mark Galeotti (ed.), *Global Crime Today: The Changing Face of Organised Crime* (London: Routledge, 2005), pp. 117–27.

69 Laura Bicker, 'Drugs, arms, and terror: A high-profile defector on Kim's North Korea', *BBC News*, 10 October 2021.
70 John Katsilometes, 'Sneak peek: Mob Museum set to open, with plenty of larger-than-life figures to greet you', *Las Vegas Sun*, 13 February 2012.
71 Iñigo Alexander, 'Brick by brick, Colombia demolishes the legend of Pablo Escobar', *Sunday Times*, 14 July 2023.
72 Juan Diego Quesada, 'Medellín demolishes Pablo Escobar's museum house, putting an end to the notorious legend', *El País* (English), 11 July 2023.

Bibliography

Archives

FBI Records: The Vault
George H. White Papers, Special Collections Department,
    Stanford University
Mary Ferrell Foundation
Richard Nixon Presidential Library and Museum
United States National Archive (USNA)

Newspapers and Periodicals

The Age
Arizona Republic
Atlanta Constitution
Baltimore Sun
The Birmingham News (Alabama)
Birmingham Post
Bristol Times and Mirror
Brooklyn Daily Eagle
The Bulletin (Pomona, CA)
California Eagle
Chicago Tribune

Cumhuriyet
Daily Herald (Biloxi, MS)
Daily Mail
Daily Mirror
Daily News (New York)
Daily Telegraph
Denver Post
Detroit Free Press
El País (English)
El Paso Times
Evening Standard
Foreign Affairs
Foreign Policy
Fresno Morning Republic
Gazete Duvar
The Gentleman's Magazine
Guardian
Herald (Melbourne, Victoria)
Hindu Times
Honolulu Advertiser
Honolulu Star-Bulletin
Hürriyet
Independent
Indian Express
India Today
Jane's Intelligence Review
La Jornada (Mexico)
Las Vegas Sun
Kansas City Kansas Globe
Kyiv Post
Los Angeles Times
The Times
Manchester Guardian

Bibliography

Marysville Appeal-Democrat
Miami Heald
Milliyet
The Missoulian
Le Monde
The Morning Call
National Post
New York Times
Newsday
Observer
Ottawa Journal
Pacific Commercial Advertiser
Le Petit Parisien
Philadelphia Inquirer
Pittsburg Press
La Prensa (Panama)
The Press Democrat (Santa Rosa, California)
Proceso
Le Radical de Marseille
The Record (Hackensack, New Jersey)
Reno Gazette-Journal
Reuters
San Francisco Chronicle
San Francisco Examiner
Santa Cruz Sentinel
Saturday Evening Post
South China Morning Post
South Florida Sentinel
Der Spiegel
Spokane Chronicle
St. Louis Globe-Democrat
St. Louis Post-Dispatch
St. Louis Star and Times

Sunday Telegraph
Sydney Morning Herald
Telegraph Online (India)
Le Temps
Time
Toronto Star
Traffic in Opium and Other Dangerous Drugs for the Year
Union Standard (New York)
Vakit
Vancouver Sun
Victoria Daily Times
Washington Post
Westdeutsche Landeszeitung

Books and Articles

Adanir, Fikret, 'Heiduckentum und osmanische Herrschaft. Sozialgeschichtliche Aspekte der Diskussion um das frühneuzeitliche Räuberwesen in Südosteuropa', *Südost Forschungen* 41 (1982).
Aldous, Christopher, *The Police in Occupation Japan: Control, Corruption and Resistance to Reform*, London: Routledge, 2014.
Albanese, Jay, *Transnational Crime and the 21st Century*, Oxford: Oxford University Press, 2011.
Anbinder, Tyler, *Five Points: The Nineteenth-Century New York City Neighbourhood*, New York: Free Press, 2012.
Anderson, J. L., 'Piracy and World History: An Economic Perspective on Maritime Predation', *Journal of World History*, 6.2 (1995).
Andreas, Peter and Ethan Nadelmann, *Policing the Globe: Criminalization and Crime Control in International Relations*, Oxford: Oxford University Press, 2006.

Bibliography

Anscombe, Fredrick (ed.), *The Ottoman Balkans 1750–1830*, Princeton: Markus Wiener Publishers, 2006.

Anslinger, Harry J. and Will Oursler, *The Murderers: The Story of the Narcotics Gang*, New York: Farrar, Straus and Cudahy, 1961.

Aranda, Salvador Maldonado, 'Drogas, violencia y militarización en el México rural: El caso de Michoacán', *Revista Mexicana de Sociología* 74.1 (January–March 2012).

Arias, Enrique Desmond, 'Latin American and Caribbean Drug Trafficking Groups' in Paul Gootenberg (ed.), *The Oxford Handbook of Global Drug History*, Oxford, Oxford University Press, 2022.

Armentrout-Ma, Eve, 'Urban Chinese at the Sinitic Frontier: Social Organizations in United States' Chinatowns, 1849–1898', *Modern Asian Studies*, 17.1 (1983).

Arsovska, Jana, *Decoding Albanian Organized Crime: Culture, Politics and Globalization*, Berkeley: University of California Press, 2015.

Asbury, Herbert, *The Barbary Coast: An Informal History of the San Francisco Underworld*, New York: Basic Books, 2002.

—— *The French Quarter: An Informal History of the New Orleans Underworld*, New York: Alfred A. Knopf, 2003.

—— *Gangs of New York*, New York: Thunder's Mouth Press, 2001.

Astorga, Luis, *Drogas Sin Fronteras*, Mexico City: Grijalbo, 2003.

—— 'Los Corridos de Traficantes de Drogas En México y Colombia', *Revista Mexicana de Sociología*, 59.4 (1997).

—— 'Organized Crime and the Organization of Crime', in John Bailey and Roy Godson (eds.), *Organized Crime and Democratic Governability*, Pittsburgh: University of Pittsburgh Press, 2001.

Barczewski, Stephanie, *Myth and National Identity in Nineteenth-Century Britain: The Legends of King Arthur and Robin Hood*, Oxford: Oxford University Press, 2000.

Barganier, George Percy, 'Fanon's Children: The Black Panther Party and the Rise of the Crips and Bloods in Los Angeles', PhD Dissertation: University of California Los Angeles, 2011.

Barrett, Wayne, *Trump: The Deals and the Downfall*, New York: HarperCollins, 1992.

Basu, Laura, 'Remembering an Iron Outlaw: The Cultural Memory of Ned Kelly and the Development of Australian Identities', PhD Dissertation: Utrecht University, 2010.

Baum, Dan, *Smoke and Mirrors: The War on Drugs and the Politics of Failure*, Boston: Little, Brown, 1996.

Bayly, Christopher Alan, *Empire and Information: Intelligence Gathering and Social Communication in India, 1780–1870*, Cambridge: Cambridge University Press, 1996.

Behan, Tom. *The Camorra: Political Criminality in Italy*, London: Routledge, 1995.

—— *See Naples and Die: The Camorra and Organised Crime*, London: IB Tauris, 2002.

Benjamin, Thomas, *La Revolución: Mexico's Great Revolution as Memory, Myth, and History*, Austin: University of Texas Press, 2000.

Bernstein, Lee, *The Greatest Menace: Organized Crime and the Cold War*, Amhurst, MA: University of Massachusetts Press, 2002.

Bianco, Lucien, 'Secret Societies and Peasant Self-Defense, 1921–1933' in Jean Chesneaux (ed.), *Secret Societies in China in the Nineteenth and Twentieth Centuries*, Stanford: Stanford University Press, 1972.

Billingsley, Phil, 'Bandits, Bosses, and Bare Sticks: Beneath the Surface of Local Control in Early Republican China', *Modern China* 7.3 (1981).

Blancornelas, Jesus, *El Cártel: Los Arellano Félix: la mafia más poderosa de la historia de América Latina*, Mexico City: Debolsillo, 2004.

Block, Alan, *East Side West Side: Organizing Crime in New York: 1930–1950*, New Brunswick, NJ: Transaction Publishers, 1999.

—— 'European Drug Traffic and Traffickers between the Wars: The Policy of Suppression and its Consequences', *Journal of Social History* 23.2 (Winter 1989).

Blok, Anton, *The Mafia of a Sicilian Village, 1860–1960: A Study of Violent Peasant Entrepreneurs*, Prospect Heights, IL: Waveland Press, 1988.

—— 'The Peasant and the Brigand: Social Banditry Reconsidered', *Comparative Studies in Society and History*, vol. 14, no. 4, (1972).

—— 'Rams and Billy-Goats: A Key to the Mediterranean Code of Honor', *Man* (1981).

Booth, Martin, *Opium: A History*, New York: St. Martin's Press, 1999.

Bonanno, Joseph with Sergio Lalli, *Man of Honor: The Autobiography of Joseph Bonanno*, New York: Simon & Schuster, 1983.

Bowden, Charles, *Down by the River: Drugs, Money, Murder and Family*, New York: Simon & Schuster, 2002.

Bovenkerk, Frank and Yücel Yeşilgöz, *The Turkish Mafia: A History of the Heroin Godfathers*, Preston, United Kingdom: Milo Books Ltd., 2007.

Bracewell, Catherine Wendy, *The Uskoks of Senj: Piracy, Banditry, and Holy War in the Sixteenth-Century Adriatic*, Ithaca, NY: Cornell University Press, 2015.

Brechin, Gray, *Imperial San Francisco: Urban Power, Earthly Ruin*, Berkeley, CA: University of California Press, 2006.

Breivold, Scott (ed.), *Howard Hawks: Interviews*, Jackson: University of Mississippi Press, 2006.

Bresler, Fenton, *The Chinese Mafia*, New York: Stein and Day, 1981.

Breslin, Jimmy, 'The End of the Mob' in *The Playboy Book of True Crime*, Vermont, CA: Playboy Press, 2007.

—— *The Good Rat: A True Story*, New York: Ecco, 2008.

Cédilot, André and André Noël, *Mafia Inc.: The Long, Bloody Reign of Canada's Sicilian Clan*, Toronto: Vintage Books Canada, 2012.

Cengiz, Mahmut and Camilo Pardo-Herrera, 'Hezbollah's Global Networks and Latin American Cocaine', *Small Wars Journal*, April 25, 2023.

Cheng Hirata, Lucie, 'Free, Indentured, Enslaved: Chinese Prostitutes in Nineteenth-Century America', *Signs: Journal of Women in Culture and Society* 5.1 (1979).

Chesneaux, Jean, 'Secret Societies in China's Historical Evolution', in Jean Chesneaux (ed.), *Secret Societies in China in the Nineteenth and Twentieth Centuries*, Stanford: Stanford University Press, 1972.

Chu, Yiu Kong, 'Hong Kong triads after 1997', *Trends in Organised Crime* 8.3 (2005).

Clarke, Colin, 'Politics, Violence and Drugs in Kingston, Jamaica', *Bulletin of Latin American Research*, 25.3 (2006).

Clawson, Patrick and Rensselaer Lee, *The Andean Cocaine Industry*, New York: Palgrave Macmillan, 1996.

Cockburn, Alexander and Jeffrey St. Clair, *Whiteout: the CIA, Drugs, and the Press*, New York: Verso, 1998.

Cohen, Lenard, 'Political Violence and Organized Crime in Serbia', in William Crotty (ed.), *Democratic Development and Political Terrorism: The Global Perspective*, Boston: Northeastern University Press, 2005.

Bibliography

Cole, Simon, *Suspect Identities: A History of Fingerprinting and Criminal Identification*, Cambridge, MA: Harvard University Press, 2009.

Conner, Susan, 'The Paradoxes and Contradictions of Prostitution in Paris', in Magaly Rodriquez Garcia, et al. (eds.), *Sex in the City: A Global History of Prostitution, 1600s–2000s*, Leiden: Brill, 2017.

Cowie, Peter, *Revolution!: The Explosion of World Cinema in the 60s*, London: Faber and Faber, 2004.

Creechan, James and Jorge de la Herran Garcia, 'Without God or Law: Narcoculture and Belief in Jesus Malverde', *Religious Studies and Theology* 24.2 (2005).

Critchley, David, *The Origin of Organized Crime in America: The New York City Mafia, 1891–1931*, New York: Routledge, 2009.

Cronin, Stephanie, 'Noble Robbers, Avengers and Entrepreneurs: Eric Hobsbawm and Banditry in Iran, the Middle East and North Africa', *Middle Eastern Studies*, 52:5 (2016).

Czitrom, Daniel, 'Underworlds and Underdogs: Big Tim Sullivan and Metropolitan Politics in New York, 1889–1913', *The Journal of American History*, 78.2 (September 1991).

D'Agostino, Peter, 'Craniums, Criminals, and the 'Cursed Race': Italian Anthropology in American Racial Thought, 1861–1924', *Comparative Studies in Society and History*, 44.2 (2002).

Davenport-Hines, Richard, *The Pursuit of Oblivion: A Global History of Narcotics*, New York: W. W. Norton Company, 2004.

Davis, Mike, *City of Quartz: Excavating the Future of Los Angeles*, London: Verso, 2006.

Demaris, Ovid, *The Last Mafioso*, Bronx, NY: Ishi Press International, 2010.

De Quincey, Thomas, *Confessions of an English Opium Eater*, New York: John B. Alden, 1885.
Dickie, John, *Blood Brotherhoods: A History of Italy's Three Mafias*, New York: Public Affairs, 2014.
—— *Cosa Nostra: A History of the Sicilian Mafia*, London: Hodder and Stoughton, 2004.
—— *The Craft: How the Freemasons Made the Modern World*, New York: Public Affairs, 2020.
Dillon, Richard, *The Hatchet Men: The Story of the Tong Wars in San Francisco's Chinatown*. Sausalito, CA: Comstock, 1962.
Dixon, David, *From Prohibition to Regulation: Bookmaking, Anti-Gambling and the Law*, Oxford: Oxford University Press, 1991.
Dower, John, *Embracing Defeat: Japan in the Wake of World War II*, New York: W. W. Norton, 2000.
Durán-Martínez, Angélica, *The Politics of Drug Violence: Criminals, Cops and Politicians in Colombia and Mexico*, Oxford: Oxford University Press, 2017.
Ebbe, Obi N. I., 'The Political-Criminal Nexus: The Nigerian Case', *Trends in Organized Crime*, 4.3 (Spring 1999).
Egmond, Florike, 'Multiple Underworlds in the Dutch Republic of the Seventeenth and Eighteenth Centuries', in Cyrille Fijnaut and Letizia Paoli (eds.), *Organised Crime in Europe: Concepts, Patterns and Control Policies in the European Union and Beyond*, Dordrecht: Springer Netherlands, 2004.
Eisenberg, Dennis, *Meyer Lansky: Mogul of the Mob*, New York: Paddington Press, 1979.
Ellroy, James, *American Tabloid*. New York: Knopf Doubleday Publishing Group, 2011.
Emsley, Clive, *Gendarmes and the State in Nineteenth-Century Europe*, Oxford: Oxford University Press, 1999.

Bibliography

—— 'Introduction: Political Police and the European Nation-State in the Nineteenth Century', in Mark Mazower (ed.), *The Policing of Politics in the Twentieth Century*, Providence, RI: Berghan Books, 1997.

—— 'Policing the Empire/Policing the Metropole: Some Thoughts on Models and Types', *Crime, History and Societies* 18.2 (2014).

Epstein, Edward Jay, *Agency of Fear: Opiates and Political Power in America*, New York: G. P. Putnam's Sons, 1977.

Escobar Gaviria, Roberto, *The Accountant's Story: Inside the Violent World of the Medellín Cartel*, New York: Grand Central, 2009.

Ethington, Philip, *The Public City: The Political Construction of Urban Life in San Francisco, 1850–1900*, Cambridge: Cambridge University Press, 1994.

Evans, Robert, *The Kid Stays in the Picture*, New York: New Millennium Press, 2002.

Favarel-Garrigues, Gilles, *Policing Economic Crime in Russia: From Soviet Planned Economy to Privatisation*, London: Hurst, 2011.

Fentress, James, *Rebels and Mafiosi: Death in a Sicilian Landscape*, Ithaca, NY: Cornell University Press, 2000.

Finnane, Mark, 'The Origins of "Modern" Policing', in Paul Knepper and Anja Johansen (eds), *The Oxford Handbook of the History of Crime and Criminal Justice*, Oxford: Oxford University Press, 2016.

Fiocconi, Laurent and Jérôme Pierrat, *Le Colombien: Des parrains corses aux cartels de la coke*, Paris: Toucan Noir, 2009.

Fisk, Robert, *Pity the Nation: Lebanon at War*, Oxford: Oxford University Press, 1991.

Fleming, Katherine Elizabeth, *The Muslim Bonaparte: Diplomacy and Orientalism in Ali Pasha's Greece*, Princeton: Princeton University Press, 1999.

Folsom, Tom, *The Made Ones: Crazy Joe Gallo and the Revolution at the Edge of the Underworld*, New York: Weinstein Books, 2008.

Forbes, Frederick Edwyn, *Five Years in China: From 1842 to 1847*, London: R. Bentley, 1848.

Foster, Anne L., 'Prohibiting Opium in the Philippines and the United States: The Creation of an Interventionist State', in Alfred W. McCoy and Francisco A. Scarano (eds.), *Colonial Crucible: Empire in the Making of the Modern American State*, Madison: University of Wisconsin Press, 2009.

Frazer, Chris, *Bandit Nation: A History of Outlaws and Cultural Struggle in Mexico, 1810–1920*, Lincoln, University of Nebraska Press, 2006.

Friman, H. Richard, 'The Impact of the Occupation on Crime in Japan', in Mark Caprio and Yoneyuki Sugita, (eds.), *Democracy in Occupied Japan: The US Occupation and Japanese Politics and Society*, London: Routledge, 2007.

Fulvetti, Gianluca, 'The Mafia and the "Problem of the Mafia"': Organised Crime in Italy, 1820–1970', in Cyrille Fijnaut and Letizia Paoli (eds.), *Organised Crime in Europe*, Dordrecht, The Netherlands: Springer, 2004.

Galante, Pierre and Louis Sapin, *The Marseilles Mafia: The Truth Behind the World of Drug Trafficking*, London: W. H. Allen, 1979.

Galeotti, Mark, '"Brotherhoods" and "Associates": Chechen Networks of Crime and Resistance', in Robert Bunker (ed.), *Networks, Terrorism and Global Insurgency*, London: Routledge, 2014.

—— *The Vory: Russia's Super Mafia*, New Haven: Yale University Press, 2018.

—— 'The world of the lower depths: crime and punishment in Russian history', in Mark Galeotti (ed.), *Organised Crime in History*, London: Routledge, 2009.

Galeotti, Mark and Clive H. Schofield, *Cross-Border Crime in the Former Soviet Union*, Durham: International Boundaries Research Unit, University of Durham, 1995.

Gambetta, Diego, *The Sicilian Mafia: The Business of Private Protection*, Cambridge, MA: Harvard University Press, 1996.

Gaskill, Malcolm, 'The Displacement of Providence: Policing and Prosecution in Seventeenth- and Eighteenth-Century England', *Continuity and Change*, 11.3 (1996).

Gellner, Ernest, *Plough, Sword, and Book: The Structure of Human History*, Chicago: University of Chicago Press, 1989.

Gilinskiy, Yakov and Yakov Kostjukovsky, 'From Thievish Artel to Criminal Corporation: The History of Organised Crime in Russia' in Cyrille Fijnaut and Letizia Paoli (eds.), *Organised Crime in Europe: Concepts, Patterns and Control Policies in the European Union and Beyond*, Dordrecht: Springer Netherlands, 2004.

Glenny, Misha, *McMafia: A Journey through the Global Underworld*, New York: Knopf, 2008.

Goddard, Donald, *Easy Money*, London: Panther, 1980.

Goodman, Derick, *Villainy Unlimited: The Truth About the French Underworld Today*, London: Elek Books, 1957.

Gootenberg, Paul, *Andean Cocaine: The Making of a Global Drug*, Durham, NC: University of North Carolina, 2006.

Grillo, Ioan, *El Narco: Inside Mexico's Criminal Insurgency*, New York: Bloomsbury Press, 2011.

Grünewald, Thomas, *Bandits in the Roman Empire: Myth and Reality*, London: Routledge, 1999.

Gugliotta, Guy, *Kings of Cocaine: Inside the Medellín Cartel*, New York: Simon & Schuster, 1989.

Haley, James, *Captive Paradise: A History of Hawaii*, New York: St. Martin's Press, 2014.

Haller, Mark, *Illegal Enterprise: The Work of Historian Mark Haller*, Lanham, MD: University Press of America, 2013.

Hammad, Hanan and Francesca Biancani, 'Prostitution in Cairo' in Magaly Rodriquez Garcia, et al. (eds.), *Selling Sex in the City: A Global History of Prostitution, 1600s-2000s*, Leiden: Brill, 2017.

Handelman, Stephen, *Comrade Criminal: Russia's New Mafiya*, New Haven: Yale University Press, 1995.

Hanson, Neil, *Monk Eastman: The Gangster Who Became a War Hero*, New York: Knopf Doubleday, 2010.

Hanssen, Jens, *Fin de Siècle Beirut: The Making of an Ottoman Provincial Capital*, Oxford: Oxford University Press, 2005.

Hernández, Anabel, *Narcoland: The Mexican Drug Lords and Their Godfathers*, London: Verso, 2013.

Hernandez, Carlos, 'Narcomundo: How Narcotraficantes Gained Control of Northern Mexico and Beyond, 1945–1985', PhD Dissertation: University of California Los Angeles, 2015.

Hess, Henner, *Mafia and Mafiosi: The Structure of Power*, Lexington, MA: Lexington Books, 1977.

Hewitt, Nicholas, *Wicked City: The Many Cultures of Marseille*, London: Hurst, 2019.

Hill, Peter, *The Japanese Mafia: Yakuza, Law and the State*, Oxford: Oxford University Press, 2010.

Hobbs, Dick, *Doing the Business: Entrepreneurship, Detectives and the Working Class in the East End of London*, Oxford: Clarendon Press, 1988.

Hobhouse, John Cam, *Travels in Albania and Other Provinces of Turkey in 1809 & 1810*, London: John Murray, 1855.

Hobsbawm, Eric, *Bandits*, London: Abacus, 2007.

—— *Primitive Rebels: Studies in Archaic Forms of Social Movements in the 19th and 20th Centuries*, New York: W. W. Norton, 1959.

Holt, James Clarke, 'The Origins and Audience of the Ballads of Robin Hood', *Past & Present* 18 (1960).
—— *Robin Hood*, London: Thames and Hudson, 1982.
Hsuan-Chih, Tai and Ronald Suleski, 'Origin of the Heaven and Earth Society', *Modern Asian Studies* 11.3 (1977).
Ito, Takatoshi and Takeo Hoshi, *The Japanese Economy*, Cambridge, MA: MIT Press, 2020.
Iwai, Hiroaki, 'Organized Crime in Japan', in Robert Kelly (ed.), *Organized Crime: A Global Perspective*, Totawa, NJ: Rowman & Littlefield, 1986.
Jacobs, James and Elizabeth Dondlinger Wyman, 'Organized Crime Control in the United States of America' in Letitizia Paoli (ed.), *The Oxford Handbook of Organized Crime*. Oxford: Oxford University Press, 2014.
Jankowski, Paul, *Communism and Collaboration: Simon Sabiani and Politics in Marseille, 1919–1944*, New Haven, CT: Yale University Press, 1989.
Jennings, John, *The Opium Empire: Japanese Imperialism and Drug Trafficking in Asia, 1895–1945*, Westport, CT: Praeger, 1997.
Johnson, Michael, 'Popular movements and primordial loyalties in Beirut', *The Middle East* (1983).
Jonnes, Jill, *Hep-cats, Narcs and Pipe Dreams: A History of America's Romance with Illegal Drugs*, Baltimore, MD: Johns Hopkins University Press, 1999.
Jütte, Robert, *Poverty and Deviance in Early Modern Europe*, Cambridge University Press, 1994.
Kaplan, David and Alec Dubro, *Yakuza: Japan's Criminal Underworld*, Berkeley, CA: University of California Press, 2003.
Keddie, Patrick, *The Passion: Football and the Story of Modern Turkey*, London: IB Tauris, 2018.

Kefauver, Estes, *The Kefauver Committee Report on Organized Crime*, New York: Didier, 1951.

Kent, Joan, 'The English Village Constable, 1580–1642: The Nature and Dilemmas of the Office', *Journal of British Studies*, 20.2 (1981).

Kingsberg, Miriam, *Moral Nation: Modern Japan and Narcotics in Global History*, Berkeley, CA: University of California Press, 2014.

Kirişci, Kemal, 'Turkey: A Country of Transition from Emigration to Immigration', *Mediterranean Politics*, 12:1 (2007), 91–7.

Kitson, Simon, *Police and Politics in Marseille, 1936–1945*, Leiden: Brill, 2014.

Klebnikov, Paul, *Godfather of the Kremlin: Boris Berezovsky and the Looting of Russia*, New York: Harcourt, 2000.

Kotkin, Stephen, *Armageddon Averted: The Soviet Collapse 1970–2000*, Oxford: Oxford University Press, 2008.

Knoedelseder, William, *Stiffed: A True Story of MCA, the Music and the Mafia*, New York: Harper Collins, 1994.

Kray, Reg and Ron Kray with Fred Dineage, *Our Story*, London: Pan Books, 1989.

Lacey, Robert, *Little Man: Meyer Lansky and the Gangster Life*, Boston: Little, Brown and Company, 1991.

Lait, Jack and Lee Mortimer, *Chicago Confidential*, New York: Dell Publishing House, 1950.

Laite, Julia, 'Traffickers and Pimps in the Era of White Slavery', *Past and Present*, 237 (November 2017).

Lange, Katrin, '"Many a Lord is Guilty, Indeed for Many a Poor Man's Dishonest Deed": Gangs of Robbers in Early Modern Germany' in Cyrille Fijnaut and Letizia Paoli (eds.), *Organised Crime in Europe: Concepts, Patterns and Control Policies in the European Union and Beyond*, Dordrecht: Springer Netherlands, 2004.

Lee, Erika, *The Making of Asian America: A History*, New York: Simon & Schuster, 2015.

Lewis, Charlton M., 'Some Notes on the Ko-lao in Late Ch'ing China', in Jean Chesneaux (ed.), *Secret Societies in China in the Nineteenth and Twentieth Centuries*, Stanford: Stanford University Press, 1972.

Lintner, Bertil, 'Chinese Organised Crime' in Mark Galeotti (ed.), *Global Crime Today: The Changing Face of Organised Crime*, London: Routledge, 2005.

—— 'The Shans and the Shan State of Burma', *Contemporary Southeast Asia*, 5.4 (1984).

Lombardo, Robert, *The Black Hand: Terror by Letter in Chicago*, Champaign, IL, University of Illinois Press, 2010.

Lupo, Salvatore, 'The Allies and the Mafia', *Journal of Modern Italian Studies* 2.1 (1997).

—— *History of the Mafia*, New York: Columbia University Press, 2009.

Lupsha, Peter, 'Transnational Crime versus Nation-State', *Transnational Organized Crime*, 2. 1 (Spring 1996).

—— 'Towards an Etiology of Drug Trafficking and Insurgent Relations: The Phenomenon of Narco-Terrorism', *International Journal of Comparative and Applied Criminal Justice* 13:2 (1989).

Maas, Peter, *The Valachi Papers*, New York: G. P. Putnam's Sons, 1968.

—— *Underboss: Sammy the Bull Gravano's Story of Life in the Mafia*, New York: HarperCollins, 1997.

Macauley, Melissa, 'Entangled States: The Translocal Repercussions of Rural Pacification in China, 1869–1873', *The American Historical Review* 121.3 (June 2016).

Malcolm, Noel, *Rebels, Believers, Survivors: Studies in the History of the Albanians*, Oxford: Oxford University Press, 2020.

Mandić, Danilo, *Gangsters and Other Statesmen: Mafias, Separatists, and Torn States in a Globalized World*, Princeton: Princeton University Press, 2021.

Mansfield, Stephen, *Tokyo: A Biography*, Tokyo: Tuttle Publishing, 2016.

Marrus, Michael, *Mr. Sam: The Life and Times of Samuel Bronfman*, New York: Viking Press, 1991.

Marshall, Jonathan, *Dark Quadrant: Organized Crime, Big Business, and the Corruption of American Democracy*, Lanham, MD: Rowman and Littlefield, 2021.

—— *Drug Wars: Corruption, Counterinsurgency and Covert Operations in the Third World*, Forestville, CA: Cohan & Cohan Publishers, 1991.

—— *The Lebanese Connection: Corruption, Civil War and the International Narcotics Traffic*, Palo Alto, CA: Stanford University Press, 2012.

Marchant, Alexandre, 'The French Connection as an Illicit Trade Network' in Paul Gootenberg (ed.), *The Oxford Handbook of Global Drug History*, Oxford, Oxford University Press, 2022.

Martin, Brian, *The Shanghai Green Gang: Politics and Organised Crime, 1919–1937*, Berkeley, CA: University of California Press, 1996.

Martínez, Oscar J., *Ciudad Juárez: Saga of a Legendary Border City*, Tucson: University of Arizona Press, 2018.

Maruko Siniawer, Eiko, 'Befitting Bedfellows: Yakuza and the State in Modern Japan', *Journal of Social History*, 45.3 (2012).

—— *Ruffians, Yakuza, Nationalists: The Violent Politics of Modern Japan, 1860–1960*, Ithaca, NY: Cornell University Press, 2008.

Mattson, Kevin, 'What the Heck Are You Up To, Mr. President?: Jimmy Carter, America's "Malaise", and the

Speech That Should Have Changed the Country'*, New York: Bloomsbury, 2009.

McBride, Joseph, *Hawks on Hawks*, Berkeley: University of California Press, 1982.

McCaa, Robert, 'Missing Millions: The Demographic Costs of the Mexican Revolution', *Mexican Studies/Estudios Mexicanos*, 19.2 (2003).

McClintock, James H., *Arizona, Prehistoric, Aboriginal, Pioneer, Modern: The Nation's Youngest Commonwealth Within a Land of Ancient Culture*, Chicago: S. J. Clarke Publishing Company, 1916.

McCoy, Alfred, *The Politics of Heroin in Southeast Asia*, New York: Harper & Row, 1972.

McGirr, Lisa, *The War on Alcohol: Prohibition and the Rise of the American State*, New York: W. W. Norton, 2015.

McMullan, John L., 'Criminal Organization in Sixteenth and Seventeenth Century London', *Social Problems* 29.3 (1982).

McShane, Larry, *Chin: The Life and Crimes of Mafia Boss Vincent Gigante*, New York: Pinnacle Books, 2016.

McWilliams, John, *The Protectors: Harry J. Anslinger and the Federal Bureau of Narcotics, 1930–1962*, Newark: University of Delaware Press, 1990.

McWilliams, John and Alan Block, 'All the Commissioner's Men: The Federal Bureau of Narcotics and the Dewey–Luciano Affair, 1947–54', *Intelligence and National Security*. 5.1 (1990).

Mermelstein, Max, *The Man Who Made It Snow*, New York: Simon & Schuster, 1990.

Merrill, Dennis, *Negotiating Paradise: U.S. Tourism and Empire in Twentieth-Century Latin America*, Durham: University of North Carolina Press, 2009.

Meyer, Kathryn and Terry Parssinen, *Web of Smoke: Smugglers, Warlords, Spies and the History of the*

International Drug Trade, Lanham, MD: Rowman and Littlefield Publishers, 1998.

Mihalopoulos, Bill, *Sex in Japan's Globalization, 1870–1930: Prostitutes, Emigration and Nation-Building*, London: Routledge, 2016.

Moore, William, *The Kefauver Committee and the Politics of Crime, 1950–1952*, Columbia, MO: University of Missouri Press, 1974.

Morgan, Kenneth, *Australia: A Very Short Introduction*, Oxford: Oxford University Press, 2012.

Morgan, William P., *Triad Societies in Hong Kong*, Hong Kong: Government Press, 1960.

Mortimer, Lee, *Around the World Confidential*, New York: G. P. Putnam's Sons, 1956.

Moscow, Alvin, *Merchants of Heroin: An In-Depth Portrayal of Business in the Underworld*, New York: Dial Press, 1968.

Murray Jones, Peter, *The Peasantry in the French Revolution*, Cambridge: Cambridge University Press, 1988.

Nesvig, Martin, 'Forbidden Drugs in Colonial America', in Paul Gootenberg (ed.), *The Oxford Handbook of Global Drug History*, Oxford, Oxford University Press, 2022.

Newark, Tim, *Lucky Luciano: The Real and the Fake Gangster*, New York: St. Martin's Press, 2010.

Newsday, *The Heroin Trail*, New York: New American Library, 1973.

Nicholls, James, *The Politics of Alcohol: A History of the Drink Question in England*, Manchester: Manchester University Press, 2009.

Nuzzi, Gianluigi, *Blood Ties: The 'Ndrangheta: Italy's New Mafia*, London: Pan Books, 2012.

O'Callaghan, Sean, *Damaged Baggage: The White Slave Trade and Narcotics Trafficking in the Americas*, New York: Roy Publishers, 1970.

The Opium Trade, 1910–1941: Vol. 5, 1927–1941, Wilmington, DE: Scholarly Resources, Inc., 1974.

Oxenboell, Morten, *Akutō and Rural Conflict in Medieval Japan*, Honolulu: University of Hawai`i Press, 2018.

Öztan, Ramazan Hakkı, 'Tools of Revolution: Global Military Surplus, Arms Dealers and Smugglers in the Late Ottoman Balkans, 1878–1908', *Past & Present*, 237 (November 2017).

Paoli, Letizia, 'The Italian Mafia' in Letizia Paoli (ed.), *The Oxford Handbook of Organized Crime*, Oxford: Oxford University Press, 2014.

—— *Mafia Brotherhoods: Organized Crime, Italian Style*, Oxford: Oxford University Press, 2003.

Paoleschi, Marie, *Le Milieu et Moi*, Paris: Fanval, 1987.

Pasley, Fred D., *Al Capone: A Biography of a Self-Made Man*, Garden City, NY: Garden City Publishing Company, 1930.

Pembleton, Matthew R., *Containing Addiction: The Federal Bureau of Narcotics and the Origins of America's Global Drug War*, Amherst: University of Massachusetts Press, 2017.

Perl, Raphael, 'State Crime: The North Korean Drug Trade' in Mark Galeotti (ed.), *Global Crime Today: The Changing Face of Organised Crime*, London: Routledge, 2005.

Philips, Gene D. and Rodney Hill (eds.), *Francis Ford Coppola: Interviews*, Jackson, MS: University Press of Mississippi, 2004.

Phillips, Rod, *Alcohol: A History*, Chapel Hill, NC: University of North Carolina Press, 2014.

Piccato, Pablo, *City of Suspects: Crime in Mexico City, 1900–1931*, Durham: Duke University Press, 2001.

Pierrat, Jérôme, *Une Histoire du Milieu: Grand banditisme et haute pègre en France, de 1850 à nos jours*, Paris: Denoël, 2003.

Pietrusza, David, *Rothstein: The Life, Times, and Murder of the Criminal Genius Who Fixed the 1919 World Series*, New York: Basic Books, 2010.

Porter, Edgar, *Japanese Reflections on World War II and the American Occupation*, Amsterdam: Amsterdam University Press, 2007.

Portnov, Andrii, *Dnipro: An Entangled History of a European City*, Boston: Academic Studies Press, 2022.

Prigge, Steven, *Movie Moguls Speak: Interviews with Top Film Producers*, Jefferson, NC: McFarland and Company, 2004.

Raab, Selwyn, *Five Families: The Rise, Decline and Resurgence of America's Most Powerful Mafia Empires*, New York: St. Martins Griffin, 2006.

Ramirez Pimienta, Juan Carlos, '"El Pablote": una nueva mirada al primer corrido dedicado a un traficante de drogas', *Mitologías Hoy* 14 (2016).

Rappleye, Charles and Ed Becker, *All-American Mafioso: The Johnny Rosselli Story*, New York: Doubleday, 1991.

Reece, Jack, 'Fascism, the Mafia, and the Emergence of Sicilian Separatism (1919–43)', *The Journal of Modern History*, 45.2 (1973).

Remnick, David, *Lenin's Tomb: The Last Days of the Soviet Empire*, New York: Random House, 1993.

Restall, Matthew, *Seven Myths of the Spanish Conquest*, Oxford: Oxford University Press, 2003.

Reuter, Timothy, 'Plunder and Tribute in the Carolingian Empire', *Transactions of the Royal Historical Society*, 35 (1985).

Ringdal, Nils Johan, *Love for Sale: A World History of Prostitution*, New York: Grove Press, 2007.

Risso, Patricia, 'Cross-Cultural Perceptions of Piracy: Maritime Violence in the Western Indian Ocean and Persian Gulf Region during a Long Eighteenth Century', *Journal of World History*, 12.2 (2001).

Bibliography

Roberts, Jon and Evan Wright, *American Desperado: My Life – From Mafia Soldier to Cocaine Cowboy to Secret Government Asset*, New York: Crown, 2011.

Robinson, David M., 'Banditry and the Subversion of State Authority in China: The Capital Region during the Middle Ming Period (1450–1525)', *Journal of Social History*, 33.3 (2000).

Roldán, Mary, *Blood and Fire: La Violencia in Antioquia, Colombia, 1946–1953*, Durham, NC: Duke University Press, 2002.

Rose, Caroline and Alexander Söderholm, 'The Captagon Threat: A Profile of Illicit Trade, Consumption and Regional Realities', *New Lines Institute for Strategy and Policy*, April 2022

Rosen, Jonathan and Roberto Zepeda, *Organized Crime, Drug Trafficking, and Violence in Mexico: The Transition from Felipe Calderón to Enrique Peña Nieto*, London: Lexington Books, 2016.

Rubin, Barry, *Revolution Until Victory?: The Politics and History of the PLO*, Cambridge, MA: Harvard University Press, 1994.

Ruff, Julius, *Violence in Early Modern Europe*, Cambridge: Cambridge University Press, 2001.

Russell Pasha, Thomas, *The Egyptian Service 1902–1946*, London: John Murray, 1949.

Rumpelt, Alexander, *Sicilien Und Die Sicilianer*, Berlin: Allgemeiner Verein für Deutsche Literatur, 1902.

Russo, Gus, *The Outfit: The Role of Chicago's Underworld in the Shaping of Modern America*, New York: Bloomsbury, 2001.

Ruvoli, Joanne, '"Most Thrilling Subjects": D.W. Griffith and the Biograph Revenge Films', in Dana Renga (ed.), *Mafia Movies: A Reader*, Toronto: University of Toronto Press, 2011.

Saga, Junichi, *Confessions of a Yakuza*, Tokyo: Kodansha International, 1991.
Salazar, Alonso, *Pablo Escobar, El Patrón del Mal*, Doral, FL: Aguilar, 2012.
Salvetti, Patrizia, *Rope and Soap: Lynchings of Italians in the United States*, New York: Bordighera Press, 2017.
Sanders, Holly, '*Panpan*: Streetwalking in Occupied Japan', *Pacific Historical Review* 81.3, (2012).
Saviano, Roberto, *Gomorrah*, New York: Farrar, Straus and Giroux, 2007.
Shawcross, Tim, *Men of Honor: The Confessions of Tommaso Buscetta*, London: Collins, 1987.
Schatzburg, Rufus and Robert Kelly, *African American Organized Crime: A Social History*, New Brunswick, NJ: Rutgers University Press, 1996.
Schneider, Eric, *Smack: Heroin and the American City*, Philadelphia: University of Pennsylvania Press, 2008.
—— *Vampires, Dragons and Egyptian Kings: Youth Gangs in Post-war New York*, Princeton: Princeton University Press, 1999.
Schneider, Jane and Peter Schneider, 'Civil Society and Transnational Organized Crime: The Case of the Italian Antimafia Movement', in Felia Allum and Stan Gilmour (eds), *Routledge Handbook of Transnational Organized Crime*, London: Routledge, 2014.
—— *Reversible Destiny: Mafia, Antimafia and the Struggle for Palermo*, Berkeley: University of California Press, 2003.
Schoenberg, Robert, *Mr. Capone*, London: Robson Books, 1995.
Schwartz, David, *Roll the Bones: The History of Gambling*, New York: Gotham Books, 2006.
Schwartz, Rosalie, *Pleasure Island: Tourism and Temptation in Cuba*, Lincoln: University of Nebraska Press, 1997.

Seal, Mark, *Leave the Gun, Take the Cannoli: The Epic Story of the Making of The Godfather*, New York: Gallery Books, 2021.

Seligman, Scott, *Tong Wars: The Untold Story of Vice, Money, and Murder in New York's Chinatown*, New York: Viking, 2016.

Shpayer-Makov, Haia, 'Detectives and Forensic Science: The Professionalization of Police Detection' in Paul Knepper and Anja Johansen (eds.), *The Oxford Handbook of the History of Crime and Criminal Justice*, Oxford: Oxford University Press, 2016.

Neil Larry Shumsky, and Larry M. Springer, 'San Francisco's Zone of Prostitution, 1880-1934', *Journal of Historical Geography* 7.1 (1981).

Silet, Charles (ed.), *Oliver Stone: Interviews*, Jackson: University of Mississippi Press, 2001.

Simpson, George, 'Frontier Banditry and the Colonial Decision-Making Process: The East Africa Protectorate's Northern Borderland Prior to the First World War', *The International Journal of African Historical Studies*, 29.2 (1996).

Smith, Benjamin, *The Dope: The Real History of the Mexican Drug Trade*, New York: W. W. Norton and Co, 2021.

Smith, Chris, *Syndicate Women: Gender and Networks in Chicago Organized Crime*, Berkeley: University of California Press, 2019.

Spraggs, Gillian, *Outlaws and Highwaymen: The Cult of the Robber in England from the Middle Ages to the Nineteenth Century*, London: Pimlico, 2001.

State of New York, *Report of the New York State Joint Legislative Committee on Crime, Its Causes, Control & Effect on Society* (1970).

Stevens (ed.), George, *Conversations at the American Film*

Institute with the Great Moviemakers: The Next Generation*, New York: Knopf, 2012.
Stiles, T. J., *Jesse James: Last Rebel of the Civil War*, New York: Knopf Doubleday, 2010.
Stille, Alexander, *Excellent Cadavers: The Mafia and the Death of the First Italian Republic*, New York: Vintage, 1996.
Streatfield, Dominic, *Cocaine: A Definitive History*, London: Virgin Books, 2002.
Tambe, Ashwini, *Codes of Misconduct: Regulating Prostitution in Late Colonial Bombay*, Minneapolis: University of Minnesota Press, 2009.
Thomas, Donald, *The Victorian Underworld*, New York: New York University Press, 1998.
Thoumi, Francisco, 'Colombian Organized Crime: From Drug Trafficking to Parastatal Bands and Widespread Corruption', in Dina Siegel and Henk van de Bunt (eds), *Traditional Organized Crime in the Modern World: Responses to Socioeconomic Change*, New York: Springer, 2012.
—— *Political Economy and Illegal Drugs in Colombia*, Boulder, CO: Lynne Rienner, 1995.
Tilly, Charles, 'War Making and State Making as Organized Crime', in Peter Evans, et al. (eds), *Bringing the State Back In*, Cambridge: Cambridge University Press, 1985.
Tong, James, 'Collective Violence in a Pre-Modern Society: Rebellions and Banditry in the Ming dynasty', PhD Dissertation: University of Michigan, 1985.
Tuğ, Başak, *Politics of Honor in Ottoman Anatolia: Sexual Violence and Socio-Legal Surveillance in the Eighteenth Century*, Leiden: Brill, 2017.
United States Senate, *Alleged Assassination Plots Involving Foreign Leaders*, Washington DC: US Government Printing Office, 1975.

Bibliography

—— *Federal Drug Enforcement: Hearings Before the Permanent Subcommittee on Investigations of the Committee on Government Operations*, Washington: US Government Printing Office, 1975.
—— Hearings before the Committee of the Judiciary, *Organized Crime in America*, Washington, DC: US Government Printing Office, 1984.
US House of Representatives, *Final Report of the Select Committee on Assassinations of the US House of Representatives*, Washington DC: US Government Printing Office, 1979.
—— *Treasury Department Appropriation Bill for 1944*, Washington: US Government Printing Office, 1942.
—— Committee on International Relations, *The Challenge of Terrorism in Asia and the Pacific*, Washington, DC: US Government Printing Office, 2003.
US Senate Permanent Subcommittee on Investigations, *Organised Crime and Illicit Traffic in Narcotics*, Washington DC: US Government Printing Office, 1964.
Valdés Castellanos, Guillermo, *Historia del narcotráfico en México*, Mexico City: Aguilar, 2013.
Valdez, Al, 'The Origins of Southern California Latino Gangs', in Thomas Bruneau, et al. (eds), *Maras: Gang Violence and Security in Central America*, Austin, TX: University of Texas Press, 2011.
Valentine, Douglas, *Strength of the Pack: The Personalities, Politics and Espionage Intrigues that Shaped the DEA*, Waterville, OR: Trine Day, 2009.
—— *The Strength of the Wolf*, London: Verso, 2004.
Van Onselen, Charles, *The Fox and the Flies*, New York: Walker & Company, 2007.
van Wees, Hans, 'The Mafia of Early Greece: Violent Exploitation in the Seventh and Sixth Centuries BC', in

Keith Hopwood (ed.), *Organised Crime in Antiquity*, London: Duckworth, 1999.
Varese, Federico, *The Russian Mafia: Private Protection in a New Market Economy*, Oxford: Oxford University Press, 2001.
—— *Mafia Life: Love, Death, and Money at the Heart of Organised Crime*, Oxford: Oxford University Press, 2018.
—— *Mafias on the Move: How Organized Crime Conquers New Territories*, Princeton: Princeton University Press, 2011.
Vitaliev, Vitali, *Special Correspondent: Investigating in the Soviet Union*, London: Hutchinson, 1990.
Vladimirov, Katya, 'Red Buccaneers: Soviet Criminal Enterprises, 1950s', *Canadian-American Slavic Studies* 35.2–3 (2001).
Kim Wagner (ed.), *Stranglers and Bandits: A Historical Anthology of Thuggee*, Oxford: Oxford University Press, 2009.
Wakeman, Frederic, *Policing Shanghai, 1927–1937*. Berkeley, CA: University of California Press, 1995.
Walker III, William O., *Opium and Foreign Policy: The Anglo-American Search for Order in Asia, 1912–1954*, Chapel Hill: University of North Carolina Press, 1991.
Walston, James, 'See Naples and Die: Organized Crime in Campania', in Robert Kelly (ed.), *Organized Crime: A Global Perspective*, Totawa, NJ: Rowman & Littlefield, 1986.
Walkowitz, Judith R., *City of Dreadful Delight: Narratives of Sexual Danger in Late Victorian London*, Chicago: University of Chicago Press, 1992.
Warren, Earl, *Report of the President's Commission on the Assassination of President John F. Kennedy*, Washington, DC: US Government Printing Office, 1964.

Bibliography

Webb, Gary, *Dark Alliance: The CIA, the Contras and the Crack Cocaine Explosion*, New York: Seven Stories Press, 1998.

Wells, Roger, 'Popular Protest and Social Crime: The Evidence of Criminal Gangs in Rural Southern England, 1790–1860', *Southern History* 13 (1991).

Weng, Peng, *The Chinese Mafia: Organised Crime, Corruption and Extra-Legal Protection*, Oxford: Oxford University Press, 2017.

Werth, Nicholas, 'The "Chechen Problem": Handling an Awkward Legacy, 1918–1958', *Contemporary European History*, 15.3 (2006).

White, Richard, 'Outlaw Gangs of the Middle Border: American Social Bandits', *The Western Historical Quarterly* 12.4 (1981).

Whiting, Robert, *Tokyo Underworld*, New York: Vintage, 2000.

Wilson, Stephen, *Feuding, Conflict and Banditry in Nineteenth-Century Corsica*, Cambridge: Cambridge University Press, 2003.

Woodiwiss, Michael. *Organized Crime and American Power*, Toronto: University of Toronto Press, 2001.

Yalçın, Soner, *Behçet Cantürk'ün Anıları*, Istanbul: Doğan Kitap, 2007.

Yalçin, Soner and Doğan Yurdakul, *Bay Pipo*, Istanbul: Doğan Kitapçılık, 2003.

—— *Reis: Gladio'nun Türk Tetikçisi*, Istanbul: Doğan Kitapcılık, 2007.

Yalman, Ahmed Emin, *Turkey in the World War*, New Haven: Yale University Press, 1930.

Yongming, Zhou, 'Nationalism, Identity and the State-Building: The Antidrug Crusade in the People's Republic, 1949–1952' in Timothy Brook and Bob Tadashi Wakabayashi (eds), *Opium Regimes: China, Britain and Japan, 1839–1952*, Berkeley: University of California Press, 2000.

Zaidi, Hussain, *Dongri to Dubai: Six Decades of the Mumbai Mafia*, New Delhi: Lotus Collection, 2012.

Zheng, Yengwen, 'The Cultural Biography of Opium in China' in Paul Gootenberg (ed.), *The Oxford Handbook of Global Drug History*, Oxford, Oxford University Press, 2022.

Acknowledgements

Several people helped make this book possible. My thanks first go to Simon Sebag Montefiore for his kind willingness to introduce me to Georgina Capel and the wonderful people at Georgina Capel Associates Ltd. To my utter amazement, Georgina took a chance on me and proved an early believer in this book. It was through her that I had the honour and privilege of meeting Kris Doyle. The faith Kris readily placed in this project was a genuine gift for which I will forever be grateful. His team, including Oli Hunt, Florence Garnett and Kerri Sharp, helped to shape this text into something that reads beautifully. I am equally indebted to Ben Loehnen for his invaluable edits and his support to bring this book to the US market. I am so, so honoured and proud to be a part of the Simon & Schuster family.

Of course I cannot close without thanking my family. As in every part of my life and work, my wife Mariana and my children Amaya and Sebastian provide me with the love, care and support that make me whole. I thank my parents, Tom and Dedee, for their love and for putting me on this earth. And, of course, I cannot close without remembering my grandparents, Dot and Charley Fitzpatrick. Not a day goes by without me closing my eyes and imagining myself back with you both on Zulette Avenue. Thank you.

Index

Accardo, Tony 136, 325
Afghanistan 295, 303, 311–13, 317
Ağca, Mehmet Ali 303–4, 318
Al-Qaeda 311, 312
Albania 16, 23–4, 26, 90; gangs/mafias in 300–308
alcohol 43, 45, 62, 64–7, 70, 74, 116, 123–6, 129, 142, 181, 262, 266, 321–3; Prohibition, US *see* USA
Algeria 144, 186, 234
Ali Pasha of Ioannina 15–18, 21–4
Ali, Mohammed 16
Aliyev, Haydar 288, 289
Amsterdam, Netherlands 78, 79, 174, 175, 292
Anastasia, Albert 203–5, 207, 208, 211, 212, 221
Andreotti, Giulio 239
Anslinger, Harry 74, 140–43, 146–8, 171–3, 175, 179, 184, 189, 198–9, 206, 208, 249
Apache 26, 134, 181
Apalachin, Mafia meeting in (1957) 207–9, 221
Arellano Félix brothers 256, 269
Argentina 190–91, 260
Arkan 30
Armed Revolutionary Forces of Colombia (FARC) 263, 316–18, 322
Armenian Revolutionary Federation 90
artel system 292
al-Assad, Bashar 316
Atatürk, Mustafa Kemal 144, 147

Atlantic City Mafia meeting (1929) 126–7, 150
Avilés Pérez, Pedro 256

Babyface Nelson 135
Balkans 15, 16, 23, 29, 65, 90, 146, 202, 224, 301, 308, 317; Wars (1912–13) 143, 300
bakuto (gamblers) 103–5, 165
ballads 31, 184, 261, 262
bandits/brigands 13–43, 46, 50, 76, 79–80, 89, 97, 111, 134, 149, 181, 193, 218, 261, 298, 299; social banditry 29–32
Bangkok, Thailand 174, 198
Barnes, Nicky 277
Bath, Somerset 48–50
Batista, Fulgencio 139, 197
Baybaşın, Hüseyin 306
'Beak, the' 2–3
Berezovsky, Boris 290–91, 295
Berlusconi, Silvio 326–7
bin Laden, Osama 41, 311, 312, 320
Bingham, Theodore A. 61–2
Birth of a Nation (film) 115
Bitches' War (*suchya voina*) (1945–53) 293–4
black hand mafiosi 62, 114–15, 124, 141, 148, 206
Black Hand, The (film) 115
Black Panther Party 278
Blakey, George Robert 227, 229–30, 246
Bloods (gang) 277, 279–81, 334
Bogotá, Colombia 263, 265, 270, 318
Bolivia 249

413

Bonanno, Joe 128–9, 185, 190, 193–4, 223, 231, 232
Bonaparte, Napoleon 38, 48, 81, 85
bootlegging 124–8, 131, 134–7, 139, 142, 207, 323–4, 342
Borsellino, Paolo 238
'boss of bosses' 150, 262
Bowery Boys 59
Brando, Marlon 6, 216, 217, 260
Brent, Charles 68–9
Brezhnev, Leonid 285–6, 288, 289, 294
Britain 16; Egyptian independence from (1919) 142; gambling in 49–54; 'gin craze' 67; Hague convention (1912) and 70; Hong Kong and 96, 97, 101, 170, 243, 244; Jamaica gains independence from (1962) 271; Krays and mafia in 153–6; national lottery 48–9; opium's emergence as a global commodity and 65; prostitution outlawed (1885) 55, 58; police in 55–6; Robin Hood and *see* Robin Hood; Sicily, troops occupy 84–5; slave trade and 69; urban population, growth of 36
Bronfman, Sam 322–4
brothels 46–8, 50, 55, 58, 61, 98–9, 107, 110, 131, 149, 159, 168, 182–3, 189, 243
Brother (film) 299
Broughton, Lord (John Hobhouse) 15–17
Bruno, Angelo 154
Buchalter, Louis 'Lepke' 136, 203, 221
Buenos Aires, Argentina 56, 59, 169, 190–91
Buhari, General Muhammed 276
Bulger, James 'Whitey' 230
Bulla Felix, legend of 19
Bureau of Investigation, US 135
Bureau of Narcotics and Dangerous Drugs (BNDD), US 199
Burns, Tommy 121
Buscetta, Tommaso 222–3, 237–9
Butler, Josephine 55
Byron, Lord 15–16; 'Childe Harold's Pilgrimage' 15

caïds (bosses) 145, 146, 148, 149, 187, 190, 196, 216, 234

Cairo, Egypt 47–8, 50, 142
Calabria, Italy 185, 192–3, 203, 238, 239, 240
Calderón, Felipe 329–30, 332, 333
Cali Cartel 266, 269–70, 321
California, US 44, 57, 109, 110, 112, 119, 137–8, 279–80, 325, 334–5
Camarena, Enrique 'Kiki' 267–8
Camorra 9, 73, 77, 79–86, 88–93, 95, 108, 113, 192–3, 195, 235–6, 238–9, 271, 293, 321, 328–9
Canada 111, 124–6, 186, 190, 246, 273–4, 322–3, 340–41
Cantú, Esteban 181
Cantürk, Behçet 303, 306
capitalism 5, 8, 22, 212, 217, 244, 290, 324; mafia capitalism 332–9
Capone, Al 9, 10, 60, 74, 101, 108, 117, 120–24, 127–9, 130–37, 141, 160, 194, 224, 232, 260, 320, 324, 326, 338, 341
Captagon 316
Carbonari 81, 85
Carbone, Paul 145–6, 148–9, 186, 190, 233
Caro Quintero, Rafael ('Rafa') 256, 262, 267, 268
Carrillo Fuentes, Amado 256, 269
cartels, Latin America 22, 149, 152, 182, 184, 220–22, 247–8, 252–71, 275, 297, 316–17, 321–2, 325, 326, 330–36, 342, 343; *cartelitos* (mini-cartels) 270; term 253, 254, 270. *See also individual cartel name*
Carter, Eunice 136
Cartouche, Louis Dominique 20
Casalesi 329
Casino (film) 245
Castellammarese War 128, 129, 131, 210
Castellano, Paul 3, 3*n*, 208, 212, 229
Castellano, Philip 212
Castro, Fidel 190, 197, 208, 214, 250, 259
Catholic Church 195, 212, 233, 237, 261, 262, 332
Çatlı, Abdullah 304, 318
Cesari, Joseph 271
Charlemagne 17
Chávez, Hugo 339

Index

Chechnya/Chechens 26, 39, 293, 295, 298–300, 307, 312, 317
Chee Kong 109
Chiang Kai-shek 100, 147, 170
Chicago, US 60, 117, 123, 125–7, 130–32, 134, 136–7, 149, 155, 194, 206, 208, 211, 214, 232, 248, 296, 324–5, 338; Chicago Outfit 60, 136, 214, 324, 325
China 7, 24, 26, 31, 41, 51; Chinatowns 57, 71, 110–12, 165, 176; Chinese Exclusion Act, US (1882) 111–12; Civil War (1927–49) 39, 101, 170, 172; clientelism/*guanxi* and 338–9; crime syndicates aide Beijing in monitoring activities of Chinese nationals abroad 338; emigration from/Chinese immigrants 46, 57, 68, 71, 109–12, 121, 169, 175–7, 182; First Opium War and 65–6, 77; gambling in 50, 57, 58, 245–6; Great Leap Forward 171; Green Gang 97–102, 147, 149, 170, 173–4; heroin trade and 102, 172, 173, 175; Hong Kong and *see* Hong Kong; Kennedy assassination and 216; Macau and 244–6; market capitalism and 244; Ming dynasty 94; new regional and national mafias continue to grow in 338–9; opium and 65–71, 102, 111, 119, 143, 147, 171–2, 182; prostitution in 55, 58, 98, 110; Qing dynasty 38–9, 65, 68, 77, 94–7, 108, 109, 171; Republic, foundation of 96, 97; Second World War and 101–2; secret societies development in 95; sensational works detail threat of Chinese gangs 175–6; tongs 9, 71, 77, 98, 108–12, 115, 147, 175, 176, 177; triads and *see* triads
Chiu Chau syndicates 173–4, 177
Church, Frank 214
CIA 163, 173, 184, 197, 199, 200, 214, 215, 216, 246, 250
Ciaculli Massacre (1963) 194, 196, 236
Ciampi, Carlo Azeglio 246
cinema. *See individual film name*
Ciudad Juárez, Mexico 181, 183, 255, 268, 332

Civil Rights Movement, US 212–13, 215, 226, 229, 278
Clinton, Bill 246, 307, 311
cocaine 66, 68, 70, 152, 189, 220–24, 248–81, 297, 316, 325, 326, 337, 339, 343
Codling, Errol 273
Cohen, Mickey 178, 183, 205
Coke, Christopher 'Dudus' 334
Cold War (1946–91) 151–3, 157–8, 171, 174, 196–7, 204, 217–18, 224, 239, 246, 250, 282, 284, 287, 306–7, 327
Colombia 7, 202, 221, 248–52, 254–8, 262–6, 269–71, 316–18, 326, 343; Palace of Justice attack (1985) 263–4
Colombo, Joe 212, 213, 229
Colosimo, Vincenzo 'Big Jim' 126, 130–31
combinations, criminal 120, 123, 127, 204
Condor, Operation 255
Confidential series 204, 205
Congress of Vienna (1814–15) 69
Coppola, Francis Ford 5–8, 212–13, 216, 217, 236, 260, 265, 341
Corben, Billy 220
Corleone, Sicily 113, 137, 236, 246
Corsica/Corsicans 26, 40, 144, 145, 146, 186, 188, 191, 233, 234
Cortés, Hernán 17, 18
cosche or clans, Mafia 82, 87, 88, 113, 194, 196, 216
Cotroni, Vincenzo 185–6, 190, 191
Crips (gang) 277, 278–81, 334
crook villages 20
cryptocurrency 328
Cuba 138–9, 140, 185, 190, 197, 208, 214, 215, 216, 250, 251, 254, 259, 261, 272, 277, 340; Bay of Pigs invasion (1961) 214, 250; Havana *see* Havana
Cuccia, Don Francesco 92
Culiacán, Mexico 260, 261, 262, 268, 332; Battle of 333, 336
Cuocolo trial (1912) 91
Cutolo, Raffaele 235

D'Agostino, Antoine 186
Dalitz, Moe 139

415

Dalla Chiesa, General Carlo Alberto 237
De Palma, Brian 119, 260, 261
De Quincey, Thomas 64; *Confessions of an English Opium-Eater* 63-4, 66
DEA (Drug Enforcement Administration) 253, 254, 265, 266, 267
Dead Rabbits 121, 122
Death to Kidnappers (MAS) 263
Defferre, Gaston 186, 187, 197, 233
Del Gracio, 'Little Augie' 118, 143
Democratic Party, US 61, 121, 122, 125, 130
Desert Inn Resort and Casino, Las Vegas 139
Dewey, Thomas 136, 139, 140, 147-8
DFS (Mexico's intelligence service) 267-8
DIA (Italian elite anti-mafia force) 239
Díaz, Porfirio 181
Dnipro/Dnipropetrovsk, Ukraine 281-4, 286, 289-92
Dragna, Jack 137, 178, 208
Du Yuesheng 99-102, 147
Dulles, John Foster 167

East India Company 65
Eastern Europe, rise of mafias in 152, 281-309
Eastman, Monk 121, 122, 123, 124, 129
Egypt 16-17, 23, 47-8, 50, 142, 145, 188
Eiji, Ijichi 105
Eisenhower, Dwight D. 164
El Chapo (Joaquín Guzmán Loera) 331-3, 336
El Salvador 334-6
Elder Brother Society 95, 96
Eliopoulos, Elie 118-19, 141-6, 148, 149
Elizabeth I, Queen of England 48, 49
Ellroy, James 8, 344
Eminoğlu, Hüseyin 188, 302
Erdoğan, Recep Tayyip 4, 337-8
Escobar, Carlos 269
Escobar, Pablo 9, 224, 247-9, 251-4, 256, 259-60, 262-6, 269-70, 306, 320, 336, 342-3

Escobar, Roberto 249, 251, 262, 342
European Union (EU) 302, 305, 327
Evans, Robert 5, 325
Exner, Judith 215

Falcone, Giovanni 237-40
Federal Bureau of Investigation (FBI), US 2, 3n, 94, 140-42, 178, 198, 204, 207-9, 215, 225-7, 230, 246-7, 265, 297, 311, 325
Federal Bureau of Narcotics (FBN), US 140-42, 146-7, 150, 171-5, 178, 184, 189, 198-9, 206, 276
Félix Gallardo, Miguel Angel 255-7, 260, 262, 266, 268, 270, 330, 331-2
Fetisov, Slava 297
Financial Action Task Force (FATF) 326
Fiocconi, Laurent 271
First Opium War (1839-42) 65, 77, 95
First World War (1914-18) 38, 58, 60, 68, 70, 77-8, 90-92, 108, 113-14, 116, 119-20, 124, 143, 144, 181, 281, 317, 321
Fitzpatrick, Charles Charley 1-2
Five Points Gang 121-2, 124, 126, 129
Flamingo Hotel, Las Vegas 138, 341
Florida, US 137, 191, 220-21, 253, 256, 259, 274, 296
Flying Dragons 176
Fonseca Carrillo, Ernesto 182, 256, 261, 268
Forbes, Frederick 76-7
Four Deuces, Chicago 131
France 7, 16, 20, 37-40, 48, 53-5, 65, 81, 98-100, 132, 142, 144-5, 148-9, 157, 186-9, 197, 201, 218, 233, 234, 246, 291
Franchetti, Leopoldo 87-9
Francis the Belgian 233-4
Francisci, Marcel 202, 233
Fratianno, Jimmy 214, 228
Freeh, Louis 297
Freemasons 77, 80-83, 85, 90, 109, 196
French Connection 180, 185, 188, 190-91, 198, 200-202, 208, 226, 233, 249, 270-71, 277, 302, 314

Index

French Connection, The (film) 201–2, 208
Freud, Sigmund 66

Gadariya, Rambabu 40–42
Galante, Carmine 190, 193
Gallo, 'Crazy' Joe 154, 228–9
Gambino family 203–4, 221, 229, 231, 247, 288, 325
gambling 2, 14, 22, 43, 45, 47–62, 64, 67, 77, 82, 86, 93, 96, 98, 100–111, 122–6, 130–31, 138, 139, 144–5, 148–9, 154–5, 160, 164–5, 167–8, 170, 176–7, 182, 185, 188, 191, 205, 207, 208, 211, 243, 245, 283, 295, 303, 319, 320, 323, 342
Gamur, Raimondo 82
Gangster Museum of America 342
'gangster' term 123
Gangsterismo in America 206
Garibaldi, Giuseppe 85, 86, 89
Gemayel family 315
Gendarmerie Nationale 39
Genovese crime family 208, 209, 226
Genovese, Vito 7, 208, 210, 217, 226
Ghost Shadows 176
Giancana, Sam 136, 208, 214, 215, 325
Gigante, Vincent 'the Chin' 3, 225–6, 232
Global Initiative against Transnational Organised Crime 327
'Global Organized Crime: The New Empire of Evil' conference (1994) 246
globalisation 62–4, 78, 157, 196, 224, 307, 328
'godfather' term 7, 152, 166, 216
Godfather, The (film) 5–8, 118, 152, 158, 165, 166, 212–14, 216, 217, 219, 233, 260–61, 279, 285, 289, 325, 344
Godfather II (film) 340–41
González, 'Pabloté' 183
Goodman, Oscar 341, 342
Gorbachev, Mikhail 282–3, 286, 290, 294, 296, 299
Gordon, Waxey 125
Gotti, John 3, 225, 229–31, 247–8
Gravano, Sammy 'the Bull' 230–32

Greco family 194, 196
Greece 15, 16, 18, 29, 47, 118, 142–5, 148, 189, 190, 300, 327
Green Gang 97–102, 147, 149, 170, 173–4
Greenberg, Big Maxey 125
Griffith, D. W. 115
Guadalajara Cartel 255–7, 261, 267–8, 270, 330, 332
Guérini, Antoine 149, 186, 189, 202
Guérini family 149, 150, 186–8, 189, 197, 202
Guérini, Mémé 186
Guerra Cárdenas, Juan 330
Gutiérrez Rebollo, Jose de Jesús 268–9
Guzik, Jake 131, 136

Hacısüleymanoğlu, İsmail 303, 304
Hague Convention (1912) 70, 147, 339–40
Hands Over the City (film) 195
Harlem numbers racket 127–8
Harrison Act (1914) 123
hashish 188, 189, 314, 315
Havana, Cuba 139, 185, 190, 208, 250, 290, 340
Hawaii, US 106–8, 167, 168
Hawks, Howard 117–18, 120, 133, 213, 260–61
Hearst, William Randolph 142, 146
Heaven and Earth Society 94–5, 171
Hennessey, David 112
heroin 4, 6, 66, 70, 74, 102, 105, 118, 119, 143–8, 168–9, 172–5, 178–91, 193–4, 196, 198, 200–202, 208, 226, 233, 236, 249, 254, 257, 265, 270–72, 275–7, 301–6, 311–15, 317, 318, 325, 331
Hezbollah 315–16, 322
highbinders 111
highwayman 26, 38
Hindus 27–8, 319
Hirohito, Emperor 106, 158–9
Hobsbawm, Eric: *Primitive Rebels: Studies in Archaic Forms of Social Movements in the 19th and 20th Centuries* 29–31
Hoffa, Jimmy 208, 209
Hong Kong 54, 96–7, 101, 102, 157, 169–78, 243–5, 336
honour culture societies 27

417

Hoover, J. Edgar 135, 140–42, 198, 204, 207, 208, 226
Hop Sing 109, 110
HSBC 326
Huang Jinrong 99
Hughes, Howard 118
Hung Fat Shan 170

Ibáñez de Sánchez, Blanca ('Delicia Herrera') 249–50
Ibrahim Kaskar, Dawood 318–19
Ichiwa-kai 242
ikka (families) 103, 104
immigration 9, 23, 33, 34, 43, 46, 56–8, 66, 68, 71, 80, 96–7, 106–10, 113, 115, 120–23, 125, 130, 136, 141, 144–5, 162, 169, 176, 182, 186, 188, 213, 232, 234, 248–9, 251–2, 259–61, 273–4, 280, 296, 301, 303, 305, 319, 335
In Little Italy (film) 115
Inada, Wataru 'Jackson' 168
India 7, 25, 26, 27–8, 40–42, 48, 58, 144, 275, 318–21
Indochina 144, 187
industrialisation 14, 35–6, 38, 39, 42, 46, 51, 80, 91, 157, 281
initiation rites 82–3
Institutional Revolutionary Party 333
Internal Macedonian Revolutionary Organisation 90
International Brotherhood of Teamsters 208
Iran 26, 64, 65, 142, 303, 315–16
Ireland/Irish 1, 3, 33, 90, 111, 121–2, 131, 150, 174, 206, 273, 300, 318, 321
Irey, Elmer 134–5
Irish Republican Army (IRA) 273, 318, 321
Istanbul, Turkey 4, 7, 16, 23, 24, 90, 143–6, 187–8, 190, 198, 302, 303, 304
Italy: abolition of monarchy (1946) 195; Allied occupation 191–2; anti-mafia movement/fight against corruption and organised crime (1990s) 4, 237–40; Berlusconi as leader of and 326–7; 'clean hands' campaign 238–9; clientelism culture of 192; first major government crackdown on Mafia 194; First World War and 91–2; Italian Communist Party 195; Marshall Plan and 192; migration from 113; Mussolini rules 92–3, 120, 191; Napoleon invades southern Italy (1806) 81; origins of mafia in 73–4, 75–6, 80–93; post–Second World War 195, 234–40; prisons nurture Camorra and Mafia 95; Second World War and 93; unification of 73, 84–5; 'years of lead' 240
Ivankov, Vyacheslav 296–7

Jack the Madman 233–4
Jack the Ripper 42–3, 55
Jamaica 224, 271–4, 276, 321–2, 334
James, Frank 30
James, Jesse 30–31
James-Younger Gang 30–31
Japan 7, 19–20, 25, 39, 55, 58, 68, 73, 100–108, 147, 150, 157–68, 170, 178, 192, 218, 240–46, 259, 297
Jasso, Ignacia 'La Nacha' 183
Jews 59, 121, 125, 129, 143, 144, 148, 150, 174, 178, 206, 207, 282, 296, 323
John Paul II, Pope 237, 304

kabadayı 302, 303
Kaduna mafia 275–6
Kanun of Lekë Dukagjini 308
Karkov, Gennady 'the Mongol' 294, 295, 296
Keane, Larry 'Killer' 2
Kefauver, Estes/Kefauver Committee 148, 204–9, 341
Kelly, Ned 33–4
Kelly, Paul 120–24
Kennedy, John F. 209–11, 215, 216
Kennedy, Robert F. 204, 209, 213–14
Khomeinei, Ayatollah 315–16
al-Khoury, Sami 189–90, 197, 198, 314
Kidd, Captain William 25
Kim Jong-il 339
Kishi, Nobusuke 164
Kodama, Yoshio 102–3, 105, 163–4, 166, 167, 241
Korshak, Sidney 324–6

Index

Kosovo 30; Kosovo Liberation Army 302, 303, 317; War in (1999) 301, 302, 317
Kot Siu Wong 170
Kray twins 153–6
Kuchma, Leonid 289
Kurds 302–6, 317; Kurdish Workers' Party (PKK) 303–6, 317
Kvantrishvili, Otari 'Kvazho' 295–7
Kwong Duck Tong 109

La Cosa Nostra 14, 209–12, 222–3, 227, 239, 246, 260, 271, 275–6, 281, 287, 297, 307, 321, 327
La Familia Michoacána 331
La Guardia, Fiorello 136, 146
La Mara Salvatrucha (MS-13) 334–5
La Résistance 148–9, 186
La Rocca, Antoine 145
'La Violencia' 248
LaBarbera family 194
Lait, Jack 204, 205
Lansky, Meyer 125–6, 129–30, 137–40, 150, 179, 185, 203, 205, 208–9, 222, 340, 341
Lara Bonilla, Rodrigo 264
Las Vegas, US 138–9, 154, 208, 228, 250, 296, 324, 325, 340–42
laudanum 63, 66
Laz migrants 188
Lazishvili, Otari 289–90
Le Milieu 145, 149, 186, 233
League of Nations 70; Advisory Committee on Traffic in Opium and Other Dangerous Drugs 142, 146
Lebanon 155–6, 187–90, 197, 198, 275, 302, 318; Beirut 155–6, 187–9, 198, 318; Bekaa Valley 189, 314, 315; Casino du Liban 197; Civil War (1975–90) 314–16, 318
Lehder, Carlos 252–3, 264, 267
Leo XIII, Pope 80
Lombroso, Cesare: *The White Man and the Coloured Man* 57, 89
London 28, 38, 42–5, 49, 54–6, 59, 65, 69, 71, 78–9, 96–7, 133, 153–5, 169, 174, 175, 271–3, 291–2, 300, 328
López Obrador, Andrés Manuel 329, 333

Los Angeles, US 137, 150, 168, 178, 183, 208, 214, 228–9, 258, 261, 277–80, 296, 324–5, 334
Los Zetas 316, 330–33, 335
Louis XIV, King of France 55
Louis XVI, King of France 81
Louisiana state lottery 60
Lucas, Frank 277
Luciano, Charles 'Lucky' 124–5, 128–9, 136, 139–40, 143, 147–8, 150, 179, 184–5, 193, 203, 204–5, 208, 221–3, 230
Lyon, Louis 146

Maas, Peter 222
Macau, China 244–6
Machii, Hisayuki 167
Machine Gun Kelly 135
Madrid, Miguel de la 267
Mafia, American. *See* USA
Mafia, Sicilian: Buscetta shepherds through postwar era 222–3; cinema and *see* cinema; expelled American mobsters influence on 192; first major government crackdown on, Ciaculli Massacre and 194, 196, 236; cinema and 195, 213, 216; cocaine trade and 271; heroin trade and 173, 196, 197, 233, 236–7; Italy's prisons nurture 95; kidnapping and ransom foundational to 193; law enforcement and *see individual agency name*; Luciano and 125; Marshall Plan and 192; migration from Italy into US and 113; Mussolini and 92–3; origins of 73, 75–7, 83–90, 206, 209–10, 212, 284, 321; politics and *see* politics; power wanes at end of twentieth century 223; reverence for old code of conduct vanishes 231–2; Riina's war against Rome 236–9; rituals associated with 82–4; Rome adopts more effective measures against 237–40; ruling council 194; Second World War and *see* Second World War; term and concept, origins of 11, 13, 29, 62, 73–4, 75–80, 82–93, 213, 216; US Navy and 139–40

mafias: advent of global 117–50; high tide of old 153–219; origins of 75–116; pre-history of 15–43; twentieth-century, end of and 220–309; twenty-first century and 310–44
Mafiosi of Vicaria Prison, The (play) 88
Magaddino, Stefano and Gaspar 126
Malverde, Jesús 31, 261–2
Manley, Michael 272–3
Mann Act (1910) 123, 135
Mao Tse-tung 101, 102, 170, 171–2, 244
Marcello, Carlos 7, 209
marijuana 147, 201, 251, 254, 255, 256, 265, 269, 272, 276, 331
Marley, Bob 272
Marseille, France 7, 144–6, 149, 173, 186–90, 194, 196–8, 200–202, 216, 223, 233–4, 236, 270, 302, 321
Marshall Plan 192
Masseria, 'Joe the Boss' 124–5, 128–9
Matranga, Charles and Tony 112
Matta Ballesteros, Juan 266
Matthews, Frank 276–7
MCA 324, 325
McCarthy, Joseph 204–5
McClellan, John/McClellan Committee 208, 209, 210, 227
McCoy, Alfred: *The Politics of Heroin in Southeast Asia* 173–4, 177, 196–7
Mean Streets (film) 232–3
Medellín Cartel 220–21, 224, 247–9, 251–7, 259, 263–7, 269–71, 275, 301, 342–4
Meiji, Emperor 104
Meltzer, Harold 'Happy' 178–80, 182–3, 190, 214–15
Menderes, Adnan 197
methamphetamine 161, 167, 339
Metropolitan Police 55–6
Mexico 7, 17, 21, 31, 44, 52, 57, 64, 111, 138, 140, 178–85, 190, 200–202, 216, 224, 248, 250, 254–8, 260–62, 267–71, 276, 284, 307, 316, 326, 329–36, 339
Mexico City 52, 180, 182, 183, 190, 198, 254, 284, 331, 332, 335–6

Miami, US 137, 220, 221, 248, 251, 252, 257–9, 261, 265–7, 273
Michel, Judge Pierre 233–4
Michoacán, Mexico 331
Milano, Peter 168
Milošević, Slobodan 336
Moll Cutpurse 79
money laundering 247, 299–300, 315, 326, 329
Monte Carlo, Monaco 49, 54, 245
Montreal, Canada 185, 186, 190, 191, 193, 322, 323
Moran, Bugs 131
Morello, Giuseppe 113–14, 124, 128, 137
Moretti, Willie 2–3
Morgan, W. P. 169–72, 177
Mori, Cesare 92–3
morphine 66, 102–3, 143–7, 184, 187, 189, 193, 200, 315
Mortimer, Lee 204, 205
Moscow, Russia 2, 37, 266, 283, 284, 286–96, 298–9
Mumbai, India 318–20
Munday, Mickey 221–2
Muni, Paul 118, 133
Murat, Joachim 81
Murchison Sr, Clint 207
Murder Inc. 136, 203, 211
Musketeers of Pig Alley, The (film) 115
Mussolini, Benito 92–3, 120, 191
Mustache Petes 128
Mzhavanadze, Vasil 290

'Ndrangheta 193, 195, 235, 238, 239, 326–7, 331
Naples, Italy 73, 75, 81, 84–6, 89, 91, 93, 121, 145, 191, 193, 195, 234–5, 240, 314
Napoleonic Wars (1803–15) 49, 69, 84–5
narcocorrido (tribute ballad) 184, 262
narcoterrorism 316–17
Nash, Richard 'Beau' 49
Nasrallah, Hassan 316
Nasser, Gamal Abdel 17, 188
National Hockey League 297
national lottery 49
National Museum of Organised Crime and Law Enforcement 'The Mob Museum', Las Vegas 341

Index

nationalism 30, 53, 81, 89, 90, 96, 100, 105, 147, 170–72, 262, 278, 279, 303, 304, 319
Nationalist Action Party 303, 304
NATO 195, 302, 312
Ness, Eliot 134–5
New Camorra Organisation (*Nuova Camorra Organizzata*) 235
New Orleans, US 60, 209, 250; lynching of Italian men (1891) 112–13, 113*n*
New York, US 1, 61–2; as birthplace of modern mafia 113–14, 124–30, 131; Castellammarese War 128, 129, 131, 210; Chinatown 110–12, 176–7; Commission 194, 208, 210, 230, 236, 251–2; first mafia family in 113–14, 124, 128, 137; Five Families 108, 129, 136–7, 186, 190, 203–4, 205, 212, 229, 230; Hip Sing and On Leong war in (1904) 110–12; homicide rate 179; Krays in 153–4; La Guardia and 136, 146; migration from Italy into 113; 'organised crime', origins of term and 61–2; Police Department 111, 112, 113, 120–21, 123, 128, 176–7, 199, 201, 203, 226; street gangs of 121–4
Nicaragua 266
Niceforo, Alfredo 89
Nigeria 7, 224, 271, 274–5, 308
Nitti, Frank 131, 136
Nixon, Richard 6, 199–202, 213, 214, 255, 265
nomads 25–6
Noriega, Manuel 266–7
Norman's Cay 252–3, 266
North Korea 339

O'Banion, Dean 131
Ochoa family 221, 252–4, 263–4
omerta (code of silence) 76, 230, 240, 308
On Leong 109–11, 175, 176
'open cities' 137
opium 45, 46, 63–71, 77, 95, 96, 98–102, 105, 109–11, 119, 123, 142–4, 147, 170–73, 178–80, 182, 184, 187, 189, 190, 197, 199, 200–202, 224, 254–6, 303, 311–14, 331, 339
organised crime: origins 13, 44–71; term 10, 61, 62
Oswald, Lee Harvey 210–11
Ottoman Empire 15, 16, 17, 21, 23–4, 26, 30, 38, 48, 64, 90, 143, 144, 188, 281, 302, 317
oyabun (local boss) 160, 163
Ozu, Kinosuke 160, 162–3

Pakistan 303, 312–13, 320
Palermo, Sicily 75, 84–8, 92, 193–4, 223, 236–8, 246, 342, 343
Palestine Liberation Organisation (PLO) 317–18
Panama 45, 46, 191, 266, 270
Panama-Pacific International Exposition (1915) 45, 46
Paramount Pictures 5, 211, 212
Paris, France 20, 37–9, 45, 55, 145–6, 189, 198, 201, 233, 275
Pasley, Fred 132–3
Pathans 319
Patriarcas 230
Peker, Sedat 337–8
Peña Nieto, Enrique 332
pentiti (mafia defectors) 237–9
Peru 249, 251, 316
Philippines 68, 69, 178
piracy 24–6, 69–71, 97
pizzo (payment) 82, 86, 89
police 4, 21, 33, 37, 38, 41, 43, 46, 50, 51, 54–8, 61–4, 70, 71, 82, 85–8, 90–93, 99, 100, 101, 105, 106, 111–15, 118, 120–21, 123, 128, 140, 142, 161, 162, 164, 169–70, 176–8, 188–90, 194, 197–9, 201, 203, 218, 221, 226, 230, 233, 235, 237–41, 244, 255–6, 264, 267–8, 270, 277, 278, 280, 283–4, 291, 294–5, 297, 299, 304, 306, 318, 331, 333, 334, 338, 341
Profaci family 154
Prohibition, US (1920–33) 70, 74, 114, 116, 120, 123–7, 129, 131, 135–7, 140, 142, 150, 156–7, 171, 181, 182, 185, 190, 211, 228, 259, 322–3, 329–30, 340–42

prostitution 9, 43, 45–8, 50–58, 60–62, 64, 67–8, 82, 91, 93, 98–100, 107, 110, 111, 123, 131, 136, 145, 149, 159, 160, 164, 167, 168, 170, 171, 176, 182–3, 186, 188–9, 191, 228, 243, 269–70, 273, 296, 297
protection racket 17
Puzo, Mario: *The Godfather* 5, 211–12, 285

qabaday 155
Quevedos family 181, 183

race/racism 57–9, 67, 115, 168, 204, 261
race wire 60
Racketeer Influenced and Corrupt Organisations (RICO) Act 227–31, 246, 247
Reagan, Ronald 265–7, 315
Reefer Madness (film) 147
Reese, Thomas 'Tootie' 279
Remnick, David 288
Richardson family 154, 155
Ricord, Auguste 190–91
Riina, Salvatore 'Toto' 236–9, 241, 264, 328
Rivard, Lucien 190
Roberts, Jon (Joseph Riccobono) 220–22, 229, 254, 258; *American Desperado* 222
Roberts, Nat 221
Robertson, Frank: *Triangle of Death* 175–6
Robin Hood 19, 31–3, 135, 261
Rodríguez Orejuela, Gilberto 269, 270
Rodríguez Orejuela, Miguel 269, 270
Roman Empire 18–19, 47, 48
Roosevelt, Theodore 69, 101
Rosi, Francesco 195
Rosselli, Johnny 126, 137, 214, 215, 324–5
Rothstein, Arnold 125–6, 134, 138, 203
Rotwelsch ('cant of thieves') 79, 80
Royal Navy 65, 69–71, 76–7
Ruby, Jack 210–11
Ruef, Abe 46
Russell, Thomas (Russell Pasha) 142, 145, 146
Russia 7, 26, 37, 41, 59, 90, 111, 131, 224, 281–5, 287, 291–300, 306–7, 312, 322, 328, 336–7

Sabiani, Simon 146, 148, 149, 233
'Sailor' (Alexander Milchenko) 283, 294
Salinas de Gortari, Carlos 268
Salinas, Raúl 268
Salvatore Giuliano (film) 195
Samper, Ernesto 270
San Francisco, US 44–6, 51, 52, 57–8, 109–10, 138, 169, 175, 176, 184, 212
Sandinistas 266
Saratoga 138
Saviano, Roberto: *Gomorrah* 328, 329
Scarface (film, 1932) 8, 117–20, 132–3, 213, 260–61
Scarface (film, 1983) 119, 260–61
Schultz, Dutch 128
Scorsese, Martin 232, 233
Scotland Yard 42, 56
Seaga, Edward 272, 273, 334
Seagram's 322–4
Second Mafia War 237
Second World War (1939–45) 73–4, 93, 95, 101–2, 104, 110–11, 139–40, 147–9, 150–52, 170, 177, 180, 182, 184–6, 188–91, 193, 198, 218, 234, 245, 249, 289, 293, 298, 324
Sekban, Ihsan 188, 189, 190, 197, 302
Semyonov, Youlian 216
Shan independence movement 172
Shanghai, China 69–70, 77, 97, 98–102, 149, 170
Shining Path 316
Shower Posse 273–4, 321–2, 334
Sicilia Falcon, Alberto 254–5
Sicily 5, 29, 73, 75–7, 79, 82–95, 106, 108, 113, 125–9, 131, 136–7, 141, 148, 173, 191–7, 203, 206, 210, 212, 213, 216, 221–3, 233, 236–40, 246–7, 271, 286, 293–4, 296, 299, 308, 321, 327, 342. *See also individual place name*
Siegel, Bugsy 125, 137–9, 182–3, 341
Silver, Joseph 59–60
Sinaloa, Mexico/Sinaloa Cartel 182, 183, 254–6, 261, 331–3, 336

Index

Sinatra, Frank 153, 185, 260
slavery 30, 55, 57, 68–70, 110, 282; white slavery 58–60, 62, 111, 135, 142, 145, 148, 149, 189
Smith, Al 125
socialism 91, 92, 288
Society of Regulators (The Hounds) 57
Solntsevo 296
Sopranos, The (TV series) 3, 4, 10, 83, 310–11
Soviet Union 7, 39, 202, 204, 211, 216, 224, 231, 266, 281–301, 306, 312, 324
Spada, André 'Tiger of Cinarca' 40
Spirito, François 145, 146, 148–50, 186–7, 190–91, 198, 233
Spook Hunters 278
spook-gangster nexus 336–7
states: bandit gangs and 14, 17–27, 31, 34–7, 39–43; clientelism and 338–9; Cold War campaigns against organised crime and 218–19; collective response to mafias 246–7; deep state (*derin devlet*) 305, 306, 308, 344; 'failed' or 'failing' 307, 332; gambling and prostitution, stricter legal regimes imposed upon 50–55, 60, 61, 62, 64; legitimacy of relationship between ruler and ruled 18, 21; mafia states 288–300, 308, 313, 329–40; nationalism and *see* nationalism; new mafias as expressions/extensions, of innately flawed states 307; organised crime connections with 197, 214–15, 337; power, mafias history and physical limits of 9; spook-gangster nexus 336–7; war, mobilisation for 17, 38, 91–2; weaknesses or limits of, successful or endemic gangs and mafias and 14
Stead, W. T. 55
Stroessner, Alfredo 191
Suey Sing 109, 110
Sullivan, 'Big' Tim 122–3, 125
Sullivan, John L. 121
Sun Yat Sen 96, 97
Susurluk incident (1996) 304–5

Sutton, Willie 36
Syria 23, 187, 189, 315, 316

Taiwan 162, 167, 176
Takenaka, Masahisa 241–2
Taliban 312, 313, 322
Tammany Hall 122, 125, 128
Taoka, Fumiko 241–2
Taoka, Kazuo 161–3, 166, 240–41
Taoka, Mitsuru 168
Taranto, Leon 144–6, 148
Tennes, Jacob 'Mont' 60–61
Teochew, or Zhouzhou 174
terror-crime nexus 317–21
Terry, Belaúnde 316
Thailand 172, 173, 174, 175, 297
Thatcher, Margaret 273
36th Chamber of Shaolin, The (film) 94
Three United Society 94
thuggee 27–8
Tijuana, Mexico 138, 182, 183, 254, 255, 256, 260, 268, 269, 332
Tilly, Charles 17–18
timber mafias 312
Toei Studios 165–6
Tokagawa 104
'Tommy guns' 131
tongs 9, 71, 77, 98, 108–12, 115, 147, 175, 176, 177
Torrio, Johnny 126, 131, 132, 137
Towne, Robert 165
Trafficante, Santo 208, 214, 250, 254
Trails, Armitage: *Scarface* 132–3
Tranquilandia 252, 264
triads 7, 73, 77, 78, 94–103, 108–12, 147, 149, 168–77, 218, 243–5, 297, 307, 309, 328, 336, 338
Trollope, William 75–7, 86
Trotsky, Leon: *Stalin's Gangsters* 284
Truman, Harry 6, 148
Turkey 4, 7, 23, 134, 142–4, 146–8, 178, 180, 184, 187–90, 197, 200–202, 216, 233, 300–308, 311–12, 318, 337–8

Ukraine 281–4, 288–9, 328
United Nations (UN) 172, 246, 312, 313; Convention Against Transnational Organized Crime 246–7

Untouchables (film) 134, 260
urbanisation 14, 36, 51, 52, 96
USA: American Civil War (1861–65) 30–31, 66; American Mafia, fall of 226–33; American Mafia, international spread of 134–41; American Mafia origins 73–4, 112–34; American Mafia profits 228; Anastasia killing 203–5, 207, 208, 211, 212, 221; Anslinger and birth of narcotics trade 141–50; Apalachin, Mafia meeting in (1957) 207–9, 221; capitalism, mafia 332–9; Capone and American mafia *see* Capone, Al; Castellammarese War 128, 129, 131, 210; Chinese Exclusion Act (1882) 111–12; CIA and the mob, pact formed between 214–15 *see also* CIA; Cold War and *see* Cold War; Congress 2, 59, 70, 101, 106, 111, 115, 123–4, 200, 215, 216, 226–33, 265–6, 276, 320, 326; crime bill (1968) 226–7; Department of Justice 199, 213, 227, 265; Department of Treasury 134–5; Hollywood *see* cinema; Kefauver Committee 204–9; Kennedy assassination 209–11, 215, 216; Krays in 153–5; Las Vegas, mafia in *see* Las Vegas; McClellan Committee 208, 209, 210, 227; migration from Italy into 113; New York, mafia in *see* New York; 9/11 311, 320, 321; Prohibition *see* Prohibition; rapid growth of creates tantalising marketplaces 151, 156–7; Senate 7, 148, 173, 175, 176, 177, 198, 203–4, 206, 209, 210, 214, 215, 216, 227, 267; *Sopranos, The* (TV series) and 3, 4, 10, 83, 310–11; tongs in 108–12; Turkish dope arrives in 184; Vietnam War (1955–75) 173, 187, 199, 213, 221, 232;
Volstead Act (1919) 70, 116; War against Terror 311–12; War on Drugs 141–50, 198–203, 265–7, 315; Warren Commission 211, 215; Watergate scandal (1972) 214, 326; Watts Riots (1965) 278

Valachi, Joseph 83, 209–11, 216, 222, 227
Valentine's Day massacre (1929) 131, 136, 341–2
Valley of the Wolves (TV show) 4
Veerappan, Koose Munisamy 40–42
Veidt, Conrad 118–19
Venezuela 277, 337–9
Versailles, Treaty of (1919) 70, 78
Vitaliev, Vitali 282–4, 286, 287, 294
vory-v-zakone (thieves-in-law) 224, 292–6, 298, 300

Wan Kwok Koi ('Broken Tooth' Wan) 245, 246
war, mobilisation for 17, 38, 91–2
Washington, Raymond 278, 279
Wasserman, Lew 324–5
waste dealers 329
We, the Undersigned (play) 286
Western Union 60
Winchell, Walter 206, 207
Winter Hill Gang 230
World Series: (1919) 125, 203; (1951) 205
Wu Tang Clan 94–5

yakuza 14, 73, 77, 78, 103–8, 156, 158–69, 218, 223, 240–43, 271, 297, 307, 309, 321, 328
Yamamoto, Hiroshi 241–2
yardies 273, 274
Year of the Dragon (film) 169
Yeltsin, Boris 291, 295
Yugoslavia 90, 187; Civil War (1991–2001) 30, 300, 301, 302, 336

Zampa, Gaëtan 'Tany' 233–4
ZR/RIFLE 214–15